IMPULSIVE MEDITATIONS

Out Of My Life And Thought

R. Garner Brasseur, M.D.

authorHOUSE®

AuthorHouse™
1663 Liberty Drive
Bloomington, IN 47403
www.authorhouse.com
Phone: 1-800-839-8640

Published by AuthorHouse 10/16/2012

ISBN: 978-1-4772-6305-1 (sc)
ISBN: 978-1-4772-6306-8 (e)

Library of Congress Control Number: 2012916291

TABLE OF CONTENTS

"A CONCEPT OF MIND"

(Title of Gilbert Ryle's book)

R. Garner Brasseur

MODES OF THOUGHT: Now it is true that one's own modest and unpracticed meditations have a decided tendency to become somewhat of the nature of aimless wanderings which then effectively spare one the effort of the deliberate hard work of goal oriented and productive thought processes. A sort of self entertainment under the pretext of a virtuous activity. This particular form of thinking is known as reverie, "our spontaneous and favorite kind of thinking". Its course is determined by hopes; fears; our spontaneous desires - their fulfillment and frustration; our likes and dislikes; our loves, hates, and resentments. "All thought that is not laboriously self-controlled and directed, will inevitably circle thusly about the beloved Ego". I would not wish to suggest that we mere mortals ought never pleasure ourselves with vacant revels and daydreams, but that rather, as in all things, we are better served by a course of balance and proportion even in our waking hours of repose.

The other three types of thought identified (see "*The Mind in the Making*", by James Harvey Robinson) are as follows:

Decisions - We resent having to 'make up our mind', a more difficult and laborious thing than reverie. Though certainly laborious, it does not necessarily add anything to our knowledge.

Rationalizing - Finding arguments for continuing to believe as we already do. We are wont to acknowledge the 'real' reasons for our beliefs: they are concealed from ourselves, as well as from others. They are unconsciously absorbed from our environmental culture; whisperings of the voice of the herd. And we spontaneously resent the imputation that any of our conceptions are subject to the need for revision.

<u>Reason</u>; or Creative Thought - that peculiar species of thought which leads us through doubt, skepticism, and intentional reappraisal of oneself and one's ideas, to the possibility of changing one's mind. It makes things look different from what they seemed before.

Also, throughout each day, a great many questions and curiosities cross our minds. 'Idle curiosities'. We wonder, and may take a superficial look at something or another. If not matters of immediate concern, we needs must pass these by, and attend to always the more immediate. Constraints of time, and always some absolute limit upon our stores of each day's energy.
RGB

Information Overload

I read a nice article by Seth Lloyd in the April, 2007 edition of Discover magazine pg. 55-57.

The article points out that in the 1700's there were perhaps not more than a thousand people in the world whom we might call by the name of scientist. In our own times their numbers are in the millions: and by 2200 there could be a billion of them. They study, investigate, and theorize on every subject than can be approached scientifically. They publish in thousands of scientific journals and papers. The result is runaway growth in scientific information. However, about 99.8 percent of their ideas and theories prove to be wrong. And of the other 0.2 percent, a large part is useless. By way of example, we are told that there were 34,510 papers on the human genome in the "*Science Citation Index*", but that the great majority of them have been cited fewer than ten times. And, of course, those that have never been cited do not even appear in this index. It suggests that the amount of useful scientific information is far smaller than the number which scientific journals would suggest.

In the mid 1700's the French compiled a voluminous scientific "*Encyclopedie*" of knowledge, but it included a great deal concerning such things as theology and black magic, that we would not consider in our time to be scientific. In our own times, with computer access to the web, there is an unprecedented opportunity to generate and disseminate information inflated by vast quantities of hot air. Information on the 'photosphere' is absolutely immense, and there are trillions of documents on the internet. We drown in information and misinformation. One needs must struggle to avoid being swept away in the massive currents of 'bits' while striving to glean the precious few pieces of information we can actually use. "The vast quantities of trivial information create a sea of noise when people try (via Google search, for instance) to seek out really important information."

All of this is not to say that there are not some very useful bits of information within the mountain of dross with which we are confronted from our scientific sources. Of course there are. But we must recognize that the proportion of truly useful information within Dross Mountain is becoming ever smaller. It behooves us to become ever more selective and to work more diligently at our meta-analysis in our attempt to come up with that which is both valid and useful.

It has been said that the primary function of life in the universe is to glean those few bits of useful information from the great quantity of gobbledygook. That life has evolved to separate a faint signal from a sea of noise gives us reason to be hopeful. The first organisms learned to cull useful bits of information out of the cosmic chatter and evolved mechanisms to protect the important information contained in their genetic code from the depredations of heat and noise. Then, by reproducing, passed that information on to their descendants.

Making the initial discovery in science is like striking gold, and those nuggets still lie about us for the taking. But once the new goldfield has been worked to maturity, large scale efforts are then required to leach out the few grams of useful information from the residual tons of dross.

Roosevelt G. Brasseur, MD
3/15/07

QUOTATIONS FOR CONSIDERATION TO A CHILD OF TOMORROW

As it seems to me, one's first and fundamental responsibility in life, is towards one's comprehension of the world, universe; and the complex familial and social situation into which one is born. And towards one's own mental advancement.

A people who has many proverbs, maxims, and epigrams in current use will be less given to talking nonsense.

- "Yesterday, this day's madness did prepare; tomorrows silence, triumph or despair."
- "Enough is as good as a feast"
- "Too much sunlight makes a desert."
- "Many a man becomes the slave and prisoner of his own opinion of himself; a fame won by their own deeds."
- "All of the flowers of all our tomorrows, are contained in the seeds of today."
- "Everything has got a moral; if only we can just find it."
- "In each moment of limited understanding and insufficient data, one must make decisions - just as though he knew what he were doing."
- "The child too is father of the man."
- "The energy of one's life is limited. In the expenditure of that

capital, the one great evil is dissipation; the one great prudence is concentration."

- "The greatest discipline; self-discipline."
- "The virtue of the mind in not in flying high; but rather in orderliness."
- "In all things a best method; and a right time."
- 'The Iron Rule' and 'The Silver Rule' are co-equal with 'The Golden Rule'.
- "The sweetest victories, are those fashioned from defeat."
- "Pay homage to Art, Beauty, and Truth; but the greatest of these is Truth."
- "Everything is good, which but takes away one plaything; or one delusion more."
- But one virtue is required by all—-civil decency.
- "Manners are minor morals; no man can fully resist their power."
- Require of thyself, a daily solitude for thought and reflection.
- "Fite illiteracy!"
- A concise general maxim—-reciprocity.
- "Passions are true Phoenixes; as soon as the old one is consumed, the new one rises forth from its ashes."
- "Men of intemperate habits cannot be free; they are fettered by their own passions."
- "The line dividing good and evil between various men, cuts through the heart of every human being."
- "Passions in themselves, are not evil; that arises from their unbridled indulgence."
- "If wanting to know be a sin, it constitutes both our guilt and our innocence." Camus

Spoon River Meditation

by R. Garner Brasseur, M.D.

I had intended this Saturday to attend rounds and lecture on Herpes Simplex Keratitis, but already by Thursday, I had abdicated that position and resolved to flee to the mountains. For I felt I must restore my 'wa', by communicating with that which is eternal. And so I left the office shortly after 5:00 P.M. on Friday and drove over to the second hand store to buy a cot and a sleeping bag that I had previously become aware of. I then retired immediately to the house, had a quick sandwich, loaded my gear into the pickup, and departed about 7:00 P.M. Wishing to get away from the heavy traffic as soon as possible, I took the freeways 495, 66, and 81. By 11:00 P.M. I had passed the Mennonite college in Harrisonburg and was into the first ridge of the Appalachian Mountains. It was a beautiful clear night. The traffic was light, it appears that very few indeed of the of the big city folks often get out into areas this rural. About midnight I stopped at the edge of a roadway turnoff, where I backed the pickup into the edge of the underbrush, and prepared to spend the night in the camper. I had some fear and uncertainty about this, as it had not yet become a common experience for me. But I wanted to reassure myself, by the experience, as to the ease and simplicity of the thing, so that I might do it more frequently.

Already, the coolness in the air nipped one slightly. I expected it to be cool indeed by morning. As I open up the $5.00 canvas cot, I discovered one of the center legs to be broken off. That would make the cot essentially useless, except that in my particular situation, it was actually an advantage. For it enabled me to push the cot directly to the edge of the pickup bed, with the broken stump resting firmly on the elevated wheel well, at the center edge of the pickup box. Fortunately, I had bought an extra blanket and sweatshirt with sweatpants. And still, it was cool enough that 1 roused myself in the night to void, and put on my jacket then too. That night's cold weather then gave me no further trouble, and I slept well.

I awoke at 9:00 A.M. to a bright clear day. And there was not much traffic out here in this back country. I stopped at Franklin, right nearby to where I had spent the night. There I had a couple of hotcakes for my breakfast, in a local privately owned restaurant. Such luxuries as that seem to be disappearing from the access to common-man, by the influx of the chain eateries such as McDonalds, Roy Rogers, and Burger King. I then headed southward on Hwy 220, I had traveled only ten or twenty miles, when I began to experience the great calling, with waves of ever increasing urgency. There was not an outhouse to be seen, nor anyplace along that highway, of any assured privacy of underbrush. For the villages there are small, and the population is largely strung out along the local highways. Under the pressure of progressive distress, I finally had to elect to turn off from the main thoroughfare, onto a more rural road, hoping there the home-sites might be more sparse — and the underbrush more dense. And so it was. Within a few minutes I had stopped the pickup and was scurrying up the hill and through the underbrush, heading for the denser cover of some trees. In that urgent rush I had peeled off my jacket and dumped it in my wake, and was already working at my belt while in full flight toward a particular spot that seemed to offer some promise of cover from the necessity of my embarrassment. Ere long I was relieved and comforted, and the world once more seemed a much more interesting and pleasant place. I retrieved my jacket from the underbrush as I headed back towards the pickup. Descartes noticed that we seem each to have to deal with both an inner world and an outer world. Under usual circumstances, we accustom our attention to a certain proportion of awareness to each. But under urgent conditions of physiologic stress we can become very much less aware of our external world, and the only thing of the whole universe or eternity that seems important, or, of which we are aware, revolves about this stress point, within.

Recovering my awareness of that external world, I descended to the road through the ankle-deep leaves, rocks, and fallen trees and branches. Then drove some twenty miles through these progressively rural roads. They narrowed, then the paving ended and the gravel tops became like a washboard as I crossed a ridge, into a new and separate community — defined by that ridge, and whose roads by degree, again improved. Already at Warm Springs, I thought I perceived an uncomfortable influence of suburban strain. Five miles further, at Hot Springs, I was stunned and disappointed to be landed into a commercial resort area, peopled for the weekend by golfers and sunbathers, cloistered together in knots and bunches, with their expensive and polished Mercedes, BMWs, and sports cars, parked upon and filling the asphalt-surfaced lots. I was fearful to turn around, lest it cost me ten dollars to do so. I chanced it, regardless, and returned to Warm Springs, then on westward via Hwy 39 to Fenwick - a curious little town, crowded uphill by a river and a railroad, in a little valley, so that one side of its main street is six or eight feet higher than the other, I stopped there hoping I might get a haircut, but the barber was just locking up for the day, as I approached his shop. I drove northward then on Hwy 55; then eastward on 20 and 15. I stopped in Craigsville at a flea-market, located in an out-doors-movie-theater. The earthen drives and ramps were black with some glistening black patches scattered randomly. Close inspection revealed them to be buried boulders and rocks of anthracite coal, smooth and polished by the traffic of automobiles, through the years. I took the liberty of pocketing a piece, for my rock collection.

Near the midpoint of my Hwy 15 drive, as I approached the top of a ridge, I came upon an old white church facing downwards toward the highway. Behind and on both sides of the chapel, running upwards toward the ridge, was a well-kept patch of grass, implanted with, perhaps, two hundred gravestones in the usual assortment of size and shapes. And there were wilting flowers, perhaps several days old, upon a dozen or two of the graves, one of which had been freshly dug. I pondered as to the possible meaning of the flowers, thinking perhaps it might be a custom to visit and tend graves on All Saints Day, but I finally supposed the explanation was merely that many of the local folks had been here to attend a recent burial, and had left flowers upon the graves of their own departed kin during that same funeral event. The ancient white church was a little dilapidated, but had a relatively new coat of paint. The windows that face the highway were shattered, but the others were all intact. I wandered alone about the gravestones, reading the inscriptions, considering the names and speculating about their individual family connections and their age and circumstances at death. Several family names were very common among those gravestones - Hamrick, Cogar, etc. That country is supposed to have been pretty much settled up by the Scotch, Irish, and Germans. The old church appears to be in much the same condition as are the gravesites, though it doesn't appear that the building is used for anything except, perhaps, an occasional funeral oration. Not surprisingly, I was in a melancholy mood, wandering there alone - except for the invisible company of the saints - a mere hour before sunset on a lovely autumn day. The fallen leaves stirred occasionally by the whiff of an occasional breeze. Enmeshed with my thoughts, were vague recollections of Edgar Masters' "*Spoon River Anthology*", and a sweet calm reverie concerning my own inevitable departure and planting.

I left that clearing of the departed, enriched by the glow of all the mellow thoughts I had enjoyed there; and imagining myself to have honored, and to have been honored there, by dint of a quiet solemn sojourn. From there, I drove over the ridge and left the setting sun behind me. I drove another twenty or thirty miles in the valley, stopping at a restaurant in Bartow, and the taking a motel room there for the night. A nice little facility, there by the Green Brier River. Changing back to standard time that night made the night unusually long, and I treated myself to a long hot shower and a full night of quiet rest. The next day about 9:45 A.M., I departed and headed back to Chevy Chase, stopping several times to inspect some geological formations and the ever migrating rocks on slopes, and in the riverbeds. I stopped at several flea-markets on my return from the weekend outing. Arriving back at the house in Chevy Chase about 5:00 P.M., I unloaded my gear, and then napped an hour and a half, before driving out to attend a Unitarian discussion group from 7:30 P.M. until 9:00 P.M. It was an informative session and offered me the rare opportunity of a interesting discussion.

R. Garner Brasseur, M.D.

10/28/85

THE GENESIS OF DELUSION

By R. Garner Brasseur

In 1970 a group of we adults decided to get together in one car and drive to Roseburg, in order to see the Ashland High School football team play that evening. We departed about 6:00 P.M., at that time of the year when the daylight hours rapidly decline. None of us knew precisely where in Roseburg, the football stadium was located. Darkness was just upon us as we approached the city. We turned from the main freeway to enter the town via the old highway, which passes into the heart of the city. We half expected to pass close enough to the stadium, that we would be able to identify it from the towering lights and stadium bleachers. We were not surprised then, when from a distance, we were able to identify the towering lights that lit the bleachers and the grass-covered playing field. It seemed as though our arrival was timely, for neither team was yet to be seen upon the playing field. Perhaps we were vaguely smug, that our general plan for locating this site was so readily effective. As we approached within a block or two of this site, we saw that the bleachers facing us seemed already filled with spectators, their distantly small round faces stacked row above row, to the top, As we had reserved seats, we were not worried about our seating arrangements.

As we saw no cars parked along this old highway - now, but an access road to the city - we supposed that there was public parking space directly adjacent to the stadium, We turned off into a well used gravel road, expecting that it might take us directly into the immediate area of the stadium. But, in the space of a few seconds upon that new-found road, one visual shock succeeded another! I was dumb, in awe at what I suddenly began to comprehend - and then immediately became certain. Here was a rough green field, not greatly different in size from that of a football field. It lay between two piles of logs, stacked one upon the other, to the height of, perhaps, thirty feet. The cut round ends of these logs faced the open field. From a certain distance, the cut ends of these stacked logs, one upon another, do indeed vaguely resemble the white to reddish appearance of Caucasian faces. These overhead lights though, illuminated an open space, upon which trucks and heavy equipment could operate, in order to stack and - later - remove these logs from the pile. Indeed, we were upon the premises of a lumber mill, with but a handful of workers scattered about, at this hour of eventide.

I perceived that my jaw had dropped - in wonder - opening my mouth, as I rapidly computed the sum of the evidence before me. Then I noticed - to my amazement - the evidence of surprise and confusion upon the face of each of my fellow travelers. They and I had each, separately experienced the same vivid illusion! Like myself, they had each come abruptly to the startling end of that group delusion.

The lesson of that experience was dramatic, rich, and instructive. It is one of the most vivid personal experiences that I own, of an optical illusion leading spontaneously to a completely erroneous conclusion. The predisposing expectations in the minds of the beholders, and the stages of its progressive development, would seem to be ideal as a model, from which one might simulate such dramatically instructive experiences, as a teaching device. That is suggested by the simultaneous nature of the experience, among all those present, within that one automobile,

That experience is also easily the clearest personal experience that I have, relating to the phenomena of group delusions. Certainly our goal and our common expectations, as well as a myriad of chance effects and timing predisposed us, as a group of individuals, to each come individually to this one erroneous conclusion.

RGB

Fatima

I recall reading the story of the 'Miracle of Fatima' (played out in Portugal, about 1917). A large populace of the surrounding area, and many from abroad, were drawn to this small community by the news of strange and miraculous occurrences. And there can be no doubt that many of them shared vaguely common expectations. Those spectators were stressed in their journey, by fowl weather and by the urgency of their individual hopes and fears. There was idle gossip and exaggeration of all manner of disconnected and irrelevant incident; in short, a plethora of imaginative ideas tinged with vague expectations. The priestly scribes undoubtedly had some hopeful preconceived thoughts and ideas that colored the content of what they wrote, concerning what the pilgrims are said to have reported and claimed to have seen and heard. No doubt even some outright fibs were told under the informality of those circumstances - some say that occurs even in courts of law until this very day; and under oath. Thousands awaited; and many - we are told - saw some rather unusual color displays as the sun struggled to break through the mist and clouds. (One might certainly expect some similar refraction phenomena such as 'sundog halos', 'glories', and rainbows.)

The priest who has written the story (in retrospect of several years), had gotten his details from many of those who were alleged to have seen something strange - most of these were undoubtedly among the parishners of his own congregation, there in Fatima.

Undoubtedly, many of those who came to witness the anticipated Fatima 'miracle', went away wet, cold, and disappointed. Most perhaps, saw nothing they would call miraculous - or even much unusual. They drifted each their separate way back home, and forgot about this event of no consequence. They wrote no dramatically interesting stories of their non-experience; and would be surprised that many - if any - should claim to have seen or experienced anything different than themselves. They died in the course of time, failing to have taken the time to describe the event, minute by minute - since any such exotic claims would seem to them, preposterous. Having now failed to receive these many reports of an alleged event that they were unable to affirm, we are then left with the dubious claims of (only) those who are 'said to have' seen or heard something unusual and inexplicable. The evidence supporting the claims of the Miracle of Fatima is subjective, only. Gossip, exaggerations, hopes, fears, ignorance, leading questions, expectations; perhaps even some outright fibs.

Hysteria, and illusions; all contribute to the processes whereby the ordinary - under circumstances adequately permissive or encouragement - is given some license to parade as extraordinary. Such evidence as there is - biographical testimony, only - may well permit its instatement, even in our courts of law; since no persons trouble themselves to find out what experiences of an unusual nature that one didn't have. No scientific inquiry however, would condone the instatement on the basis of such evidence as that.

No one of sound mind and reasonably broad experience of life, would doubt that we are subject to illusions and delusions, Many, perhaps, have had experiences similar to mine, such as to assure them of the reality of group illusions, and to guess at some of the circumstances which might predispose to them. Throughout the world and in all times, hopes and promises - far the majority of which never come to fruition - serve almost as well as full payment in hard cash, in the here-and-now. A great many medical problems and illnesses are hysterical in nature, and can be alleviated or cured by subtly confronting the patient's erroneous belief with the negating evidence of his own sensory or motor system. Hysterical blindness is perhaps among the most easily demonstrable examples of such a situation; this perhaps because of the profound faith that people develop, concerning that which they can see - for we rely upon our visual, more than any other of our senses. Seventy percent of our sensory perceptions are mediated through the visual system. So profound is our visual confidence - in most people - that systematic demonstrations of its evidence has been known to confound and alter even the most deeply embedded of delusions and superstition. Of course, the visual system too, can be hoaxed, and is subject to skillful deceptions; as evidenced by optical illusions and magical tricks. And It has taken mankind hundreds of years of experience; and has required the integrity possessed by only the occasional magician, or stuntman (such as Houdini) and the slow progress of science, to finally convince us that even the evidence of our eyes, cannot be accepted non-critically, and needs must be verified by our progressing skills of reason, and a rigidly systematic method of experimentation and demonstration.

RGB

Leopard Men

Albert Schweitzer, in his book, "*More From The Primevil Forest*", tells us of an odd and a much more lethal group delusion of his experience in Africa. A deadly delusion, of fearful consequences, which had spread over the whole of the west coast of Africa in his time. Bands of 'human leopards' had begun to propagate throughout the area increasingly for several years. Some districts had been so terrorized by these creatures that people feared venturing even out from their huts after dark. The perpetrators were men who were deeply possessed by the delusion that they were leopards, and that because of that, they regard it as their obligation to kill men. In the sway of this delusion, they attempt to emulate the leopard, going about on all fours, with the claws of leopards attached to their hands and feet. When they catch their victim, they kill him by severing his carotid artery, as do leopards. We are told that they are involved into this delusion, involuntarily by roving bands of members of this cult. The cult members prepare 'a magical potion' which is made from the blood of one of their victims, and concocted in a human skull. The potion is then slipped into the ordinary drink of some superstitious local fellow. "Then he is informed that he has drunk the potion, and therefore is from that time, one of their band. Nor does any one of them resist." "They are all alike, then dominated by the belief that the magic potion has some magic power against which no one can successfully fight, and so they obey unresistingly. The next step is a command to take one of their brothers or sisters to some place where he or she can be attacked and killed by the members of the band. Then the novice must himself start killing."

Orders were given to put an end to this business, and 90 likely suspects were jailed. In detention, they are said to have poisoned one another rather than fess-up to their guilt.

We, in our times, are much more acquainted with delusional situations in which a group of devoted followers is led by some charismatic self-appointed authoritative figure who leads his group into some form of social chaos; sometimes to their own death and destruction. Some such examples being The People's Temple group of Jim Jones, the Charles Manson affair, or the Waco, Texas situation. Such as these being common occurrences throughout the past millennia. Some of the more successful having survived to become known in our times as 'religions'. The distinction between 'cult' and 'religion' being somewhat hazy in the minds of we most.

RGB

Suddenly Blind

One evening I was called to the hospital emergency room to see a patient alleged to have gone blind. I was told the patient had awakened from sleep into a state of blindness. The details were vague and fuzzy.

As I drove to the hospital, I considered what the possibilities might be, to explain this patients problem. The vital signs (pulse, blood pressure, respirations, and temperature) were all normal. Nor was there any history of trauma, nor was the patient in pain. Basically I had two fundamental possibilities to consider. First, that the patient had not really, after all, lost her sight as I had been told. (Do not be harsh with me for being skeptical). The second possibility was that she had lost her sight, or at least a significant part of it. It could be a very serious matter indeed.

Upon arrival at the hospital and seeing the patient from across the room, it was immediately clear to me that here at least, was nothing life threatening or even physically painful to the patient. Nor was there the quality of drama in the situation. My heart went out to her in sympathy, as my questioning revealed some of the painful details of her troubled life. I only stroked the edges of the specifics enough to be certain of the essence of the details, for I didn't want to traumatize her psyche by roughly tugging at the painful roots of her story. She was but a mid-teenage girl - so young already to be feeling such deep sorrows of life. She had discovered what causes babies and had recently become a mother. She was not married nor had prospects of marriage. No, she wasn't in school presently. She lived at home and had to take care of that child. Mother or not, this poor young girl was still basically a naïve child. Undoubtedly felt miserable and guilty in the eye of the family. But where else was there for her to be? She had recently been under pressure to take a job to help bring in support for herself and the child. This plain and backward sort of girl was working at Wendy's (hamburgers etc.) and having to face the public - where she was not entirely anonymous. And the story progressed with other depressing details, as you might well imagine.

I held my hand in front of her. She said she could not see it. She said the could not see my light which I shined into her eyes. I had reason to doubt this, for her pupils constricted briskly; but I specifically did not wish to imply that she was not being truthful - especially there - in front of her worried mother and all. So I guided her down the hallway and through some doorways where I could examine her eyes more closely, in order to assure myself that I was overlooking nothing. I grasped her by the shoulders to guide her steps, and walked her ahead of myself. I purposely tried to guide her close enough to the doorsill, that she would bump her shoulder. Despite my misguidance, she handily sidestepped that obstacle. Her mother had the impression that I was being careless, so tried to get in front of me and the girl to prevent her being injured. I deftly cut out the mother by moving across her flight path as I watched her out of the corner of my eye. Thus was I able to repeat the experiment; with again the same result. Then I walked her directly towards a stool, and she sidestepped that, but with less ease. My eye exam turned up nothing objective to confirm her subjective blindness. So, I walked her back and dropped my guiding hands from her shoulders several steps before she reached a dividing curtain petition. She sidetracked two or three steps on her own, so as to be able to walk through the parted walk space of that curtain, even though it would not have injured her to walk into the curtain. Isn't psychology interesting with all its subtleties and the delusions it presents to us?

Indeed, this girl was not blind. But that does not mean that I will be able to convince either the girl, or her mother of that fact. Nor do I wish to set the mother against daughter over this small fraud. So I gave the girl a prescription for some pills which perhaps she might regard as the magical cure for her imaginary illness. An bogus cure for an imaginary illness. It was a sedative of very small dosage. I sent her home with instructions to rest. She was to return to the office for follow-up the next day.

The hospital charge, plus my bill perhaps cost them a hundred dollars that day. When I saw her at the clinic the next day, I was told her vision was almost completely restored, she told me. She did, in fact, have a slightly amblyopic left eye, but this was no handicap to her (in as much as she had functioned that way all of her life) and is irrelevant to the central issue of her alleged blindness.

In all honesty and charity, I must further point out that the girl was not outright fraudulent. For there is a subtle difference between "malingering" on the one hand, and "hysterical blindness" on the other. That difference has to do with how deeply the girl herself, had actually begun to believe the game she was playing. Perhaps she was only looking for a reason not to have to report to work, to a job she dreaded. Perhaps then the told her mother a little fib, and under a concerned interrogations found that she had to support the first lie with a second fib; then the second with a third etc., until the matter quickly escalated out of control and she found herself uncontrollably forced into the E.R. scene in order to save face etc.

"Oh what tangled lives we lead,
When first we practice to deceive"

One might speculate that having now determined that the girl is not blind, we might perhaps now gladden their hearts with these good tidings. The problem though is that they already believed the opposite (on that first day in the E.R.). Had I the artistic gift for showmanship, and a fortuitous coincidence such as sudden lightening bolt, an earthquake, or an eclipse of the sun, I might have pulled off one of those sudden cures that folks so like to rave about, and which they might easily therefore accept. Most usually though, a firmly held false belief, like unto a bad habit (or a skunk, or a porcupine) must be respected for the thing that it is and for the power it has to remain unmoved. No man dare boldly pitch it out of the attic window for fear of the consequences and unpleasantness that such an act can generate. Rather, it must cautiously be coaxed down the stairway, unhurriedly, one step at a time, then out the closest door.

RGB

Beco of Lourdes

I was recently reading of "The Eight Great Appearances of Our Lady", and specifically concerning the vision as it is alleged to have appeared to a twelve-year old girl, by the name of Mariette Beco, in the Belgian village of Banneux, in 1924 - or was it 1933(?). One really can't be sure of the year from reading the twenty-six page section of the book devoted to that story. The narrator introduces us to the setting, and similarly describes the terrain and the history of the area; and of the family. All are so objectively presented - and integrated into the whole of the story - that he immediately has our confidence, account of that clear and tidy presentation; despite our lingering uncertainty as to the precise year. Perhaps that detail will become more clear as we continue into the story. The details of the running commentary carry us along into the details of the first encounter of Mariette, with 'Our Lady' - as though we were almost eye-witness observers ourselves. Seeing a peculiar light in the front yard of the family home, Mariette blinks - perplexed. We - the readers - already know; before Mariette does, what this strange light shall be reported to have been. We, ourselves, always willing and hopeful for the miracle, though it never seems to be a miracle to one's own benefit - are almost tempted to whisper encouragement to Mariette. Three days later, at the alleged second appearance, she wanders out the cottage door - as though in a trance - and kneels prayerfully beside the gravel footpath. Besides (seemingly) ourselves, the father, a brother, a cousin and two other village men are said to have been witness to the events of this second encounter. Suddenly, in reverence and adoration, Mariette lifts her arms forward and up, towards the tree-line of the evening horizon. And behold(!), there is a beautiful radiant lady, dressed in white, with a blue sash at her waist. She is, perhaps, twenty feet from Mariette, walking upon a white cloud and unsupported pedestal. As she approaches, her knees can be seen to move beneath her gown. As she speaks, her lips can be seen to be in motion, in conversation with Mariette, though she wears a transparent cloth about her head. She seems to be unaware of the others that are present, in silent observation. Mariette makes reply. The apparition recedes, though still speaking to Mariette. Mariette follows and stops to kneel, pray, and question - whenever the radiant lady pauses. At the last stop - beside the road - still in front of the cottage - Mariette is directed to a previously unknown spring of fresh water. There she dips her arms and prays; still in conversation with the beautiful lady; to a total of about thirty-five minutes at this encounter. Some instructions - about a chapel, about healing waters; exhortation to "pray much". The encounter ends then. Mariette remains, kneeling in prayer; and reciting her rosary for an additional five or ten minutes. She returns to the cottage fatigued and stuporous - unnoticing of the bystanders who silently make way for her. She is later seen to be in prayer at the bedside in her room, for a long while. The following day she asks her father the meaning of certain French words which were spoken by "Our Lady", and with which she was unfamiliar - for the Walloon dialect differs somewhat from French. She has been particularly concerned about the dilapidated condition of her father's Catholic faith; and it shall later transpire that his faith has been greatly invigorated. Be aware that we ourselves are not witness to this event: in the ambiguities of the narrative style, it only almost seemed as though we were. The narrator has drawn us into it, as it were; and we needs must now withdraw ourselves, in order that we maintain a decently objective perspective, concerning this dubious 'fact' of history. As it turns out, it is furthermore also the case, that (the father, the brother, the cousin, the two village men, and - later - the mother, a physician, and other unnamed 'witnesses' to subsequent encounters) each witness has testimony of very limited applicability. None of them - were actual witness either to the apparition; nor hearers of any of the dialog. We are assured that Bishop Kerkhof's investigation does list some twenty well substantiated 'miraculous cures' (of the alleged healing powers of that newly established spring of water) between May, 1933 and 1938. Miracles said to be in consequence of the apparition of "Our Lady of the Poor" which is attributed to the child, Mariette Beco. The site was approved - along with the Cult to the Virgin of the Poor, in 1941 - by the official Catholic Church hierarchy, with the approval of the Pope. There was also a very great 'secret' which was imparted by "Our Lady", to Mariette. 'A secret' which she has never indulged to anyone what-so-ever. So what is the point of the alleged and forever unknowable secrets? The world and the universe are teeming with such secrets.

RGB

Artistic License

There is a fanciful tradition in artistic style, that seems to enter from old Rome, passes through into Christian Art, and seems not to be extinguished until the Renaissance of European Art. It almost makes one wonder about the sanity of those who sponsored the production of those works of art. The works depict very fanciful goings-on in the heavens and in the spirit world. Chubby child nudes are depicted as floating about the sky, usually in attendance upon some mortal or group of mortals, who are firmly grounded to the earth. There are adult-like spirits, usually gowned, and apparently dependant upon feathered wings to keep them aloft. Those wings perhaps evolved by evolution, from their scapulae? There are (first, celestials; next demigods i.e. Mary; and later, 'saints') - beings with 'halos' of circular lights about their heads. Occasionally horses and chariots are to be seen in the productions, among the clouds. Was there a time when the sky-folks were commonly and abundantly present at the goings-on of earthbound mortals? Or were the ancients so ignorantly and superstitiously out-of-touch with reality, that they commonly imagined they actually saw such sky-folk? Did they see these things ubiquitously and as a cause of the chaos in the world and in their individual lives; or as spirits in sympathy with their plight; or as explanation of the inexplicable? But, perhaps it was a form of propaganda, whereby was encouraged - in the masses of men - a myth with some power to constrain them to their impoverished and downtrodden condition.

Look now at such religious "historical methods" of the past:

"Where I have not found any history of any of these bishops, and have not been able by conversation with aged men, or inspection of the monuments, or from any other authentic source, to obtain information concerning them; in such a case, in order that there might not be break in the series, I have composed the 'life' (of the saint) myself, with the help of God and the prayers of the Brethren." (written by Agnellus, the scholarly 9th century Bishop of Ravena)

If the historians are to be believed, there were reports of specters and visual portents in abundance, as well as panoramic vistas of peopled and spirit populated gatherings and goings-on in the heavens; to which people were not uncommonly, witness. Yet, the writers themselves, as historians, seem not personally to have seen such things; nor do they give us even second-hand accounts of the people that did claim to see such things. The historian's reports of such things are couched more vaguely - as, "there were reports of specters and portents having appeared to many people in the (such and such) area," The historians even sometimes strike a more personally disconnected note, concerning these reports; indicating that they have some reservations about the factual basis of these reports; though as historians, they somehow feel obligated to report that there were such reports. Concerning the matters, mentioned in the above paragraphs, there is something that seems to us misleading. Not only do these things not square with reality; but they are not even realistic, from the point of view of the framework of reality - as we experience it in our times. Novels and historical novels, for example, are commonly written, depicting events and experience that is not - nor even pretended to be - the actual experience of persons of flesh and blood, who now or once actually lived and had those experiences. They not uncommonly, however, portray a certain reality concerning times, events, persons, and places - of times past or present. In that sense, they are realistic. Their fictional characters, respond to situations in those settings, much as we might expect - knowing as we do, somewhat of human nature; with its propensity to human weaknesses, corruptibility, passions, and the tendency to aspire to certain ideals. History itself, in fact, can never give us completely valid details, even though the historian generally holds historical veracity to be among the foremost of the goals and ideals toward which he strives. It may well be the case, however, that some writers deceptively pretend to be historians, in order to mislead us by way of the confidence with which we hear them. Otherwise though, it seems not probable that any man, or society of men of responsible character would speak of these highly improbable happenings as bona fide reality to a whole world that can see it as patently not true. Nor that they would endorse its veracity into posterity, to men who would know of the lie - by virtue of the continuous nature of reality into their own times, whose laws of nature must correspond also to times past. Such writers would certainly then be judged to distain. Responsible men would surely by preference, endeavor to be to be judged to have had sound character, heroic tendencies, and valid grasp of reality. How then shall we view and interpret their endorsement of this obviously erroneous information? As noted, the historians of the times, when writing of these things, absolved themselves of the responsibility of their personal endorsement of these dubious historic events. The likes of Julius Caesar, or Cicero, would surely not traffic in obviously disreputable reports. Even the prophets of the various religions seemed to report their 'seeings' and messages as coming to them through dreams, or subsequent to having been stunned by light (perhaps lightening, or a variant of migraine syndrome, or severe keritstill from sun-burned corneas, etc.), or in a trance - induced by who knows what . . . epilepsy, mescaline, peyote, hemp, or simply, ethanol spirits ….?

How shall we explain the blatantly false endorsements? Sculptors and the decorative stone masons probably saw themselves as absolved from responsibility by virtue of the necessity of carrying out orders of the authorities in charge - as soldiers absolve themselves from mayhem and murder, by the convenient myth of resting the responsibility upon the shoulders of their commanding officers of the next higher grade above themselves. Nor can there be any doubt but that official delusional religion or superstitious beliefs were felt to be politically expedient. Fictional histories might very probably constitute a part of the mechanism of that intention. The cultured elite, of course, would not then be expected to take it seriously, so long as they were not actively subversive toward its general diffusion and propagation. After a few centuries of entrenchment however among the Roman Church officials, clergy, and monks, some did begin to take this fictitious history seriously; and despotically to expect all citizens to do likewise. That though, I expect to be in consequence of a chronic state of progressive ignorance and depression that afflicted the entire Roman Empire - the result of unimaginably devastating recurrent epidemic disease which swept the empire for centuries, leaving them no hope of health; and chronic fear of inexplicably gruesome death. That prolonged influence, perhaps, underlies the disturbed outlook upon reality that so long manifested its influence on sculpture, painting, fanciful literature, and decorative masonry; and supported various distortions of history. It likewise fortified and prolonged individual delusions, group delusional systems, and the propensity to visual hallucinations. One can determine from a photograph, the relative location of the camera with which it was taken. Similarly, historians have a certain view of history, such that we can see from the emphasis, detail and portrayal of the characters, that they favor one group against another. Or, they have a certain personal view of history - of which their exposition is a biased, supporting document. Some are obviously, patently biased. Others manage a more objective style, by analytically focusing upon the nature of the controversy and the history of its origin, that brings forth this challenge and response which constitutes history; and by enumerating the data and facts that exemplify the contradictions. The historical sources - whether witnesses, archeology, or historical documents - are always limited; so that even objective intentions are limited by that fact alone. Regarding long periods of historical time, dogmatic and dictatorial institutions, national governments, and individuals have had their peculiar and individual reasons for intentionally wishing to alter and distort the veracity of history - to make it appear other than what it was. Books have been burned, libraries destroyed, fictitious histories written. Witnesses have been bribed, imprisoned, or killed. Historical data has been deleted from the record or distorted from proper context; all, to expedite that intent - to alter the appearance of history unto posterity. And to stymie the efforts of historical research to obtain untainted and valid historical information to those such as who might eventually wish too enquire. Through all of this intentional and unintentional obscurity, we are obliged to read between the lines, in order to obtain what seems to be a more probable course of events and set of data; and a reasonable interpretation of history. In this attempt, we are aided if we may reasonably presume: l) that human nature has remained essentially unchanged through historical times, 2) that the laws of nature remain similarly unchanged, 3) to the extent that we avail ourselves of access to a diversity of historical texts, documents, and archeological sources.

RGB

MIRACLES

A man's perceptions in life ought ideally improve and come more nearly into alignment with the way things really are. Generalizations are helpful and of use to the extent that they can be verified by individual instance. Specific knowledge and experience applied to specific problems is more productive of success than vague and generalized dogmatic notions.

What shall we say of miracles, so highly touted in various religions as proof of the truth and validity of that very same religious text in which they are recorded. One recalls the discussion between Hotspur and Merlin. Says M., trying to intimidate H., "I can summon and command the very devils from Hades!". Says H., "So can I. So can any man! But will they heed?" The claims of miracles are absurdities which become obvious when confronted with rational inquiry. They melt into nothing when confronted with the problem of definition and called upon to show proof. That we never were previously stunned by that absurdity is simply due to the fact that we were bombarded and brainwashed with that nonsense before the age of development of any of our rational faculty.

Miracles that are a part of the text of other religions (than the one to which we were accustomed) have no such power to enchant us. The fact of their absurdity is often immediate and spontaneous to even the rational mind. As a high school student (and as a non-Mormon), I was humorously affected by the palpable absurdity concerning the story to the effect that Joseph Smith had a pair of magic spectacles which enabled him to decipher and translated some golden plates of ancient script into English. This alleged miracle he then passed off as "*The Book Of Mormon*" and a sacred text of revelation onto that group of believers; and to thousands of people over already five generations. Insofar as can be determined, these people are in all other respects capable, intelligent, and progressive folks.

Such alleged miracles seem so absurdly unlikely that we at first can hardly believe that otherwise sane people in our advanced society can actually and seriously maintain such a view. Yet, we are highly affronted and shocked when they turn the tables on us concerning our foolish, hand-me-down articles of faith and belief. Und so geht es, immer! Always able to see the follies in others; peculiarly blind to our own.

We gradually discover that the whole human race is similarly afflicted with compartments of insanity. And these compartments can be troublesome for us to attempt to put aright. We soon learn, simply to change the subject and avoid tampering in these pathologically dangerous realms of concepts as casual conversation topics.

We recall some of our nightmares and dreams, and other irrationally fixed ideas which at one time troubled our own individual past. But we have now recovered from some of these, and can recall that recovery was also itself uncomfortable. Hence we have a sympathy for the small insanities of others, and silently wish them a speedy recovery, while changing the subject to something less controversial

The entire human race seems transfixed with assorted legends of miracles past, and the hope of some to come that will specifically favor themselves. The word itself--miracle--is rarely even defined by those all too ready to contest the subject, with themselves having carried out not any significant analytic process whatever. There are legendary miracles, there are miracle drugs, there are miracle performances in athletic contests, there are all manner of scientific and technological miracles. So the word itself has taken on various and rather loose meanings.

Religious miracles commonly revolve about whether or not an alleged act or occurrence has resulted from the suspension of natural laws (which strictly govern and limit all other acts and occurrences). At least this is the case in the New Testament. Whereas in the Old Testament, miracles center more frequently around the alleged accurate predictions of natural disasters. Concerning the first variety of miracle, the implication is that natural law and order (the laws of nature) have been perfectly designed and attuned. That then, upon occasion, a white Deity or perhaps a black Deity, reaches in from outside the system and dramatically suspends a law of nature, so that what results is completely out of context with the manner in which we would suppose. That based of course upon our limited knowledge and experience of those laws. What a weary dream!! And almost as overworked as the concept of romantic love.

The performance of magic, and the miracle, would appear to have somewhat in common. We have 'magic' tricks, and magic shows composed of these tricks. We are fortunate that magicians are more open and honest than priests, for many a magician has occasionally divulged the secrets of their tricks so that we do not make the error of proclaiming them miracles. The magician and his magic show then tend to stimulate our thinking, rather than to lull us into ignomious stupor, as seems the case when just such similar tricks are proclaimed as miracles.

We no longer regard earthquakes, volcanic eruptions, typhoons, floods etc. as fortuitous miracles in support of some particular version of history. And would-be prophets find difficulty in the here and now, to predict these things accurately. Such predictions seem to us to have been more reliable in times past, for under those conditions they can write their predictions retrospectively. Interestingly though, the eruption of Mt. Ste. Helens was scientifically anticipated. This however, by scientists - not priests - and no miracle was thus proclaimed.

Neither is the fact that person A meets person B accidentally on a journey, a miracle, even if they do have a mutual acquaintance. For under such rules, any meeting whatsoever would by a miracle; and so even for every non-meeting. Nor is sickness, nor recovery; nor death, nor life itself for that matter to be considered a miracle. For it is all in accordance with the laws of nature so far as we can tell.

Nor, finally and most assuredly, can we accept as miracles, the mere stories, tales, and myths of miracles. For a story of a miracle is not any miracle, any more that a picture of a man, is itself a man. Nor have you or I ever seen any one to arise from the dead, though it must be allowed that some near to death and some even thought to have been dead have occasionally later been found to be alive.

We might conceive that nature as a whole, and the laws which govern nature, are miraculous in their immutability and perfection. But this, only if they are unalterable nor have ever been suspended, for such a change nullifies their supposed immutability. And if the laws of nature are not precise, then our only source and text of truth (reason) is and remains forever hopelessly uncertain and we are thus then deceived by the Deity himself, rather than by the fallen angel.

To presume that some persons among mankind are in direct communication with the Deity strikes me as an absurdity, though the claim is by no means uncommon. There is nothing deity could communicate to them, except what they already have the intellectual capacity to understand. If then, what they understand, they subsequently communicate to you and I to understand, by virtue of our intellect, then, how shall we explain our understanding? Will it be in accordance with the laws of nature? Or shall we again say this is yet another miracle? For if a miracle, it is another interruption of the laws of nature. Etc. It seems then hardly economical for a Deity to have created natural law and order, if he is forever at the beckon call of myriads of petitioners throughout eternity, to have to interrupt the motions and interrelatedness of the laws of nature. Far worse, of course, is that it strikes me as something akin to immoral - to halt the perfection and continuous flow of those laws of nature. For then, the complainers (unhappy to God with their portion) and the stoics would be deprived of the validity of their one natural source - reason - for the observing and testing of reality, by which their powers of reason might guide them on toward truth.

RGB

METAPHYSICS

(that which is above and beyond the tangibility of physical reality)

To encounter and deal with real problems in the course of one's life presents always the possibility of having to turn one's attention to philosophy - that is to say, metaphysics. It seems doubtful however, that one can - by beginning with metaphysics - translate anything of use towards the solution of the problems of this real world. (See, "*The Black Swan*") What use to argue so meticulously from erroneous premises.

Recall the poem by John Saxs, (*The blind men and the elephant*). Six blind men of Indostan who reported each their separate conclusions of what they thought an elephant to be: The first, who touched upon the broad side, exclaimed 'twas very like a wall. The second came upon the tusk and said 'twas rather like a spear. The third who grasped upon the trunk allowed 'twas much more like a snake. The fourth chanced then to touch the knee - believed it very like a tree. The fifth who happened at the ear opined it more resembled a fan. The sixth who seized upon the tail thought it rather like a rope.

"And so these men of indostan, disputed loud and long: each in his opinion, exceeding stiff and strong. Though each of them was partly right, yet all of them were in the wrong!" And so, we see that multiple points of view, if each is accurate, can oft' be fit together and reconciled so that each view can be seen to be true in itself, yet really being only a part of a larger truth or more sophisticated reality.

Not all reported observations of course can be reconciled, though perhaps all accurate views might be . . . ultimately. There are many reasons for distorted and erroneous views (most, perhaps, from a pausity of accurate information and mistaken premises). Those that will not fit, may require to be reexamined. (So too, perhaps, ought those that do fit.)

As we journey through life we each have our separate experience of reality, each with unique experiences which are personal, and based partly on what is real and true to one's subjective experience. Subjective differences and variance of perspective of experience (between separate observers) with the same entity, gives to each a slightly different outlook on life and reality. The sum total of the difference of their perceptions is apt to be quite more than their different actual experiences can explain. Yet, in concept, it should be possible to iron out these wrinkles, and eventually come upon a unified concept that will later be provable by extended experience.

A man does not leap from the foot of a mountain to its summit in a single bound. Rather, he goes slowly and cautiously, one firm step after another, with determined resolve, to continue until that goal has been achieved. The approach is general - the difficulties are individual and not all foreseeable. The internal mental life can be elevated and carried forward only in a similar step-by-step fashion. Gradually our beginning concepts are enlarged, reworked, and replaced. The concepts of yesterday are not adequate for the understanding and solution of today's problems. The first class repairman of the Model "A" Ford would require considerable extra experience and training to become proficient in the analysis and corrections of problems in the Ford of 1983 vintage. Just so, our hand-me-down and even our self-constructed concepts needs must be abandoned, as we reach upward and lift ourselves toward an ever more realistic view of how things are, were, or shall be.

We are indeed subject to 'that-which-is-greater-than-ourselves'. This we acknowledge readily enough with but the briefest recollection of the myriad examples which frustrate our every day, and each waking hour. Perhaps I am currently partial to designating that as the "The Force", as it was called in the movie "Star Wars". I am also inclined toward the word "Deity", for it seems through the years not to have become the trademark of any special sect. The expressions "nature" or "natural law" are perhaps even better, in my view, for they hint specifically of an operational concept of what is otherwise commonly designated vaguely as "Allah", "God", "Buddha" etc. The non-trademark (generic) expressions allow one more easily to deal with the concept openly and afresh. To use such generic expressions in conversation and in writing, keeps us aware that one does not subscribe to one or another of the currently common religious views of that-which-is-greater than ourselves.

One might easily suppose that a part of that which is 'greater-than-ourselves' constitutes a part of our own very beings. Just as we incorporate within ourselves, somewhat of the bodies of all plants and animals that we consume; so also do we bear a trite of the substance of our parents and linear ancestors. One also incorporates into the mental aspect of his being, the intangible stuff - superstitious notions, methods, beliefs, ideas, ideals, concepts, and attitudes from our ancestors and our society. It does not seem likely that without this transfer of that mental-philosophical-psychological material, that we (left alone and entirely to our own devices) would be much elevated in our existence beyond the cattle of the field. The tradition of learning seems rooted somehow within our very genetic structure, and magnified by our cultural habits of family, clan, and tribe.

Everywhere about the world, in all peoples, has arisen this awareness of that-which-is-greater-than ourselves. The intangible deity. And the metaphysicality of the wide universe. The general notion is that the intangible deity is separate from, and above nature and the laws of nature - which may or may not be the case. This awareness is given expression in various superstitions, magical rites, and the early beginnings of all religious practices - so multiple in diversity. Not always at a conscious and intellectual level, peoples and tribes have recognized the unifying potential of shared beliefs and have thereby organized their cultures socially, around a mythical-religious-philosophical system of concepts of a deity; and rituals of activity seemingly intended to court the favor of the deity - or placate what they deem to be evidence or potential of his wrath. A peoples' collective experiences and knowledge of seasons, of agriculture, of hunting, of warfare, or psychology etc. then flow into, and unite with their evolving religions. These things they believe. Such a religion then represented their knowledge - imbedded in myth; and was a thing of utilitarian value. Such a body of mythical notions would gradually be acquired, and then taken over by perceptive 'specialists' (priests and shamen) as the history of the tribe progressed. Both the magical-superstitious and the knowledge-wisdom within a religion do have a tendency to lose their flexibility. On the one hand then, the religion retains some utilitarian value to the extent that its wisdom and knowledge are aligned with reality. On the other hand, the religion is a distinct disservice in that new knowledge and more useful concepts are disbarred by the inflexibility of a previously formalized system of superstition, belief, and ritual.

At another stage in an involving society (in conjunction with its religion) is the development of political-military leadership to police and regulate the tribesmen and to protect, control, and extend the tribal interests against its neighboring bands, in the inevitable competition for the natural resources to sustain life and avoid enslavement. The political-military leaders then become rival to the priestly leaders for status within, and for control of the tribe. Insofar as physical prowess, the priests have little ability to protect their status. However, the military-political leaders need the assistance and support of the priests in order to sustain their power to mobilize tribal warriors for defensive and offensive contest against the threat of neighboring tribes. Thus, there comes into being an uneasy but vital truce between the priesthood and the political-military governors of the tribe.

The formalities of the priesthood then tend to become less vital (more symbolic) as compared to the propagation of old beliefs and superstitions, which are more able to compel and retain the loyalty and blind faith of the tribesmen. A larger emphasis of the 'elect' priesthood is then placed upon their ability to compel and control the will and assent of the tribesmen - along with 'the tithe', or its equivalent . . . the power of money. Religion's wealth and status function to counterbalance the military-political powers of the state, for the maintenance and protection of their own status against inside and outside tribal usurpation.

Thus then, are the trustees of the supernatural and of the natural powers, within the tribe thereby united in uneasy truce to perpetrate status, power, and control within the tribal system.

RGB

Inscriptions Upon The Tabla Ransa

Our primary knowledge comes to us through our sense organs, to facilitate our perception of the potential assets and threats of the outer world in which we are immersed. Those first quiet impressions existed in times prior to our feeble evolving powers of reason and recollection. Our power to recollect sensory impressions is weak, and I am appraised of this truth daily. My ideas concerning this topic were precipitated in discussion with members of the Lunar Society some decades ago. Today I have had intermittent recollections of what I wished to write concerning these matters. But, just now, as I sat down with pen and sense of urgency concerning something I intend to write, I was forced to search and ponder with effort, just what it was that (sitting here with pen) that I had hopes of expressing.

The reality of materials of the outer world is confirmed by probing their related manifestations with our various sensory faculties. As infants and unsophisticated toddlers, we begin by investigation of things close at hand. What we see, we try to get our hands upon, in order to test its sounds, its surface texture, its smell, and its taste. We correlate these things with our most sophisticated sense - sight. Eventually, by sight alone - we are able to imagine and predict some of an object's characteristics by visual impressions.

As infants, our genetic and sociologic endowment from our forbearers gives to us a period of grace and protection in which to grow both physically, socially, and intellectually. There seems a variation in proportion of these encouragements from tribe to tribe, and between different families within a tribe. Some of these measures, customs, and practice are useful. Some are, or tend to become counterproductive and in need of correction. The specifics of physical skills and weaponry changes from age to age. Culture too, changes but only slowly and with diversity around the world. A long and adult life can be lived within the framework of cultural patterns and examples with but a minimum and uncertain resort to ever the powers of reason. The powers of the mind remain however, as a large and muchly untested reserve for the understanding of the world of nature, of man, of the mind ,and of its powers. The relatively untapped powers of the mind--and its capacity to recall, to integrate and to reason, lead to the slow and progressive cultural changes of mankind.

The perceptive mechanisms of man fit him to function as a scientific investigator of reality. It is as though mankind were designed and destined as scientific and analytical beings, above all creatures.

Concerning things familiar, we gradually forego repeated in-depth analysis in lieu of presumptions based upon visual and-or auditory input. We are thus, unnecessarily misled and mistaken on occasion, but the uncertainty factor is small, compared to the savings in time and effort. Still, regarding the unfamiliar and new, we resort to the more complete and fundamental examination technique until those new categories are also familiar among the things with which we are acquainted.

We develop a language of our own, closely related to those among whom we live. Nouns and verbs in phrases, then sentences, communicate to us a new category of information, ideas, concepts, and theories. Language greatly facilitates our exploration of the tangible world, as we exchange information concerning our individual perceptions and experiences. Certainly, without language, we would not have access to information concerning the metaphysical. What we read and are told, we still must test to the extent that we have time, facilities, and the equipment with which to confirm what we learn. Central and vital to the whole process, must always remain our sense of doubt and skepticism along with curiosity. Learning becomes more sophisticated as we learn to project our retina upon the surface of things afar through telescopes and by the analysis of minor changes in their emanations of electromagnetic phenomena. Besides surface phenomena, we begin to detect internal structure and process through percussion, deep palpation, X-Rays, infra-red, ultraviolet, etc.

Working with concepts, ideas, and theories, our testing becomes progressively more challenging to the point where we reach the frontier of our intellectual capacity. But frontiers recede, and what we now can only tentatively accept today as knowledge, remains hopefully to be established (or disestablished) in future generations. Some ideas and truths are so elusive of verification and documentation, that only one man will once, at last, discover that method of proof, by serendipity, or by consuming a large portion of his life in the achievement.

The natural universe seems quite filled with objects, phenomena, and truths, most of which has probably not yet made its first impression upon any human consciousness. It must be the case, that there are no incompatible realities. Yet, man's explanations and operational concepts are only in their infancy and stir deep controversy among mankind. Poor, dim, and juvenile creatures, as we are, we tend to envision the all of that-which-is-greater than ourselves by the heavy over-application of mythology. We cling to these incomplete systems with passion and fervor because they seem to be of some assistance in our need to understand. The myths are often given undue status by the fact that it becomes politically and economically expedient for individuals and groups to manipulate the masses of mankind through these perpetuated distortions of truth.

And yet, every now and then, a mind here or there, from our dimwitted species, will burst into flower, given a unique experience and proper background of family tradition, exposure to ideas and encouragement. Such a mind brings progress, beauty, and rejuvenation of ideation into the world. It would happen more often perhaps, if individual lives were not so filled with time-consuming struggles, with passions, with learning a trade, with earning a living, with supporting the unsupportable, with fighting wars, with having to recover from illness and injury, with the performance of rituals, with haggling over prices, with doing good (and evil). Yet the ability to think and reason can be finely tempered by firsthand experience in all of these things - experience in solving life's problems. Second-hand experience (conversations with others) can broaden our perspective view and sharpen reason. Not less useful is 3rd hand experience (the written examples, experience, and the views of others). Its potential for benefit to our rational powers of the mind, is decisively powerful to the extent that multiple and diverse reading materials are available, first - and then actually made use of. Given such access, only personal interest and determined quest, along with a doubting disposition can predispose one toward truth. For all ideas, ideals, and concepts are controversial.

There is a time for doubt, just as there is also a time for belief. Myriads of gadgets and gizmos, as well as ideas, ideals, concepts, and philosophical systems are offered up for sale to the weary pilgrim - for a price. The price is always high and the claims of the product are not infrequently exaggerated. Nor with any purchase, is it ever apt to fulfill the unreal expectations of the pilgrim. And so, it is well to doubt before one commits to purchase. For much of what is offered for consumption has but little or no value; and some of it is hazardous to life, limb, and soul. A thorough-going skepticism, properly exercised and trained, can save one time, money, and grief aplenty. The price to be paid is a chunk of one's life. For honest money is gotten only by the expenditure of one's time and energy.

The time for believing is after one has made the purchase. For confidence and optimism can contribute heavily to whatever success one has with only marginally satisfactory merchandise. With that of lesser quality, the euphoric expectation may often be the only benefit to be derived from the purchase. Why deny oneself even those small moments of bliss by the now premature exercise of doubt?

The time for doubt is oft recurrent, as when proven experience tells one that little or nothing of value has been derived even after extended attempts at satisfaction with the purchase. Likewise when the promise of satisfaction promises forever to be somewhere in the future - but never in the here and now. Then, one must 'gird-up' one's intellectual loins, begin anew to exercise honest doubt, and decide to act. Having decided the merchandise is useless, one must either find someone dumber than oneself (the bigger fool theory) on whom to unload the junk, or toss it into the dung heap.

RGB

ROMANISM

Contesting nations of amalgamated peoples confronted one another militarily-politically now and again. Advancing technologies of warfare and mechanized weaponry soon became the critical factor in the outcome. Accurate information and technical experience were in contest with myth and metaphysics for status. Secular education was soon to advance above religion-philosophy account of its pragmatic value, though mysticism and superstition were allowed and even encouraged to prevail among the masses.

One day however, knowledge began to divorce itself from religion; and courageous doubters of men from among the masses began then to pursue and acquire knowledge. Where knowledge came forward, religious dogma found itself in retreat. But the mass of men is yet intimidated by religion, which early in the lives of individuals, beclouds the advancement of minds, with myth and superstition.

The length and energy of individual lives are limited; and - besides the inevitable mating game - mere mortal man's whatever occasional intent and encouragement toward contemplation and learning, are easily diverted by trinkets, cosmetics, movies, flashing lights, deafening noises, and the mania for owning things. Therefore, no great numbers of mankind regularly accustom themselves to the pursuit of knowledge, though they regularly pass by the portals thereof. Blinded are they . . . by their hand-me-down insights which shut out the lights of the universe. And deafened by their own noise, to the whisperings of the natural world. And their superstitious concepts tend to hardened into concrete by early and regular attendance of religious rituals and sophistic repetitions of cults and clergy.

And these leaders themselves may indeed believe their own myths, just as a hypochondriac may mistakenly believe that he has a serious physical ailment.

Should a war be lost, the native military-political leaders might then be disposed of, and replaced with men of the conquering tribe. A conquered people under certain circumstances, could be more easily dominated, controlled, and taxed if the conquerors could establish a quiet liaison with the religious leaders of the conquered tribes to assure them an ongoing status.

Not all religious leaderships however were predisposed to such clear and pragmatic dealings, so that state religions were sometimes broken; and a totally recalcitrant peoples might be banished into disbursement or carried off into slavery.

A savvy military-political group at the head of a strong and conquering nation might find itself allied with also a progressive priesthood and happen upon a new mode for the control and redirection of the will and consent of the conquered peoples. As between the Romans and the Sabines; and the Etruscans. Confederated Tribes had a tendency to become, 'nations', in which however, the forces of tribalism persist as an always active undercurrent. Religious systems might be combined and reworked; and then propagated officially throughout the dual realm. The new coalition could enlist the very strength and wealth of a conquered nation to comply with the best interests of both the conquerors and the conquered. Tribes were thus welded and became as one in historical legend, strength, wealth, and will. A reading of ancient Roman history well documents just this process.

It is well for us to recall certain historical background information concerning Rome. For Rome has heavily influenced Europe and the New World.

- Rome was primarily a military-political state, united and directed by authoritarian law.
- The objective of Rome was and always has been, to conquer the world and to control and direct mankind and the nations of the earth.
- To achieve these ends and to maintain and further their control, they have always done whatever they felt necessary

and expedient to their cause. The city of Rome itself was first founded under Romulus by force of arms and strong military tradition. The subsequent king, Numa aroused in these peoples a strong sense of law and of religion.

- The Romans originally united the tribes of their own peninsula by war and treaty. They early recognized the unifying effect of religious myth among soldiers and citizens who might cling to promise of accruing benefit in a strong common homeland.
- The Romans early recognized that the cross-currents of contesting religions and religious beliefs worked mightily to the disadvantage of their plans for the unification of their peoples into a firm and stable military-political force. With contesting religions there were always cracks in the texture of nationalism that forever threatened to become chasms. For the prophets, seers, and madmen are always afoot and stirring up the tribes, one against the other on the basis of vague but forceful emotions. How can one send a united army abroad when the constituents are forever at the throats of one another?
- To overcome this emotional and fundamental issue, they generally offended none among local gods and sects! Rather, they enshrined and honored each of these gods and housed them in Rome. They were loosely matted together into a national religion of sorts. The religion was contrived and designed, and supported by the state. Priests were appointed and there was an official calendar of religious events to occupy the time and the minds of the citizens.
- As opposing states and nations were overrun, their leaders were disposed of and their citizens hauled off to Rome. Their religious leaders and mythological Deities were eventually made over into saints, and fragments of their religions not infrequently incorporated into that of Rome.
- Between the rigors of war, and the rituals eternal of religion, the rude masses of men were kept occupied with more of less of success. For the rude masses of men must be so occupied, lest they themselves destroy their state with bickering and exotic excesses.
- At a later date, the kings were proclaimed to have been Deities. Still later, the Caesars themselves (and during their

very lifetimes) were regarded as Deities. They had the license and the power to make it nearly believable. That it was not true, mattered little to them, compared to its pragmatic value and benefit.

- Israel presented the Romans new and uncommon difficulty. Here they met the most bigoted and prejudiced people on the face of the earth. These were the Jewish people, whose god cherished no one but Jews. Nor did the Jewish people want the Romans to accept their god.
- Saul attempted to save a remnant of Jews from annihilation under Rome, by putting forth the image of a peaceful Messiah, rather than the Jewish military-political Messiah which Rome would in no wise abide.
- The result of the furor in Palestine was this:
- The strongly political Messiah advocates (Zionists) were decimated in the destruction of Jerusalem. Those that survived Jerusalem were later eradicated at Masada or hauled off to feed the lions in Rome.
- The oppositional and defiant Jehovah was remythified by an off-beat Jewish sect and given the new image of a now peaceful Messiah. Paul, of Tarsus, seems to have been the primary author and advocate of this more congenial and peaceful 'Messiah' - a form more acceptable (less threatening) to Rome by dint of a Hellenistic philosophical paint job. This new version of Judaism was subsequently designated with the appellation of 'Christianity', and trans-located **to Rome.** There, to co-mingle, compete, and amalgamate, with the multiple other local and imported religious sects immigrated to Rome from throughout the Roman Empire.
- For political reasons, it later (about 325 AD) became expedient for Constantine to make the new Messiah's image into the foremost Deity when again the deity of Caesars became a more difficult illusion to uphold. In fact, the mythical history concerning the person of Romulus (Rome's founder), as told by Livy (who died in 9 BC) seems in many respects much the same as the stories we are told of the person of Jesus. A strange coincidence - and you can wonder which then has the weight of precedence. The king Numa (succeeded Romulus) in fact

even created the position of pontifex (pope) to guide and direct the state religion of Rome hundreds of years BC.

- The Christian religion is a continuation of that strong and Roman tradition of license and expedience. The Catholic Church is the author of a "New Testament" (the peaceful Messiah) intended to supersede the failure of the Old Testament (the warrior-political Messiah) and to subvert the weight of its ancient influence to the new cause. Some say the writings of the gospels was begun perhaps 60 or 70 AD. Some say it was more like 200 or 300 AD. Perhaps even, they are in part but extracts of materials written originally in BC times by Essenes or Gnostics; or even by one of the early Pontfixes (concerning the mythicised life of Romulus). They certainly are not freehand eye-witness accounts, or detailed and accurate as historical documents. Even Christian Scholars are forced to concede that Matthew and Luke seem to be somehow dependent upon Mark. And all three, seem to draw material from some unknown source of sayings. Nor are these alleged saying of Jesus all original.

There were some 17 centuries of book burnings, library destruction, and the hauling off of books and documents for hiding (in caves, and into the Vatican library), in order to make the N.T. appear original and without peer. And after suppressing criticism stringently for centuries, the 18th century and thereafter suddenly blossomed out with some {60,000?) biographical accounts and analysis of the life of Jesus, built upon some few shreds of residual extant data. Albert Schweitzer, among the most studious of men, evaluated and summarized this data and made his own well considered comments in his book, "*The Quest for the Historical Jesus*". There are widely disparaging views among those 60,000 authors, and all have some 'evidence' of one sort or another to support their views.

Christianity is certainly not the religion of Jesus. (Nor is Buddhism the religion of Buddha). Many wise and worthy sayings are dredged up from ancient legends and attributed to the person of Jesus. They could just as well have been attributed to Uncle Remus. The Christian religion might better be termed "Paulism", for he seems to have served as its primary organizer; and to have fabricated a good part of its early doctrine. Yet, surely, "Romanism" would be a more nearly accurate designation as to its most significant utilitarian evolution; and representative of whom it was originally designed to serve.

Such then, is my personal and reconstructed view of the historical reality of Christianity. It is only an outline, and a general view; and I continue to try to update it as mandated by the continued flow of information, experience, and reason.

60,000 diverse biographical sketches (and perhaps a great many more, that were intended, but never saw completion) attest that I am not the first or only one to be dubious concerning all of the propaganda leveled at mankind concerning religion. What is strange, is that despite widespread dissention, they still have any following whatever. Yet, on the other hand, so do all ancient religious forms and practices persist. So does pantheism, animism, and druidism remain present, even also, among present Catholic and Protestant populations.

Priests and politicians continue mutually to support each other's base of power for their own ends. In times of national crises, religion along with nationalism must be drummed upon to bring the mass of men under arms. The church has made of itself, a large part in the social life of its members. And, religious rhetoric and dogma stand in place of a personal mores, for the majority perhaps, of mankind.

I am not down particularly upon Romanism (either the Catholic or the Protestant variety) more than any other religion. For they are all filled with absurdities by the time they are completed into their 'authoritative' and scriptural forms. Nor, if the world were purged of Romanism would our religious-philosophical problems and controversy be ended. For Romanism would merely in all probability be replaced by some other religious sect of authoritarian bent. Perhaps then the Mohammedan sect would set themselves up into that void. Or perhaps the Mormons, the Zoroasterans, the Janists, or the Taoist etc.

Because of the human propensity to cling to forms and avoid the effort of intellectual responsibility, it may always be the case that some religion or another will dominate, control, and direct the lives of the masses of mankind. Nor are any of these forms; nor is tradition without at least some little merit. These religions and forms as scaffolding, are useful to provide a structure for the shaping of individuals into an integrated society. Highly important indeed, especially where large populations of people are crowded together.

If there is a purpose in life, perhaps it has to do with evolutionary transcendence. For mankind, and individual men display this in their history and in their individual lives. Therefore it seems perhaps best that the predominating religion of society, display tolerance to the occasional skeptic and professed 'prophet'. Best, to allow them as self-elected, unpaid servants to think, aspire, and transcend as they see fit, and to keep the manifold sources of assorted embers of truth alive. For their personal growth and transcendence tends also to draw the sluggish authoritarianism system belatedly upwards too.

As to a life hereafter; how would I know about a thing like that? Let that be as it may; for those who claim to know, seem not to agree. Perhaps the world would be the better off, if we cease pretending to certainties of knowledge and information - of which there can be no certainty.

RGB

Durant And Voltaire

As Will Durant ("*Christ and Caesar*") puts it, "History could not come into its own until theology gave way." "Voltaire produced the first philosophy of history - the first systematic attempt to trace the streams of natural causation in the development of the human mind" "for he was interested to know by what steps men passed from barbarism, to civilization." Precisely the matter that interests me, also! Having all of us made that trip - or part of it - in the course of our own lives, we all, perhaps, have some vague recollection as to the landmarks by which we passed.

In Ancient History, the Greeks seem to have inherited and cultivated a facility for rational thought and logic. Perhaps that was because they had some culturally advanced neighbors, and because their curiosity was stimulated by conditions that made it necessary for them to travel widely. They evolved a long tradition of able thinkers, enabled even to make progress against their own culturally inherited religious bias and superstitious ignorance. The Greek culture was subsequently merged into the more unified and universal Roman Culture. There, for a time, it was nearly eclipsed by a tidal wave of physical, economic, political, and religious churning - from which it emerged and continued with the Roman culture, into the Western European, Eastern European, and American cultures - subsequent to the renaissance.

RGB

OF AN ESSAY BY J.W.KRUTCH

by R. Garner Brasseur, M.D.

Once the yoke of universal Catholic Religion was sufficiently diminished, rational thought was progressively freed of some of its restrains. Joseph Wood Krutch takes up the trail of its conflict and evolution from that time - in his essay "The Phantom of Certitude". The early Greek Philosophers had only begun their observation of nature, and had barely started to combine some of those observations with reason and logic. Under the Romans, authoritative dogma had been insinuated into the rational process and logic - to the exclusion of every other influence. Their technological progress was slow and relatively insignificant, as they were preoccupied with war and politics; and later, obsessed with a religious version of politics.

Francis Bacon (1561-1626) looked out upon the ruins of the past. Centuries; whole civilizations had passed, with hardly even a significant modification of methods of heating or lighting. He saw theological metaphysics as sterile and counterproductive to all human accomplishment. Protestant denominations had finally escaped the dead hand of Catholic dogmatism, but yet remained essentially devoid of productive thought or action. The new and the old authoritative sources now merely disputed in their sterile deductions and conclusions, concerning some vague hereafter. Meanwhile, people lived mean and tragic lives, worn by unabated strife, endless labor, and loathsome disease. Francis Bacon espoused a new course; and exhorted his enlightened colleagues to contribute their efforts toward other goals; by way of new methods of thought and outlook. Men were beginning to put aside the fruitless spinning of pure logic, and to set aside the pursuit of the unknowable hereafter. The art of sailing had become a rational technical feat through continuous centuries of trial and error experience - culturally transmitted from generation to generation; and from civilization to civilization. Access to accumulated and to newly acquired data; technical skill in applying that data; and shrewd observation enabled perceptive and astute men to achieve consistent success in navigation. Likewise, architectural engineering was evolving into a learned science - on the basis of reasoned thought; tempered by centuries of experience; and guided by abstracted principles of that past experience; and current experimentation in design. Agriculture too, like Architecture and Navigation had evolved slowly and by degree, so that the fact of its having become a science, went almost unrecognized until this time. Francis Bacon seems to have become aware that these accomplished arts had become transformed into sciences - and considered that success as being, possibly, the result of the combining; 1) the observations of natural phenomena - nature's experiments, 2) the successes and failures of controlled experimentation, together with 3) a rational method that embraces cause and effect relationships. Theology and Metaphysics continued, of course, but without the efforts of Francis Bacon - whose effect on science was largely that of exhortation and encouragement. The evolving scientific method would eventually impact upon Metaphysics too, but with only slow and indirect progress - by calling into question the dubious nature of their authoritative premises, generalities, and conclusions; and by diminishing the sphere of their influence in the affairs of mankind. Until then - indeed, even until now - men have continued their attachment to their historically inherited religions which they presume to have been those of their ancestors; and by voluntary rote affirmation. It could hardly be denied to offer some economy and utility to the order of their lives. For the whole social structure of their lives - for generations - had centered about the social activities connected to the church. And one of the major modes of the transmission of the mores of their communities, comes from the doctrinal teachings of their various religions. The religions, though, are pretty much interchangeable in this regard. In our own society of present times, the public schools and the homes are of at least equal importance to religion - in the transmission of mores. Yet, the un-disprovable teachings of a fiery hereafter, still incline most folks to maintain the cost of their overly expensive religions. For each congenital believer, of each religion, the phantom of certitude spares them the burden of contempt of their fellow parishioners; as well as the time, and the energy which would be required of each, for a personal enquiry into the veracity of that which they are said to believe.

Men of science were necessarily confronted with the intimidation of dogma and a firmly entrenched religious establishment, in their quest of nature's truths; and in formulating tentatively, what seem to be the laws of nature (the evidence of which being based upon their observations and experimentations). But, their ingenuity in applying these new found facts and laws of nature to the production of goods and services (that have gradually and largely enhanced the quality of life) enabled them to proceed, even against the grain of popular prejudice and dogma. A clergy, content with the status quo - and comfortable with the phantom-of-certitude concerning their beliefs - reluctantly retreated to within the boundaries imposed upon them by the advance of science; and its application to technology, Not only were the sciences being developed, one by one, but they were even beginning to merge with one another - so that it was beginning to seem as though they might be a unity. Physics, for example, is necessarily an important consideration, as it pertains to the advanced studies of Chemistry - and vice versa. Advanced biological study requires a familiarity with both Physics and Chemistry. Astronomy becomes a combined study of celestial objects, intricately related to both Chemistry and Physics; related also, on a different scale of magnitude, to Geology, It would seem, if this trend continues, it may well proceed directly into the fields of Theology and Metaphysics! So it was - says J.W.Krutch - that the bright young T.E.Hulme wrote his book, "*Speculations*". The book begins thusly, "One of the main achievements of the nineteenth century was the elaboration and universal application of the principle of continuity. The destruction of this concept is, on the contrary, an urgent necessity of the present." Thus, did he clearly acknowledge to theologians and metaphysicians, the issue that was putting them to great disadvantage to science and valid history in the modern world. In response to that, there was a renewed effort on the part of metaphysicians, to reestablish themselves on firmer ground; and there was a renewed vigor in the old assertions of the clergy.

By way of perspective in the controversy over this issue, it must be pointed out that Christian Theological Metaphysics has always held the upper hand - of political power for persecution and punishment - over slowly evolving secular scientific thought and method. There are no instances of a scientific gathering of men of science, in order specifically to enquire into the beliefs of individual theologians or clergymen, nor whose judgment constituted a sentence of banishment - or even death. Ecclesiastical theology, on the other hand, has always been very oppressive of scientific men merely because they disagreed with his scientific ideas - fearing these might undermine their own beliefs and authority. At least from the time of Ancius Boethius (AD 480-524), science and all other potentially controversial issues were severely scrutinized by the Christian ecclesiastical hierarchy in Europe. Islam, on the other hand, embraced a tradition of broad intellectual pursuit, beginning about one hundred years after the death - of their prophet. Not until the beginning of the eleventh century Renaissance of politics in central and northern Italy, did a scientific philosophy begin to be resurrected in Europe; and then, only haltingly. Padua, Bologna, Paris, and Oxford gradually became university centers of learning, despite their being crowded by continuous scrutiny from religious authority. Paris became the premiere center for receptiveness to new thoughts and ideas, though even its great scholars were harassed. Peter Abelard (1079-1142), Albert the Great (1195-1280), Maricourt (about 1269), Thomas Aquinas (1225-1274), all encountered no small amount of difficulty from the church. Nor did religious reformation suddenly open the minds of Protestant Ecclesiastics. The scholar Michael Servetius (1511-1555) found himself in the hands of Calvin, in Geneva; where he was burned at the stake. Finally, in London (1662), was formed the Royal Society for the Promotion of Natural Sciences (see essay of Thomas Huxley), which was under the protection of the king. Similarly, in Paris, in 1666, was founded the Academie Royal des Sciences. Thus was eased some of the oppression against the sciences. Even so, such studies as those of Wallace and Darwin were met with great hostility on the part of the clergy. Though in our day science is generally accepted with relative calm, this seems largely by virtue of the wealth of goods it produces for a greedy materialistic society. It is, however, roundly berated account of the evil of its by-products; though that has as much to do with the metaphysical short-sightedness of society and individuals, as it does with science.

But to continue now, concerning the re-fortification of "the-will-to-believe", whose new hope for certitude of old beliefs was rekindled by the energy of such new words as those of Hulme. Certainly, science was slower to produce its benisons than many of its overly optimistic proponents had prophesied; and there were alarming consequences of technology which seemed adequate cause for some disappointment. But, it is <u>not</u> the case, that science produces atheists; though that same open-mindedness which seems to benefit scientific thought and progress, tends also to predispose these same minds to enquire into other areas of thought - including Religion and Metaphysics. Even so, to question and doubt authoritative religious dogma is hardly an innovation in this world; nor indulged in, only by minds considered to be scientific. There have been at least dozens - perhaps hundreds - of populations of so-called 'heretics', that have arisen and been successfully exterminated by the Catholic Church in Europe and in the Americas. Many others have been successful in eluding that fate - mainly only since the Protestant Reformation. And, in truth, I don't personally know even a single atheist—-which I find, not surprising. For one might have thought that the phantom of <u>atheistic certitude</u> might be as demanding as the phantom of <u>theistic certitude</u>, as to presumptuousness - and might be a whole lot of more risk to one's body - though not perhaps, more risk to the soul. The simple fact is that the unknowable hereafter simply remains unknowable. Agnosticism seems to me immanently more affirmable than either atheistic or theistic certitudes.

The great problem with Metaphysics is that individuals tend to become 'vested' in the system that they inherit, adopt, or invent. In any of these instances, they feel morally obligated to a system which they knew from the start, to be a moral system. Having tried in good faith to live some of its tenants, they conceive that they are to some degree, an embodiment of that system; to which they have voluntarily accepted with no coercion whatsoever. Thereby, have they received its whatever blessing, and have been be-knighted with a fashionable respectability, which they otherwise previously lacked. They have been certified, as it were - into a remnant society of the elect. They may conceive themselves as responsible, perhaps, to one another; whose attachment to the same faith, is partly in deference to their own certainty concerning that faith. Whatever might be their veiled doubts and disillusionments, how then shall they stand at the next alter-call to announce that they now rescind their commitment to that system to which they volunteered last week at this hour? In any case, it comes to this: being now proclaimed, inducted, and vested into the society, therefore they tend to be more interested in maintaining a general vague certitude concerning complex and esoteric issues. Issues for which they have little time or heart. Certainly no heart for having to begin once more at square one. And they are largely aware that the social philosophies of religions are generally vague enough to enable them to continue to squeeze through the portals from month-to-month, despite the occasional new-found truths they might acquire. Scientific thought and curiosity take a somewhat different perspective, for here, the object is to arrive at truth; though it is generally agreed that only the approximations to that objective, are the best one can hope for (i.e., tentative truth). More than that, science ultimately requires its truths to be objectively affirmed in the real world; or, eventually give way to a greater truth that more nearly does so. The 'pragmatism' of Wm. James, containing as it does, those elements of uncertainty, and of the tentative, was specifically congenial in its open-mindedness, to men of all religious persuasions. And Wm. James himself saw vague religious forces at work in the psychodynamics of men's lives. He attempted to delineate and define some of these forces, as he described them (in his "*The Variety of Religious Experience*"). He saw these forces as the common ground of all religions. Also, as it happens, science was beginning to confirm the reality of a certain . . . uncertainty, even in science. The work of Max Planck and Niels Bohr suggested the operation of 'probability' factors (and hence, uncertainty) at the atomic and subatomic levels in Physics. In mind of these things, and armed with Henri Bergson's notion of 'intuition', the new metaphysicians set out to isolate man and metaphysics from the bonds of continuity - with which science threatened to enclose all subjects. Metaphysicians reasoned that, the science of mere possibilities has no obligation to concern itself particularly with that one possibility which happens to be reality. That possibility (unfathomable reality) they would abandon to science; as they hoped, now, to establish unto themselves the possibility of a metaphysics disconnected from a continuity with reality. A quiet island of their own, as it were - where they need not fear encroachment from science. Here, they might resist the dreaded implication that man is a part of nature. And having thus surveyed their new promised land, and having vaguely set their sights upon its distant horizons, most of them were content to merely presume their promised land had been won (without the exertion of a battle) and continued their business as usual, with this mere new confidence in old assertions. Thomas Aquinas' "*Summa Theologica*" was resurrected from six centuries past, and widely again read and admired. For on the basis of pure logic, he was able to compile a code of behavior concerning the minutiae of conduct. Joseph Krutch says the work is naive, and causes one to smile at some of his conclusions, for the entire work was written without the testing of its deductions by reference to any external facts. So that while its logic may be satisfactory; yet, it fails in its intent - from want of the corrective virtue of alignment to reality. For error is exponentially amplified at every step in a sequence, so that error near or at the base of a chain of reasoning, or event, rapidly progresses to chaos (see "Chaos", in Sc. Amer. Dec.'86). To cite the example: consider the case of an expert pool player (i.e. 'Minnesota Fats'). Though highly skilled in the predictive accuracy and coordinated skill of technique, concerning the game of pool, his miniscule initial error brings on chaos. 'Fats' is given a cue ball and instructed to drive the cue ball into the table cushion. But, he is first to call his shot; that is, to indicate the initial position of the ball, the cushion it shall strike and the precise point of initial deflection from the cushion. Furthermore, he is to predict the precise course that the cue ball shall follow thereafter. Presuming that the ball lost no inertia or speed, how long would the ball follow the predicted course? Because of the exponential amplification of error, it turns out that before the lapse of one minute, the actual course of the ball shall be completely chaotic, compared to the predicted course - if 'Fats' has neglected to take into account even so small a force as the gravitational attraction of an electron, located so remotely as the edge of the galaxy. And so because of the amplification of error, one begins to get some grasp of why it is, that the astronauts like to have their on-board computers in a healthy state of function. That is how they manage to escape death caused by small errors . . . so that they can die of huge stupidities, instead. For the computers make continuous corrections of predicted necessary thrust force for each stage of the flight trajectory, in response to nearly instantaneous collection and integration of up-dated data from tracking systems.

In any case, though, the 'will-to-believe' took new courage in the promise offered by this counter-possibility, whereby there seemed some possibility that Religion, Theology, and Metaphysics might inhabit a newly discovered, unassailable Masada, where the progress of science might not threaten their cozy nitch. Though thought had never been observed, except in conjunction with physiologic processes, and is therefore considered by science to be a physiological phenomenon; yet, metaphysics simply denies that. Denies that dead matter passes into living matter, and that living matter passes into thought, by a continuous process. There is reason to suspect that morality arose from an imputed sacrosanct authority, attributed to slowly evolving customs; based, on the day-to-day experience of living men, living together in their various societies. Yet, metaphysics preferred merely to deny that possibility. Instead, they cling to the medieval hope that metaphysical certitudes (rather more comfortable than the hard truths of natural science) could be arrived at by pure thought. In short, Metaphysics is rather a grasping at straws, in that her advocates are wishing to be "freed from the necessity of referring their conclusions to the test of external fact." In a complex world with little time for thought; and against a cultural background nearly destitute of experience with thought, it is not surprising that men might commonly turn to the metaphysics of past generations; wishing to repose, in a supreme confidence in her. It is the same sort of psychological adjustment to which most of us find resource, when we travel by airplane. Yet, we know that metaphysics was "demonstrably wrong in so many of the certitudes of the past, which science has unquestionably upset". As to the metaphysical certitudes pertaining to the unknowable hereafter, it is at least possible that some one, or the other of them could be correct. But which among those mutually exclusive assertions shall we select; and upon what basis? And what of "intuition", as a working tool (a direct perception of things in their eternal aspect and relationships)? Where is the cutting edge of so vague an instrument? And how may it be said to be of value; producing, as it does, chaotic inconsistency among the multitude of perceivers? The unknowable hereafter remains unknowable, for the present - at least, to those of us on this side of the River Styx. Our speculations upon the subject are, perhaps, best tempered by probability considerations. Certainly though, one cannot arrive upon specific religious or metaphysical certitudes merely on the basis of pure logic, alone. One must generally begin with the dogmatic premises of that particular religion, in order to arrive at their particular certitudes. And so it may be the case, that metaphysics is merely "the art of being sure of something that is not so", and pure "logic, only the art of going wrong, with confidence".

Though Wm. James was a philosophically kindly man, and tolerant to the beliefs of others; yet, he was knowledgeable concerning the progress of science in his day. And his principle of pragmatism was much more demanding and rigorous - as he applied it to his own effort (to grasp reality) than is commonly perceived. The clergy and theological metaphysicians commonly interpret it to mean, "if an idea or belief is comfortable or useful, and it cannot be disproven; then, for practical purposes, it is 'as though' that belief or idea were true". And James himself, tolerantly allowed of this loose use of the concept as a defense of one's right to a 'will-to-believe' whatsoever would be useful and not inconsistent with the known facts. But Wm. James did not condone one's right to believe just whatever one simply wished to believe. For Science applies the principle of pragmatism more precisely, asking of any hypothesis; 1) can it be disproved? and then (if that question is answered, 'no') 2) is it more useful than any other which has been proposed. If yes, then it may be used (tentatively) as a valid possibility. Wm. James and science would both probably agree however, that there is a distinction between such a tentative hypothesis, and the truths which may emerge when more facts are discovered. Since "consistency with proven facts and fruitful workability are the only characteristics by which we would ever be able to recognize truth if we found it. They consequently should constitute a part of the definition of truth itself."

R. Garner Brasseur, M.D.
Feb. 5th 1987

Entropy

by R. Garner Brasseur

Not a common expression, I suppose. I have heard the word and encountered it occasionally in my reading over the past twenty years. Rarely, it is a topic of conversation - but only rarely and briefly. Few of us among the general mass of mankind seems well enough versed with that concept to enable them to discuss the subject comprehensively. We are indebted to Rudolf Clausias for that term - Entropy - and the concept which he numerated first in about 1850. It has come to be known as "The Second Law of Thermodynamics": no device can deliver work out of a closed system which has but a single energy-level potential. That law seems to rest upon the observation that "heat will pass spontaneously from a hot body, to a cold body" (from a high level of potential energy, to a low level of potential energy). It turns out that of all forms of energy, heat is the most disorderly.

Now, "The First Law of Thermodynamics" is more or less equivalent with "The Law of Conservation of Energy". It says that one cannot get more work out of a system than the equivalent of energy which it contains. Indeed, one is destined always to get less! The entropy concept (of the Second Law of Thermodynamics) deals with that specific or relative quantity of energy by which one seems to be 'short-changed' in converting a source of energy into work. For, in any spontaneous process, the amount of <u>un</u>available energy of a system increases with time - a measure of entropy, therefore. And yet, that energy has not been lost; simply unavailable - by dissipation, apparently. So that, by combining the First and Second laws of Thermodynamics, it can be said that: in any closed system, the total energy content remains the same, while the total entropy increases with time. Supposing that that the mass and energy of the universe are currently in a state of expansion (dissipation) subsequent to 'The Big Bang' - entropy might be explicable on that basis. If so, we might anticipate that the fueling of the systems, which provide us energy, may become more efficient once the universe achieves its maximum expansion; and begins its phase of contraction toward some remote incipient recurrent big bang.

On a statistical basis, the general entropy or running down of the universe seems to be the generally accepted status of 'that which is', at the present time. This general decline, dissipation, and running down are generally felt to be equated with increasing chaos, and a decline in the forces of increasing organization. If indeed true, it would be an argument (for example) against the Theory of Evolution - not however, a good argument; for it is easily circumvented. Though our sun (for example) and the universe (in general) could both be powering down; yet the earth and its systems continuously capture energy from that which is being dissipated from the sun and cosmic radiation. Therefore, life on earth is not in an isolated state or progressive decline, dissipation, and chaos; for it is powered and supplemented from a beneficent outside energy supply. And there are undoubtedly a great many similar 'back-water' places throughout the universe where silt is similarly deposited; even though (in general) the currents of time and the river are indeed making progress in transporting the land into the sea.

RGB

Maxwell's Demon was a delightful device of fiction for demonstrating the possibility of escape from the inevitability of entropy. Considering heat as a kinetic phenomenon, one would say that the particles of gas which are heated, have more energy and move faster than those gas molecules which are cooler. If two flasks of the same gas (one heated, the other cold) are connected, the two will diffuse into one another (molecule by molecule) so that their average energy per molecule is the same. This, even though in each of the two, there will still be some that have a high energy (hot) and some that have a low energy (cold). And more, perhaps, will have intermediate levels of energy. Supposing now that we were to place 'Maxwell's Demon' at the point of connection between the two flasks. The demon's task is to catch every fast moving (hot) gas molecule that approached his station (at the point of juncture between the two flasks and toss it into flask "A". soon then, flask "A" would contain all the hot gas; and flask "B", the cold gas. So long as the demon continued faithfully to perform his task, the flasks would then maintain their temperature differential.

I was reading "*Post-Historic Man*", by Roderick Seidenberg (Beacon Press), wherein he suggests that - perhaps life itself is the functional genetic equivalent of Maxwell's Demon. The genetically transmitted ability, that is, to maintain integrity of the individual, against the relentlessness of entropy. To be sure, we lose eventually (perhaps our demon getting tired, falls asleep at his station). On the other hand, though we as individuals drop off eventually; yet, the genetic strain of the species (man, for example) is continuous, even backwards through the whole of evolution. Furthermore, genetics and evolution do not move backwards; but lead progressively to higher forms and increased organization. And such evidence as has come to light, supports the general concept of evolution of the species. Indeed, as is proper, the theory itself must (and has) changed to be compatible with objective evidence.

We are accustomed to distinguish what appears to be purposeful behavior into instinct and intelligence: the later, man attributes primarily to man, who is said to have intelligence - in addition to some rudimentary instinctual behavior patterns. On the other hand, it would be difficult to demonstrate that the two are not the opposite ends of the same continuum. I have been the occasional witness to some actions that have every appearance of the rational intelligence, in creatures as lowly as the spider and the cockroach. Throughout history, some men at least, continue to demonstrate (in their thought, word, and deed) impressively rational and intelligent behavior. Undoubtedly, all men of normal intelligence use that intelligence to some extent or another. Few though, seem regularly attuned to its direction in their lives. Indeed, a large proportion of the lives of all men are guided by ritual and habit; that, possibly founded in turn, upon instinct, experience, custom, and reason.

Language first, and then writing, has enabled man to slowly accumulate some information and abstract some wisdom from experience; and to expand and transmit that experience from generation to generation. The method of reason applied to this early vague and uncertain information enabled some men to acquire power in the politics of war and peace; and some measure of wealth in commerce. Mere circumstance of opportunity; and chance in confrontation were often of equal or greater importance in determining their relative fate among those contestants.

The powers of reason are indeed useful to those favored by fate and circumstance. But despite the accumulation of eminence, wealth, prestige, and power into the hands of intelligent men; yet the progress of man has been slow and halting, concerning industrial technology and the scientific basis upon which to minimize disease, and generate and transmit energy. For reason can function to its maximum effect and efficiency only in proportion to its store of, and access to, valid information - and the disregard of that which is invalid. With the advent of the scientific method in the past three centuries, mankind has for the first time begun to approach a new condition wherein the informed intelligence may have begun to dominate the more or less static nature of instinct. The instinct will abide, no doubt; but man is launched and going forward into the universe at an accelerating pace. Of course, there seems some risk that he may destroy himself in his own laboratory; but that risk may diminish once colonies have been established in space. The risks of adventure cannot be eliminated, though they can and must be reduced. Preservation of the individual seems never to have been a part of nature's scheme for man. The emphasis seems rather to have been for the preservation and non-entropy of the species.

RGB
9/4/87

"CATACLYSMS OF THE COLUMBIA"

From my reading of that book
(by authors John Allen, Marjory Burns, and Sam Saigin)

The geology and the mechanisms of the geological features of eastern Washington's Channeled Scablands was gradually documented and worked out by a Mr. Bretz, who began his field studies of the area about 1912. The geological features of that area were eventually linked to the intermittent release of massive accumulations of water behind the glacial ice-dam obstruction located at the site of what is now Idaho's Lake Pend Orielle and the mouth of the Clark's Fork River which opens into Lake Pend Orielle. Behind the dam of glacial ice, about 500 cubic miles of water accumulated up into and beyond the valley of the Clark's Fork to form what is now referred to as the ancient Lake Missoula. The current site of the city of Missoula lay then about 950 feet below the surface waters of that Lake Missoula. One of the arms of the massive lake extended up the Flathead Valley and Lake area to beyond the city of Kalispel, Montana. A southern arm of the lake extended up the Bitter Root Valley to far beyond the town of Hamilton; while up the valley of the Clark's Fork itself, the waters extended far to the east beyond Drummond and up as far as Deer Lodge.

Intermittently, beginning somewhere about 12,000 to 15,000 years ago, the dam of glacial ice would be lifted up (floated) and partly torn away by the sudden rush of a massive volume of water flowing down the Clark's Fork Valley at a rate approximating nearly ten cubic miles of water per hour, rushing along at speeds of from thirty to sixty miles per hour. From the mouth of the Clark's Fork River, at its entrance into Lake Pend Orielle, the wall of water raged southward twenty miles, and then southwest along the Purcell Trench (where now is located Highway 95), and thence across Rathburn Prairie into the Spokane River Narrows west of Post Falls, Idaho. The south shoulder washings of the deluge silted up the outlet of the Spokane River west of Coeur d' Alene, Idaho, bringing about the formation of what is now the beautiful Lake Coeur d' Alene, which is the source of the present day Spokane River. The rushing flood then proceeded forty miles down the Spokane River to a high narrow area of obstruction where the floods topped the high ancient volcanic plateaus. From there the waters roared pel-mel across the broad plateau, scooping out a multitude of channels in the layers of hard basaltic rock of eastern Washington in the wake of the mighty weight and volume of those massive recurring floods (now known as the Bretz Floods, or the Spokane Floods).

One hundred fifty miles to the southwest of Spokane lies another obstructing basaltic ridge where the mighty Columbia River is forced to negotiate the Wallula Gap narrows, just south and east of Pasco. Here again the rushing flood waters were briefly slowed until they overtopped this obstruction too. Then the deluge surged down the Columbia River Valley, tumbling into the series of ever deepening canyons as the waters churned and gouged ever more deeply into the already spectacular Columbia Gorge through the high Cascade Range of mountains which crest a hundred miles inland from the Pacific Coast. In the descending rush, the flood waters denuded the areas of their top-soils while ripping and scouring the calumniated layers of basaltic rock to further widen the confining walls of the gorge. Spewing from the all too narrow gorge just before the Columbia makes a right angle jog to the north beyond Portland, the torrent of waters spread and tumbled into the lowland of the broad Willamette Valley of Oregon which lies between the Coastal and Cascade Mountain Ranges. There the great excess of Columbia waters spilled southward as far as Albany, fifty miles distant, and making of that lowlands a great but transient lake whose surface waters lay 400 feet above the streets of what is now Portland, Oregon.

Perhaps forty to seventy such dramas were enacted at intervals of a hundred to a hundred sixty years. The Columbia River volume at times was thus some sixty times that of the current volume of South America's great Amazon River, and a volume larger than all of the other rivers of the world combined. Each such flood lasted perhaps but a few days, or a couple of weeks, before the whole cyclical process of re-accumulation of waters into Lake Missoula was again repeated, in preparation for a subsequent deluge. In the aftermath of these floods, some two thousand square miles of eastern Washington State has been scoured clean of its previously thick top-soils and vegetation; and an additional thousand of its square miles carry significant gravel deposits. The spectacular topographical changes of the Columbia Basin and the Columbia Gorge are now understood to be of a cataclysmic nature. That is to say, they are changes that have occurred in consequence of a series of very brief, episodic, mighty, floods, with relatively very little change occurring through the long intervals in between those floods, nor since these floods. The effects of wind erosion are relatively very small, even over long intervals, compared to the weight and force of the mighty torrents of water. Geologists who study the processes of water erosion tell us that the brief annual flood of a river moves at least ninety percent of the soil and rock that is moved along its bed in an entire year.

The gathering and piecing together of this geological information into a unified concept of cause and effect that is supportable by the visible evidence of what remains, has been a slow and painstaking process that has not finally succeeded in convincing the vast majority of geologists until only very recently. Now finally, generally accepted only since about 1956, as the accumulating evidence has continued to mount, and as the pieces of the puzzle have slowly been fitted together.

Another similar mighty, though less spectacular flood has left its similar traces and signature in the valley of the Snake River of southern Idaho and down through Hell's Canyon. The Great Salt Lake of Utah was once a great deal larger and deeper than is its current mere remnant. Its waters likewise did break through a barrier of glacial ice in the Raft River Mountains just west of Snowville, Utah, to send its deluge of water northwards into the Snake River Valley. In subsequent eons of time, the Great Basin that houses The Great Salt Lake has become very arid, and that huge lake has evaporated into a stagnant and relatively small pond that is highly charged with salt and alkaline minerals.

There is a huge batholith of acidic light weight rock material that occupies central Idaho, to the north and to the east of the course of the Snake River. By virtue of its relatively light weight, it essentially floats atop the surrounding and underlying heavy basaltic rock and magma. Its buoyancy lifts it to a great elevation. Its weight nevertheless presses mightily upon those supporting basalts, inducing those basalts repeatedly to burst through a relatively thin crust of rock, and to issue forth as lava flows, along the southern and westerly peripheries of that great batholith.

Thus, the Snake River Valley is a mass of sheeted layers of lava flow, piled one atop the other to a great depth through their eons of episodic outpourings. To the west of the batholith, it would seem that the pressure to induce the flows of molten lava is even greater. Beginning about sixteen million years ago, and for a relatively active period of about ten million years. a series of about two hundred separate flows of lava have issued forth to flow west by north, burying much of eastern Oregon and eastern Washington to an accumulated depth of nearly a mile in some places. These flows in Washington, have crowded the Columbia River north and west toward the roots of the bases of the earlier Cascade Mountain flows. It is these flows, in eastern Washington that have subsequently been carved up into to the appearance of great scabs upon the face of the earth - hence called the Channeled Scablands.

R. Garner Brasseur, M.D.
9 August 1998

EXTANT UNIVERSE

by R. Garner Brasseur, M.D.

In the beginning was the question - "to be, or not to be". The question persists and all of creation vacillates as it has been playing out its steady course now 13.5 billion years and perhaps not yet but half finished. 'Creation' is now in a phase of its evolution that is marked by the presence of a star-studded sky. A period that is compatible to the existence of what we call 'life' - which is probably scattered about the universe - but known to you and I with certainty to exist at least here on planet earth. A long period of time existed before the stars began to coalesce from the cooling soup (plasma) of subatomic particles. And those particles ever so gradually cooled and coagulated into the atoms of Hydrogen which constitute the bulk of the mass of our universe. As cooling continued, those Hydrogen atoms began to attract one another, to clump and clot irregularly into hydrogen clouds - in like manner as we observe the vapors of earth's sky form into knots and masses of vapor that periodically obstruct our view of the sun, the moon, and the stars of our sky.

But no. No stars yet existed to produce the life-giving energy we call light. Light, a form of energy that appears to be the obverse aspect of matter itself. All was darkness and stifling heat as the speed of the movement of the plasma particles and the Hydrogen atoms slowly diminished. The accumulating Hydrogen clouds grew heavy with promise as do the cumulus clouds of summer as they join to form towering formations that become thunder-clouds and inevitably produce turbulence and rain in our advanced times here on earth, within the evolving universe.

Why? When? What? Where? And how? Questions that eventually

precipitate within the mind of mankind, once having produced language from mere brute sounds. Questions that are implied, even though and when not being asked. Implied before man ever asked them. Evidence accumulates to the mind from sensory and motor systems that interact with man's external world and the necessity of his having to interact in a dangerous and unforgiving world and among its multitudinal life forms. The inescapable realities with which he must forever compete for the essentials of his existence.

About a hundred years ago Einstein began to pull together what he had studied and learned - and from his experience and reflections - into some theories that led him into some thought experiments. They, in turn, led him to hypothesize the existence of such an entity as 'a black hole'. Not a thing that anyone had ever seen, but even just such a thing as a shadow can cause one to suppose that there needs must exist a mass to explain it, even though not being able directly to visualize it. Yes, this world and universe is a mysterious place.

Other learned minds have dabbled with and added their insights and calculations to suggest that perhaps black holes do exist, and with the advance of telescopic technology have then come up with observations that seem to validate the existence of these black holes. And they have speculated with oddities of reality, such as to suggest that the faster one travels in space, the slower time passes; and have some observations and calculations that seem to establish the fact. And now they tell us that the closer one physically approaches a black hole, the ever slower passes time, until as one were to approach and then disappear beyond the black hole accretion disc and disappear into the black hole, the clock would stop and time itself would cease to exist. The more interesting part of this, is that the void that existed (or should we say, that was non-existent) before the time of the 'big bang' was the equivalent of a black hole. That being the case, time itself did not exist before the big bang. That being the case, the question of what existed before the big bang is a meaningless question. But that does not mean that "to be, or not to be" is not forever a question that is implied. A question that would have to have been implied even beyond the boundary of eternity itself, just as it is for your existence, and mine.

And to add to this enigma, we are given now to understand that atoms themselves seem continuously suddenly to materialize out of nowhere. While others, inversely, cease suddenly to exist. To be; or not to be . . . .

Eventually the knots and clots of Hydrogen gravitationally attracted together into such a heat-producing weight, that some pairs of the Hydrogen molecule fused together at the core of the mass with such violence as to produce one atom of Helium from the two atoms of Hydrogen - along with a byproduct of a single beam of light. And there was light! Emanating from what we would then call a first generation star. A process which was then evolving all across the far flung universe: the eras of stars had begun.

But the core of even so massive an object as a star eventually comes to the end of its supply of Hydrogen, so that the Hydrogen to Helium reaction does no longer produce enough energy to counterbalance the weight of the overlying mass. Being then squeezed by weight, the temperature of the core rises enough to permit a similar fusion between atoms of Helium, to produce Carbon-12 and Oxygen-16 and enough additional light and energy to counterbalance the mass of the star. And when the substrates of that reaction become depleted, other and gradually larger molecules are produced up to those of the weight of Iron. And then, as the weight of the star can no longer be opposed, the star suddenly collapses with such force that the additional heat of the explosion produces even many others of the heaviest 92 elements even as the star is ripped apart and flings its outer mass into the relative vacuum of its surrounding space, enriching the interstellar Hydrogen gas clouds with its newly created atoms. From these enriched gas clouds, the second generation of newborn stars arise in the same process as that by which the first generations stars arose. Some of them much larger than previous stars, besides being heavier from the inclusion in their mass of some proportion of elements heavier than mere Hydrogen. After they in turn first use up their supply of hydrogen, they, having heavier elements in their mixture, in turn can fuse even the ever higher weight atoms as their greater weight can produce ever higher temperatures. The second generation stars too, cycle down to the end of their life spans and produce even greater explosions account of their higher weights and temperatures. Thus, the ever heavier atoms are again commingled with an ever more enriched interstellar gas clouds. The process seemingly continues on to ever weightier and hotter subsequent generations of stars. But from the very beginning, of the big bang, all of those positive forces of matter and energy were pitted against the invisible negative forces we call by the names of dark energy and dark matter (presumably interchangeable with one another?). So that like a car which at 80 mph has suddenly run out of fuel, it is destined ere long to come to a stop. Thus, from the very beginning it was destined to come to this stop. We might say that the equation was balanced.

Not all of the vaporous gas cloud from which a star is born is included into the body of the star, but some remains as a spinning disc encircling the new star. This cools and condenses into a variable number of what eventually become the planets and their moons, as well as stunted bodies of mass that become the asteroid, comet, and interplanetary dust of each particular solar system.

Meanwhile, the universe as a whole continues to expand and cool, so that the interstellar clouds are too dilute to permit of any new forming stars, and the final generations of stars explode and wink-out as the final sources to the production of light, and the universe becomes a dark and cold. Long before that final fate, the universe will have become uninhabitable by any form of life whatsoever.

And just as before what is called 'The Big Bang' is said to have occurred, so also after its consequences have dissolved into nothingness there continues to be the metaphysically implied "to be, or not to be"; as well as why? when? what? where? and how?

"God only knows."

R. Garner Brasseur, M.D.
16 August 2011

MAYFLY
(Larva, Adult, And Beyond)

by R. Garner Brasseur

I am given to understand that some half-dozen years preceding my earliest recollections, I came into this world as "a quivering lump of clay - not far removed from a beast that day". Not much advantaged above the station of the lowly larva or earthworm, but equipped with compulsions even as these are. Not exempted from the necessities which are visited upon every creature of earth: the necessity to eat and breathe; and the necessity to beget. The urge to explore and inquire. These things being so, then - like the earthworm - I stirred and wriggled in my perceptive dark earth-bound mortality, and set forth presently on the great adventure of existence, where even just to see the obvious requires of one a constant struggle. [paraphrase from Alan Devoe's essay, "Life and Death of a Worm"]

But the history of the universe, the world, the evolution of man and the murk of his unrecorded and controversial versions of his more recent history is an immense tome through which even a dedicated bookwork is not likely ever far to penetrate in the brief span of a single lifetime. The life of the adult mayfly is but a single day; the span of a man's life is scarcely more. But just because I have not taken nor had sufficient time to comprehend 'the all', does not absolve me from the duty of putting forth at least some little symbolic effort at so grand a conquest. A goodwill gesture to my fellow mortals; and perhaps a moral obligation? And thus, my fitful and discombobulated efforts proceed next to the following recollection.

I stopped by the local junior college in southern New Mexico one Friday night to attend one of their series of special movies. Playing was

"Arsenic and Old Lace". I myself acted a minor role in that productions when I was a junior in high school. Yet, my memory of it is dim. I had a few small lines to learn, and a few cues to remember. It seemed to me a complex and difficult thing to coordinate and I recall that it troubled me considerably. I was anxious and fretful, not at all sure that I would do it right.

I had the same reactions and feelings when I played minor parts in "The Red Mill", and in "The Pirates of Penzance". I lived and felt toward those roles and uncertainties, somewhat also as I lived and felt about my life. I awaited, to be assigned a particular role, but never aspired in advance to play this part, or that. In point of fact, of course I never knew the plot or the story in advance. I only knew that such-and-such was going to be produced, and that because I was a member of this class, or belonged to the choir, that I was more or less expected to participate in some way and perhaps play some specific role. But I always presumed that "they" (the teachers/ the other members of the group?) were in a position to know what part I ought to play and would give me valid instruction and cues to enable me to accomplish what was required. I maintained more or less a general sense of security that I could pretend a satisfactory performance.

Strangely though, in the case of "Arsenic and Old Lace", I really recall but little of the plot. I found that out the night I recently saw the production in film. Seeing it, in fact, convinces me that the problem is not that I have forgotten. The fact is that I never was well acquainted with plot or with the production as a whole. I was perhaps so absorbed in learning my little lines and cues, that I failed to grasp not only the message, but even a rudimentary perception of the overall plot.

How exactly similar with my life as a whole! For I had no notion of who I was, of what part I should play, what cues to look for, or what words or lines to use, having once recognized a cue. For I had the general notion that I ought cooperate affably and accede to play whatsoever role was decided upon for me. The deciding factor as to which part I played (be it central or insignificant) was merely whatsoever was expected of me. I only need be told, and then to have the moral support of my associates in the fulfilling of that role.

Other people, it seemed to me, were persons in their own right, with specific identity and specific characteristics. As though they acted specifically out of a knowledge of exactly what was to be said and done. Each act, gesture and word seemed so appropriate and so correct that it seemed the very fulfillment of predestination.

My own situation I perceived of, as that of an outsider, now come to this arena of activity as an observer. Always a bit envious of the reality and certainty of their roles, compared to only the tentativeness of my own. Yet, the circumstances of my life seem to have situated me in just this position. There was nowhere to which I might withdraw, for my parents, daily trundled me off to school, off to sell newspapers, out of the house to play etc. I saw that my brothers and sisters were caught up in the same routine of their daily lives. Yet, I had no complaints to register. It simply was the way things were, and we youngsters were travelers on that road.

Only within the family did we have places of certainty. One was the oldest, one the youngest, one the favorite, one the smartest etc. The family itself however, was always forever relocating into some other town. As individuals we were each newcomers to separate peer-group school mates and to a new society of beings, from well established families abiding here since ageless time and treading their beaten paths of certainty. I vaguely envied their established orbits and places - apparently eternal - of warmth and light. Among them, I was a wanderer - such as a meteor or a comet - here amongst them, yet not really a part of their planetary system.

Within the universe, some such wanderers occasionally become favored and captured, to become another of that cluster of a particular planetary system and settle comfortably into an orbit of their own. Most though, sweep on through, lingering here for but a brief turn before drifting back into limbo. They similarly encounter another planetary system here and there until one day their molecular existence as an entity is eroded into non-existence by pressure of heat and time or a spectacular collision with one of their kin...

I do not doubt that my view applies generally to the lot of the millions of mankind in each their individual existence. The outsider is likely to experience a sense of self-consciousness and clumsiness - as the newcomer to a group - however loosely that group be associated. Perceives and somewhat envies their advantage of person and place while neglecting to consider their individual private unhappiness, disadvantage, and discontent. One neglects to realize that oneself - as an outsider - also has unique advantages and characteristics that may make him to some degree the envy of others. For in their closeness, they too are bound by regulations that impede the doing and becoming of what they sometimes fancifully wish. In short, the laws of their being bestow upon them advantage and disadvantage peculiar each unto himself. They too have their small satisfactions and sometime large envies. For them, as for me, every advantage is a trade-off for some sort of a disadvantage and limitation. The word responsibility, comes to mind.

And so, we as individuals are plagued and frustrated by our personal limitations and disadvantages. I would not imply that we are all equally endowed with the same equivalent proportion of assets. For many by virtue of inherited wealth and gift of genetic endowment have relatively unencumbered lives. So also concerning the fortuitous circumstances as to the land of one's birth and time in history.

There remains nothing for one to do with this - one's own life and circumstance - but to live it out; and to make the most of it. Just so, do we also play out a hand of cards, with no complaint or mention of the weaknesses of that hand. I have no way to approach life except through reason and persistent attempts to grasp and understand.

RGB

To Be, Or Not To Be

In the beginning I was engulfed in an amorphous totality with no detail whatever to impinge upon my obtunded natal consciousness. None of this into which I had been precipitated was of my choosing. I was not a volunteer. Was but "a quivering lump of clay - not far removed from a beast that day". The functioning machinery of my existence had been turned out in the fullness of time; as is the engine of a motor vehicle, from a lump of metal. Precipitated into a family, a neighborhood, a community, a nation, a world of millions. There to be shaped and nurtured into some one or more of a host of potential possibilities and uses, by the times and circumstances of my being; and by the society of similar creatures with whom I have gradually come to recognize as having a great deal in common with myself and with one another.

In my childhood and early youth my parents and siblings directly and indirectly swept me into the current of daily routine and activities. I bobbed along sort of treading water in that current of daily routine with no plans or agenda of my own and with only the vaguest perception that perhaps in some distant future day I might be what was called 'an adult' with the liberty and freedom to own an independent life and perhaps be in charge of directing the ongoing goals and objectives of my own little batch of children. As best I could discern, that seemed to be the way things were headed for all of us youngsters - 'in the fullness of time', as the expression goes. And that somewhere 'in the by-and-by', even that would come to an end, and I would probably go to heaven - wherever that was.

As the seed of an acorn becomes an oak in the presence of a nutritious soil, atmospheric gases, a favorable climate, water, and sunlight (and circumstance); so also had I gradually attained a form and being in accordance with the possibilities and limitations of my genetic inheritance. There was a lot for me to learn in my first few busy years, just to enable me to establish rudimentary communications with those few about me. I wouldn't had survived, if they had not treated me kindly. And through the years I have gradually become half-civilized, and neat, and clean . . . and well-advised. But in a few years, I found myself outside the nest, with no tangible assets, and having to make my own way in the world. Being broke, cold, hungry, and without a home is a lonesome business - and depressing. As I had strength, good health, and coordination; and had acquired a general sort of education, and a modest capacity for communication and understanding, it seemed like there might ought to be some way that I could put those things to some use, so as to acquire the bare essentials of sustaining a living. Since I was not yet quite desperate enough to beg, and my limited education left me aware that thievery and robbery might leave me in even further difficulty, I needs must give consideration to the possibilities of somehow earning my way along. Endowed as I was with no inheritance, I pondered as to how I perhaps myself ought give consideration to the necessity of the alternative of work. It was a hard and desperate business, this work - yet there seemed to be a great many who managed to sustain themselves with little or no apparent labor. How did they manage to get by without that necessity? At least until I might figure that out and emulate that achievement, I needs must "get to crackin".

Though there seemed generally to be a lot of work that needed doing; yet there seemed to be a good many people who had an aversion to work: but were so desperate to have it done, that they paid the able and willing in 'coin of the realm', in order not to have to do the work themselves. And so I enquired about, to learn from the laborers, just where and how one might find some such work for which the more well-to-do might pay a man. Fate always enters into to these arrangements, and I did then begin to find enough income to sustain myself. But the work was fatiguing, and increased my appetite, so that I ended up having to do more work than what I had supposed, to satisfy my caloric needs. And once then enabled by work to sustain myself with my basic needs, I then began to acquire additional 'appetites'. I was no longer content just to eat the bread and go without the meat. I was lured by music, theatre, and the dance. Entertaining companions became an additional expense. Soon I was living beyond my means as this cultural inheritance was making its demands upon me - in addition to the demands of genetic inheritance. Expenses were rising.

The physical work proved to be hard and tiring, and I was becoming ever more aware that I did not actually enjoy the work itself by which I was sustained. Confronted as I was with the realities of this world, questions began to arise into my consciousness. Though I had been gifted with the machinery that constitutes this body - and 'a being' - I had never had access to the instruction manual pertaining to the design, operation, and maintenance of this being, and its various parts. This business of 'being' had gotten to the point of making a lot of demands upon me. And I was beginning noticeably to have to exert myself to keep up with these demands. Evolved from work and demands and from appetites was also now this matter of 'concerns' that was beginning to weigh in upon me. Was I irrevocably now economically enslaved? Was there no possibility whatever of escape from the burdens of doing the will of others? Perhaps there be alternatives? Perhaps another way to go about this so as not be so overly encumbered with the necessity of quite so much labor. Perhaps one could find work that was not so physically demanding. Work that was not so repetitious and boring. Work that was not so intellectually taxing: thinking, too, turns out to be laborious and tiring. Might one find some type of work that was 'enjoyable'? Perhaps one might find a job with a higher rate of pay, so as to require of one less of his time and effort. Perhaps one might find what is called a 'sinecure' - a well paying 'position' with a comfortable office and a staff of underlings - such as a government 'appointment'. Preferably an appointment such as might accord one with a sense of importance; such that one might be treated deferentially just everywhere one might wish to wander at his leisure.

Is everyone - or even anyone - enamored with this business of working for a living? If so, why do we so look forward to the ever next holiday; why hanker in anticipation for the upcoming vacation period and sabbatical; why the dangling carrot to keep one focused on retirement in the by-and-by?

Nothing to do but work
Nothing to eat but food
Nothing to wear but clothes
To keep one from going nude

Nothing to breath but air

Quick as a flash 'tis gone
Nowhere to fall but off
Nowhere to stand but on

Nothing to comb but hair
Nowhere to sleep but in bed
Nothing to weep but tears
No one to bury but dead

Nothing to sing but a song
Ah well, alas and alack
Nowhere to go but out
Nowhere to come but back

Nothing to see but sights
Northing to quench but thirst
Nothing to have but what we've got
Thus through life we are cursed

Nothing to strike but a gait
Everything moves that goes
Nothing at all but common sense
Can ever resolve these woes

Ben King

Well, economic reality is an ever present factor that confronts we mere mortals. The earth is not abundantly fruitful apart from the sweat of man's brow that ensues in consequence of his endless toil and endeavor. Shelter from the elements is a necessity to man's survival and comfort, and none such exists in nature. And the clothing necessary to obviate the nakedness of man needs must be garnered by his own inventiveness and time-consuming effort. No, nothing at all but common sense can ever resolve these woes!

Our reality is comprised of the sum total of interrelated and interconnected subjects and objects and of our perceptions. One must finally not only realize, but also accept that one will not be able to study all of 'that which is', nor develop all of the many possibilities to which he has been genetically endowed. Nor drink to the dregs all . . . of even just one field of knowledge. No time for that. "No time to stand beneath the boughs/ to stare as long as sheep and cows . . . . "

And at the back of the mind, one wishes eventually to have done something of value - something perhaps even ennobling. Would like to know what is the nature of the game going on behind the scenes of our 'being', existing, and individual actions.

"Thus at the flaming forge of life
Our fortunes must be wrought.
Thus at the sounding anvil shaped,
Each burning deed and thought."

Even a lone shipwrecked sailor (with something near equivalent to a high school education, say) washed up onto a desert isle of sufficient natural shelter and supply of food and water, would end up considering what he might do with himself in his spare time. (Exclude the possibility of rescue or escape in this thought experiment.) Inevitably, he would eventually take some steps to make himself more comfortable, but what then after that. Though he has never taken an interest in books, this marooned fellow might now read some . . . if he had them. If he had some paper, he might write one. Would we say he has absolute freedom - or that he is imprisoned? As with you or I, in the here and now, neither - and both. His situation excludes him from much of that to which he is ordinarily inclined. Would he be driven to madness in his solitude? Or might he preoccupy his mind with reading, study, writing, local observations of day and of nightly phenomena, philosophy . . . . Might it eventually occur to him, that though a castaway by fate, he might at least leave behind him:

"Footprints in the sands of time; -Footprints, that perhaps another,Sailing o'er life's solemn main,A forlorn and shipwrecked brother,Seeing, shall take heart again."Might he "then, be up and doing,With a heart for any fate;Still achieving, still pursuing,Learn to labor and to wait."

The general nature of one's existence has the possibility of leading one into the most common and ordinary employment in physical labor or a trade, though there is also some possibility of finding one's way into one of many specialties, professional and non-professional. But, one must spend long years of self-disciplined labor and effort in maturing and in learning something from which one can earn a living.

To reiterate, one must finally not only realize, but also accept that one will not be able to intellectually encompass all of 'that which is', within his limited time for study; nor develop all of the many possibilities to which he has been genetically endowed. Nor drink to the dregs all of even just one field of knowledge. Never time enough for that.

I am inclined to suppose that no man - reviewing his past life from some whatever 'hereafter' - would be pleased to suddenly then become aware that he had frittered away his life devoted to the study and learning of mistaken ideas, erroneous concepts, and groundless religious systems.

Say, for example that there were such a thing as 'a final judgment' in 'a hereafter'. There, the Hindu - for example - would be confronted with that now obvious fact (that their beliefs had been based on nothing more than mythical tales and mistaken legends). Called upon then to explain themselves, to 'the grand inquisitor' what might they reply in the way of mitigating circumstances to get themselves 'off the hook'? Well, there is always the plea of "innocent by virtue of insanity". After all, some 10% of the population is mentally unstable with psychosis or severe characterological defects. Some such pleas perhaps as "I was born and raised with that system of belief"; or, "my life was so preoccupied with the desperate business of the earning of a living, that it left me no time to study and ponder concerning the beliefs into which I was born"; or, "it was dangerous, or made life difficult to go against the grain of our common beliefs".

'Innocence by virtue of ignorance' would seem to be the most logical and probable of 'explanations' one might offer to any such 'grand inquisitor'. And - surely an 'acceptable' explanation. Though it is true that valid information and knowledge have been gradually increasing for several hundred years, most of what is potentially knowable has by no means yet yielded to investigative research. Thus, ignorance and misinformation prevail (only slightly diluted) not only among we of the 'unwashed masses' but still holds sway among even the 'the best and brightest' of minds whose authoritative investigations are narrowly focused into specific fields of knowledge. For the expertise and knowledgebility of even the minds of bright, well-intended, and honorable men does not automatically extend widely outside of their specific fields of expertise. And they too can plea, that they are at least putting forth an effort to break free of 'the all prevailing ignorance'.

RGB

Health Maintenance

To brother, Duane--

I am delayed in my intended response to your letter in large part because of your fervent message concerning health maintenance. In addition to your written document, I recall that we discussed this general subject in our visits during the past year. And I vividly recall that you introduced me one by one to the various herbs, extracts, and supplements to which you have had recourse in recent years. When you had completed your presentation, I was a little astounded at the number of bottles that stood arrayed upon your table top. I have no cause to doubt that you are sincere in what you advocate; nor that you have been remiss in your effort to validate your views with an honest research. I appreciate and am touched by your concern to offer to me your best advice from your most recent tentative conclusions in this matter of health maintenance. And I philosophically agree with you about the fundamental importance of maintaining a healthy life style and an adequate nutritious diet. Based on what you showed me, and considering my limited knowledge of the specific active ingredients of those substances, I have at this time no cause to impugn the potential benefits to our systems of any one of them. Neither do I disregard your personal testimony as to the benefits of any one of them specifically. It is on the basis of such personal testimonies that we can begin to evaluate the potential benefit of any such substances. But a thorough scientific evaluation is a complex and time consuming business; and we are best advised to defer our final judgment, nor confer our final validation until our information is complete. However - since our lives are short and the tedious process of full validation is long - there is nothing to prevent our personal experimentation with these various substances, in the hope that one or the other may convey to us such benefit as we require. Provided, of course, that there is adequate empirical evidence and testimonial experience to reasonably assure that the substances are not known to be dangerous.

And so, the problem with the use of these substances being based on testimonial is that when it comes to checking these things out, our research is - of necessity - limited indeed . . . . Limited, in fact, to other testimonials; because the scientific and definitive information is nowhere available. Has not yet been completed . . . often, perhaps not yet even begun. Pragmatically, the other main problem that I have with testimonial recommendations is that I have so many of them, and one's time is so limited that there simply is not time enough to permit a perusal of the testimonials - themselves, each, a highly dubious source.

Having reviewed and reflected upon my own views concerning cancer, it is my tentative view that the major causes of cancer are primarily 1) cigarette smoke 2)cosmic radiation and 3)dietary. There are many other causes, including harsh chemicals and radiation from radioactive elements of our earthly environment, but items 1 and 2 each constitute about 30% of the cause. Each of them is within our individual ability to control or limit. Dietary factors pertaining to our general health may also eventually be within our ability to control, but what we know about them is only of a general nature - too much fatty food and too much alcohol are certainly a part of that. As far as I know, the eating sugar does not cause diabetes. What you have said about the weakening of individual immune systems certainly increases our susceptibility to all of the above causes of cancer . . . as is clearly evident from our experience of AIDS.

It would be erroneous to say that the treatment of cancer by surgery, radiation, and chemicals is not advancing. A part of that advancement has to do with gradually discovering which of the three is the most effective for any specific type of cancer. Another has to do with the slow development of more effective and less traumatic procedures; and with the development of more effective chemicals. No one denies that fortifying the immune system will also be very beneficial to the treatment of cancer - another approach that is slow in developing. Once I have concocted the "divine elixir", that too, may be beneficial. But we are a primitive - and only slowly developing species of creatures; so all of these things will take time. The Sept 1996 issue of Scientific American is devoted to the subject of cancer. I am enclosing to you some copy of a couple of those articles for your perusal.

Dr. Whitager seems to be fudging at the game he has invented specifically to 'wow' us pilgrims. It isn't outright lying, just sort of a slight-of-hand operation. "WHAT HE WOULD DO IF HE HAD CANCER". He cleverly selects an irrelevant case in order to demonstrate what seems very unlikely to be true if he were to select a more realistic example. He proposes unto himself the situation in which he has a proven case of lung cancer . . . the very worst and most hopeless of all the malignancies. It generally manifests itself suddenly - although it most probably been present and worsening for quite some while. When once it has become detected it is usually so far advanced that nothing at all - that any therapy can actually benefit - has any chance whatever of arresting the problem . . . or, of even retarding its inevitable and speedy march to resolution (in death). We can see then, how this evasive maneuver might seem to support his radical skepticism concerning a generality of hopelessness for all forms of cancer whatsoever - since it applies already to the full thirty percent of all cancer (which is lung cancer). In the case of lung cancer, I suppose that I myself would do much as he suggests he would do - since the well recognized and nearly always hopeless outcome is usually always the same. Supposing however that newly evolving techniques and medication were soon to demonstrate that we could now effect a 50% five-year-survival rate. That sort of scenario, for example, has already come to pass concerning some forms of leukemia. Or, supposing that Dr. W's annual sigmoidoscopy exam had, this year, demonstrated an early and histological proven colon cancer. I don't believe that he would resort to the multitude of herbs and supplements as his only reasonable recourse.

But the matter of health maintenance is a subject quite apart from that of cancer treatment; though it seems to me that our state of information concerning both is rather nothing more than in its beginning stages. However, the matter of health maintenance is a lifelong project which we each must face. Yet, it seems to me that our individuality in the matter of digestion and assimilation of nutrients is so prominent that only the most general of guiding principles would seem to apply. So our situations are such, perhaps, that we needs must each be personally involved in a certain amount of dietary experimentation - for which the only reasonable guides would seem to be the various testimonials that come our way. That, coupled with our individual digestive experiences, reported to us by our innards subsequent to our every experimentation. Coupled with that, there is in fact at least a little firm factual information for our guidance, such as the things that have been discovered pertaining to vitamins, essential proteins, and trace minerals, for example. Said information having been only recently acquired by our struggling race of creatures - within only the past 150 years, more or less. A further evidence of just how primitive our species of creatures truly is. I believe that I do vaguely recall having given you some information concerning this material you call "prostata". And that I happened across that information not long after I had become aware of this new prescription medication, "Proscar". I have never used either of them . . . but I am beginning to think that perhaps the time in now about ripe for a beginning trial of one of those. So. I'll borrow back from you that recommendation for "Prostata".

I read your "Code of the Plains Indian", which is not far off the mark of my own vague view on this subject. As you have indicated, it is also transcendentalist. And as I lay dying some 10 months ago, I was in no way tempted to abandon that code in favor of the Roman prejudice. But to speak of that reminds me that I am living on borrowed time; and that I had best get to cracking on these projects that I had hoped to complete - and get on to the exploration of some of the others that continue to tempt me. My life - its direction, aspirations and meager little accomplishments - have certainly turned out a great deal differently than I would ever have anticipated. As it seems to me, the influence of, and interactions with my four brothers - yourself, Gene, Vic and Phil - loom as certainly among the most positive and (taken together) continuously guiding influences of my entire life. Each of you contributing to me something of his own particular genius and outlook. Exhortation, encouragement, admonishment, and interaction - it seems all to have flowed so inevitably. Including always into our communion, great thoughts and ideas, great music, great literature and the remembrance of great minds and our own worthy friends and teachers. ("And Little Orphan Annie says that when the blaze is blue; and when the lamp wick sputters and the wind goes 'woo-o'. And you can hear the crickets stop and the moon is gray; and the lightnin' bugs and dew is all squinched away. Well then you better mind your parents; and your teachers fond and dear. And cherish them that loves you. And dry the orphans tear. And help the poor and needy ones 'ats gathered all about. . . .). Ah, yes . . . we five idealists. Regularly and fortuitously humbled by the harsh realities of life; and the grim necessity of wrangling a living. Yet, "clinging desperately to some rag of honor" . . . as Stevenson has put it. "And gentlemen of England now abed, shall think themselves accursed they were not here. And hold their manhoods cheap whiles any speak, that fought with us . . . upon St.Crispins Day." (Shakespear).

And so I speak of these impressions now, remembering that in the final extremity, I may not again have the energy nor opportunity to do so.

RGB
1997

CONVERSATIONS WITH NATURE

(Scientific Method)

by R. Garner Brasseur

Even from the earliest days of a person's memory, one can recollect fragments of one's life-long conversations with nature. A spontaneous and universalized dialog into which one enters beginning at the instant of one's earliest moments of consciousness. Nature speaks to her child, sometimes gently and sometimes harshly throughout its waking hours: even as a mother does continuously speak, interacts, and remains attentive to the child. And the nature of the child is such as to perceive that there is an inevitable message directed to him both **from the mother and from the immensity of nature** (mother nature) into which he has been conceived. *Consciousness might well be defined as a driving determination to interact with nature and the beings and creatures which inhabit the seemingly ever expanding reality of nature and of one's own being.* "One can observe a lot by just watching", as Yogi Berea puts it. Early within one's tiny cosmology of beings are those that are attentive to his needs and wishes. Stimulus and response. The newborn voices it's primordial discontent and perceives a satisfying response. Learns next to coo, in gratitude. The beginnings of a mortal career. Ere long, the infant begins to discern that there are self-serving potentialities within himself, and that his attendants are encouraging and tempting him to learn the use of his own appendages and voice so as to interact more efficiently. To admit him to the companionship of their shared poverty, misery; and mite of information and wisdom. Learns to identify with them by the reciprocity of his own behavior. Becomes first, one . . . with his mother. And then gradually recognizing his own separate identity from her as he comes to recognize the other separate beings of his intimate circle whose attentiveness is sometimes substituted for that of the mother. The complexity of it all no doubt confusing, but familiarity with the reality induces his acquiescence to 'that which is'. Beyond the infant self, beyond the crib, beyond the nursery and the home are the ever enlarging spheres of unfamiliar extended realities with which one is yet to be acquainted in trial and error through the years and decades of one's mortal existence. Coteries of being which are much less conciliatory to one's wants and wishes than those of one's nativity and intimate acquaintance. Groups that are commonly indifferent and not uncommonly hostile to one's presence.

There are some few mortals with whom we communicate in the course of a life-time. A communication of words, ideas, stories, concepts, action, and inaction. Words have meanings, though what is said can often be well neigh devoid of meaning, erroneous of content; or of the nature of misinformation that can injure and destroy. They can encourage or uplift. When we are spoken to, are we listening? When we speak, are we being listened to? Words are cheap. Do we weigh and evaluate what we hear? I expect we are much more apt to weight and evaluate what we see - actions speak louder that words. Yet actions too can be deceiving and their meanings are not necessarily easy to discern among our fellow mortals whose various private agendas are so commonly apt intentionally to mislead us.

We are generally well advised to ally ourselves with those who seem to have common interests and purpose with our own, presuming that our acquaintance with them is adequate and sufficient to give us some assurance of our prejudice and a common loyalty to our cause. But, in any case and even under the best of circumstance the nature of our dealings with fellow mortals is such that we can never know but what those fellow mortals may be unknowingly - or even intentionally - misleading us into error. We must always be judging their motives as well as the validity of their ideas. Needless to say, continuously evaluating our own ideas also. Always aware to be assured that our own best interests are being served or at least that those self-interests are not sacrificed to the preferential interests of those whose agendas may well benefit from our being so misled.

Beginning with the utter helplessness and dependency of our infancy, we gradually broaden our perceptions towards an existence in a state of interdependence with the fellow beings of our genus - with allegiance of the first order towards our immediate family and friends and progressively more remote allegiance to extended family, clan, tribe, race, and out towards the edges of mankind as a whole. A priority that tends to become confused by the supra-imposition upon it of various superstitions and systems of beliefs ('idols of the theatre'). In the concreteness and intimacy with persons near at hand in the routine of daily living we are highly attuned to the matter of 'the ongoing conversation' with people and often neglect to take cognizance of another 'ongoing conversation' that we individually maintain with nature throughout our lives - even when we are not aware of it. A conversation whose mighty importance to us is often all but ignored by us by virtue of the fact that language in the intimacy of our small social groups tends to preoccupy our conscious existence. And yet the reality of our ongoing conversation with nature is so vital to our experience that its mere mention immediately recalls to us the relevant pervasiveness of its reality. The conversation with nature is the primary instructive and moral influence of our lives. At best, our linguistic communications with one another does nothing more than to point out to us some small fragment of the source and structure of the reality (of Nature) - of that in which we live.

In fact, we mere mortals are individually a part of the nature in which we are imbedded, and the bounds of what we may accomplish and perceive are limited and circumscribed by the laws of that nature. The world in which we live is a textbook of data and information of times past and present from which we can also gain some insight into the probabilities of the future. History itself is but a sequence of contingencies that have acted upon preceding events within the realms of possibility and probability.

Do we have an obligation or anything to gain from the study of history? Does our individual history and personal experience have anything of importance to teach us? Can human intelligence decipher the clues of history and experience so as to come to any certain or probable explanations? Can we mere mortals influence the course of events and consequences into the future? Can our own acts and studied opinions influence the course of even our own individual lives? Do we have an obligation to be intelligent; and does any such obligation oblige us to seek and advocate for truth? In a world of misunderstanding, lies, deceit, misinformation, and contradictions, is it not implied that we must maintain a high level of skepticism? Are we mere mortals ever capable of freeing ourselves from at least some of our own ignorance and superstition? Are there not questions the answer to which is eternally unknowable to mortals? Is there any answer so certain as to be incontrovertible? Do not all men manifest (in some sense) a faith throughout the course of their lives? Is it not in fact inescapable? Does fate have a hand in the course of our individual lives? Is there any objective proof of the existence of a soul in homo sapiens or of the non-existence of either a tangible or intangible soul in other creatures? Why does organized religion maintain so much antipathy towards science? Are either of the two infallible?

RGB

EVOLUTION

Among the sciences, there is overwhelmingly wide support for the concept of the evolution of species, including the evolution of our own species - Homo sapiens. That evidence continues to mount as scientific data continues to accumulate subsequent to the monumental observations and deductions pertaining to the theory as presented to us originally from two independent nearly simultaneous reports of Darwin and Wallace. "We know that evolution must underlie the order of life on earth because no other explanation can coordinate the disparate data of embryology, biogeography, the geological record, vestigial organs, and taxonomic relationships" (see "*Wonderful Life*", by Gould p.282). There are those who demur from the well established reality of evolution on the basis of religious beliefs, the poetical writings of which suggest to them that an unseen and unproven God has created the many individual species of life on this earth at one unique moment at some time perhaps as recently as 4,400 years ago. Those who support this theory of Creationism appear perhaps unanimously to be immersed in fundamentalist religion - which in itself suggests what motive lies at the bottom of those beliefs. From among this group emerges the notions of 'Intelligent Design' as antithesis to evolution. 'Intelligent Design' being a separate special and unique creation of our species of Homo sapiens (to explain man's supposed endowment with 'soul') and seeming at least to permit of some possibility for the 'theory' of evolution to have produced the other varieties of life.

It was Socrates who seems to have originated the conception of the 'soul'. That conception seems to have dominated European thinking ever since. For more than 2000 years it has been the standing assumption of civilized European man that he has a soul. It remains an assumption. Nothing more. An intangible something which is the seat of his normal waking intelligence and moral character; "and that, since this soul is either identical with himself or at any rate the most important thing about him, his supreme business in life is to make the most of it and to the do the best for it." (A. E. Taylor, "*Socrates*")

"The direct influence, indeed, which has done most to make the doctrine (of the soul) so familiar to ourselves is that of Christianity – but when Christianity arrived into the Greco-Roman world it found that the general conception of the soul - which it needed - had already been prepared for it by philosophy – by Socrates. "It is absent from the literature of earlier times." (According to A. E. Taylor, in his book, "*Socrates*", pg. 79) "Socrates created the intellectual and moral tradition by which European man has ever since lived."

Though there is not a whit of evidence to support it, there remains the unlikely possibility that mankind could have been transplanted among earth's life forms from some distant planet (which, even were it true, does nothing to resolve the fundamental question of man's origin - and there exists abundant evidence to indicate that man is closely akin to "the beasts of the field" which are native to planet earth). There are recent myths believed by many people concerning UFOs manned by aliens from other worlds. And a large body of testimonials to support such claims, though as of yet, no hard evidence to substantiate any such claims.

The Creationists seem to have their own separate science and coterie of scientific believers from private citizens and from their own religiously affiliate bible schools and Church Universities funded by religious organizations. They seem generally not to trouble themselves with scientific research to back up their self-serving notions of Creationism, but rather, manifest a penchant for sophistic reinterpretation of honest scientific data by the forcing of square pegs into round holes and devising obtuse arguments in attempt to align evidence into conformity with their predetermined conclusions. They have occasionally written to Scientific American to inquire why it is that the Creationist articles are not being accepted for publication. A recent response to that question (Scientific American, April 2005) is worthy of being read by the readers and students of both science and science fiction.

While the scientific community must at times budge and make some alterations in their interpretations to the theory of evolution in the face of newly acquired facts, observations, and sound discussions, Creationism runs a course of dogmatic assertion and never finds cause for any valid readjustment to their predetermined conclusions. Imagine it; mere beliefs of fatuous certitude in the minds of millions - to whom there seems never cause for even the slightest correction.

There seems no possibility that Creationism will ever conform itself to within the limits of what scientific findings can continue reasonably to demonstrate. No basis for even an intellectual discussion that can hope to close the ground between Darwinian evolution and Creationism. For in the ground-rules for any such discussion, the Creationists will inevitably insist that the "sacred writings" of their religion must be accepted by the discussants as evidence of a quality and reliability to trump each and every controversial conclusions which science can present in support the theory of evolution. For the view of creationists is that anything that they suppose God to have said or remotely implied in vague 'scripture', is more dependably accurate and to the point than what reasonable arguments (based solely on scientific findings and data) can put forth. The essential premises of Creationists includes the certainty of the existence of their notions of God; and that the words of their religious manuals are God's words that have come to them in book form from the writings of mere mortals whom he is said to have sanctified and authorized to this task. Sort of like "channeling". The product of that middle-man effort is thus 'certified' (to the minds of believers) as to its validity by what they view as the highest authority to which mankind has been subjected. Thus it is that Creationist views of the origin of species have no possibility of ever being meaningfully discussed between Creationists and those of secular authorities in scientific research and teaching. Thus it is that Creationist 'scientists' and teachers have little trek with their secular counterparts.

RGB

Darwin's Conversation with Nature

Far prior to the appearance of Charles Darwin and his monumental studies and writings on the evolution of species, mankind had long been involved in the process of selective breeding of plants and domestic animals to better serve the needs and tastes of mankind. The improvement of quality as well as quantity were both a part of this ongoing process, the tradition and methods of which have been passed along from generation to generation. Enlarging populations impose an economic demand for ever more in the way of food and clothing. As civilizations arise, they encourage the inevitable distinctions that produce the several socioeconomic classes which constitute their populations. And from those advantaged classes the matter of 'a demand' for taste and quality then arises. Thus, from the natural change and development of organized societies of men there arises from them the selection and betterment in what is ever becoming an improved science of horticulture and animal husbandry. From earliest times - apparently - ever the unspoken presumption of inheritable potential within the domestic stock. And that potential for improvement then being acted upon to select the best in volume as well as in quality. The exercise of selective judgment to produce the upgrade in native stocks was in accordance with man's own judgments based upon his experience and fruitful practice from generation to generation.

Through the ages it has become apparent that one line of domestic stock did well in one particular climate and ecological situation but no so well (compared to a variant stock) where the climate and ecology were rather different. In an alternative situation, another variant stock might be better suited to productivity for other purposes (i.e. dairy vs. beef production) and despite less ease of handling (docility) for example.

Surely people noticed these things and they became topics of discussion among at least the more advantaged and enlightened persons within societies. Charles Darwin seems to have grown up with such notions as a part of his cultural heritage. We know for example that such notions were already in the writing of and concerning both Darwin's own father and his grandfather. With learning being a part of Darwin's cultural tradition and with his studies pursued in biological fields, it is therefore not a great surprise that Darwin should pursue themes of his cultural background and traditions as provided him by fate and the want of any other occupation, in order to seize the opportunity to become a naturalist aboard the H.M.S. Beagle. A contract that demanded of him a daily routine of regular industry such as to make of him perhaps the ideal candidate for exploration in the field of natural history. Natural History then, even as yet today, is a field well open to innovative investigation. And so it is that Charles Darwin opened himself up to a life-long occupation and pre-occupation in 'a conversation with nature'. Nature had long been prepared to answer just such questions as he might pose as he sought for answers in his attentive observations and systematic methods.

He based his theory of natural selection on three observable facts of nature and on two deductions from those facts (see *"Evolution"*, by Julian Huxley, p.14). The tendency for organisms to increase in a geometrical ratio (the offspring are generally more numerous than their parents). Second, in spite of this increase, the numbers of a given species actually remain more or less constant. He thus concludes that there is some sort of struggle for existence that somehow constrains their numbers. His third observation of fact is that of variation from individual to individual within a species; and from this fact and his first deduction (the struggle for existence), he further deduces that some sort of natural selection must occur to eliminate much of the progeny. On a broader scale, he then supposes that the surviving variations within the species accumulate through long periods of time to produce the separation of related creatures that eventually we come to recognize as *Genus* - groups closely related morphologically that no longer interbreed.

Though Darwin was unaware of the work of G. Mendel (on the genetic inheritance and variability in peas), and less aware than in our times of ongoing genetic drift in populations, yet he had intimations of both from his 'conversations with nature'. His observations and studied conclusions led him to a theory of evolution based upon this ongoing genetic drift (coupled with natural selection) within the populations which display variants of that species. As to the force and mechanism by which that some of the variants attain survival in a hostile world, he offered the suggestion that those most suited and best fit to an ever-changing environment were more apt to survive than those that were less able to adapt to ongoing changes in environment. "The survival of the fittest" as the expression goes: a force which is surely relevant to some degree. He did not exclude pure chance as being also relevant.

Neither did he exclude vast exterminations of whole populations of species as a mechanism to extinction to many species. Whereas we in more enlightened times have come to recognize at least five such major extinctions which have cleared the planet of all but the residual fragmentary fossil evidence to bespeak their past existence as species. Extinctions that have been produced by cataclysmic geological and astro-geological calamities such as to have exterminated an estimate total of 99% of species that have ever existed. Of the species having once existed, those five calamities are estimated to have extinguished: 65 million years ago, 17% of families; 210 million years ago, 23% of families; 250 million years ago, 64% of families; 375 million years ago, 19% of families; and 440 million years ago, 25% of families. And there are now said to have been 148 additional lesser extinctions in addition to other extinctions of which we may never uncover any fossil evidence. The mechanisms of some or many specific extinctions may often have come to pass from pure chance, as opposed to "survival of the fittest" - i.e. "survival of the survivors". But such evidence as exists certainly supports the notion that the diverse forms of animal life evolved in a certain sequence from simple life processes, into one-celled organisms, into multi-cellular life forms; onward into creatures with diversity of tissues for specialized purposes and then into those creatures with higher specialized organs for locomotion, digestion, excretion, and organs of perception. And finally organized into a CNS to further facilitate the accumulation and integration of information such as might enhance man's 'conversation with nature'.

We mere mortals gain some firsthand experience of the aging process that bedevils our existence; and of the tenuous nature of that existence from day to day and year to year. We also inevitably discover how astonishingly rapid proceeds the process of putrefaction and decay of the soft tissues of animal life once life has departed from the corpse. Though the hard tissues such as bone may be readily preserved by burial for many centuries and even millennia, such is not commonly their fate - or at least not frequently encountered from prehistoric times and beyond the beginning of earliest civilizations. For under natural conditions the bones are gnawed and trampled by the beasts of the field and are most apt to lie at or near the surface of the earth where weathering to decay proceeds much more rapidly. And yet, surprisingly, accidental deep burial and partial preservation of the skeletal hard parts does occur with enough frequency to preserve to us a fossil record that can be dated back to over 3 million years. A record however which is very fragmentary and incomplete the further back in time we follow it out. For who knows upon the surface and subsurface of this wide earth just where they might happen to lie? Such finds are mostly accidental finds from sub-soils and geological formations of sediments that are by chance currently being secondarily now eroded - as was the case with the important Burgess Shale deposits that came to light in British Columbia, in the early 1900s. Some such rare finding as have even revealed information concerning the anatomy of soft parts in occasional fossils.

From my own personal and limited experience, I am astonished that anything whatever of skeleton or soft parts should ever become available for our perusal, let alone whole extensive museums and collections of such material which can be classified and related to one another through eons of time. My limited studies and readings of scientific books and journals convinces me that this 'reading' of the fossil record is not a figment of the scientific imagination. And the fossil record continues to expand.

To actually study human anatomy and the comparative anatomy of other animals can hardly leave the unbiased observer without the distinct impression of the uncanny similarity of the structure and function of man to that of many other creatures. The study of embryology adds even more to that impression ("ontogeny recapitulates phylogeny"), and quite broadens the thesis in one's own mind. The phylogeny of plants is much more uncertain than that of higher animals. (see H.S. Harrison, P.396)

And so it is with the theory of evolution: every scientific discipline points one towards the theory and reinforces it from a different angle. A convergence of independent bodies of information that sometimes make only little modifications but that always strengthens the theory. **Is not that the essence of the nature of proof?**

And then in the mid 20th century the very structure and the function of DNA and RNA was discovered and published to the world. Does any of that ongoing research confound and destroy the theory of evolution?

Or rather, does it add to an already overwhelmingly extensive basis for its support? Of course, the sciences have no special concern or intention of being supportive to the evolution theory. It just happens that their unbiased conclusions point in its direction. They would just as willingly prefer to support the fundamentalist notion of Creationism or of Intelligent Design or of the Special Creation if their final impressions pointed in those directions - but they don't. Can one run a decent study by starting with predetermined conclusions and then expect nature's part of 'man's dialog with nature' to falsify its testimony in support of a delusion?

When we can study actual adaptive evolution with the aid of fossils, as with the hooves of horses or the molar teeth of elephants, we find that it is steadily directional over tens of millions of years, and must therefore have involved a very large number of steps. It is improbable that such progressive adaptations can have arisen without the operation of some agency which can gradually accumulate and combine a number of contributory changes. And natural selection is the only such agency that we know.

More recently we hear of Symbiogenesis, which recognizes that every visible life-form is a combination, or community of bacteria. Such mergers between different kinds of organisms are thus said each to be a big leap forward in the process of evolution. Perhaps, the single most important force behind evolution, no matter that it be an uncommon occurrence. Nevertheless, it does not negate the importance and necessity of the smaller and incremental steps in the process of evolution; nor of the mechanism of natural selection from molecular alteration of the DNA.

R.A. Fisher says that natural selection is a mechanism for generating a high degree of improbability. Adaptation as seen in nature demands natural selection to explain the origins of these improbabilities. Fisher's statement also has a bearing on the "argument from improbability"

Natural selection is efficient in its way - at the price of extreme slowness and extreme cruelty. But it is blind and mechanical.(p.485 Huxley) Next, (see Gould p.290) on contingency in human history. Laws in the background; contingency in the details.

Whatever factors were concerned in the ancient evolution of modern man, the upper limits of his powers and aptitudes of mind were not determined by the struggles for existence. Natural selection however could be and doubtless was operative in bringing about the evolution of speech and conceptual thought, with their corollaries of rational control in the practical sphere, freedom of association between the different compartments of mental power. Once however this higher level of mental attainment was reached, the so-called higher faculties immediately became possible. They are implicit in the general type of brain organization required for speech and conceptual thought and are therefore correlated characters in our beings since then.

- - - - - - - - - - - - - - - -

Says H.S. Harrison in 1936
Concerning Human Progress
J. Royal anthropology Inst. 66:1

As to what constitutes "evolutionary progress", Huxley suggests it is a raising of the upper level of biological efficiency - this being defined as increased control over and independence of the environment. (p.564)

Man is lately evolved to the position of dominant type of creature on this earth. He owes this position to a combination of unique properties, notably bi-pedalism, the capacity for conceptual thought, and true symbolic speech. For domesticating other animals, and for making adaptive exosomatic progress, conscious purpose based on human values is needed, as dominance of mind that has come with man marked a critical point in evolution.

The raw material available for evolution by natural selection falls into two categories - mutation and recombination (of genetic DNA and RNA structure).(P. 21)

Evolution not only need not occur by a series of sharp single steps, but is not commonly likely to do so.(P. 68) All that natural selection can assure is survival. It does not assure progress in any specific occurrence.(P.466)

The arm of a man, the wing of a bird, and the flipper of a whale can be shown to be built on a common plan; and it is deduced that the reason they are all built on a common plan is because they are descended from a common ancestor. (P.513)

Evolution can be viewed as a series of blind alleys - some very short, and others very long.(P. 571)

RGB

THE ORPHANATORIO

(From my journal of March 1997)

I drive westward in southern California, across Hwy 8 to Hwy 94, and then south to Tecate. There I gas up before crossing into Tecate, Mexico (population about 40,000) about 6:00 PM. Account of rather vague information from the Mexican Border guard, I am under the impression that the mission (where Miette and Bart are working) is near the village of Guadalupe. From there, another bum steer leads me further astray into San Anton, Salazar, and even up to La Mission. I then search my own journal pages (this journal - Jan 22, 1997) to discover that I am looking for Carmen Serdon. So I have to back track and find that place, which is about 10 miles north of Guadalupe. The last 6 kilometers are up a washboard road before I finally arrive at Carmen Serdon. The entire village seems to have retired with no lighted windows or street lights to be seen when I arrive at about 11:30 PM. So I just pull off to the side of the road (actually only 2 or 3 blocks from the mission) and bed down for the night in the front seat of the pickup. I arise about 7:00 AM in the morning, and stop to talk with one of the locals to discover where "the mission de los Orphanatorio" is located - just where I had surmised - only 2 blocks distant - an enclosed complex of buildings. There I stop for a little breakfast with them and talk about 1½ hours with my daughter, Miette; and then let her get back to her duties while I read a couple of hours and then have a little siesta. About 4:00 PM, Miette, Bart, one of their associates and I drive to Tecate. There we eat out at a Chinese restaurant and then drive back to the mission. I had this captive audience in the car and did my best to keep their ears full. About the probable source of all the orphans; the history of "orphan trains" in the U.S. in the early 1900's; about Tuberculosis, Plague, and Echinoccocus; about Subaru cars; some stories of Miette, in her former years; about brothers Phil's and Gene's "perpetual motion" machines; about my recent talk with Jauhn and his family. About "The Flight of the Phoenix" movie ; about flying saucers etc. I then catch up on my journal notes while they go to a friend's place for some dessert.

I climb into the sleeping bag in the pickup camper to end my day about 11:00 PM. After a cool night, I was up next day about 7:00 AM. I take a hike for exercise and then wear my jacket while reading in the warming morning sun. Soon Miette and Bart arise, and we then drive up through Tecote to El Cajoun. There we have breakfast at an IHOP - greatly overpriced because they insist on serving one enough for two breakfasts. Again I end up doing most of the talking. Phil's swing bike; about a trip with Jauhn; on the intensity of Pierre; on 'poisonous' oxygen; about poisonous foods; on the "divine elixir"; on gravity; on space travel; on my uncertainty as to the strange things people tell me. How a lie is a poor substitute for a truth; on the certitudes of belief; that I have no answers . . . only questions; on our primitive race of mere mortals; on man's first flight in 1750; about the first climbing of mountains about 1850; about the necessity of aligning our opinion of reality with its actual reality; about the moral corrective force of reality; about enterprise; about my escape from the grip of cancer; about the priority of my projects - number one being the writing of my autobiography and then on to various other unspecified projects. We parted about 1:00 PM. And I depart north on Hwy 15 to get an oil change, and then stop at a rest area near Boron, CA, to watch a comet in the night sky.

RGB

LIVINGSTON

by R. Garner Brasseur

I read an interesting biographical analysis of the life of David Livingston (1813-1873) - Livingston, by Jim Jeal. In time, the life of Livingston corresponds almost precisely with the life of John Stuart Mill (1806-1873). Significant, because both were champions of the rights of the individual, and of social progress. It seems certain that Mill would have known of Livingston though it is not likely he would have recommended of his career choice or efforts. It is much less likely that Livingston would have known of Mill. If he had, he likely would have disapproved of the man. This however, because of Mill's differing personal religious philosophical views - not because of his intent in political action.

Had Livingston and Mill ever met and known each other it seems likely they would have been on good terms, though perhaps not in their earlier years of life, say up to age thirty five or forty. Livingston was a prig and a bigoted fundamentalist by dint of background, upbringing, and education. He obtained a good, though not a comprehensive education to prepare himself for his work in Africa. He became a physician, and to that extent he was acquainted with science; but science was not far advanced at that time and the parasitic diseases of Africa were among the least well understood.

In the earlier years of my own life, I acquired the vague notion of Dr. Livingston as a missionary personality of much the same caliber of steady determination as Dr. Albert Schweitzer. But whereas Schweitzer lived out his mission in his only medical facility in his one facility on the Congo River, Livingston undertook the additional heroic task of the exploration of the mysterious 'dark Africa', where he became lost and eventually found by an even greater explorer of Africa, Henry Stanley. In the vague perceptions of my youth, the legend of Livingston almost fuses with that of Dr. Schweitzer. The essence, of my impression of Livingston seems now to have been somewhat off the mark. A maverick sort of missionary, one might say. Not too much in common with the erudite Schweitzer, though both were men of great determination and energy.

Livingston was very much a self-made man, having acquired his education and training by dint of a headstrong, self-determination in the face of vast odds mitigating against that probability. There are many elements of his life circumstances, and of his background that lead me in many ways to identify with Livingston, and that make the analysis of his life a thing, for me, of great fascination.

The man himself in many ways, very much reminds me of my brother, E.V.H.Brasseur. I sometimes wonder if E.V.H.B. might not, in fact, have been the very reincarnation of David Livingston: both, men of durable physiology and of iron will. David's father before him was similarly headstrong and individualistic. Young David was the eldest son among seven children. His labouringly impoverished parents took great pride in their family. They dressed them better than one would have expected, and encouraged them to acquire education. The social church was strongly influential in their lives. In short, despite the reality of poverty in their lives, the family maintained a biased and unrealistic optimism for improvement in their personal lives, and for the expectant improvement of social conditions in mother England.

David Livingston had been taught at home to read and write before he began to work in the textile mill at age ten. He worked six days a week, and fourteen hours per day. He worked part time at odd jobs on his day off. Daily, after work, he attended school for two hours to continue his education. He would then read at home until his mother chased him off to bed. He read on the job to the extent that that was possible. He aspired to be a physician though his father did not approve. At age twenty-one he read a tract describing the need for medical missionaries. His father, then seeing the tract, consented to David's plans for entrance into a medical school. Family scrimping, part time work, and some funds from a wealthy parishioner at last enabled him to attend medical school. He was eventually accepted by a mission society and given some theological training before being sent out into the mission field at age twenty-seven. He was not a polished product and the mission society had some hesitation about accepting him, but his medical training swung the balance in his favor.

And I was particularly interested in this story because of it's parallels in various aspects to that of my own family. For we were likewise dressed well each Sunday, and sent to church and Sunday School regularly. The stories of the church heroes were given to us as models. The missionaries, and especially the medical missionaries, seemed the ultimate to which one might aspire. Our congregations in the west were yearly visited by these stalwart moral beings who were alternately home on summer leave from the foreign mission fields of their labor. Especially the summer Bible Camps made the missionary and his self-dedicating achievement the center of our admiration. I believe I may have carried these notions and vague ideals at the back of my head as potential vocations since the highly impressionable age of eleven or twelve.

The ever churning and aspiring David Livingston finally then achieved fulfillment of a dream that was very nearly an impossibility. Not only did he become a missionary, but he went one-up on nearly all of them, by dint of his additional medical training. He was sent then to South Africa, and there began to manifest so many of his characteristic personal traits and attitudes that remind me so much of E.V.H.B. After a lifetime of lauding and nearly worshipping the missionary, Livingston is finally privileged to interact and fellowship with them in the South Africa mission field. He lives with and travels with them under severe and strenuous conditions of travel in those days. Though anxious to be at one with them, his immediate and continuous experience of them is that they are puffy, narrow-minded, and weak of endurance. They are forever entered upon intrigues of status and power among themselves. To Livingston, their accomplishments begin to seem miniscule.

He begins to see that in reality, the missions are not at all the mighty world-moving force that the local congregations at home make them out to be. He abides there among these highly regarded missionaries and begins to perceive them as querulous and rather ordinary. Perceives to his astonishment that there are no crowds of humble black folks awaiting and crowding near in great expectation of the words and wisdom of the born again and enlightened white missionary.

Travel is tedious, difficult, and expensive. At best, one can make ten miles a day. It takes him two months to arrive at the first mission station, once landed in Cape Town. He is vaguely concerned as to how he can fully justify all this expenditure of time while the supposed hoards of black folk dwelling in darkness are awaiting yet to be baptized; and taught about the Christian God and how then to begin to learn to live in brotherly love. Difficult and slow as travel is, he begins to realize that he, in fact - among these lesser missionaries - has a uniquely conquering endurance and will for such tasks. He, afresh within this new environment, is amazed at the harshness of this stark land. But he is not intimidated. His determined strength of will and endurance is the secret of all that he is yet to accomplish. His inner resources and determination enable him to conquer every obstacle—-and he is destined to encounter many. He refuses to submit to the brutal reality of any obstacle and is ever quick to devise and put into action a plan to overcome. His enemies, when not defeated by his determination, are awed at least into a curious admiration of the man. Even while attacking an obstacle, he is also devising another contingency plan, should this first approach fail. He is a diarist, observing always all manner of conditions and objects relevant to his goals for further reflection - and analysis - before entry into his journal at each day's end.

He is keen of observation through necessity of attention to details; and yet he is confronted with such a vast unknown that he inevitably misses a good deal. His ideas and theoretical speculations are generally quite good. But diseased, dark, and superstitious Africa inevitably takes its toll upon him. He is pressed by illness, pressed for time, and embroiled in political difficulties to the extent that he begins often to neglect to make relevant observations. Unexpected consequence arise. He has a tendency to make naïve deductions, and twist his information to conform to those naiveties. But even wholesome and perceptive deductive theories must necessarily often be tried and revised before satisfactorily answering the requirement of reality. He tends to jump to erroneous conclusions; and his failure then, to put these conclusions to further tests adds to the monumental difficulties of his assault upon vast unexplored Africa. He is so intent to complete his tasks and the progress is necessarily so slow - but his resources so limited - that he feels constrained to supplement his limited findings with wild guesses, trusting then in God to allow their validity.

There are some rather strange inconsistencies that have crept into the being of David Livingston. He is God's servant but he turns the tables on God, expecting God to uphold the accuracy of his wild guess-work. He is patient, kind, and understanding of the Negro; but harsh, critical and unforgiving in his judgment of his white compatriots. He comes especially to dislike missionaries but is generally unable to get along with any of what he considers to be white prigs. Of necessity, he must suppress (as best he can) his hostility toward his fellow missionaries and their disappointing missions; for he himself is dependent upon their meager support. He comes especially to love the challenge of exploration he has found in Africa. Though he has been remarkable in his determination as a student, he has never been an exceptionally good student - only mediocre. Still, he maintains a very superior attitude toward missionaries and of the common English public, to say nothing of the harsh officials of the mission societies. Though never having proven himself to have been an outstanding student, still he is quite perceptive in the field. He sees the problem of the Negro and how all of their cultural practice runs against the Christian philosophy. Thus, he is content then not personally to convert the Negro, but to help the negro improve his ignorant condition and his life situation; and to free him from the condition of slavery. Livingston comes to want for himself a commission to rove about Africa finding areas suitable for missionaries and colonists to settle. Unrecognized to David Livingston is the fact that his experience in his new reality (subsequent to his disillusionment with Christians and their missionary efforts), has changed his outlook. He has become an explorer; and a pragmatist; and a humanitarian. But the remnants of his illusionary religion do not qualify him to work in the strict definition of a Christian missionary.

The one art he masters is that of effective letter writing. He writes continuously, in volume, from out of dark Africa. He has an intuitive knack of knowing how to put people on the spot, on the basis of their own professed philosophy. He knows how to play one against the other. He perceives the methods of the mission society in milking funds from congregations and comes to see how (as a hero of England's congregations of common men) to squeeze the mission society. He is aware that the man of the congregation back home is also a strong force of sentiment in the public opinion; and knows that sentiment can influence the actions of parliament. He has, through letter writing and through his explorations, stirred up considerable controversy in the missions fields, mission society, the geographical society, the home congregations, and the man on the street.

He returns to England, as if in triumph, to a host of questions among the many groups with which he has been in contact. He has come to be THE authority on Africa, with new proposals for African missions, and for African Colonies. All await him for enlightenment upon his geographical findings, the condition of the Negro natives, word of his contact with the natives, and information about the secrets . . . of dark Africa.

In England - the missionary returned to the people - he is widely acclaimed and sought after for speaking engagements. He continues to play one interest group against another. He writes a book for the popular enlightenment, playing up the details and facts that benefit the ends he seeks for his own further opportunity for personal income support and expeditionary funding. He plays down a great many details and facts that stand in his way. In the end, he achieves what serves his personal interests. He becomes perhaps, the transcended missionary, no longer relegated to the fruitless and boring daily routine of the ordinary missionary in the field. He becomes the African spokesman and statesman! With still the missionary image (a pragmatic image). He directs the lesser laboring class missionary to go here, or go there, in accordance with the perceptual insights of David Livingston. He is paid more handsomely now, by the state, and is no longer dependent upon the mission for their miserable gratuity. In him, the interests of the church and the interests of the state have become fused. Livingston(!!) - the national hero, national saint, and explorer - seeking out the natural resources of Africa, to the benefit of all that believe him (and in God). Though his life be hard, though his labors and days be long - what of this?? For he must play out his unique role in the manifest destiny of the white man of the British nation. "Whist ye not . . . .?" "A light onto the gentile . . . .!"

Strangely though - and enigmatically - back on the frontier his whole master plan is doomed to failure account of a great number of ill-advised presumptions based upon his misperceptions of realities. The lives of men and women - white and black - are lost, needlessly, because of his inability to acknowledge the incompleteness of his information, and the inadequacy of his 'certain knowledge' concerning risky health conditions. Perhaps though, he is only guilty of neglecting to take a personal interest in, and concerns for those that are to come forth as ordinary missionaries, and are depending upon the veracity of his judgments and pronouncements.

Inside the head of Livingston, there was obviously considerable uncertainty, confusion, and ignorance which he refused to acknowledge nor deal with. For now new political reasons he is regarded as a national hero of sorts; as well as a saintly humanitarian. In truth though, he is greatly over-rated in this regard. In reality those illusional images are allowed to persist, more or less unchallenged in the perceptions of the folks back home, to protect this Jack-Armstrong-like Christian image, in order to get some mileage from the many cubic feet of natural gas (verbosity) for which a dear price has been extorted. The real basis of his fame is more properly in the field of exploration, his reputation as a pious instrument in the colonial expansion of England must remain untarnished to the extent that be possible.

Certainly no one can deny that Livingston heroically achieved stature by dint of personal achievement in the face of magnificent obstacles and against all probability. His background of narrow-mindedness did decline in the face of his first-hand personal experience. Certainly that alone is enough to earn him a share of immortality.

And Livingston's exploits paved the way for an even larger and more comprehensive exploration of darkest Africa by his successor, Sir Henry Stanley. That autobiography, well worth one's perusal.

R. G. Brasseur, MD
10/21/84

Prayer Mechanisms

(Leverage of prayer)

by R. Garner Brasseur
4 March 1986

Scanning the channels of a TV set in the motel this evening I happened across a program in which a priest was discussing the miracles associated with Sister Ste. Frances Cabrini. I gather that she has recently been elevated officially into sainthood by Papal Decree. She is now the only American to have attained sainthood. Think of it. There are at least some few thousands of saints, and only one American finally now among them. And to have arrived there ahead of any American male candidate! What does that say about the condition of mortality in America? You might think it would speak loud enough to bring at least some of the damned Yankees to their knees, and to their senses. But will it?

Sister Cabrini is said to have founded some seventy hospitals and foundling homes. I recall there being a Ste. Cabrini hospital in Seattle, (I served a brief clerkship there when I was in medical school), but I was entirely ignorant of the many and fine accomplishments of this humble sister of mercy. The priest's TV talk went on to suggest that 'we good Catholics' should now call upon this new saint, in prayer, to procure miracles and blessings through her - now well entrenched - cosmic influence and connections. What he implies is that the chain of influence in this new hot-line to the deity is as follows: Ste. Cabrini -> Holy Mary -> Mary's son, Jesus -> God Himself. One must expect that perhaps these chains have a certain potential to generate cosmic forces - as for example in a game of crack-the-whip. Suppose for example that I have in mind a certain worthy and needful potential beneficiary for the object of my prayer request. We might even perhaps now design some new logic into our scheme, in order to lever a new advantage into the intended beneficence, by lengthening the chain of request as follows: the hopeful beneficiary -> me -> you -> a priestly sub-intermediary (perhaps the one now enlightening us on this subject, since he seems to be so well informed on the technicalities of the subject)-> Ste. Cabrini -> The Holy Mary -> Mary's Son -> The Deity Himself. Then, if the motor mechanism is even, say, half as long as the pathway of request, why . . . then we might easily generate enough momentum to whip the recipient of the request over the moon.

Most of these yarns are originally whispered about from ear-to-ear among the poor and naive parishioners; the functions of the priest being only to nurture what-ever is good and potentially advantageous to the church, by endowing faith with a heavy handed permissiveness towards this noise and these buzzings. This particular priestly elucidation was of interest to me primarily because the priest himself was giving us the authoritative details on the history of the newly recognized Saint Cabrini. And he took the time and trouble to sort of perjure himself, by speaking of the alleged facts of a particular tragedy, the details of which cross directly into the heart of things concerning which, I possess a certain familiarity.

The miraculous story is that of an incident alleged to have occurred at Cabrini Hospital in Seattle. The details of an Ophthalmologic disaster which was resolved in seventy-two hours by supplying a relic to the victim, and by the prayers of the Catholic sisters through the intermediary of the departed Ste. Cabrini - > Holy Mother Mary - > etc. Briefly, it is alleged that fifty percent Silver Nitrate (rather than the standard one percent) was accidentally poured into the eyes of a newborn infant in the delivery room. The eyes were "immediately eaten out of their sockets" by that strong acid; and "deep pits burned down inside the cheeks and into the chest cavity". The Ste. Cabrini nuns prayed, completely restoring the child's eyes in twenty-four hours. But the child then got 'double-pneumonia', and was doomed. Again, the sisters prayed through the night. And, within seventy-two hours after the initial injury, this child had miraculously been restored to perfect health—and perfect vision, too! Now, how could anyone doubt a jovial old priest who would share with us, a wonder such as that?

R.G.B.
March 1986

GIVE THE MAN TIME

by R. Garner Brasseur
Written in about 1992

I recall an essay, by William James, "The Evil That Good Men Do". And we all have first-hand, and second-hand experience of good intentions, gone awry. St. Paul writes of the disappointment that troubles him, as he so often falls short of his own expectation; and ends up doing that, which he does not want to do. A theme eternal - familiar to the experience of all. To recognize or acknowledge its veracity, is to do honor to one's own opinion. Carelessness and ignorance are the cause of many an accident; coupled often with good-natured horse-play. Chance, coincidence and fate, too, generally enter into the equation of detrimental accident. In the realm of politics, nothing has wreaked more havoc and mayhem against mankind, than has religion ... and the supposedly good intentions thereof, I would place nationalism only second, upon that list. The tools of this well-intended evil are none other than ourselves - in our roles of 'believers' and 'patriotic citizens' exhorted into ill-considered policy, actions, and reaction - by 'leaders' who lust for power, action, and drama. It is not to be implied that the common man and citizen is any paragon of virtue or wisdom; nor, in general, superior to his leaders in these things. This genus and species of creature is known as Homo sapiens; abbreviated Homo sap. The term. Homo, refers to man; while sapiens, suggests sagaciousness, wisdom, or knowing. By strange irony, the abbreviated form of sapiens (sap.) - has come to mean something quite the opposite of sagaciousness; something akin to simplemindedness. Thus, the ambiguity of the abbreviated form - Homo sap. - is probably a more accurate description of our race of creatures, in general; though it does seem also to be the case, that we creatures do have a certain individual capacity for sagaciousness; a capacity not overly exercised, however. The Germans have a expression that seems to touch near to the heart of the problem of man's intellectual limitations. "Ve gett too soon alt; und too late schmardt". That seems, at least to me, to be a large part of the problem. Some other parts of the problem are these; 1) inadequate discipline, 2) a lack of self-discipline, 3) inadequate cultural tradition, 4) a late and weak beginning of the learning process, to the individual, 5) prevalence of superstition, prejudice, and "bunk", as obstacles to the learning process, 6) obviously, then, an inadequate method of teaching. What, more easy to explain that, than 7) an inadequate accumulation of information on the subject, or an inadequate theory - something that requires rethinking and experimentation.

Dewey says that the task of education is to free the mind of bunk. Undoubtedly, the presence - in the minds of pupils - of that bunk, is among the foremost obstacles that confronts the educators of our youth, I am not sure that educators would all agree with that. Certainly, they would not agree as to what, specifically, constitutes bunk. For, their own minds too, like yours and mine, are overburdened with deeply imbedded and cherished bunk; bunk which they teach by innuendo and deference. As to even the approved curricula themselves, their relevance and validity are not all certainly established. Perhaps "The Educational Value of Doubt", an essay by Dean Martin, is a more fundamentally valuable principle to learning, than is "the freeing of the mind, of bunk", for it is a straightforward maxim, which one can easily own; and which one can at all times apply - to every situation of life; and to everything whatsoever that is proposed for one's learning.

The daily insecurities and seasonal insufficiencies of this life - along with culturally and hormonally driven wants and desires - have continuously produced the man-of-action, in a world of limited supply. And, supply has always been limited, by the withholding of surplus, in good times; and by natural austerity, in times of drought. One's empty granary calls him forth to its filling, against the prospects of a lean season to follow. When overflowing, it brings him forth in arms, to protect that store. Always, the necessity of focusing one's plans and actions upon the feeding, defense, and well-being of himself and his family; with some secondary concern, too, towards his friends, and his countrymen. Little, is the time - and rare the chance - for free and open conversation; nor, for reading and writing; or for private thought and reflection. [Looking about, one can see that our human nature has led many even to want guarantee of success into eternity. In our modern society many seem to have outgrown the mere earthly expectation of living-happily-ever-after.] In Plato's Phaedo, Socrates and Simmies are involved in a discussion. Socrates touches precisely upon the condition of mortality which I have often pondered:

> "Now, as to the acquirement of pure knowledge? Is the body a hindrance or not, if it is made to share in the search for wisdom? What I mean is this: Have the sight and hearing of men any truth in them, or is it true, as the poets are always telling us, that we neither hear nor see anything accurately? And yet if these two physical senses are not accurate or exact, the rest are not likely to be, for they are inferior to these. Do you not think so?
>
> - - - - - - - - - - - - -
>
> "But it (the man) thinks best when none of these things troubles it, neither hearing nor sight; not pain nor any pleasure, but it is - so far as possible - alone by itself, and takes leave of the body, and avoiding, so far as it can, all association or contact . . . .
>
> - - - - - - - - - - - - -
>
> "For the body keeps us constantly busy by reason of its need of sustenance; and moreover, if diseases come upon it they hinder our pursuit of the truth. And the body fills us with passions and desires and fears, and all sorts of fancies and foolishness, so that, as they say, it really and truly makes it impossible for us to think at all."
>
> - - - - - - - - - - - - -

But the thoughtful Socrates isn't getting much help from the overawed Simmias, who merely assents to each of the intermediary conclusions; though each should obviously be challenged. Socrates, himself, is probably a bit discouraged at the fruitlessness of this exercise. We, of course, need not agree with the conclusion to which he arrives - that the body is merely a hindrance to the complete knowledge and self-awareness of one's being. For the argument runs and leaps about, on the basis of confusion of terms; and is based upon some strange concepts, and upon words which own more than one possible definition. In so far as I am aware, such evidence as exists, suggests that the rational thought processes are a function of the organ we call the brain. The mind is not an entity, either spiritual or physical, but, rather, the function of an organ - the brain. This function, or capacity, to think is a very important tool to man in his competitive struggle for the upper hand - against the forces of nature, the beasts of the field, and against his fellow man. And against his own actions and policy, which are not infrequently self-defeating of his own best interests and his moral and intellectual progress.

The intellectual and rational capacity of the human brain is generally adequate to assure to the individual, a certain measure of protection against a hostile world; a world where threat and danger are an omnipresent reality. However rude and elementary the concepts which one acquires, that intellect must relate the reality of one's individual vulnerability, to the reality of the danger of one's environment and circumstance. We expect each individual to grasp the primacy of that concept, as a fundamental mandate for his own survival. That is the least elemental notion which will suffice. We expect our children to - at least - be able eventually, to fend for themselves. One's self-concept is not a single concept and abstract perspective on his various (real or imagined) traits, and characteristics; the sum total of which can never be held in focal awareness at any one time. That sum is experienced but not perceived.

Only the occasional benefactor of the human race has bequeathed to our race some little wit, wisdom, and light such as to encourage (every now and then) another pilgrim into the continuation of a tradition of inquiry; and dedication to veracity. Its most fruitful manifestation seems to be a thorough-going skepticism; and a breaking-away from the old and established dogmas. Such benefactors to the race, are the likes of Confucius, Socrates, Buddha, Plato, Galileo, P. Bacon, Abelard, Spinoza, Ethan Alien, T. Huxley, Darwin, Jefferson, Descartes, Hume, Einstein, Schweitzer, Mark Twain, Mencken, Emerson, Thoreau, etc. Nor should we exclude a long tradition of fine and energetic historians who have labored to elude some of the narrow views, whose weight has always been a constraining force upon their efforts; Livy, Josephus, Voltaire, Burckhardt, Toynbee, Pirenne, Gibbon, and Herbert Mueller . . . to name but a few. One marvels at their accomplishments, as one ponders the reality of a perspective such as that set forth by Robert Louis Stevenson's, "Pulvis et Umbra". And yet, they might each have accomplished, even more; but for the marked limitations of their fixed, and mere mortalities, the limitation of the time of their days, and of their years.

There is a moral aspect, too . . . of this rational process - as alluded to by Thomas Huxley, Pascal, and Benjamin Franklin. Huxley points out these common religious notions, with which he disagrees (as do I, with him). That barbarious people are of the conviction that:

1. authority is the soundest basis of belief.
2. that merit attaches to a readiness to believe.
3. that the doubting disposition is the bad one; and that skepticism is something of the nature of a sin.
4. that when good authority has pronounced what is to be believed and faith has accepted it, reason has no further duty.

Yet, says Huxley, "It is the unquestionable fact is that improvement of natural knowledge is effected by methods which directly give the lie to all of these four ubiquitous convictions; and assume the exact reverse to be true."

"Thought makes the whole dignity of man; and the endeavor to think well is <u>the</u> basic morality", says Pascal. And from Benjamin Franklin we have this, "As the happiness or real good of men consists in right action; and right action cannot be produced without right opinion, it behooves us, above all things in this world, to <u>take care that our opinions of things be according to the nature of things</u>. The foundation of all virtue and happiness is in thinking rightly."

The sands of time run out, for individual man; and comes the time for one to weep. To weep, when it is done - "for being done too soon . . . for being done." Has anyone ever seriously lamented having learned or accomplished too much of value, in one's limited span of time? Rather, each has had cause to lament the dearth of his personal fund of knowledge and understanding. We are familiar with the experience of seeing a play, an opera, or a movie. The action is strung together in a sequence of "scenes". Each of the scenes is a small, but significant portion of the drama of the life of the individual; or of the plot, as it unfolds to our attention. The production may run its course in, say, ninety minutes of actual time; but we can gather from the context, that the actual span, which it represents, may be that of several days sometimes weeks, months, or years - generations, even. What, then, of all the time left un-staged - between the scenes? That may largely be considered to belong to the category of, <u>perfunctory</u> - done without care or interest, or merely as a form or routine (see Webster's Dictionary, Second Ed.). Interestingly, this is how we generally view our own lives, too - if we ever reflect back upon them at all. We recall the significant events of our past life; or recall -by category - those portions relevant to a particular subject, or question under consideration . . . the good, the bad, the joys, the pains . . . . Thus does pass the major portion of the time which constitutes one's life (presuming, of course, that time runs continuously uniformly - or at least approximately so). Yes, the major portion of one's life spent - as it were - in a merely perfunctory manner . . . in preparation for the transient, significant scenes, the memory of which, constitutes one's life - in retrospect. The most of one's life is thus a preparation - a long preparation. The first thirty, forty, or fifty years seem almost as though they had some purpose, each phase preparing us for a subsequent life task. "The first 40 to 60 years of life give us the text; the final years supply the commentary", says Arthur Schopenhauer.

The infant prepares the child; the child prepares for the adolescent; the adolescent prepares for the young adult, etc. The ambiguity arises once the children have been raised to the age of their majority. Until then, each new stage of a person's life has been a sort of advancement. But now, at age fifty-five or sixty, one is looking commonly into a period of declining vigor and health; though the rational and intellectual faculties may remain strong. Those employed in the professions, and others who have cultivated and maintained an active mental life, can continue the pursuits of the mind for perhaps yet, up to several decades; provided they are not overtaken by overwhelming nor catastrophic, physical or CNS disabilities. And, provided they can find within themselves, the interest and motivation to do so. Yes, a period of years with a sort of golden potential, for one to pursue one's own interests and ideas—-economic and physical health permitting; and, provided one recognizes that potential. "While individual man is always finite, one of the most significant things about him is that he seeks the infinite. There is a spirit in him that transcends nature, history, reason, and self - a spirit that belongs to eternity." (says Herbert Mueller)

The world's populations of our times, and through ages past, are and have been merely drifting passively through space, with no particular clue as to where they are headed. Their troubled individual years are preoccupied with the business and problems of life. Meanwhile, the mindless stars, planets, moons, meteors, cosmic dust, and energies continuously describe and repeat to us, the immutable laws of the universe. They are not forbidding; they nod and beckon to us for attention. In our ignorance of what they would readily divulge to us, we continuously strain to injure ourselves against the immutably unforgiving statutes of reality. Statutes, whose regularity and impartiality we might, rather, use - to further our own best interests; and define to ourselves, a larger destiny. As to the unseen and unheard-from Deity, who many suppose to exist above and beyond the universe and its natural laws; I regard that as a mere prejudice, which the bigots of each religion call by the name of faith, (as it exists in themselves) but, called by the name of superstition, (as it exists to those of religions other than their own). My own prejudice leads me to suspect that a portion of the Deity may well abide within me - within each one of us - and that the natural laws of the universe have something to say to us, about finding our pathway through the stars, and through our own being to the Deity, within.

> "The spacious firmament on high,
> With all the blue ethereal sky,
> And spangled heavens, a shining frame,
> Their great original proclaim.
> The unwearied sun, from day to day,
> Does his Creator's power display;
> And publishes to every land
> The work of an Almighty and.
>
> Soon as the evening shades prevail,
> The moon takes up the wondrous tale,
> And nightly to the listening earth
> Repeats the story of her birth;
> While all the stars that round her burn,
> And all the planets, in their turn,
> Confirm the tidings as they roll,
> And spread the truth from pole to pole,
>
> What though in solemn silence all
> Move round this dark terrestrial ball?
> What though no real voice, nor sound,
> Amidst their radiant orbs be found?
> In reason's ear they all rejoice
> And utter forth a glorious voice,
> Forever singing, as they shine,
> This hand that made us is divine."
>
> *-a verse by Addison*
> *as quoted by Thomas Paine.*

- - - - - - - - - - - - -

Few conceive of any immediately foreseeable reason for mankind to want to escape his earthbound condition. Yet, it is obvious that adequate reasons have already been proposed; and the first steps into space have already been taken. In 1969 an American man - Armstrong - became the first man known to have set foot on the moon. And now, President Bush informs us that the U.S.A. plans to place a man on the surface of Mars, by the year 2015. The history of the moon, still legible upon its impact-cratered surface - and its allusions to the history of the earth might, at any time, make it seem a prudent thing, to have acquired that capability; if one but considers the continuity of history into the present and future.

In the past couple generations, the opportunity and necessity for the education of increasing numbers of people is becoming a reality. There is progressively less need for man as a beast-of-burden, in a technologically advancing society, where the requisite physical forces can be more efficiently and economically supplied by machine and robot. Technology increasingly requires of workers that they attune and discipline their individual minds to understand systems so as to enable them to solve technologically complex problems; and diagnose problems in their technological equipment. But technology and its equipment changes, so as to require of us an on-going character to our individual educations. The most willing and able will set themselves to the task of a more thorough-going knowledge, in a wide field of inter-related sciences, so as to assure the exchange of information and fruitful application of theory and method, from one to another among the technological and scientific fields. It has been said - and I suspect it may be true - that there are more scientific minds alive in the world today, than the total of those that have ever previously existed in the history of the world. There seems a definite tendency for a person's interests to broaden and enlarge into other fields of interest beyond that in which one is employed to earn one's living. This, somewhat proportional to one's available free time; but also, proportional to the moral influence to which he has been exposed. And related to his cultural background, and his circle of acquaintances. There is, perhaps, a natural current that favors such a drift and spread of interests, on the one hand; and on the other hand, one's cultural background and one's acquaintances may either facilitate, or retard that current of one's interests.

It is generally thought that wisdom and sagacity accumulate to one in consequence of acquired knowledge and experience that one accumulates with time. I think that we can find some examples of that in almost any community. Logically, one would certainly expect that it might be so.

Unfortunately however, I do not see evidence that it is the usual and customary trend, progressively into advancing old age. For man is afflicted with a detrimental aging process, which, throughout the abbreviate course of his life, brings with it the incremental demise of the function of his various organ systems - including the structure and function of his central nervous system (CNS). Though unproven, it may be the case, that the aging process is largely - or even entirely - secondary to continuous exposure and susceptibility to trauma, disease processes, and toxins. These, perhaps, cumulative in nature. Even presuming that the aging process is merely expedited by those influences, the possibility still exists, that the aging process can be greatly diminished - to provide one an infinitely longer productive and useful life. Were one's life span extended by a factor of four, for example, he could live that span of productive life with but one period of formal education - the same, or even less, than what is ordinarily required of us now; provided only that one were properly disciplined to a continuous process of self-education. In the history of the race, but one in ten persons has ever attained unto the age of sixty-five years, under even the most favorable of circumstances. Currently, however—-in this country-—it is anticipated that eight of ten may do so. New possibilities for human accomplishment and personal achievement then arise; if we can continue to extend the time, the resources and the will of a people, toward such goals. The limitations to man's accomplishments and attainments has always been that of a want of determination, a want of intellectual grasp, and inadequate flow and evaluation of valid and fruitful thought, ideas, and concepts. As Gilbert Ryle put it, the complaint ought not to be that the intellect is too weak, too dull, or too clumsy a tool; but rather, that one "approaches death before he has learnt all its uses".

As things now stand, the larger part of the years of one's life are preoccupied (in the most fortuitous of circumstances) with the learning of arts and skills that may prepare one for the possibility of a productive mental life; when - and if - the winds of fortune endow him with adequate health, time, and opportunity to utilize the potential of his intellectual capacity.

One's life can be lived on any of a number of planes of perception and being; commonly alternating between several of those planes of existence. The most rudimentary, is the vegetative existence such as one occasionally sees in the nursing home; one whose cerebral cortex has died from some accidental period of anoxia, but whose brainstem (vegetative functions) continues to adequately regulate its cardiovascular, respiratory, and metabolic functions. Far at the other extreme is one such as Stephen Hawkins, whose body is all but completely disabled, but whose active mental processes and interactions are far the predominant portion of his being. An influential being.

I might suppose that my own ancestors even of only a few generations past probably lived out their lives in plane of existence not far removed that of beasts of burden.

Yet, I know too that they were engaged in the ideological struggles of their times, so that a community and familial tradition of thought and discussion of ideas has been evolving. Thought . . . whose outcome may transcend, one day, into a dialog of inquiry, investigation, and discovery; and into communication of sufficient motivating influence and established tradition such as to enable the short-lived individual to attain in a few short years, that knowledge that the entire race of mankind had been able to acquire in painful slowness over only the last few millennia of its existence. That experience and knowledge are the enabling force that may, hopefully, expand the possibilities of his being towards enrichment, broadening, and prolongation of our healthful productive being and accomplishment.

RGB

The Public Philosophy

by R. Garner Brasseur

J. Bentham, James Mill, and John Stuart Mill were strong advocates of social justice. What they said and did; and what they wrote, had a very significant impact upon the improvement of working conditions and the quality of life for the common man, beginning in the early 19th century, in England. Their impact created ripples that soon transmitted to all of Europe and the western societies of the new world. Their great guiding principle was that of utilitarianism - "the greatest good, for the greatest number". Their Jacobean ideology held that the interests of the community are no more than the sum of the interests of the several who happen to compose it, at any particular instant of time. Bentham said that "the happiness of the individuals, of whom a community is composed - that is, their pleasure and their security - is the end; and the sole end, which the legislatures ought to have in view."

Walter Lippmann (in his book, "The Public Philosophy") acquaints us with the view of Edmund Burke, which is opposed to "the greatest good ..." principle of utilitarianism. Burke indicates that besides the happiness and the security of the individuals of whom a community is at any moment composed, there is also the happiness and the security of the individuals of whom - generation after generation - it will be composed. In this view, "The People" (as in, "We, the people of . . .") is the stream of individuals, or the connected generations of changing persons. Those (of any particular nation already dead, those yet living, and those yet unborn are involved in a sort of partnership (corporation, or entity) of mutual trust. Thus, 'The People' live on, while individuals come into it, and go out of it. That sacred trust of continuity (from ancestors, through us now living and into posterity) is the binding matrix that makes a man, a citizen; and one of 'the people'. Any affirmative process on the part of the individual, effectively confirms his signature to that partnership (or corporation, or entity) of national ideology. Such affirmative action might be that of informed voting, dying for, or serving his country in the interests of it's defense; or reading, writing, and reflecting upon the principles and problems of the nation.

Burke's view, I think, is a more comprehensive view of democratic government than is mere utilitarianism. For Burke's view implies a measure of rational responsibility of a citizen - to his country. Nor does that responsibility to his country, pre-empt his responsibilities to his own family, nor to his own personal concerns or interests. It does complicate his life however, in that it may (at any moment) require of him some individual thought and soul-searching. And this brings us to Walter Lippman's notion of a public philosophy. He means by this, that the individual citizen (in the casting of his vote and in the use of his whatever measure of influence) ought to be forever mindful not only of his own personal interests as opposed to those of some other citizen, or group of citizens, or corporations of the here and now; but that he has a sacred contract to uphold public philosophy. He is, as it were, a trustee of the interests and rights of generations of citizens yet unborn; and of those departed. He needs must, and ought to uphold that government which will preserve some seeds of freedom to the future sons of men, just as our ancestors preserved some rights and freedoms to us, having first wrested them free by increment through many generations of sweat and bloodshed. Why ought each voter and citizen to consider and act as I have suggested? So that government of the people, by the people, and for the people should not perish from this earth. And in order to keep alive (each citizen - by conscious, and personal initiative) that public philosophy which alone can perpetrate that government; and the benevolence of it's ideals of justice and freedom.

In truth, a public philosophy is rarely to be found among the ranks of the citizens of the U.S.A., in this age. It may not have been common in past ages either. Yet, it must have existed in the minds of the men who framed our constitution. And Lincoln seems to have been aware of a public philosophy. Presidents (of this country), in fact, are by tradition, supposed to be the living embodiment of a public philosophy. They are sworn to uphold the constitution and are officially expected to eschew all connections with special interest groups. Officially, they are even to be above those private interests peculiar to the political party from which they are elected.

The senators and congressmen however, are very much susceptible to the pressures of special interest groups. For they very much need the support of their constituents to achieve election; and re-election. If they any, as individuals, have a public philosophy, they are hard pressed to fend off their electors upon the basis of any of it's principles. And each legislature, is under pressure from the plurality of voters (by whom they are elected) to effect some legislation to benefit this and that private and special interests, in the here and now. By rhetoric and compromise, they patch together some new legislation, or modify some old. They hope it pleases, or at least satisfies their constituents, or at least that the constituents do not become implacably irritated. But any president with a public philosophy is apt to give the legislature a great deal of harassment and opposition in the legislative process, for his interests and concerns relate to the rights and prerogatives of the individual citizens of the past, present, and future; and for the public interest at large.

The public interest may be presumed to be what men would choose if they saw clearly, thought rationally, and acted disinterestedly and benevolently. That individual voters and citizens not infrequently fall short of this ideal, tends to erode the foundations of our democratic republic. Unless the individual voters and citizens develop, and maintain an awareness of a public philosophy in regards to their voting responsibility, it seems probable that the force of our democracy shall end - by force of bankruptcy and chaos.

R.G. Brasseur, M.D.
dated about 1983

To Have, Or Not To Have

by R. Garner Brasseur

There are those who are said be "the haves", as opposed to the majority of us who constitute "the have-nots". 'The haves', become generally accustomed to being served, in addition to enjoying perpetual access to the 'feathered nest' into which they were conceived and hatched. We, among 'the have-nots' are destined to be 'of service' to 'the haves', as well as in reciprocity to also those among our fellow 'have-nots'. The notion of equality among we mere mortals has long been an ideal towards which we aspire. And - with some gradual success from century to century - so that we ordinary folks live generally longer, easier, and more comfortable lives from generation to generation. At least that is how it is and appears to be for us here inside the USA. But it is not the situation universally among the nations of the world. So while you and I are among 'the have-nots' of this nation, we are citizens of the foremost of 'have' nations of this world. Much better than being 'have-nots' in a 'have-not' nation. Even among 'the have-nots', there seems destined always to be some who are more equal than others. And (among both 'the haves' and 'the have-nots') in the course of time, one may rise or fall in his degree of 'equality' in accordance to one's personal intentions, efforts, economic prudence, personal virtues, and fate.

But we, 'the have-nots', most seem inclined to make for ourselves at least somewhat of a life, as best we can, from what little is available to us. Most settle into whichever first occupational opportunity opens onto them and make their way by hand-to-mouth through life in common with their native peers. Must spend long years of daily time in labor to bring home the bacon and daily bread. Occupied and preoccupied with the cares of life and burdens of existence. Some eventual hopes and aspirations perhaps, for one or another of one's offspring. Comforted perhaps, by some vague hope of somehow getting past the pearly gates into the unknowable hereafter. To what may they aspire, once landed there?

But another reality is that even we, 'the have-nots' are mostly all of adequate intellectual potential and mostly physically able enough that we might each aim and aspire higher than we do, might become somewhat 'more equal', if only we had given the matter more consideration, and focused on the more distant - rather than on the more immediate satisfactions. Most get swept up into someone else's agenda, rather than thoughtfully evolving their own. We are well advised to take note of whether any such agenda has merit - and to whose benefit. Yes, there is something to be said for giving heed to the advice and agenda of the thoughtful friend or relative - such as might be concerned and willingly to trouble himself to be of benefit to one's best interests.

Yet another reality is that those from among 'the haves', do have much the same needs and psychodynamic make-up as do those of we, 'the have-nots'. Though they are spared the necessity of laboring for hire, they too needs must have something to occupy their time, and strive towards goals and objectives to which they are wont to aspire. One might say that they are generally more apt to be preoccupied with ideas, thoughts, concepts, and mental manipulations. But they must at least strive to hold and retain the great wealth and advantage they have already acquired by virtue of an inherited privileged status in our society.

Both 'the haves' and 'the have-nots' are always at least vaguely aware that one's life on this sphere continues to be brief, brutal, and hazardous.

Earthquake, deluge, prairie-fire,
Against mere mortal man conspire.
From fate and chance be no appeal,
When mighty wind and wave prevail.

'Twas brute to brute and nail to fang,
On Serengeti's teeming plain.
Though agile youth escape today,
From predator the fate of prey.

Still, un-suspect the ranks of men,
By microbe hosts were yearly thinned.
While from the sky and mountains roar,
Fire, ash, and bolts of Thor.

Life stark and brief let each amend,
Eternal pathway to transcend.
And harness skill toward small advance,
In daily life to better chance.

RGB

- - - - - - - - - - - - -

When all is said and done, we must come to recognize that each life is faced with its own particular difficulties. And that all are not equal in any sense, though in this nation there has generally been some intent and some effort to put us on an equal par before the law. An ideal that undoubtedly is destined never to be fully accomplished. Nor will any political system ever succeed in equalizing our economic circumstances. We certainly wouldn't want to be equally destitute. And were we all equally wealthy, where would we find anyone to serve our interests? Whatever the prevailing political climate, there is but little we individually can do to effect much change in it. About the best we can do is to make an effort to recognize the realities in which we are immersed, and make what adjustments we can to get by as we must.

A reasonable agenda? To perhaps free oneself from the superstition and ignorance which are obstacles to one's rational purpose; and an obstruction to one's view of reality.

RGB

THE SIT-IN

by R. Garner Brasseur

There are so many evil agendas at play in Washington, D.C. and across this nation in the past few years that it begins to concern me, and in my semi-retirement I find myself being ever more absorbed in the details that leak out - now that we have Glenn Beck and The American Heritage Society to bring us access to the back-room scandal of politics that has always been afoot - and becoming ever worse and more a threat to the best interests of this nation and its citizens. I am astonished by both its scale, and its ubiquitousness. The recent election (2011) has enabled the citizens to give the forces of evil a bit of drubbing, but more needs must be done to get the progressive socialists, the communists, and the Soros 'one-worlders' out of our legislative bodies. I thought I might run for an office myself, but I am not well known, and hardly apt to find myself ever nominated to an election ticket within the limited time of my few remaining years. Besides, I am too old to be given any such elective recognition. But should you or any of your acquaintances elect to evolve any plan that could shoe-horn me into the presidency or lesser sort of governing office, I would take the job and set about a thorough 'house-cleaning'. No, I don't really want to, but I would take it on. A sacrifice I would be willing to make.

The Wall Street sit-in crowd may well have some valid basis towards which they make their protest, although they seem unable to iterate precisely just what their protest is actually about. They seem to have a only a vague sense that there is something amiss in an economic system that leaves them in the years of their youth and middle age with so much burdensome individual debt, and poor prospects for employment such as to offer them much hope of working themselves free of the economic morass into which they are mired. This, while having become well aware of the huge affluence and economic privilege they perceive especially as symbolized by the wealth that flows through the hands of 'big money' operators and operations of Wall Street. Their demonstration however has been usurped by union thuggary and a vast free-loading element, and thus degenerated in mob misbehavior.

The sit-in crowd seems just now to be discovering what has been the economic-political reality of the country for the past 150 years. Government with always economic ramifications; and an economy with always political ramifications.

By a hundred years or more past, the USA already had a well established hereditary propertied class. Great wealth in the USA is no longer ordinarily gained by the input of one's great effort, legal or illegal, but comes from being named an heir to fortune. Almost every single wealth-holder in the upper 0.5% of the population arrived to wealth by this route. And some who are heirs, are heirs many times over. Owing to intermarriage among the wealthy, property holdings tend to concentrate into ever fewer hands.

It is not that the rich take from the poor, that which belongs to the poor, but that they sponsor, support, and underwrite public arrangements, such as the tax structure, that makes any different outcome impossible. (see "*The Rich And The Superrich*" P. 835)

The progressive tax system is in fact the final obstacle that decisively protects the <u>old established wealth</u> from any much possibility of being invaded by the occasional chance 'newly wealthy' - with whom they have not much in common.

Entering into business for oneself in the United States has always been a highly risky affair. "Many are called, but few are chosen". Most who remain in business do so on the thinnest of margins. Many are hopelessly in debt and in imminent danger of folding as economic tides wax and wane.

As for the legislative voices that are calling for a tax-the-rich policy, the measures they propose are misguided, for they are not aimed at the rich and the super-rich, but aimed rather at the hard working middle-class who are just now struggling for a toe-hold to enable them to escape their economic mediocrity. In so doing, they are actually potentially the major providers of jobs to the disaffected masses who originated the Wall Street 'demonstration'. To over-regulate and over-tax these potential major employers is counter-productive to those desperate for employment; and to economic recovery of the nation.

Mark Twain says: "There is no distinctly American criminal class, except for congress." We recently hear more of the gloomy details of that with the revelations that our 'representatives' have been always able and willing participants to 'inside trading'. Which goes a long way towards explaining how it is that they manage to enrich themselves quite beyond what one would expect even with their generous annual incomes of $174,000.00 per year. We are informed by Beck of such other delicious tidbits such as that the House Members have their own private House Bank which was forced to close because they 'bounced' 8,331 personal checks. Having then pledged to fix the problem of the House Bank, it then reopened. And they again promptly bounced 4,325 additional personal checks. Naturally, they are not exposed to any such inconvenience as that of having to pay overdraft fees. There appear to be other scams to which they are party, but one becomes numb to the scandalous principle of the thing if we allow the list to become overly lengthy. The issue between political conservatives and radicals is not weather God exists - for this issue is of interest to neither - but what the effect is on the populace of belief or disbelief in God. Religion is seen by both as an adjunct to repression and inhibition. (ibid. p. 836) "Money is their God. And how to get it . . . that is their religion." (As Mark Twain puts it) Well, it ain't as though money is everything; it's just that everything can come to seem like nothing without it. Having been broke and desperate on a number of occasions in my life, there seems to me to be a measure of truth in that.

Salary of retired US Presidents .... $450,000 FOR LIFE
Salary of House/Senate members .... $174,000 FOR LIFE
Salary of Speaker of the House .... $223,500 FOR LIFE
Salary of Majority/Minority Leaders .... $193,400 FOR LIFE
(pretty good retirement benefits!)

You wouldn't think the income so meager that many of the younger members of congress end up sleeping on fold-away cots in their offices. Perhaps it is more of a convenience to them, as they have intermittently irregular hours and odd-hour committee meetings. They have their own gym where they can work out and shower, as well as good food available to them from their own cafeteria. And it is probably more of an economic strain on the younger members who haven't yet acquired much ill-gotten wealth.

Average salary of a soldier DEPLOYED IN AFGHANISTAN - $38,000 Average income for seniors on SOCIAL SECURITY - $12,000

I hear Donald Trump indicating that the net assets of the United States is something in the range of 280 trillion dollars. And that our current national debt is 15 trillion - and growing alarmingly. There is one matter concerning this country's financial status of which I have never seen an estimate. I know that during WW-II this nation was spending vast resources on 'lend-lease' to Russia, England, and France. And after WW - II we spent other vast sums to rebuild all of Europe from the ruins of war. And that the 'Marshall Plan' spent additional vast sums of American money to reindustrialize Europe. I am aware that additional vast sums of taxpayer dollars since then have continuously gone towards many 'underdeveloped' nations around the world through the USAID Program, which is generally acknowledged to have been a failure. And more, that we contribute also in vast sums to many countries for military and economic support - especially to Israel, Palestine, Egypt. And that even while providing all of this, we supply military protection to Japan, and all of Europe, so that they are spared the expense of having to supply their own military protection. I have not yet begun to come to grips with the accounting system that puts a reckoning upon all of this shifting of economic aid and assistance that seems ultimately to be coming from the American taxpayer. I am left to suppose that the final tally would probably indicate that The United States of America would most likely have more accounts receivable than accounts owing.

Or is it possible that there is no accounting of the American wealth which has been, and is being sent to nations and causes abroad? That would obviously be quite disadvantageous to our American citizenry. Bogus paper money being printed by 'the fed'; each dollar of which diminishes the purchasing power of my every asset and savings.

It would however, help explain how it is that the "most productive workers in the world" (the American worker) get but 2 weeks of vacation yearly, while in Europe they get 6 or 8 weeks; why our work week is 40 hours while in Europe they work only 32; why retirement in the USA is age 65, but as young in some European nations as age 52 etc. And offer some clue as to how it is that European cities have been twice in the past century been reduced to rubble in world wars among themselves, (and from which they were extricated by the USA) and have twice risen from the ashes with seemingly little adverse consequence to their current economic conditions.

We know in this country that we wage earners are paying, for the money comes from our paychecks before we even see it. Secondly, the tax rate is generally on an upward climb. Thirdly, the costs of everything keep going up (inflation) even as the package contents of what we purchase are decreasing, and it is necessary to get an occasional ungenerous pay raise to keep the folks from rioting - that, of course puts us into an ever higher tax bracket. Fourthly, new fiat money continues to be printed and there-by continues to dilute the value of our every dollar. The value we thus continue to loose seems to be dribbling up to the wealthy corporations and families, for we can see that it is not dribbling down to us po' folk. And in addition to these things, Americans are encouraged and seduced by matching employer contributions to invest in IRA and Roth retirement funds, where Wall Street manipulations are able to 'harvest' some of what would otherwise be profits to aid in the retirement assets to which they aspire. (by leveraging natural price fluctuations into boom and bust cycles from which enterprising brokerage firms and investment bankers intermittently engage in 'profit taking')

Hitler (see "*Mein Kampf*") and Griffen (see "*The Creature from Jekyll Island*") are not the first to suggest that the politically powerful wealthy entities at the top of the economic feeding chain of this world find it sometimes useful to facilitate and prolong the intermittent wars between nations. Why? The profits of war do facilitate the business of 'profit taking'. But, as the mega-wealthy already control most of the wealth of the world, perhaps there is some other reason behind this. Human nature – being what it is – does have a propensity to be envious. The vast majorities which constitute the middle and lower classes poses always somewhat of a potential threat to arise, to "level the playing field". War, and rumors of war, are powerful distractions to avert any such economic leveling. In addition to that, the reality is, that the burgeoning populations of the world do continuously strain the world's resources. War, along with disease and epidemics, does provide a mechanism for holding the world's population in check.

I vaguely recall having read the "*Report From Iron Mountain*" (unintentionally leaked to the public in 1967) some thirty five years ago. But I have much forgotten its contents and have long since lost track of my copy of the book. But I now come upon a book ("*Rescuing a Broken*

America", by Coffman) which reminds me of some of what that report iterated. That 'report' apparently having been put together by some elitist 'jet set' supra-nationalists or others of their ilk with a theme somewhat of the same nature as "*The Protocols of the Elders of Zion*". That is to say, expounding somewhat on the principles by which the elite 'governors' (and 'the abundantly wealthy' whom they serve) might manipulate and control 'the great unwashed masses' of we 'children of a lesser God'. Useful and necessary actions and deceptions useful to their long term objectives such as to achieve and maintain the advanced 'new world' society from which they would reign over us common folk of the masses.

- They considered as useful, the threat of external war to distract the nation's population from internal problems.
- Considered war itself and the necessary military spending to be the only force with enough wasteful inertia to perpetuate poverty and thus to keep the people divided into classes and thus forever in contest with one another.
- They considered ongoing war as almost necessary, to keep the poor in poverty
- Consideration of a substitute for war, should peace evolve.
- A shadow government of 'the elite' experts in fields such as social science, history, economics, international law, cultural anthropology psychology, psychiatry, math, astronomy to conjure up threats or perceived threats to substitute for war should that become necessary. Alternatives such as UFOs, space exploration, or 'warmism'.
- As a useful alternative to war, perhaps exploiting pollution and protection of the environment as being the need for ongoing austerity among the masses.
- The poor to be kept dumbed-down and in bondage - like serfs.
- An ongoing pretext of welfare without any actual benefit to the poor - so as to maintain class distinctions and promote unending class warfare.

There was some furor over the report back in those years when I first became acquainted with the it, but the population as a whole is not much accustomed to reading and 'the leak' was not widely discussed. Like myself, most of the few to have heard any discussion of the report, soon forgot about this mere rhetoric. The major media is said to have denied its authenticity; and, as with "*The Protocols of the Elders of Zion*" little much was ever henceforth heard of the matter. However, shortly thereafter, there insidiously soon evolved to the public mind a concern about 'the environment'. And in 1969 congress passed The National Environmental Policy Act; and in 1970, The Clean Air Act. And in 1972 created the Environmental Protection Agency (EPA)and passed the Clean Water Act. Now, thirty years later, the EPA has morphed into a monster which, under the Obama regime, is stifling the economic development of our nation and contributing greatly to the ruination of our very economic life blood.

RGB

The Abundantly Wealthy

by R. Garner Brasseur

"*The Rich and the Superrich*", by Ferdinand Lundberg was published in 1968. I first read it in 1970 - over 950 pages. My poor powers of comprehension permitted me only a vague understanding of this mass of information. Enough at least to inform me that my own very limited first-hand experience of the political-economic reality of the world was in no way contradictory to what had been so nicely now researched and written for my perusal. I think I grasp it all a little more clearly as I now again go through the book forty plus years later.

In 1968 there was said to be perhaps 90,000 millionaires (0.6% of the population). But that was when my current $15,000.00 model of 2004 pickup would have cost a tenth of what it costs today, and gas was 35 cents a gallon.

For the really poor man imbedded in a poverty culture, the outlook for personal achievement is bleak. (p. 833) He needs constant help and encouragement. In my own generation, the need to finance a medical education privately out of even a middle-class income operated to exclude men of genuine talent from out of the lower classes (such as were my brothers and me. (p. 825)

No - not that the rich take from the poor, that which belongs to the poor, but that they sponsor, support, and underwrite public arrangements, such as the tax structure, that makes any different outcome impossible. It has all come about on a historical basis, and a reading of history does not disclose to us the alternative possible outcomes.

- In the United States, 20% of all wealth in the country is said to be government owned.
- The bottom 50% of the population own 8.3% of the wealth
- The bottom 92% own 48%
- The top 1.6% own 32% of all assets, and nearly all of the investment assets (income producing assets). The investment assets are what give economic control and produce to the wealthy the bulk of their enormous incomes. Their holdings concentrate on the leading corporations, not the 'paper tiger' corporations.

The wealth of the rich and the superrich (those with several million dollars or more) in 1968 was being held in: stocks 65%, Tax exempt bonds 8.5%, real estate 6.7%, cash 4.3%, govt. bonds 4.2%, mortgages and notes 1.8%, insurance 1.8%, other bonds 0.8% and misc. 6.8% (p. 84) Generally speaking, it was income earned on their invested assets, rather than based on labor and day-wages. Income which when not entirely elusive of any tax whatsoever, are subject to much lower tax rates than is earned income. The IRS tax code is progressive, so that the wages and earned income of the wealthy would indeed be at a considerably higher rate than that of we ordinary earners. That though, is irrelevant, since they are able to arrange for their own remuneration by accepting their portion in discounted stock shares options, bloated business expense accounts, corporate credit cards, and many corporation 'perks'.

Within the past hundred years or so, there have been quite a number of million dollar (and even some multi-million) fortunes earned and established - mostly in oil exploration and dealings, some yet in real estate, and more recently in silicone-valley technology. But keep this in mind, "a man seldom gets rich without ill-got gain - as a horse does not fatten except by feeding in the night", unless with the help of inherited wealth. (p.806) But even some of these, like Bill Gates' Microsoft would not have been possible without significant pre-existing family money and connections.

The DuPonts, Rockefellers, Mellons, and the Fords seem probably at the top of the heap of the many families of super wealth. All have been in the United States for generations, the oldest and probably wealthiest being the DuPonts.

Characteristics of the fortunes of the super wealthy;

- It generally controls and revolves around one or more important banks.
- It controls ownership stake in from one to three or more of the largest industrial corporations.
- It has established and controls - through the family - one to four or more super foundations designed to achieve a variety of worthy purposes, as well confer vast industrial controls through stock ownership and extend patronage-influence over wide areas.
- It has established or principally supports one or several major universities or leading poly-technical institutions.
- It is a constant heavy contributor to political parties. Money discreetly transferred so as to avoid any impropriety such as might possibly suggest anything akin to bribery.
- It has extremely heavy property holdings abroad so that national, foreign, and military policy is of particular interest to it.
- It has vast indirect popular cultural influence because of the huge amount of advertising its corporations place in the mass media.

Among the rich and the super-rich, there are thousands of family and private holding companies that keep the business holdings and fortunes of the very wealthy under a central direction. And to prevent the dissipation of the 'nest-egg' principle by the economically undisciplined among the inheritors. Part of the annual interest of the income is often spread among scores of hundreds of cousins, aunts, and in-laws.(p.225)

There are also a great many trust funds held in large banks, which concentrates that industrial voting power under the boards of directors of the banks, making the banks into large economic powers in the nation. (p.229) It is the super wealthy themselves who occupy most of seats of the boards of directors - thus spreading their mighty influence indirectly through a variety of mechanisms.

We can see that the rich and the super-rich seem to have cornered the majority of the nation's wealth, and it seems ever increasing to be going into their voluminous barns. They absolutely own and control all important economic enterprises in America. It seems more to be their fortuitously inherited wealth, rather than their laborious effort that increases their wealth. 'Wealth at work' - it earns wealth. What services do they provide other than the profitable lending and the counting of their wealth unto their own profit? The rich do not appear motivated by any particular motive other than to rule and continue to increase their inherited wealth. They have come to call themselves by the name of philanthropists. A euphemism which has come to be widely used in the mass media when referring to all the wealthy. A misnomer, which seems to be based on the fact that they donate money to a wide variety of endowments. Some small part of those such benisons of their various foundations do go out to various not unworthy uses, but the main benefit of such trust fund endowments is that it enables them (by various tangled tax-law loop-holes) to escape what would otherwise be a high burden of taxes to themselves. A complex but self-serving arrangement.

That the American people choose their own rulers is an idea that will die hard. We are a nation mostly of free and equal employees - better circumstances than in Russia in that we have a longer leash. All but the rich and the super-rich belong to the category of poverty (the bulk of American citizens) which includes anyone who does not own a fairly substantial amount of income-producing property or does not hold a well-paid securely tenured job. The bulk of us are wage-earners, and even with a strong income, can become destitute overnight if deprived of our jobs - a strong encouragement to mindless conformity.(see "*The Rich And The Superrich*" p. 23)

As to how and why the IRS code favors the wealthy, that is because the wealthy are indeed the ruling class in America. Though the tax code is written by our elected representatives and bureaucrats, the individually wealthy and wealthy corporations have ready access to, and influence upon the writing of the tax laws, that has allowed for the insertion continuously here and there of special clauses and exemptions to benefit the wealthy. After all, it is the wealthy who decide which specific politicians are to be candidates for elections. Naturally they hand-pick candidates who are apt 'congenially to accede' to various ongoing measures that are beneficial to the themselves. Not much need for the powerful to break the law, when - instead - they have laws written to serve their purposes. The candidates in turn are directly and indirectly remunerated by the wealth of wealthy individuals and corporations such as to make them electable. It is campaign money that does eventually decide which from among our grasping politicians will eventually 'represent the people'.

There is no process of estate reduction of the super-wealthy taking place in the USA through taxation, as is commonly suggested. Few heritable estates pass to institutions, but many pass indirectly as well as directly to heirs through various arrangements such as delayed-action trust funds, private investment holding companies, endowments, and foundations. The indirectly conveyed portions are operated by the heirs for their own beneficial interest. (ibid. P. 27)

Most people in the United States, including many outstandingly intelligent and highly trained are much like the participants to a game of dice in which the opponent throws a long series of 7's and 11's, losing seldom; but when the dice change hands, it develops that the dice follow the laws of randomness and show no such runs of 7's and 11's. In a real dice game, most such losers would quickly conclude that the dice were loaded, and that they were being cheated.

Now, if the social dice were not subject to manipulation from behind the scenes, would so many people be so far under par in the matter of money and property? Might it be said that they lacked ambition and wit? But could that be said to be true of Nobel laureates, university professors, and trained professional classes whose pay in comparison with corporation executives and big dividend recipients is absurdly meager?

Are we to suppose that highly trained professionals have acquiesced in their relatively niggardly compensation? In fact though, they do make largely unheard sounds of disgruntlement, much as though they were complaining futilely against loaded dice. (a paraphrase, see ibid. p. 333)

The 'old wealth' are long accustomed to social deference and a pampered existence. Besides having interbred among themselves, they have become accustomed to maintaining always a certain social distance in regal mansions upon their secluded familial estates.

The newly rich (P. 790) have no such education, experience, nor subtile nuanced refinements in riches such as to enable them to fit in well with 'old wealth'. They tend to be restless and more energetic, as well as often eccentric. And with their advancing wealth, they too are able to avail themselves of the rich man's tax loops to further their ambitions. Even so, I am led to understand that their wealth is only rarely apt to approach that of the wealth of 'old wealth'.

Even with our smaller tax rates, most members of the labor force in the USA manage their livelihood at something approaching a 'hand-to-mouth' existence. And even with a bit of a raise or an occasional bonus, would not be able to save their way out of poverty because - hazards apart - the system of advertising consumer goods often operates upon them with coercive effect. Able himself to resist the blandishments of the advertisers, an employee finds that his wife and children more readily succumb. Importune him to make rash purchases for their delight and put him in the position of niggardly churl for counseling prudence. "All the other families have one, why should we be different?" At the end of his career, he has not made the grade, but is given the gold watch for forty years of service before being ushered off to live on a few hundred dollars per month from SS. His children often look at him as a flop, speak of him disparagingly. (ibid. p. 835)

Are these things some of what lies behind the vague notions of those protesting at Wall Street?

- - - - - - - - - - -

"Good sense is of all things in the world most evenly distributed among men, for each one believes himself so well endowed with it that even those who are the most difficult to please in all things are generally satisfied with their share of good sense."(ibid. p.879) The rich man like the non-rich, believes his own mind is as good as any and its way of operation to be in no particular incorrigible. But having rarely in the course of their privileged lives faced truly humbling experiences of life, the rich tend to have rather an exalted opinion of themselves. Beyond their ability to cling to inherited wealth, there arises few if any from among them of outstanding accomplishment. No professional athletes, artists, writers, poets, editors, musicians, physicians, attorneys, professors, explorers, or Nobel laureates. Neither do they enter into the professional ministry.

Is this class of privileged persons any happier or more content that we of the huddled masses? There is no reason to suppose so, though they are not deprived of any of life's luxuries and comforts. They too are destined to encounter illness and injury. They too perceive slights and personal insults. They too are constrained and encounter limitations from at least among those of their own class in matters political, economic, and social. They are said to have a much higher rate of divorce than what is average in this country. Not uncommonly divorced as many as five or even up to ten times in a lifetime. There must certainly be some disappointment and unhappiness connected with that.

A fundamental philosophical difficulty of the rich consists of acquiring a sense of worthwhile function (and getting the world to agree with his self estimate). Difficulty stating any function for themselves that is disassociated from their economic ruler-ship of the nation and hanging onto the family fortune.

The super wealthy evidently do not believe that being the beneficiaries of huge trust funds has undermined their own characters, or that establishing trust funds for their children will distort the children's characters. I suspect they may be correct in that matter. The honest earning of a large fortune is probably also not in itself an unworthy goal or accomplishment, for that matter. There is always the possibility of spending some of it on worthy projects, after all.

It must be the case that at least some of those who have come into possession of old family wealth have personal religious beliefs or could even be said to practice their religion, though our author has the impression that they are generally not more than superficially religious church-goers. One can see that it might be hazardous for them to be too deeply involved with religion, for the beckoning coffers tend to crowd even us po' folk for ever a little bit more. Religion tends to be seen by the super wealthy elite as a part of the political process of keeping the common man in chains and submissive to higher secularists, often in clerical garb.

The children of the rich and the superrich are early separated from us common folk by attending special schools, but the schools tend to be democratic in that they take in students from an intentionally wide social spectrum - many of whom are subsidized by scholarships. It gives them some little experience of lesser mortals, you know. The education of the best of these private schools is no better than that offered by the better public schools, but the classes are smaller, better supervised, and there is more attention to keeping even the slower students up to par. A well motivated student in a good public school could learn as much out of that experience as he could at one these private schools. I once spent a week at one of these private schools in Rhode Island where some of their faculty taught us senior citizens a few courses. A pleasant comfortable setting and nice personnel. Those born into wealth, of course tend generally also to attend 'ivy league' colleges. Beyond the years of their education, there is at least one private central club of the wealthy in every larger city which constitute the societal control of the elite. The most important of these exclusive clubs being in New York, for obvious socio-economic reasons. The elite deign also to co-mingle with men of public affairs - approved artists, musicians, columnists, professors, writers, lawyers, editors, and even book-reading executives - with whom they needs must have dealings outside of the private world of their super-wealthy elite.

RGB

Return To The Future

by R. Garner Brasseur

I am tentatively planning to depart from Washington D.C. right after the first of the year. Though the disorganization and oppressiveness of the clinic is so great, that I doubt our mutual incompatibilities will endure the strain that long. I had planned to return to the mountain for renewal this weekend, but the recent flooding conditions of the Appalachians and the early wintry conditions there, along with the semi-loaded condition of the pick-up camper, combine to make that prospect seem unwise. So I arose at 9:00 a.m. and drove via highway 495, to Fairfax in northern Virginia to stop at a library book sale. On that journey of 25 miles, I noticed that the lovely fall color changes of the trees, that everywhere crowd between the living areas, are now in approximately the same state as were those of the mountains of the eastern part of West Virginia when I was there four weeks ago.

Returning, I stopped at a second hand bookstore, and then went to a Catholic Church School Bazaar, where I bought a colorful scarf and mittens for my grandson. Came home then and napped from 4:00 p.m. until 6:00 p.m. I had hoped then to read and write, but felt instead that I might benefit by a little diversion. I therefore went to a movie "Return To The Future" that Pierre had recommended. Then I bought a few groceries; and returned to the house by 10:00 p.m.

But the movie, "Return To The Future" was messing with my imagination and leading me into some insights for contemplation. I wonder if there is not perhaps a current of truth in the concept of the actions that it presents us. The story concerns the effect of one generation of a family upon another generation of the same family. And it portrays the alternative course that lives may take, in consequence of heroic deed, exhortation, encouragement, and inspiration. Marty, an eighteen year old high school student of 1985 is acquainted with a scientific inventor who finally perfects a machine, which then takes Marty back thirty years in time, to this same town as it was thirty years ago when his mother and father were high school students there. He meets his strange and timid father whom he recognizes (but who in turn cannot know him - as his son - because he has not been born yet). Marty saves his father from being struck by a car, but himself is hit in his stead. He is taken into the home where he is unconscious nine hours, and regaining consciousness discovers his mother - whom he recognizes to be such - but who is the teen-age girl in that family at this point in past historical time. She is infatuated by Marty, and completely uninterested in Marty's father. Marty and the scientific inventor have two problems. One, is to effect a match between these two 1955 high school students who are to be his parents. The other is to get a supply of power—-from a bolt of lightning—-adequate to transport Marty back to 1985.

These two objects accomplished and he arrives back to 1985 just in time to witness - as a second alternative self - his own mode of departure which initiated his adventure back into 1955. Yet, his now second alternative self, remains behind in 1985, and scurries over to aid his injured friend, the inventor. Marty then goes home to bed and arises in the morning to discover to his surprise that the lives of his parents and his siblings are all being lived on their now alternative and much more positive, happy and successful modes. All of this change from the previous state of things in their lives, is apparently in consequence of the influence he imparted to their lives on his journey into the past. Their relationships (the parents) and their individual beings are thus much more positive, and presumably, that effects the outcome of the enhanced person-hood of each of the siblings.

The concept of the possibility of traveling through time, into the future and the past, has been with us a long while - perhaps for thousands of years. For people must always have wished that they could change the past, recognizing the cause and effect relationship between things present and things past. The idea in itself however, does not have any scientific basis of reality - nor does it seem even remotely possible that any serendipitous invention will ever bring time travel into being. And yet, much of what was once thought impossible, has already evolved into existence.

It occurred to me however, that it is very common for us, as individuals, to affect the lives of one another - both for the good, and for the bad. The advancement of the arts and sciences - and the continuation myths and superstitions - give evidence of that. Each individual, no matter how seemingly well known and widely esteemed has but a limited small number of persons with whom he is intimately connected. These few lives, he can effect positively, if he will. Perhaps he can effect them negatively too, but with generally less overall effectiveness because of the idealizing influence of society and it's institutions. Also because once injured by us, those we might influence then tend to withdraw themselves from our influence. But, for the most part, most folks perhaps give no concern or thought to the matter, and simply live their lives from day-to-day with no special intent or effort - nor with any intentional policy toward influencing positively, the lives that they might touch. The sociologic influence of familial customs, beliefs, and behavior has almost the force of genetically inherited traits, in their influence upon the lives of individuals. The views and concepts of religions and state are often intimately combined with that of family, and their influence often concomitant with that of family. The standard education is perhaps not much more than the merest broadening of those two influences of state and religion. Yet, the education brings to each individual the chance and possibility, that each might very greatly alter his views, the concepts, the trends, and the direction of his individual life - by exposing oneself to specifically narrow channels of thought, or to broad and open horizons of ideas, concepts and thoughts.

For centuries, it has been convenient and useful for the church and state to proscribe official beliefs, concepts, thoughts, and ideas. Yet, continuously, some few are somehow advantaged by chance or personal and family connections to have looked and thought more broadly; and to have advanced their personal frontiers toward new ideas, concepts, and hopes. This, in their actions and in their writings, remains to all future generations, as communications that may contribute to the enrichment and broadening of future individuals. Remain as the foundations upon which knowledge can be built and extended. Thus, by laboriously concentrating the energies of our lives into the various forms and branches of knowledge and experience, these influences may be transmitted to our own subsequent generations. And thus, this energy of their lives and our, which might have expended into useless idle conversation, or in climbing mountains etc. comes to us as a new force in our lives - or as a fulcrum, for more advantageous leverage. So also may we conserve a part of our energy and genius, to impart to future men, in the form of inspiration, motivation, energy, and power.

R. G. Brasseur, M.D.

11/9/85

Akrazia

(Acting against one's better judgment)

15 January 2011

Awoke this morning having had this vivid dream reminiscent of an experience I had at age 14 in Miles City, when I bolted out of a classroom and considered running away from home, rather than having to face the music for my precipitous action.

So let me then try to recall some of the details of last night's dream: I was residing at my home in a comfortable community, I can't place the location - irrelevant. The adult Pierre was about, as a sort of concerned bystander to the goings-on. I had just had an angry confrontation with my non-descriptive spouse who had returned from work. I do not know what the contest was about, but the consequence of it was that it ended in my taking my leave of the premises - anticipating that this was destined to end in a divorce. But I was determined to 'hit the open road' and wander about at leisure in a carefree independent vagrancy in California. I was wandering about this hometown a bit, contemplating and preparing to launch out upon my journey. But cut off from my home base, how would I manage, with little or no immediately available cash to tide me along? Well, thinks I, I have little need for much money, as rambling about and living out of my pickup would not be very expensive. And besides that, I could pick up a small temporary job here and there to supply me with some of the meager wherewithal for my support. But then it dawned upon me, I did not have any of my regular medications with me; and even if I had, my current supply of meds would soon be exhausted, for I only possessed a three month supply. And how then would I get access to re-supply - with no money in my possession? Well, I returned home to find my angry spouse cleaning out the accumulated junk from a big room. A silent hostility permeated the situation, as I quietly gathered my medication supply, even as a silent concerned Pierre looked on.

The next thing I knew, I was landed to a quiet subdivision of some pretty community in California and wandering about on foot. I there encountered the adult Rod Dodson wandering about the grounds of one of his several ranchero estates. I am thinking I might prevail upon his friendship to accommodate me to a temporary transient shelter and to earn there a bit of income from a little handiwork about the place. For I did need a bit of substance, after all, to facilitate my aimless pilgrimage. At the same time, I was savoring the contemplation of the sweetness of this solitary leisurely journey which was luring me along. But it was sort of counterbalanced in my mind by the reality of this sort of desperate economic aspect of what I was getting myself into. I recall from past experience that there is a sort of depressing discomfort that comes from being broke and unemployed; despite the freedom of being able to wander where-so-ever one might wish in the idleness of it all.

It suddenly dawns upon me that there is no real necessity for allowing myself to be economically deprived in this anticipated pilgrimage, for from my home I have ready access to savings and retirement income. But I can foresee that the probability of forthcoming divorce proceedings is certainly apt to tie up my assets, even before depriving me finally from a goodly proportion of my property.

And then I find myself again back at home where a sullen spouse is still putting things in order. But she takes a moment in her repentance to say, "I'm sorry" (for whatever it was that had precipitated our disagreement). At that moment, it dawns upon me that there is another way to go about this that makes more sense. And I can now see that my solitary sojourn need not be for more than a duration of several months. For one would not want to wander about for more than, say, several months. And I am not pleased about the prospect of being cleaned out financially by self-serving attorneys and an ex-spouse. Perhaps she and I can work this out between us. I can now believe that she too might be agreeable simply to accede to my little interlude of pilgrimage for a few months rather than to totally disrupt our domestic tranquility. And so ends this little foray into the sub-consciousness of my dream state.

And here is my seventh grade experience to which I suppose the above dream has its relatedness:

The scheme of things was different here in the seventh grade in Miles

City, Montana in 1946. Instead of being situated in one room all day, we pupils were to march about from one classroom to another at the end of each class period of 50 or 60 minutes. One adjusts to it easily enough. I was always quiet and well behaved, and I was astounded to have my English teacher suddenly reproach me severely for having been whispering. In the face of so blatant a false accusation, I promptly stood right up to apprise her of the truth of the matter. But, she was impervious to my truth. Not yet realizing that most of the world is impervious to truth, I slammed my books down upon the floor and stomped out of the classroom, and out of the school. I had some long hours to think things over that day. It soon dawned upon me that I was probably destined to also have trouble at home concerning this incident. Hemmed in by trouble, as it were. An unforeseen interruption of the continuity of a life. I couldn't see an easy solution to this dilemma, so I began to give some deep thought to taking my leave from this whole territory, right yet this very day. But, where would I go, and how would I get there, and how would I weather the cold of this coming night upon an empty stomach? And there were a whole train of other questions that were destined to follow. At length I slinked on home and talked it over with mom, and she then went over to the school to get the affair straightened out on my behalf. The new morning found me back in classes, and I heard nary a word more about that little incident.

Also contributory to the above said dream, seems probably my past experience (the winter and early spring of 1986) of wandering about the state of California a few months in search of employment. That, in addition to my experience of a troublesome and long drawn-out divorce proceedings, which cursed my being for about a ten year span of time.

RGB
15 January 2011

THE TEMPLARS

(Knights of Jerusalem)

(Concerning the treasury of cash and literature they discovered at the temple mount in Jerusalem. Where has this wealth of information gone?)

I have not previously perused anything but the scantiest of information concerning the Knights Templar. A close-knit group of brothers, in-laws, and nephews out of France who wandered into history as a part of The Crusades to liberate the Holy Land. But now, Gardner's book ("*Bloodline of the Holy Grail*")(p. 254) has something to say that is a bit more informative and certainly attracts one's interest, for he indicates their quest for the Holy Grail was rewarded with success. During the crusades, various knightly orders were established, one of which was the Knights Templar which was founded some years earlier than the stated AD 1118 as the "Poor Knights of Christ and of the Temple of Solomon", said to have been established by a group of nine French knights who took vows of poverty, chastity, and obedience and swore to protect the Holy Land. They are said to have made it their function to safeguard the highways for pilgrims, but this stated purpose was perhaps a ruse. They were installed at Baldwin's palace located within a mosque on what they believed to be the site of King Solomon's Temple. Grail lore was born out of this Templar environment. Deep beneath the Jerusalem Temple site were reported to be the great stables of King Solomon, which had remained sealed and untouched since early Biblical times. The actual mission of the Templars was to find and open this area to which was said to be attached a large store-room, said to "contain the Ark of the Covenant, which in turn held the greatest of all treasures - the Tables of Testimony." These Tables of Testimony were said to contain "The Cosmic Equation": the divine law of number, measure, and weight. "The mystical art of reading the inscriptions was necessarily achieved by the cryptic system of the Cabbala." [A general rule of the ever elusive short-cut to enlightenment seems again to come into operation here. The magical key that opens the way to the 'holy of holies' becomes then dependent upon yet some other secret code, talent, or method which is possessed only by yet another privately vested concern, agency, or person. And each is then required to trust the veracity of the other. Always, the fox is guarding the chicken coup.]

The Tables of Testimony are said to have been inscribed by God Himself and given to Moses along with the Ten Commandments, to be kept along with them in the specially constructed Ark and guarded by the Levites. When the temple of Jerusalem was built, the Ark was lodged in the Holy of Holies and nothing further is said of it in the Old Testament. It is said that when the temple was destroyed by Nebuchadnezzar the Arc was not listed in the 'schedule of plunder'(?). In 1127, we are told, the Templars had retrieved the Ark and its contents along with an "untold wealth of gold bullion and hidden treasure", all of which had been safely stowed below ground long prior to the Roman demolition and plunder of Jerusalem in AD 70. Gardner says that in 1956 confirmatory evidence(?) of the Jerusalem hoard came to light at Manchester University, in the completion of the deciphering of the Qumran copper scroll.

In AD 1128 Hugues de Payens of the Templars was summoned to attend a meeting of Council at Troyes, to be chaired by a papal ambassador. [Another hungry fox enlists himself into the equation.) The Templars departed the Holy Land with the loot and traveled with it through France to Troyes under heavy guard, to where the cryptic translation was to be done. (We are left to presume that it was done.) International status of a Sovereign Order was conferred upon the Templars. The Church established the Knights as a religious Order, and Hugues de Payens became the first Grand Master.

The Templars enjoyed a swift rise to international prominence, and engaged in high level politics and diplomacy. In 1139 the pope granted them international independence from obligation to any authority save himself; and they were granted vast territories and property across the map from Britain to Palestine. Christendom was at their feet. Large private donations seemed to flow in their direction. They were tax exempt and amassed additional wealth as moneylenders and bankers to the Holy See. Even the sons of nobility flocked to the order, though the individual knights were still bound to a vow of poverty. They were associated with (attached to) the Cisterians as warrior-monks. [A fox has now gotten in among the chickens]. Within the next 25 years more than 300 abbeys were then constructed. But even more impressive then, the beautiful Notre Dame Gothic Cathedrals began to rise in Paris, Chartres, Reims, Amiens, Bayeux, Abbyville, Rouen, Laon, Evreux and Etampes. Magnificent structures, some of which took over a hundred years to complete. It seems inferred that both the Templars' wealth and their fund of cryptic information went into the construction of those awe-inspiring structures. They are certainly among the wonders of the world. But the Templars denied the crucifixion series of the New Testament, and therefore none of the decorative artwork of any of these cathedrals ever depicted that scene. Recall that they now had access to their new found wealth of ancient manuscript books, "many of which predated the Gospels, and provided first-hand accounts that had not been edited by any ecclesiastical authority. It was widely accepted that they possessed an insight which eclipsed orthodox Christianity, an insight that permitted them the certainty that the Church had misinterpreted both the Virgin Birth and the Resurrection". We can safely presume that this new information was closely guarded. Nevertheless, the 14th century inquisition brought the Templars under savage persecution.

Modern Freemasonry is generally conceded to have its origins from the private stores of new information of the Templars. Note however that the institution so known in the New World is said to be "speculative rather than operational", which I take to mean that they do not have access to any of that actual literary or financial wealth.

The Cathar sect was derived from the Gnostic factions of Judaism. In France, just to the northwest of Marseilles, they were settled in what had formed the 8th century kingdom of Septimania under the Merovingians. They also, were thought to be the guardians of a great and sacred treasure, associated with a fantastic and ancient knowledge. They were non-conformists, preaching without license and with no requirement for an appointed priesthood (apparently, in some way related to both the Templars and to the Mary Magdalene Cult?). They were tolerant of Jewish and Muslim cultures, and upheld the equality of the sexes. They were said to be probably the most cultured people in Europe, with access to education for both boys and girls. They had a Judaic Academy and were known to be adept in the occult symbolism of the Cabbala, an expertise that would have been of significant use to the Knights Templars who were thought to have transported the Ark and their hoard of treasure into this area. In 1209 the Papal army of 30,000 descended upon the Cathars. Tens of thousands were exterminated over the next 35 years.

Until 1306 the Templars had always operated without papal interference. But Philip IV of France was bankrupt and owed a great deal of money to the Templars and so he arranged for their persecution in France and attempted to arrange for their elimination throughout all of Europe. The papacy at that time was in residence at Avignon, in southern France. And under the influence of (or probably in collaboration with) the French king. Friday 13, 1307 the king's henchmen attacked the Templars throughout France, arresting 2,000 of their members, including their Grand Master, Jacques de Molay. But it had been arranged for the Templar treasure to be removed in a fleet of eighteen galleys from the port of La Rochelle (on the Mediterranean Coast). The majority of these treasure ships are said to have sailed to Scotland, which was under the rule of King Robert the Bruce, and in opposition to the Catholic Church authority. The Bruce was excommunicated to encourage the populace to throw off his reign. That did not happen, and the entire population was then excommunicated. In Scotland, the Templars were associated with the Sinclair family and involved with the construction of the Roselind Chapel of that family. The military forces of Robert the Bruce were engaged in battle and quite outnumbered by the English, yet are said to have won an astonishing victory. Said to have been made possible by the prowess of the Templar Knights.

The royal prosecutors "dragged into the light every dark superstition and fearful imagining of sorcery and devil-worship that lay along the roots of the medieval mind." "Elements of witchcraft, magic, and sorcery were taken for granted in medieval life, but Philip's use of them to prove heresy in the seven-year melodrama of the Templar's trials gave them fearful currency. Under influence of the customary prolonged methods of torture, de Molay confessed, but as he was exhibited to public spectacle for sentence to life imprisonment, he declared his innocence and called down a curse upon the pope as well as the king and his descendants - for which he was burned at the stake. Both the king and the pope were dead within the year. Thereafter, charges of black arts became a common means to bring down an enemy and a favored method of the Inquisition in its pursuit of heretics, especially those with property worth confiscating. In Toulouse and Carcassonne during the next 35 years the Inquisition prosecuted 1,000 persons on such charges and burned 600. French justice was corrupted and the pattern laid for the fanatic witchcraft persecutions of subsequent centuries." (see Tuckman, "A Distant Mirror")

I am interested to know something more about the hoard of ancient manuscripts the Templars are said to have acquired, and what it is that they might add to some necessary revisions of ancient church and secular history. Here is another cache like unto that of the "Dead Dead Scrolls" waiting to see the light of day. Where might they be lodged? The Vatican Archives would be a not unreasonable guess.

Does it seem probable that this Templar cache (in addition to 'The Dead Sea Scrolls' and the possibility of an occult collection of old manuscripts within the Vatican) of potentially informative ancient manuscripts might still provide valid information to me, and to thee? Some such unlikely things do occasionally occur. Here is another: concerning the history of Copan, I note two recent TV Public Broadcasting Program specials that deal with the lost civilizations of Maya world, in Central America. Archeological excavations and an intense scrutiny of the glyphs carved upon the monuments in Copan is said now to be providing information back to as early as AD 200 or 400, and that fully 80% of the glyphs have been deciphered. Who would have guessed that to be possible just twenty five years ago?

The history of Switzerland up until the 14th century remains vague and provincial. Hidden in the crevices of the Alps and of time. Apparently populated only by scattered small villages and mostly inhabited by farming folks with no background of military experience. But there were trade routes running east by west through which the commerce of the Templars had flowed. We are left to suppose that Switzerland's sudden rise of commercial centers along with a powerful banking industry may somehow be intricately connected to the escape from France of a goodly part of the Templar wealth and banking experience. Those templar knights escaping persecution in France with their treasures, would also likely offer explanation as to how an unremarkable rural nation would suddenly have achieved reputation of military strength. All of the details of these things remains rather secretive to the outside world.

RGB
Revised September 2011

THE U.S.A. IN CHAOS

by R. Garner Brasseur
August 2010

What is the sharpest instrument known to man? And the only instrument that actually gets sharper with each additional usage? Ans. - the human tongue.

It seems strange that one should have so few recollections of one's childhood. It is a period of intense informal learning - and of remarkable physical growth. One acquires a language and must continuously enlarge one's vocabulary. By trial and error, from a state of utter helplessness, one must learn to coordinate his own physical mechanisms of locomotion and the feeding of oneself. One must explore and adapt to the reality of a physical world and gain a working familiarity with the inescapable and unforgiving laws of nature. And one must ever learn to behave in reciprocity with those who constitute his family and the ever widening circles of his acquaintance. Learn, is the imperative. A price one must pay, or a reward one might acquire - such as to encourage one along. One's conclusions must be tentative and subject to revision. One's interactions with those about him require that he become an ever more proficient psychologist - perhaps at times, a philosopher. More from one's immediate family - but also contributed to by the round-about of one's whole society - one gradually becomes patterned to a daily routine of life. A well ingrained pattern of life such as might carry one (even) unthinkingly through each successive day of one's day-by-day existence.

And without one's being aware of the matter, one begins to acquire "a theory of mind". That is to say, one begins to see that, like oneself, those about him seem to have a great much of unspoken thoughts that cross their minds. One need not always be told this or that; for one begins to perceive some of these things. Like ourselves, others, too, are often judgmental of one another's behavior and motives - in the give and take (reciprocity) of life. Expectations of one; both as to the matter of civil decency; and as to one's 'voluntary' contributions to the shared life of the pack. For the reality is that we mere mortals are social, or herd animals. Yes, and more. Even above that reality - (perhaps partly in one's disappointment of it) - one begins to acquire self-expectations. Dreams become day-dreams. Day-dreams become vague aspirations. Some aspirations proceed to the setting of goals. But a goal without a plan is simply a wish.

Laws of nature? Reciprocity? Psychologist? Philosopher? Pattern of life? "A theory of mind"? Expectations? Self-expectations? Civil decency? To 'perceive' (does it smack of ESP?).

What does a child know of these things? What does an acorn consciously know about becoming and oak tree? Not much perhaps in particular. And yet, each comes eventually to grapple with its own destiny.

And upon such fundamentals as these, one must eventually construct one's own superstructure - which becomes one's own individual and personal life. Upon the expectations of others, and upon our eventually evolved self-expectations, we may begin to set our goals - unlikely though they be. And yet, when supported by realistic plans, some may indeed come to fruition. Like hurdles, our goals stretch out before us into the ever unknown and uncertain future. Are our dreams and goals realistic? Do we possess the time, the health, and the energy to struggle against the obstructions? Can we hold fast in the face of life's temptations and diversions? Do we have the will and determination?

Can promise then bring hope?
Can hope bring forth a faith?
Can faith give rise to courage?
Can courage bring forth effort?

R.G.B.
1997

- - - - - - - - - - - - -

But I digress. For I began this essay with the intention of a brief and elementary primer on another taboo subject. Politics. We all are subject to the winding influence of politics in our lives. Subject to . . . but with very little of say and influence in the currents of politics.

As a child and youth I neither found nor took the time for the mental calisthenics of politics. Far too deep and beyond my poor powers of comprehension. And I was necessarily preoccupied with the daily grind of school and the earning of some little income. And my immune system preoccupied with working out my defensives against the host of childhood diseases that ravaged our neighborhood.

Politics as I perceived it, seemed to be primarily rhetorical - apparently more interesting and seemingly appropriate to the folks of my parent's generation. Then, as now, there seemed to be a great deal of debate and argument over the these political matters. "Heat always passes from the hotter, to the colder body" - as does anger. A great deal of opinion and disagreement attended their discussions - more heat than light, perhaps. In that sense, it seems much the same now in my adult years also. Differing points of view, for example, such as what various religions might have said concerning the subject of Trouble:

- Taoism - trouble happens.
- Confucianism - Confucius says trouble happens.
- Buddhism - if trouble happens, it is really not trouble.
- Zen Buddhism - what is the sound of trouble happening?
- Hinduism - this trouble has happened before.
- Islam - if trouble happens, it is the will of Allah.
- Protestantism - let trouble happen to someone else.
- Catholicism - If trouble happens, you deserve it.
- Judaism - Why does trouble always happen to us?

From Zuckerman editorial
US News and World Report
of 14 Jan 1991

Is politics relevant to our lives? Certainly it is. And how one responds to political policy can make a vast difference in the consequence of one's own and family's lives. Those of my parent's generation were much more aware of that than we youngsters. They full well knew that their cousins in Russia were suffering through the deaths and agonies of, first WW-I, and then WW-II (to say nothing of the horrors of the interval under Stalin's purges, programs of starvation, and their exiles into Siberia). Meanwhile, my own ancestors had the wit and good fortune to have escaped to the U.S.

before all of that terror began. Thus, though our family was sustained on an only meager livelihood through the depression years of the Midwest, into WW-II. Yet we - unaware of our good fortune - lived in the most safe and secure situation in the entire world of those times. A thing that we perceive only in retrospect.

There is a tenant of socialism to the effect: "From each according to his abilities; to each according to his needs." An idealistic platitude which sounds friendly and nice. An idea that has been around a long time. Though many a community and nation has set out upon this course, when uncorrected, it leads to ruin, death, and destruction. In the settling of the New England colony, Gov. Bradford discovered it didn't work out. Too many unwilling to apply themselves to the drudgery of personal labor: no, not when they had free access to the communal granary. The fatal flaw of socialistic utopian schemes. Eventually the 'dear leader' is destined "to run out of other people's money" (not, or course, without first absconding with a tidy fortune for his personal comfort into retired obscurity).

And in the United States of America, is there "Trouble in River City" as that song suggests? Indeed there is. Yes, trouble in these United States of America ("with a capital T, and that rhymes with P, and that stands for" . . . politics). Trouble has been brewing a long time. Socialistic intentions get just a little toehold, and they soon progress to what is called "creeping socialism".

There were two varieties of socialism afoot at the same time in Europe for a generation or two before WW-II. Each of them - Nazism and Russian Marxist Communism - led to violence and to the death of many millions. Chinese communism produced even more violence and death, as did the communism of Pol Pot, in Cambodia.

Meanwhile, the euphemistically named 'Students for Democratic Society' (SDS) of the 1960's, (after bombing buildings, robbing banks, and causing a few deaths in this nation) seem somehow to have eluded any significant punishment and ended up as the lawyers, preachers, college professors, and financiers who have groomed and now surround and advise the Chicago community organizer - who has become the puppet and mouthpiece for their new approach to the destruction of America. I have not yet learned how this cadre of SDS incendiaries have managed to elude prison terms and are said to have become 'rehabilitated'? to now their more covert form of America's destruction through the medium of 'progressive socialism' as 'advisors', 'hatchet men', and 'czars'. Their efforts at demolition of Americanism has been so successful that they have even once again reinstituted chapters of the SDS upon a number of campuses of the nation's colleges and universities.

The USA was founded upon a very different set of principles quite opposed to progressive socialism. Aspiring to individual justice, as opposed to 'social justice'. Striving each towards individual salvation, rather than 'collective salvation'.

Why, after all these years, has my attention been drawn to all of these matters concerning state and national government? After all, at my advanced age, I might reasonable well expect that the consequences of all of this subversive socialistic politics and unpayable debt will not come due until I have shuffled off of this mortal coil. But, on the other hand, the big slam may come upon us a great deal faster than what I am wont to estimate. And even if not, neither am I agreeable to consent-in-silence that it will come down heavily upon my children and grandchildren.

The reality as I see it, is that progressive socialism had put this nation into a death-grip. But now, a new factor has entered into the equation of this death struggle. A sort of astonishment to me. For the first time in history, 'we the people' (through the medium of Fox News and Glenn Beck, supported by input from a multitude of free-lance bloggers and radio talk-show programs) have available a continuous stream of inside information to apprise 'we the people' of the scandal and the double dealings that are allowing - and even abetting - the ill considered legislation that is spending this nation into oblivion, destroying our economy, permitting the peaceful invasion of the county by aliens and armed thugs, undermining our national sovereignty, and diminishing the rights and freedoms guaranteed to 'we the people' by the constitution of these United States of America. How many nations of the world actually permit the invasion across their borders of the citizens of alien nations? Certainly none has ever before actually encouraged aliens; and provided <u>public funds</u> to feed, house, educate, and provide medical care to uninvited aliens and their offspring. If the wealth of our citizens and nation were such that it were able to support such largess, it might be done and we might take some little national pride in our generosity. But, in point of fact, the USA has become a debtor nation whose line of credit is on the verge of collapse. Who, among friendly nations or among our nation's citizens will continue to supply our daily necessities in return for mere promises - of only bogus greenbacks? What happens when the wheelbarrow is more in danger of being stolen, than is the cubic yard of devalued greenbacks it might contain?

The question is now as to whether 'we-the-people' will "heed the warning of the distant drums", and manifest the will and determination to rid ourselves of the inevitable destruction by vague socialistic idealisms, self-serving legislators, and power-grabbing demagogues. As things now stand, less than fifty percent of American citizens pay any federal taxes whatsoever. I notice for example, that there are 250,000 households in Britain in which no adult has ever held a job: I wonder if there may not be a similar proportion in our own nation. The founding fathers of this nation were long ago cognizant, that a democratic form of government could not long endure, once unproductive voting citizens outnumbered the producers within a society.

And yet, the question remains the same; whether 'we-the-people' will "heed the warning of the distant drums". Whether even those who are the major beneficiaries of governmental largess (those most dependant upon government) will manifest the will and determination to enable us to rid ourselves of the inevitable destruction of vague socialistic idealisms, self-serving legislators, and power-grabbing demagogues.

Another question is this; among the poor and dispirited voters (forever clamoring for more beneficent governmental handouts), do any significant proportion of them actually realize that the politicians and demagogues who promise so much (in exchange for their votes) will not - cannot - deliver on these promises.

There will be 'shortages', and those "shortages will be distributed among the poor" - as Stalin put it. See the following letter to my grandfather, by way of demonstration of the principle:

> From South-Russia 1923
> Michailopol, Gov. Odessa, March 25.
> From the Dakota Freie Presse, 8 MAY 1923,
>
> Dear Cousin Georg Bopple! (my grandfather)
>
> I hereby verify the receipt of the 12 dollars which you have sent to me via Mr. Sallet [a tidy sum of money in those times]. My sincere thanks and may God reward you! More I cannot say. I got the money on March 24, at which time we had consumed everything in the house and I didn't know what should happen the next day. With it I can now buy some bread and seed.
> When you emigrated to America, I owned 100 dessiatine of land and you looked up to me. Now I have nothing left, suffer with my family all kinds of difficulties, and you stand high above me. Never would I have thought that in this life I would be obliged inexpressible thanks to you. However I gladly thank you and cannot find words to express it. I had to call for the money at the post office in Kurisowo. Four years ago, that was still my address. However now I live in Michailopol and my post office

is Janowka. So I had to make a trip of 50 werst to Kurisowo and stayed overnight in Helenental. There Johann Leno told me that cousin Immanuel Bopple at Tripp also sought my address. We are profoundly grieved at my house; a year ago my dear son Immanuel was drafted into the army and we haven't heard anything from him all this time, and are unable to track him down either. My Wilhelm also doesn't write any more. We received the last letter from him from New York in September 1921. I am like Job. My land was taken from me and I am deprived of my children. My oldest son Reinhardt returned from the war not in his right mind and has been this way now for 6 years already. I would be very happy to read the Dakota Freie Presse, but I don' t have any way to pay for it. Greetings to all my relatives over there: Uncle Christian and Aunt Johanna, Uncle Daniel, and Aunt Justina, as well as all the cousins.

Immanuel Bopple
(cousin to grandfather, George)

- - - - - - - - - - - - -

Among the poor and dispirited voters clamoring for ever more beneficent governmental handouts; will they continue desperately to cling to the hope that perhaps these 'shortages' will not yet be visited upon themselves? May they well be correct in this. But hope is ought more than stop-gap complacency in the face of clear and present danger. No substitute for a reasoned and remedial action. No . . . hope is not promise; and promises - like contracts - are not necessarily destined to be fulfilled.

Obama continues each day to demonstrate that he has set himself in opposition to the will and intent of this nation's electorate. He has done nothing but stoke the racial fires and magnify the religious and social tensions within the nation. Accusing a white policeman of acting stupidly. Appointing van Jones the professional communist race-baiter to a white-house job. Saddling the nation with a host of authoritative 'czars' to replace an increasingly impotent congress. Has nominated 'the Wise Latina', Sotomayer, to supreme court; and the lying Keagan is awarded a judgeship sinecure instead of a jail sentence for her perjury.

The ongoing 'Affirmative Action' policy does nothing for the poor and working class whites who get no special consideration into the Ivy League Schools or into high profile IBM jobs since they are not beneficiaries of privilege. Blue-collar whites need not apply unless they have extraordinary grades.

Progressive socialistic policies continue to shrink private enterprise and enlarge the rolls of the unemployed now into the second year of this wayward administration. Meanwhile, government employees have increased by 250,000 (25%!) in the past two years. The average income of government employees is 111,000.00. Plus an additional cost of benefits that brings the total to 121,000.00. In the private sector it is 60,000.00. In the small bell-weather community of Bell, CA with a population of 30,000 the mayor has covertly managed to fudge up his salary to 847,000.00/ year, while even the sheriff confiscates 457,000.00/year. Teachers unions have ratcheted up their retirement benefits to 70% and 80% of the income of their working years as they continue into early retirements. Auto workers and service employees unions too have defaulted to federal bailout arrangements (to be paid by the taxpayers). Taxpayer dollars are being funneled into a Pension Benefit Relief Guarantee fund; a euphemism suggesting of promise that it will not be able to deliver.

Several states are already broke, and a good many others are destined to become so when federally mandated health costs are shifted to their already strained finances.

More recently, 'The Fed' announces it will buy up even more worthless mortgages (they already own 90% of them) and some T-bills, even as Fanny Mae and Freddy Mac continue to reach their hand into the federal till on a regular basis to buy up additional default mortgages at prices quite beyond their market values. Federal policy permit's the 'The Fed' to continue to spend, but does not require 'The Fed' to disclose the source of any such money they intend to use for said purchases - nor assets to back up any such bolus of purchasing power. The Fed, of course, will print the necessary shrinking dollars for all of this; and of course their bookkeeping system is immune for scrutiny. We yahoo private tax-paying citizens are to remain blissfully uninformed as we are led to the economic slaughter.

Unless at least a goodly large portion of the voting public still have some residual of hope for the United States of America as outlined in The Constitution and The Bill of Rights; and unless then willing - to take steps to rectify a government now run amok - we stand soon to lose our national sovereignty and individual rights. The rising standard of living long enjoyed in this nation shall also - assuredly - decline. Shall an informed American voting public willingly accede to such impoverished notions as 'Socialism', 'Social Justice', and 'Collective Salvation'!?? Shall the 'last great political hope of mankind' then perish from this earth?

So will the bloggers, The Savage Nation, Rush Limbaugh's EIB, Fox News' Hannity, and Glenn Beck have any success in abating the current tide of liberal progressive socialism? It makes an old geezer weary to ponder all this evolving economic and upcoming social chaos. I wonder if an occasional dose of Lithium will free my mind of all this futile concern over matters now quite beyond my any power to influence?

The power-mad elite of the Islamic religion are most especially empowered by those of their most radically rabid militant-fundamentalist faction - which is 'hell bent' on their ultimate mission of bringing into submission the entire population of this world. I expect it may well be true that the great majority of those of the Mohammedan Religion are not of this radical Wahhabian strain. But I am unaware of any significant Mohammedan influence or movement within this moderate strain of Mohammedanism that acts to quash or moderate the radical agenda of Islam that is once again on the rise not only in the middle east, but has slowly infiltrated into Europe and has now also been enlarging their numbers within the United States (currently already about 1% of our population). Americans as well as European citizens are beginning to perceive that - yes - these moderate Mohammedans do indeed also pose a threat to we non-Mohammedan nations and we of non-Mohammedan persuasion. For they represent what is becoming an enlarging body of what may be called by the name of 'fellow travelers'. When we were long engaged in a hot and cold war against Marxist Communism, it was well recognized that those 'fellow-travelers' were indeed clearly a significant part of the danger from Communism.

In point of fact, McCarthyism was a partial and significant factor that brought about the dispersion of the Communist Party in this nation. Submerged them from view, but did not eliminate them. They seem to have metastasized mostly into what we still call by the name of the Democratic Party - though some also exert their malevolent influence from within the Republican Party, as well. Their covert minions of deceit and anti-Americanism have long been tilting and nudging this nation into 'progressive socialism'. And have now peacefully stormed into both legislative and presidential (administrative) control of the government. Can they now be ousted by the peaceful process of a voting majority? Or shall the damage they have done (and yet intend) continue to go unrecognized and uncorrected? The fate of the nation is being weighed in the balance. "Is it that Americans are ignorantly complacent, or just indifferent?", asks the reporter of a man-on-the-street. The response . . . "I don't know, and I don't give a damm." It is not enough that the rascals be thrown out of office, for they have enacted legislation whose consequences already constitute a detrimental burden to the ongoing political and economic well-being of this nation and its citizens - and to their ongoing liberties. The potential for legislators to accumulate unseemly large personal powers and influence needs must be constrained by limitation to not more than one or two terms in office - and to the holding of never more than two offices in the course of their lives. We do not want career politicians: follow the example of George Washington, in this. Candidates for election to office of the political parties needs must be ready to sign something of the nature of "The Contract with America". Not rhetorical promises; rather, written and signed pledges. And, it is not enough that this recent "Obama-care" and other legislation recently enacted (and more yet threatening) be annulled from want for funding. These mischievous voluminous new laws of thousands of pages must be declared invalid and expunged from the tomes of legislation.

And to reiterate, from thoughtful correspondence I have received previously, I wish to second the following:

"I truly don't care if members of Congress are Democrat, Republican, independent, liberal, conservative, progressive or whatever. The self-serving must stop. The below listed proposed 28th Amendment to the U.S. Constitution would do that. This is an idea whose time has come."

> Proposed 28th Amendment to the United States Constitution:
> "Congress shall make no law that applies to the citizens of the United States that does not apply equally to the Senators and Representatives; and Congress shall make no law that applies to the Senators and Representatives that does not apply equally to the citizens of the United States. Nor shall any such past nor current law continue to be valid."

This is fair, to the point, and non-partisan. Who could be against it? Congress, that's who.

And while we are on the subject of Constitutional Amendments. We needs must also adjust The Fourteenth Amendment to circumvent the abusive practice of endowing "anchor babies" with citizenship. A recent report indicated that 12% of live births in the U.S.A. are of the nature of 'anchor babies'. Clearly, a problem.

Now, about hatred. Or is it only resentment? Or cause for suspicion about motives? Or concern about threatening and disruptive misbehavior? And repetitious accusations of this always vague . . . hatred? Need we not (as a nation, as well as individuals) strive to protect ourselves from subversive intent and influence? One gets weary of the repetitious harangue and finger pointing rituals about 'hatred' and 'racism'. It is not constructive.

The truth is that we are all bigoted, and prejudiced, and suspicious - of all who are outsiders to our individual cozy little groups of family, relatives, and some few close friends. It appears to be a part of the condition of we mere mortals (and rooted in stark realities). We are necessarily subjected to some degree of distain and suspicion even upon every occasion in which we confront and interact with one another. I find myself much more attracted or repulsed by the demeanor and character of a person than by the color of their skin. I am hesitant about those who do not display the mannerisms of simple civil decency. I tend to be a little more uneasy and guarded around strangers considerably larger than myself, and more cautious as an individual when I must confront a group rather than an individual. I can sense my own suspicion and prejudice when I am confronted with an overly friendly stranger. Regardless that I judge rightly or wrongly, my perception is that black-skinned people seem (in this nation) to be more sensitive to apparent affront than those of any other color. I do not perceive of myself as harboring prejudice towards any other skin color - either red, brown, or yellow. It is true of course that in this country, the blacks have had a struggle in their coming 'up from slavery'. Part of the reason, undoubtedly, that they seem here culturally to have been nurturing an oppositional and defiant quality to their character - "nurturing their wrath to keep it warm."

The stupidities of such legislation as "Affirmative Action" and "Hate Law" legislation mostly serve to inflame racial tensions. I do perceive the negro as having a much deeper animosity towards me as a white, than what I find in me, towards them as blacks. It appears that there are historical cultural reasons beyond me, for such perceptions as these. One might suppose that the white-black tensions might have been infinitely less, had the black man come to these shores of their own volition - and as free then, as they be now. They do not seem to conceive that they would be more content at this time to return to their native African jungles. Their self appointed race-baiting 'spokes-persons' aggravate resentment even further with their occasional rhetorical claims upon America for 'reparations'.

But a new and sinister part of the black-white racial tension is that white politicians and legislators - even more than blacks - seem to have become facile to the playing of the 'race card' for their own selfish demagogic purposes.

It does not appear that the Mohammedan influence is destined to integrate peacefully into the historical traditions of our American society. In the parallel European situation, look at the unrest, strife, and rioting that is evolving in consequence of what is happening from the inability of the Mohammedans to peacefully integrate there. Why encourage their immigration here? Why even permit it? The whole business is pointless, stupid, and avoidable. Are we not ignoring the reality? - oil and water are immiscible. Many combinations do not serve well together.

Though I have had hardly any contact with, or experience of Muslims, I do follow the news fairly closely in the past ten years or more. Listening in often to talk radio programs: and in the past 5 or 6 years I subscribe to "The Week" - a news magazine. Also, in the past couple of years I am following closely along with Glenn Beck and other Fox News programs. I must say, that I have never previously been aware of such detail in news analysis, and such scrupulous exposé, as what has become available through Fox News. Yes, I get enough exposure to news to recognize that the Muslims who occupy the middle east are churning up quite a storm there; as well as precipitating a regular storm of religious-cultural-political strife throughout the whole of Europe. And it has become obvious that that same trouble is also creeping into The USA and Canada. And now, as I write this little essay, it has seemed to me advisable to seek out a somewhat more thoroughgoing and more comprehensive source of information on the history, origins, and evolving problems concerning Mohammedanism. And so it is that I am going through a book, "*The Sword of the Prophet*" (by Serge Trifkovic), given and prescribed to me by my brother, Duane.

Though I have my own private personal religion, I do not perceive myself as being prejudiced toward persons of other religions - except that in recent years I can sense, within myself, a growing aversion to those of the Arabian Mohammedan religion - based upon the evolving confrontations which they have been nursing and precipitating about the world increasingly since the about the 1960's; and concerning their ever belligerent whining. And, of course, because the history and fundamental tenants of Islam clearly indicate and demonstrate their primary and fervent intent of prejudice and violence against all who do not submit to Mohammedanism. What is the reason for these Arabian Mohammedans wanting to expand into and among the peoples of nations with whom they refuse to accommodate themselves? There are 5 million or more already in the USA as of Y2K. Do they conceive of themselves as guests in a host country? or as conquerors?

And yet, for some reason, I do not seem to have evolved a similar disaffection for the Persian Mohammedans - who seem also to have some difficulty in getting on well with Arabians. I don't yet know how I can justify to myself that the Persian Mohammedans are less of a threat and potential problem to this nation (as fellow-travelers to Islam), given the current belligerence and a venom directed against the USA from the regime currently in power in Iran. Certainly their political and religious leaders currently in power are obviously supportive of Sharia and Jihadist fervor.

And yet the Persians, as a race, have a much longer tradition of 'civilized status' than have the more tribal Arabian peoples. And so, as to the Persian Mohammedans in this nation, I am much more willing to give them the benefit of a doubt, until such time as they manifest a fervent intent for a program of Jihad and regressive clinging to and advocating for Sharia Law. But dare we be optimistic about the possibility of a Muslim reformation that might lead to a more moderate and liberal form of Mohammedanism that accepts the separation of church and state? Keep in mind that tolerance to those who wish to eradicate our way of life can be self-destructive. For Islam preaches no tenants of religious toleration.

It is true, of course, that the early Christian religion had a similar unforgiving ferocity as we might note in the following proclamation dating from somewhat a bit prior to AD 400:

> "It is our will that all peoples under the government of our clemency shall practice that religion which the divine Peter the Apostle transmitted to the Romans . . . that is, according to the apostolic discipline and evangelic doctrine we shall believe in the single deity of the Father, the Son, and the Holy Spirit under concept of equal majesty, and of the Holy Trinity. We command that persons who follow this rule shall embrace the name of Catholic Christians. All others we adjudge demented and insane; they shall bear the infamy of heretical dogma, their meeting places shall not be called churches, and they shall be smitten first by divine vengeance and secondly by the retribution of our own animosity, which we shall assume in accordance with divine judgment."

> "We command that all churches be immediately handed over to the bishops who confess that the Father, the Son, and the Holy Spirit are of one majesty and virtue, of the same glory, and of one splendor. . . . Authors of sedition and disturbers of the peace of the church shall pay the penalty of high treason with their life and blood. Similar punishment shall be visited upon persons who may attempt to supplicate us surreptitiously and secretly contrary to this regulation of ours" (Theodosian Code 16.1.2)

Roman Catholic heavy-hand abuses persisted until the coming of the Renaissance and the Protestant Reformation shattered their monopoly of religious politics. Even then, the early Protestant denominations were similarly abusive and intolerant. But with time and the rise of nationalism as a temporal authority; and with the progressive fracture of Christianity into smaller denominations, the abuses we suffer at the hands of religion is considerably moderated. One might hope that the same sort of moderating influence might eventually settle in to some factions of Mohammedanism, however belatedly.

It is also true that Mohammed did originally advocate some conciliatory toleration concerning "The People of the Book" - both Jews and Christians. But that was early in the game when he had attained military supremacy and considered himself to have sufficiently intimidated them into complying with his intent of merging them peacefully into his fold - or at least into the periphery thereof. There were many Jewish groups and factions within Arabia at the time. It is said that Mohammad seems to have been astonished at the Jewish refusal to convert to Islam.

The result was that Mohammed's earlier favorable pronouncement evolved quickly into an implacably hostile position and resulted in Jewish expulsion from Arabia. There soon followed, an ethnic cleansing - genocide.

Zaid Shakir, formerly the Muslim chaplain at Yale University has said that "Muslims could not accept the legitimacy of the existing political, social, and constitutional order in the United States". I submit to you, that those of that persuasion do not belong in this United States of America. Not either on visitor visa, and certainly not to be accepted as applicants for citizenship to this nation.

As to Sharia Law. No . . . no compromise whatsoever to Sharia law on American soil. Nor the laws of other foreign nations. Nor newly hatched intended laws of one-world-government advocates; nor The United Nations' aspirations for legislation superseding our national sovereignty. No law other than The Constitution of the U.S.A., The Bill or Rights, and our Federal, State, and local codes of law. All . . . of both sexes, of every social class and occupation, of every race and color, and of every religious persuasion subject to one and the same civil, criminal, and tax code.

To suggest that this nation should "be compliant"(?) to Sharia seems as though to imply that we ought perhaps to recognize Sharia and the Muslim culture as being in some sense inherently superior and of higher authority than the foundations and traditions of our own county. Compliant? Oh, no. Let us not be even permissive!

Grandfather Boepple's application for Citizenship to the United States of America required his signature to the following statement:

It is my bona fide intention to renounce forever all allegiance and

> fidelity to any foreign prince, potentate, state, or sovereignty and particularly to the __Emperor of Russia__ of which I am now a subject.
>
> I am not an anarchist: I am not a polygamist nor a believer in the practice of polygamy: and it is my intention in good faith to become a citizen of the USA and to permanently reside therein.

\- - - - - - - - - - - - -

I wonder if Mohammedans applying for American citizenship in present times have yet to sign any such document? There surely ought be some effort to 'nip in the bud' at least the more obvious of potential for subversive trouble. Again, something such as:

> It is my bona fide intention to renounce forever all allegiance and fidelity to any foreign prince, potentate, nabob, sultan, caliph, or state, or sovereignty and particularly to (Saudi Arabia, Egypt, Iran, Iraq, Syria, etc.) of which I am now a subject.
>
> I am not an anarchist. I renounce all and any primary allegiance to Sharia Law and the laws of any nation, empire, or religious philosophy as binding upon me as a citizen of the USA. I am not a polygamist nor a believer in the practice of polygamy: and it is my intention in good faith to become a citizen of the USA, to abide by its laws, and to permanently reside in the USA.

\- - - - - - - - - - - - -

Muslim jurists have pronounced that Muslems may live in lands ruled by non-muslims, provided they use their presence there to further the cause of Islam. As Allah's missionaries and soldiers. To speed up the end of 'the infidel's' rule. This ideology - not mere insanity - is more probably the explanation for the recent Ft. Hood incident of mass murder by an Islamic soldier in American uniform.

In this nation we needs must expose and chastise the opinion forming 'elite' for pretending that Islam does not present a threat of serious evolving problems.

In Mohammed's time, the individual was tightly aligned to his clan and tribe. Belonging to the tribe with all its attendant benefit and protection was the key to survival and possible prosperity. "Love your tribe, for you are bound to it by ties stronger than any between husband and wife", was the line of an Arabic poet. The father died before Mohammed's birth in Mecca, and Mohammed lived in poverty with his mother until she also died when he was but 6 years of age. He then lived with his grandfather who died three years later. He was then relegated to care of his uncle for whom he served as a camel driver. Circumstance had marginalized him from his roots. And as he began to preach of his visions and gradually assume the mantle of 'prophet of God', his relatives supposed him to be deranged. He seems then to have acquired his fortune through marriage to a woman of wealth some fifteen years his senior; and increased his wealth by the managing of her business interests; thus also increasing his status in the community. This wife, and a slave whom he adopted became the first converts of his evolving religious system. Marginalized from among his own roots, his early converts seem to have been a collection of foreigners, and other similarly ostracized acquaintances. He seems only to have finally enlisted his own Mecca relatives eventually by force of arms and intimidation.

Allah is said to have conveniently informed Mohammed that "Islam has rent all bonds asunder". A necessary tenant to his evolving religious system, as he struggled against the long established forces of family, clan, and tribal loyalty that were an impediment to his unifying theocratic intentions. A tenant which Islam still proclaims. To whatever political entity a Muslim believer may belong, he is first and foremost the citizen of Islam, and belongs morally, spiritually, intellectually, and in principle, "totally to the world of belief of which Muhammad is the Prophet, and Mecca is the capital". Do we have cause to suppose that they would make reliable companion soldiers to American forces fighting against Islamic nations?

"That is not of course true for every Muslim, but it is true of every <u>true</u> Muslim", says Trifkovic. It is the central worldly demand of Islam.

Muhammad's practice and constant encouragement of bloodshed are unique in the history of religions. Murder, pillage, rape, and more murder are in the Kuran and in the Traditions. They "seem to have impressed his followers with a profound belief in the value of bloodshed as opening the gates of Paradise" and prompted countless Muslim governors, caliphs, and viziers to refer to Muhammad's example to justify their mass killings, looting, and destruction. "Kill, kill the unbelievers wherever you find them" is an injunction both unambiguous and powerful.

There were a few more items I had in mind to touch upon, but this little note has already outgrown my intentions for it.

RGB
August 2010

\- - - - - - - - - - - -

I notice a news article in "The Week" (Sept 3-10 2010) that General Motors has posted two consecutive quarterly profits, including a 1.3 billion in the latest quarter. Now they are preparing a public share offering to raise 70-80 billion in Oct. Yet I see just now a statistic on the TV screen that says they have sold 25% fewer units in the past year, compared to last year. I guess their big profits must then have come from investing into T-Bills that stimulus loan money they received from government (at the expense of the taxpayer)?

RGB 9/1/10

A FATHER'S DAY RANT

Father's day - a pretext of an excuse for a rant.

Roosevelt Garner Brasseur, M.D.

19 June 2010

Trouble in the Wind

Glenn Beck seems to have it pretty well figured out. He seems to have been on Fox News for now a couple of years, but I have only happened to stumble upon his daily TV talk program in the past year of more. Here, a modern day equivalent of pamphleteer Thomas Payne ("*Common Sense*") who awakened the population of the English colonies prior to The American Revolution. Of course, Beck too has his personal fundamentalist "faith based" agenda, but he doesn't seem intent on enforcing it upon us. One might suppose in fact that Glen Beck's audience would hardly be so large and influential without its ecumenical appeal. For, in fact, this country is, as they say, "a Christian nation". Nor do the various streams of Christian religion (in our times) seem to have any current intent of excluding others of us citizens from the benefits of a Constitutional Republican government and The Bill of Rights. Thus, a confluence of mutual interests between us agnostics, Unitarians, some of the Catholics, and the fundamentalists of this nation - concerning the importance of a unified and determined effort to preserve our government. A government of, by, and for the people.

I approach this essay with trepidation, for it deals with wealth and power - of which I have little personal experience. Why then expose my ignorance at this late stage of my life? As with the subject of private agendas, the matters are ubiquitous in the living of our lives and interactions with our fellow man. And the principles exert themselves upon even us lesser mortals, so that with one's any amount of 'free time', one is often apt to ponder their mysteries, even if only briefly, and occasionally. Now into my 78th year, I have been accumulating an ever larger experience and awareness that beckons and tempts me to reflect upon these matters more seriously. I am both tempted and intimidated by the prospect. I have read and studied what seems to me a great deal of the history of world; and of the rise and fall of civilizations. But not since December 7th of 1941 (and again in 1996) have I been so caught up for so long in what appears to be an impending and far reaching crises. The destruction of nations and the slaughter of millions within the span of my lifetime, has always before precipitated only upon foreign lands and upon other peoples.

In the end, I then finally elect to compose this essay as a project primarily to elucidate unto myself, some once reasoned account of what it is that I suppose seems to have come to pass in the worrisome political directions of this nation; and provide me with some notion of the political prospects of what lies ahead.

I have a first-hand acquaintance with the torments of personal poverty; but am un-accustomed to prison confinement and have only a reader's concept of the possibilities of the terrors of the wanton murder of millions in death chambers and by intentional starvation and maltreatment. Knowledge enough to make me wary! In this county for several years now we are becoming aware of a slowly impending economic disaster from a tumorous enlargement of welfare 'services' and from billowing 'unfunded obligations' which now have come to include the right to free health care, along with Social Security, Medicare, Medicaid, Aid to Dependant Children, food stamps, subsidized housing, etc. Additionally we pay out huge funds for Aid to Developing Nations, fund the wastage of a self-inflicted and counterproductive entanglement with the United Nations, and Police the world with our massive military machine. As if all of these things were not expensive enough, the Federal Reserve, in cahoots with the capitalistic engine of our economy has been permitted to loot the working man and citizens of their hard earned savings and personal reserve by becoming 'cozy' with the regulating government bureaucrats so that they have been permitted to neglect their fiscal restraint and responsibility. The banks and investment houses have come to act with diminished concern, because they were playing with the money of anonymous investors, and with only little of their own skin in the game. Willing thus to take the bigger risk to earn their personal bigger commission. Thus they have put the investment house into bankruptcy along with the citizen investor. Even contrary to all common sense and against the will of the voters, these failed financial institutions have been 'saved' by infusions of taxpayer dollars into their coffers. But the citizen investors have not been saved. The consequence is that the wealth of the nation has been ravaged. It seems unlikely that the voting citizen would ratify this policy of 'privatizing wealth and nationalizing the debt' - once he fully understands that this is the essence of what has happened. Both social and economic chaos seem to be on the rise. How far shall it all proceed before we begin to see riots and revolution, and blood in the streets? Do tyrants and dictators already await in the wings, ready under conditions of martial law, to imprison and eradicate the ten percent? - in order to intimate the masses into silence and inaction?

But now in the past year we have seen the president of our nation surround himself with obvious and even self-admitted Marxist 'advisors' that openly espouse the economic downfall and destruction of the capitalist system upon which this nation arose and thrived. And with the president and his ever enlarging retinue of unelected 'czars', one must suspect that the President and his administration of Chicago thugs threatens soon to make congress as irrelevant as were the senators of Rome under the Caesars. Meanwhile, the current legislature is already imposing Draconian tax measures and a non-sustainable expenses, even in the face of an un-consenting public. It begins to look as though possible, (if a lethargic public fail its duty to replace its wayward legislative incumbents in November) that militant factions and chaos could soon arise.

The TV and radio programs of Beck, Limbaugh, and some dozen others deal with current events as commentators and analysts rather than as a newscasters. A strong educational component to the information that they glean from the broad base of information and study; and ongoing research. Beck and his research staff have been prolifically rooting out the nefarious goings-on behind the scenes in American and World politics. He and Rush Limbaugh have been the primary elucidators in my efforts to decipher the cryptic meanings and translations of the ongoing streams of vague snippets and misinformation from the 'lame-stream media'. Of course there are a myriad of individual and organizational agendas that coalesce into the gooie morass we call politics. It happens at all levels of government, of course, but is potentially the more dangerous and costs the taxpayer the more at each successively higher level of government. Government, and our representatives to government are potentially ever a citizen's and a nation's greatest nemesis in their wayward policy, personal misbehavior, and surreptitious propensity to accumulate personal wealth and power. This, while eluding individual and party responsibility for their audaciousness. And the 'Manchurian Candidate' who has somehow come into the presidency, is the one person who can - at his discretion - suddenly declare Martial Law (for reasons of even dubious), as well as those of vital significance. There is ever the tendency for legislators to regard themselves as an elite class with special privileges - exempting themselves from the consequences of their own legislative constraints (which fall alone upon the populace). It is the case that "power corrupts, and that absolute power corrupts absolutely".

The ever deepening tide of political legislation becomes an unfathomable morass that churns and sways with currents and cross-currents into unpredictable forms - into unforeseeable consequences. Sort of like one of those lava lamps of plastic goop suspended in oil and that picks up energy from the enlightening bulb at its base. Producing a continuous motion of the rising and falling of unpredictably oddly shaped clouds of semi-molten hydrocarbons.

The gooie mass of politics and unforeseeable consequences of burgeoning legislation become a danger to our freedoms and economic well being. Dangerous? How so? Political models, and ideologies coalesce into political party agendas; and then into legislative programs. This nation was established on the basis of a constitution that limits the powers of the national government, preserving legislative authority and powers to the individual states. Authority which in turn is intended to be apportioned out to counties, cities, and individual citizens. Finally, and most important, The Bill or Rights is appended to the original Constitution to assure that individuals continue to own human rights that are intended to be un-abridgeable by any level of government - though yet suspendible in times when Martial Law prevails.

While there could always be some reluctance on the part of our American born U.S. troops to act against the citizens of their own nation in time of chaos, the UN's blue helmets from abroad would always remain a potential alternative to the repression of American citizens. Might even be pleased to be so obliging.

The rising conflict within the Democratic Party seems now near a boiling point. The Democratic Political Party leaders (the politicians themselves) versus the Socialists and the anarchist Marxists who have infiltrated the party. The Democratic Party has now accumulated about as much power as they have ever had and are ever apt to have. Will they make their move before the November elections to declare Martial Law in order to suspend individual liberty and uprising? That would pre-empt the growing tide of citizen discontent that threatens to curtail the agenda and legislative program of Chicago styled politicians. An agenda and threatening legislation that seems intent upon the economic destruction of the nation.

We have the additional problem that the GOP, also, has its own cadre of Marxists and "Progressive" Socialists within their ranks. As to whether our chances of sweeping the incumbent malefactors out of office are best by the founding of some kind of a new Tea Party; or more probable by the possibility of a reforming (from within) of the GOP; that remains an open question.

I confess that it remains to me a mystery as to how it happens that the-main-stream-media is either unable or unwilling to bring forth the details of the ubiquitous political improprieties and implications thereof. Or why they neglect to deal with the material even when it is once unearthed (primarily by bloggers, and the FOX News). One must presume that the controlling influence of the editors and producers is somehow in liege to the current federal governing regime.

If these tyrants are able to seize and hold power (under the guise of martial law) they will not relinquish power until or unless forced to do so by strength of arms, and civil war. They know that the mass of American Citizens will not willingly accede to autocracy and loss of liberty; nor the loss of their Constitution and Bill of Rights (which are the foundations of this nation's unique and exceptional existence); nor the confiscation of their individually acquired wealth and property. The tyrant demigods (awaiting, in the wings) already know and are full well prepared to the necessity of having to eliminate that ten percent (say, 30 million) of the population of these United States which is most actively and vociferously opposed to their "new order" of government. History is prophesy. Do not forget 'the killing fields' of even just the past 75 years of my own life. Six million Jews and additional millions of Poles and other undesirables eliminated by Hitler, 66 million deaths at the hands of Stalin, even more millions than that in the rise of Mao's regime, and Pol Pot's 1.7 million mass murders among the much smaller population of Cambodia. Others in in Franco's Spain, under Pinochet in Chili, under Castro in Cuba, and yet again in Argentina. More recently, the genocides in the Balkans, in

Uganda, the Congo, and in Darfur. I haven't yet heard the final estimate of victims under Saddam Hussein.

Don't expect any leniency from the overlords, once they have invoked martial law, and then put their hands upon us unsuspecting citizens. "The perpetrators of an injustice never forgive their victims." The same is true of both the signers of infamous 'orders' and the executioner.

For any legislator to have voted for a bill without having read the bill - is there not something amiss here? Unquestionably a dereliction of duty. I have never heard it said that such an willful irresponsibility is an act of treason against the constituents AND the entire nation. But I do suggest that it ought to be so considered.

Steps:

- Legal requirement for federal balanced budget.
- Limit on the number of federal employees and their incomes.
- End to American 'Czars'.
- End to lavish pensions and benefits for government employees.
- No union or corporations pensions shall default to government for ultimate payment.
- Firm, prompt, and definitive end to 'Cap and Trade' and other schemes and programs for the redistribution of American wealth.
- Immediately legislate to put an end to CCX (Cap and trade) on any exchange board.
- Immediately defund the recently passed health care bill.
- Then, repeal this same (recently passed) 'Obama-care' bill.
- Legislation to Constraint the Fed Govt. from authority to create or enforce these ever new and expensive 'rights'. Nor permit them the authority for use of economic substance to fund them.
- Tight and immediate control by the federal government of the Canadian and Mexican Borders with military boots on the ground.
- No consideration to the question of amnesty until a few years of experience have demonstrated border security.
- Legislation making it illegal for illegal aliens or foreigners with

visa status to foment or participate in public protests of any kind within the United States or its Territories.

- Strict immigration visa control and oversight. Enforce laws already on the books to deal with this problem.
- End to the tyranny of 16th Amendment (income tax).
- Pass a flat tax to replace income tax.
- Repeal of the 17th Amendment. Revert to process by which each state's two senators are elected by that state's legislative body.
- Proposed 28th Amendment to the United State Constitution: "Congress shall make no law that applies to the citizens of the United States that does not apply equally to the Judges, Senators, and Representatives or federal beaurocratic and special government employees. And Congress shall make no law that applies to the Senators and Representatives that does not apply equally to the citizens of the United States. Nor shall any such past nor current law continue to be valid."
- End the Federal Reserve System.
- No further federal 'bail-out funds' to Fannie Mae and Freddy Mac or any other government corporations current or subsequent.
- Strict control of size of banks and their holdings, as well the breadth of their areas of fiscal dealings.
- Definitive end to ongoing claims of reparations to any and all 'minority groups' and political factions against local, state, and federal government.
- Get USA out of the UN; and get the UN off of American soil.
- Reduced authority of Interpol and World Court - American sovereignty within America.
- Get the USA out of International Monetary Fund.
- Constraint on USA aid funding to foreign nations.
- Term limits for legislators (and create a mechanism for initiative recall of those elected and appointed).
- Term Limits for Judges (and initiative recall of those appointed).
- The banker's license to rob us blind shall be constrained by reasonable ongoing surveillance.
- But one jurisprudence system that applies to all residents and

visitors to this nation. No concession to Muslim or other foreign systems of jurisprudence.

- No, we don't want a Muslim "Dome of the Rock" in the metropolitan center of any major city. No declaration of any 'sacred sites' within the borders of this nation.
- Severe constriction of admission to citizenship of any persons of Muslim faith. Severe constraint of temporary visas to Muslims.
- Immediate funding for construction of several pilot projects of Atomic Energy Generating facilities based on current state of the art technology.
- Ending of government funding to other 'green technology' research and development projects. Require them to compete for private financing. Also, economically prudent arrangement for prize money for provable and economically feasible developments. Perhaps require the wealthiest among the wealthy, to personally invest in these 'green technologies' which they regard as the most promising.
- Immediate and extensive permission and encouragement for drilling for oil and natural gas resources on private and public lands including in the shallow waters of the continental shelf.

The players and activists:

1. The professional politicos having risen to positions of party leadership - want to continue to rule as a class of elite 'entitled' wealthy aristocrats. Having originally been elected by encouraging hopes, and promises of ever expanding 'democratic' benefices to the voting public.
2. The novice members of congress would seem to be preoccupied with learning the ropes, with distant prospects of elevation into aristocratic security and sinecure. Whipped into compliance with the composite agenda of their aristocratic party 'leaders'.

What has evolved from 1) and 2) above, is that our 'representatives' have switched their allegiance from that of the best interests of the nation and its voting citizens; to that of the leaders of the two respective parties and to the agenda of the party in power. There is a party 'platform' of some few vague 'planks' which is crafted and iterated at the nominating conventions of presidential candidates every fourth year (sort of like chapter headings) but "the devil is in the details" of the unmentioned paragraphs, sentences, words, and connotations that come into being only subsequent to the madness of political conventions. Intoxicated with power and privilege, the primary concern (private agenda) of the elected, becomes that of their own re-election. These 'representatives' become beholden to the party leaders through whom they have access to the party's election slush funds. And the adequately financed incumbent almost invariably wins out against the challenger to the seat. I am of the opinion that the nation would be best served by the imposing of term limits to members of congress. And that senators again be appointed by state legislators, rather than by general elections. Limiting the terms of Supreme Court Justices to say, 8 or 10 years with eligibility to begin at age 60.

Within the extant political parties of this nation are a multitude of groups with various political ideologies which continuously clamor and claw for expression within the politics of the nation. No nation on this earth or throughout history has fared better than has The United States of America under its Constitutional Republican Representative Government and economic Capitalism. That, despite the inevitability its inequities and shortcomings.

History informs us that Monarchy, Dictatorship, Oligarchy, Socialism, and Marxist Communism have been neither economically prosperous, nor generally considerate of the best interests of mass of common man. Nor permissive of liberty and the freedom for individual pursuit of happiness. But mankind seems to be forgetful from generation to generation, and hence these various failed ideologies continue to arise under ever new guise.

3. The liberal socialists (i.e. NAZI) utopian ideologists whose platitudes and rhetoric have hopes of sweeping them into office, from which they may eventually come peacefully into power. It seems possible that some of them are actually naïve enough to believe in the possibility of an all powerful benevolent government that would (and could) tenderly care for its citizens from 'cradle to grave'. Intend on activating their 'social justice' programs peacefully, by degree, with 'baby steps'.

4. Marxist Communists revolutionaries have infiltrated most markedly into the Democratic Party since having been forced by McCarthyism in the 1950's to disband the name of "Communist Party". Their agenda persists, covertly. They are professional organizers establishing a plethora of organizations to various high sounding 'causes' which they advocate to gain the support of "the huddled masses". The elite of said Communist leaders regard the masses as 'useful idiots' to a covert cause known only to elite Marxist leaders. Their 'useful idiots' constitute the angry violent mobs which they can summon on demand through their assorted "noble organizations", including the various "unions" (Auto Unions, SECI among the foremost of them). Indeed, the union organizational "dues" are a major source of financial support to the growing hopes and aspirations of the Marxists.
5. The unions from humble and battered beginning, have become a political force to be reckoned with. They have their own self-serving interests, and are not adverse to the prospect of resorting to riots and violence, either on their own, or under their own leadership bosses. They are not adverse to join, and stand ever ready to be manipulated into actions by either the above 'Progressive Socialists' or the Marxist Communists if they can be led to believe there is something in it to somehow serve their interests, tool.
6. We are additionally threatened by the moneyed Financial and managerial class who control the vital substance that brings action and ever increasing wealth. Capitalism, gone amok. In possession of the economic wherewithal. They are always aligned and influential with politicos, 1) and 2) above; but can and do make common cause with 3) 4) 5) and 7) when it seems to their own political and economic advantage.
7. The forgotten man - the law abiding and hard working citizen. In the end does have the vote and thus the potential power to have a not insignificant say in the formation and in the direction of the government. And the other players in game of politics all have cause to desire his vote. He has difficulty in deciding how best to vote to his own best interests. Historically, he has not been well informed, and is commonly shepherded about by the politicos, but is also susceptible to the courting of the

other groups of players in the game of politics. He has hardly known what lie or which crook to believe. But in the recent decade or more, and especially under the ever more obvious stress of the imminent economic meltdown of the nation, he has had more incentive to become more informed as his burden of tax becomes, and looks to weigh more obvious and imminent upon him. And information has come to him more easily and analytically through radio and television. Now, with the looming threat of Progressive Social Evil, and that of the Marxist Evil at the door, as well as an evolving awareness of the blundering and self-serving politicos 'wizards' (to which he has previously paid scant attention) "behind the screen" the common man and his dog, Frodo has been becoming more confident as to what constitutes the least detrimental path of government, and is beginning more to assemble together peaceably to make common cause with "the forgotten man" in the marking of his ballot, come elections day.

RGB

RE: "MEIN KAMPF"

by R. Garner Brasseur

I read the book "*The Fourth Turning*" some ten years ago. Nephew Dobie indicates he has recently been reading it. The winds of political change from generation to generation to which he refers does seem to have a vague reality that we can endorse from our own general and un-reflected experience, and that of our personal and family history. We, the second, third etc. generation Americans are mostly more distantly removed in our racial memories from the previous nations and tribes of our long forgotten ancestors. But newer immigrants to this country, and peoples of Europe seem more closely connected psychologically to the roots of their peoples. And those of the more primitive peoples such as the Chaos-stans and Africa are very much more attuned to their racial memories. And . . . more easily stirred by mere linguistic, imagined, and sometimes real, racial and tribal slurs in the (often careless) rhetoric of our nation. We are a nation, after all, of mere mortals - not saints. In the cross-currents of this nation's prejudices in ethnicity, religion, politics, unionisms, and socioeconomic categories, there exists always the ubiquitous 'injustices' of inequality, controversy, and disagreement. Injustices which, however gradually attenuated will inevitably remain - however vague and remote. And which will inevitably be reawakened from time to time in the ongoing 'dialectic' and discourse of the nation. For many politicians and unionists find it politically expedient to slander their opponents and stir up their audience against these foes - in hopes of gaining advantage over their rivals. That, with little or no regard for the class warfare and animosities which they perpetrate. Hatreds that contribute to a great deal of the criminal activity that overburdens our troubled society economically and creates insecurities that trouble the sleep of our citizens.

When one is in desperation for succor - for the very essentials of life - food, shelter, clothing, a bit of seed money to tide one over - where then to turn with some little hope of aid and consolation. Every man knows in his soul that when one is caught up in those astringencies of life, that one can yet finally hold out with at least some little hope for some relief from one's own family - even from one's remote family. The prodigal son returns home at last; as the distant relative in some far away country finds his way to the door of hope . . . of last resort - thee and me. The immediate family, and the unknown cousin or uncle are still somewhere out there, when even one's last friend has deserted or turned against one. Less likely, is the staunch friend of one's family. A co-religionist or a tribal tie is still at least a potential source to one's cause, though probably even less likely. Succor based on one's race is far less likely; and one merely of the same nationality is even more improbable in the greatest of one's desperations, in times of chaos.

In the years shortly after WW-II, when I was in high-school, I remember often hearing about Communism. Though the national politics of the times was of scant interest to me, one could not escape being aware that "the red menace" was oft in the news and seemingly on the minds of our adult population as they followed the news of the day. And we heard often about Karl Marx and about the book he had written, which seemed to be a sort of bible to the Communist Party. And ever since then, we often read and hear of reference to "*The Communist Manifesto*" (1848). But I have never gotten around to reading that book, and I know nobody who ever has. And so, what I know of Communism is only indirect, for there continues to be the ongoing recurrent references to Marx's book. And I can recall that there was persistent talk; and military 'preparedness' and actual war in opposition to 'the red menace'.

In 1950 The McCurran Act established The Subversive Activities Control Board permitting that: after a hearing the board might indicate any such organization it deems subversive (i.e. to be a part of a conspiracy to set up a dictatorship controlled by a foreign party) to be outlawed. And in 1954 the Communist Party was specifically named as falling into that category of subversively dangerous organizations covered by the security act of 1950. The Communist Party was outlawed in this country, and there was a ferreting-out of Communists in politics and in the movie industry, for example. Some Communists were given jail sentences, and some, even the death sentence in this country. Its members and sympathizers appear mostly to have crept into what has now become the ultra-liberal wing of the Democratic Party.

In the intervening years however, the constraints upon the Communist Party seem to have been loosened, and here - on American soil - we are seeing union groups and protesters parading about here and there under large red banners and large letters extolling communism (some with actual hammer and sickle emblazonments). There are those directly connected to the president and even among his white house staff who openly proclaim that they are Communists.

It did strike me as odd that despite being outlawed in the United States, the Communist Party continued to be an active political party in European countries. It seemed odd, also, that during WW-II, Communistic Russia was presented to us as an ally until the end of the war, when it soon became our foremost and ever present enemy; and a force even behind wars that involved the United States in Korea, Vietnam, and Cambodia; and the Cuban Missile crisis that threatened to involve us in a nuclear war.

Watching all of the national political wrangling and contest in DC the past few years, I have taken to becoming concerned about it. We seem perhaps to have arrived at a point of juncture where the long term fate and directions of the nation is soon to have been precipitated upon us, and it is a matter of vital concern as to how that issue will be decided. Will the body politic have the wisdom and will to shrug-off the evil and steer us clear from the progressive Socialism which has been so rapidly advancing upon us - most especially by the current Obama Administration? Or will the gathering momentum of Chicago's Marxist Coalition push us ever closer to the Internationalism of One-World-Government and loss of our national sovereignty? Are we going to revert to the principals of republican democracy with a system of Capitalism that has made the USA the freest citizenry and the mightiest industrial, economic, and military power that this world has ever seen? Or are we going to allow ourselves to slip into an advancing degenerative Socialism which history has repeatedly been demonstrated to end in chaos and failure?.

And if we have the national character and the will to protect our borders, retain our sovereignty, and cling to our Bill of Rights; will we next then have the wit to recognize that our monetary system under the self-serving cabalistic influence of 'The Fed' has long already been in the process of perverting our congressional system of government and bleeding generation after generation of our citizens of the wealth which they earn and are entitled, as they strive to maintain their individual dignity and become - and remain - self-supporting unto themselves and their offspring.

As I have had but little by way of formal education in either politics or economics, I have bumbled and suffered my way along to acquire many of its lessons in 'the school of hard knocks'. (Likewise, I am tempted to suspect that what I learned about medicine, surgery, and psychiatry as a medical student is a bit less relevant than what I have learned incidentally and from first-hand experience since I graduated from medical school.) I am aware that there are available, a good many wordy and difficult books that are available concerning these things, but I have not found them enough interesting to struggle through them. And besides, there appears to be the endless controversy between them - as to which theories are more correct in their ongoing disputations. And so, I have acquired only rough and uncertain ideas about the nuanced distinctions between things like ordinary Socialism, National Socialism, and Marxism, for example. From my rough notions, it seems to me that none of them are very attractive systems under which to have to live. Yet, one or the other among them (or some combination of them) seems about to envelop our nation politically and economically. By chance then, I happened to stumble upon the writings of a fellow who seemed to have a bit of a gift for words and a determined motive for needing to try to come up with some distinctions in these things. From his writing, I attempted to gather a somewhat clearer notion of the essence of Marxism, to which he was so adamantly opposed. The following then, deals with some of what he had to say about it and about his own brand of politics - National Socialism.

WW-II started when I was in the second grade of school and ended just as I finished the fifth grade. Though never informed of the history of NAZI Germany, even we grade school students were continuously aware and interested in the course of WW-II as it evolved. And, as with Marx's book, we were made aware of Hitler's book, "*Mein Kampf*". Another sort of 'evil tome' which we none of us ever read - nor were encouraged to read. But from the constant news reports and from various movies about WW-II, we were acquainted with the evils perpetrated by 'The Third Reich' during WW-II. (The First Reich seems to have been that of Prussia, under Otto von Bismarck: The Second Reich I guess would then have been the Germany of WW-I) And, of course, we were shocked to discover the evidence and grim story of genocide of the NATZies as they abused and killed six million unarmed Jews from Germany and the territories they had occupied during WW-II. They seem to have treated the Polish population not much differently.

I saw the movie and have often heard mention of Hemmingway‘s "*For Whom the Bell Tolls*". But only recently did I come upon the actual history behind the Spanish Civil War 1936-1939. It was a civil war between Spain‘s then recently elected Republican Government (seeking escape from the oppressive rule of Catholicism); and the revolutionary forces under Spain‘s Generalissimo Franco who had been exiled to the Canary Islands. In some sense, it was also the pretext of a war that seems to have been a sort of 'preview of coming attractions'; featuring a testing of military equipment and field tactics, in a conflict between Hitler's Germany and Stalin's Russian Communism; and which soon evolved into WW-II.

Having then read this thing about the Spanish Civil War from a book recommended to me by Pierre, a train of events overtook me, that led me into the difficult necessity of having to read "*Mein Kampf*". Massy had given me a book ("*The Book Thief*") about the experience of some German youngsters growing up under Hitler's dictatorship just prior to and into the World War-II. It whetted my appetite to look more closely into the rise of this Hitler rascal. Where better to look than Hitler's own autobiography? And so it is that I am now finished with the reading of "*Mein Kampf*". A complex, but informative book. I had no idea what had been going on in Germany prior to and during WW-I, nor what it was that Hitler was up against as he struggled to first understand, and then formulate some way of counteracting 'the red menace' which was at that time upon the verge of subjugating all of Germany under their banner; and which was aimed at world conquest. Still is!

- - - - - - - -

"*Mein Kampf*" (my struggle) seems to be the story of Adolf Hitler's experience and his attempt to perceive the nature of Communism. A struggle within himself and from his experience of the chaos and foment of his day, to grasp the nature of Communism. To formulate what were its aims and objectives; and by what means was it acting to attain its objectives. And finally, what might be done to eradicate that menace from the German states. Says Adolf, "Marxism will march shoulder to shoulder with democracy until it succeeds indirectly in securing for its own criminal purposes, even the support of the intelligentsia of the nation whom Marxism has set out to exterminate. But, if the Marxist should one day come to believe that there was a danger that from this witch's cauldron of our parliamentary democracy a majority might be concocted, which, if merely by reason of its numerical weight, would be in a position to legislate and thus to constitute a serious threat to Marxism, the whole parliamentary hocus-pocus would be at an end. Instead of appealing to the democratic conscience the leaders of the Red International would immediately send forth the furious rallying-cry to the proletarian masses and the ensuing fight would not take place in the sedate atmosphere of parliament, but in the factories and in the streets. Then democracy would be annihilated forthwith, and what the intellectual prowess of the apostles who represented the people in parliament had failed to accomplish, would now be successfully carried out by dint of the crow-bar and the sledge-hammer of the exasperated proletarian masses just as in the autumn of 1918. At one fell swoop they would make the bourgeois world see the madness of thinking that the Jewish drive towards world-conquest can be effectually opposed by means of western democracy." (p. 258)

(Within the soul of each non-Marxist, each will come to understand): "Only a very credulous soul can think of binding himself to observe the parliamentary rules of the game when he has to face those for whom those rules are nothing but a pretext. He will discard them when they prove no longer useful for this purpose." [And the stage will now be set for a more militant German nationalist opposition to Jewish Marxism].

In Adolf's view: "The Marxist doctrine is the concentrated extract of the mentality which underlies the general worldview of today. And for this reason alone it is out of the question to think that what is called our (German) bourgeois world can put up any effective fight against the Marxist. For this (his then) current (German) bourgeois world is permeated with all those same poisons, and its worldview in general differs from Marxism only in degree and in the character of the persons ruled. The (then) current (German) bourgeois world is Marxist, but he believes in the possibility of a certain group of people – that is to say, the (German) parliamentarian bourgeois – as being able to dominate the world, while Marxism itself systematically aims at delivering the world into the hands of the Jews."

Yes, "Marx used his unerring instinct of the prophetic genius to detect the essential poisons, so as to extract them and concentrate them, with the art of an alchemist, into a solution which would bring about the rapid destruction of the independent nations of Europe. All this was done in the service of his (Jewish) race".

["To extract and concentrate the essential poisons", just as now did Adolph intend to do - and did - with remarkable success. Somewhat of an overreaction, as we can see in retrospect. But we may be well advised <u>not to discard</u> his insights into the existential reality of Marxist Communism, and the 'progressive Socialism' from which it proceeds.]

Adolph's education and formative years of poverty as a young man in Vienna had filled him with the certainty that Marxist Communism was one and the same with "the red menace" that had precipitated out of the Russian turmoil. Marx himself was of Jewish extraction and it is my impression that a great many of the leading lights and leaders of Russian Communism were likewise of Jewish extraction. And from the beginning Marxism was intending itself to be a world-wide movement, to include all the peoples and races of the world. Adolph soon estimated that despite Marxist claims of being a benison to the common middle class and working man of the world, Communism was destined to be elitist and exclusive of the actual best interests of the masses of mankind.

Having been a student of German History, he looked upon its heroic military and cultural leader's with awe and was convinced that The German Race of Mankind was a culturally and physically superior race among the diverse tribes of mankind. He looked upon the sorry state of his German people as they were before WW-I, and was himself heroically involved in that war. His view was that the war had been lost by traitorous persons and misguided political movements within Germany itself. He was angered that these German people with the seeds of greatness within them, had failed to achieve the greatness to which he thought them as being able and even destined to achieve. He saw that the German State of Austria was being infiltrated by other peoples - Slavs, Hungarians, Polish, Russian, Jews etc. - as diluting out the strengths and virtues of 'the pure German stock'. Vienna and Austria had attracted these foreign peoples so that only a fifth of Austria's population was now yet composed of pure German people. And it became Adolf's view that Germany's land-poor status was obstructed by the uncomprehending leadership in Vienna, cutting the Germans off from acquiring the necessary territories in eastern Europe. Thus it was that he launched out upon a program with a newly formed political party to inspire and empower his German people with a vision of their potential greatness as a people; and a program of political action to rid them of the evil influence of non-Aryan peoples. And then to lead his 'master-race' on to acquire the territories and their rightful status of world dominance.

And we, in our times, do well to be aware that Marxist Communism has returned with a vengeance into our very own United States of America. The country has been slowly progressing into socialism, and more recently into 'Progressive Socialism', which appears to be the precursor to Marxism. A menace which under the Obama regime is already neigh onto becoming an actual dictatorship, and seemingly intent rapidly to entangle our nation into a 'one-world-government' with the loss of our national sovereignty. An economic-political quick-sand from which we may hopefully yet have time enough (and sufficient determination) to extricate ourselves. Implied, certainly, in the American Declaration of Independence from England, is also our intent at independence from all other nations and peoples of this world. Isolationalist, or at least with liberty enough as a nation to negotiate with others the terms of our voluntary alliances with them.

In point of fact, the Communist Party, per se, is alive and openly representing itself as such in southern California, with parades and red banners; and being supported by SEIU, Latinos ranting of La Raca; and some teacher's unions. And there are those within the white house and among Osama's 'czars' who openly admit that they are Communists. In early August of 2011 I note an e-mail blog saying that the Communist Party had recently endorsed Obama for presidency to election of 2012. Yes, all of this even after the 'red menace' was recognized as such, and purged (1954) by the Joseph McCarthy congressional investigating committee subsequent to WW-II. You will remember that Oppenheimer and his wife, for example, were given the death penalty for their activities and involvement with the Communist Party.

Do we as a nation understand the imminent danger of destroying our own government from within by governmental waste of our national wealth; and a destruction of our productive capacity? Are there enough voting citizens with a will and courage enough to draw back from the excessive government 'entitlements', hand-outs, redistribution of the nation's wealth, acting the part of police to the troubled nations of this world, 'foreign-aid' pouring into rat-holes, and acting as guarantors of loans to foreign entities (massive billions for which we as tax-payers have been, and are continuing to pay)?

Keep in mind also that there are subversive forces other than the obvious waywardness of congress and governmental executive regimes with which we must contend if we intend to right our ship of state. Become aware of them. The United Nations is but a vampire seeking in stealth to suck the monetary blood from America's vital being; 'cap and trade' would have provided access to but a larger and more accessible vein for that blood-letting. The U.N. has proven to be more tenacious than that toothless debating society called 'The League of Nations' that was set in motion after WW-I.

Even more problematic, is 'The Federal Reserve System', which does not even wait for the dark of night to sap our economic vitality. "*The Creature from Jekyll Island*", as it is named by author Griffen, in a book of that title. If you love your country and cherish the protection it provides you (from something more nearly akin to being naked and defenseless on the Serengeti Plaines) you would do well to become familiar with the information available through his book.

- - - - - - - - -

But more now about the life of Adolf Hitler; and his rise to power in Germany subsequent to WW-I. Let us not be too eager to suppose that he was without personal virtues and genuine empathy for his beloved German nation and its peoples. Though we are especially well apprised about "The Holocaust", let us keep in mind that equally evil genocides are a not uncommon consequence of contest within the long history of human warfare. One might make the case that massive political purges have much in common with genocides. Race and religion oft are the pretext for such discriminations. 'Categories of people' consigned in mournful numbers, by the ruthlessness of war - to the pits of defenseless destruction. We do well also to direct a portion of our pity and disgust to these categorical mass murders of millions, concurrent with and subsequent to WW-II; in Russia, China, Cambodia, Rowanda, The Congo, Bosnia, Darfur . . . .

Adolph was born somewhere about 1880 and orphaned in his mid-teens, so that his formal schooling ended, and he had to make his way to Vienna to rub shoulders with desperate workmen controlled by merciless union thuggery, and having to scrounge about several years to learn a trade, and trying to make a living. He acquired first-hand experience of reality in desperate times, living in a hovel, but avidly acquiring and studying books, and devouring newspapers - determined to acquire an education and some insight into the chaos in which he found himself. Hours of many days did he observe and ponder the activity in the parliament of Vienna. He found a few friends with whom he had discussions and debated; only gradually and incidentally acquiring what would become one of his greatest assets - a gift for public speaking. He had always had an avid interest in History, especially in German History; and was an ardent admirer of German heroic leaders, such especially as Bismarck (of the first Reich). He came to identify strongly with his German (Aryan) peoples who (in Vienna and Austria) had become a minority - about a fifth of the population. He had early and easily become what one would call a German patriot, and there was a plentitude of social and racial, as well as union-based conflict astir in that caldron of human misery in which he acquired his early political experience. He and his friends eagerly volunteered for front-line military duty with the outbreak of WW-I, where he served honorably until wounded and was sent back to a military hospital for care and rehabilitation towards the end of the war. Ever inquiring into the political folly all about him, Adolf and his comrades came to understand that the effort of the German patriots on the front-lines were being undermined and weakened on the home-front by an elite weak-spined German political class and a Jewish controlled news media to the extent that young men were being discouraged from joining to serve in the military, and there was political obstruction to the flow of armaments to the war front. In short, a sort of home grown 'revolution' to the trench-warfare stalemate of WW-I. Something perhaps like the growing home-front antipathy to the Vietnam conflict that eventually led to American abandonment of that misguided war effort.

Adolf's observations concerning the business of democratic parliamentarianism in Vienna is not very optimistic. "In the election days over and the parliamentarians have held their last public meeting for the next five years when they can leave their job of getting the populace to toe the line and can now devote themselves to higher and more pleasing hasps then the program committee space is dissolved and the struggle for the progressive reorganization of public affairs becomes once again a business of earning one's daily bread which for the parliamentarian, merely means drawing his salary morning after morning the Hon. Member winds his way to the house, and though he may not enter the chamber itself, he gets at least as far as the lobby, where there is the register of members attending the meeting. His onerous service on behalf of his constituents consists in entering his name, and he receives in return A small indemnity as the well-earned reward of his unceasing and exhausting labors."

"After the lapse of four years, or if any crisis arises in which Parliament seems faced with the danger of dissolution, these gentlemen are suddenly fired with the desire for action. They address the effect once again, give an account of the enormous labors they have accomplished, and emphasized the malicious obstinacy of their opponents. They do not always meet with grateful applause. Occasionally the unintelligent masses throw food and unfriendly remarks in their faces. When this spirit of public ingratitude reaches a certain pitch, there is only one way of saving the situation. The prestige of the party must be burnished up once again. The program has to be amended, the committee is called into existence one more, and so the swindle begins anew. Once we understand him and the inexorable stupidity of our public, we cannot be surprised that such tactics prove successful. Led by the press and blinded once again by the alluring appearance of the new program, the bourgeois, as well as the proletarian herds of voters, faithfully return to the fold and reelect their old slate. The people's man and labor candidate now change back again into the parliamentarian garb, and become fat and rotund as they batten onto the leaves that grow on the tree of public life to be transformed into the glittering butterfly after another four years have passed."

- - - - - - - -

"It may be said that the individual member of parliament may not have the knowledge which is requisite for the treatment of this or that question, yet his attitude towards it is taken on the advice of his party as the guiding authority in each political matter; and it may further be said that the party sets up special committees of 'experts' who have even more than the requisite knowledge for dealing with the questions placed before them. At first sight, that argument seems sound, but then another question arises, namely, why are five hundred persons elected, if only a few have the wisdom which is required to deal with the more important problems? That is just the point. It is not the aim of our modern democratic parliamentary system to bring together an assembly of intelligent and well informed deputies. The aim is rather to bring together a group of nonentities who are dependent on others for their point of view, and who can be the more easily led, the narrower their individual mental outlook. That is the only way in which a party policy can be put into effect. By this method alone is it possible for the wire-puller, who exercises the real control, to remain in the dark, so that he personally can never be brought to account for his actions." (p.72)

- - - - - - - -

Hitler early sees Russia as having been the proving ground of the Marxist theory of Communism, and regards Russia as being the foremost threat both to his own nation and to the world. And he regards Jewish dominated leadership as foremost both in world-wide economic matters and in Union leadership. Indeed, it is against Russia that Germany first declares war in what subsequently enlarged into WW-I; and Adolf and his companions were eager to serve in that cause. Here is what Adolf says. "Those who are in power today (in Russia) have no intention of forming an honorable alliance or of remaining true to it if they did. It must never be forgotten that the present rulers of Russia are blood-stained criminals; that here we have the dregs of humanity which, favored by the circumstances of a tragic moment, over-ran a great state, and in their lust for blood, killed and extirpated millions of educated people belonging to the ruling classes, and that now for nearly ten years they have ruled with a savage tyranny such as has never been known. It must not be forgotten that these rulers belong to a people in which the most bestial cruelty is allied to a capacity for artful mendacity and which, today more than ever believes itself called upon to impose its sanguinary despotism on the rest of the world. It must not be forgotten that the international Jew, who is today absolute master in Russia, does not look upon Germany as an ally, but as a state condemned to the same doom as Russia itself." "One does not enter into alliances with people to whom no treaty is sacred." (p.438)

"For 70 years the German state was systematically attacked by Marxism and (in essence) capitulated to Marxism (in 1918)." (p. 358) He is indicating here that the Marxist Newspaper propaganda, along with the Jewish-led labor strikes in armament plants were major contributors to the decline in support for the troops on the battlefront. "In peacetime as well as in WW-I, the Jewish-Marxist stock-exchange press systematically stirred up hatred against Germany, until one state after another abandoned its neutrality and placed itself at the service of the Allies in WW-I, even against the real interests of its own people". (p. 414)

"The real organizer of the (German) revolution (that ended the German will to continue on to victory in WW-I) and the actual wire-puller behind it, the international Jew, had sized up the situation correctly. The German people were not yet ripe to be drawn into the bloody swamp of Bolshevism, as the Russian people had been drawn. That was because there was a closer racial unity between the intellectual classes in Germany and the manual workers, and also because, as was also the case in the other states in western Europe, broadly speaking, most classes of the community had their quota of cultured persons, whereas this was not the case in Russia. In that country the intellectual classes were, for the most part, not of Russian nationality. The thin upper layer of intellectuals which then existed in Russia could be abolished at any time, because there was no intermediate stratum connecting it organically with the great mass of the people. There the mental and moral level of the great mass of the people was extremely low." "In Russia, the moment the agitators were successful in inciting the broad masses of the people, who could neither read nor write, against the upper layer of intellectuals who were not in contact with the masses or permanently linked with them in any way, the fate of Russia was decided, the success of the revolution assured. Thereupon, the illiterate Russian became the slave of his Jewish dictator who, on their side, were shrewd enough to name their dictatorship 'the dictatorship of the people'". (p. 351)

Adolf later tells us that "Before 1918 there was nothing like an organized anti-Semitic feeling. (Hitler's) party encountered difficulties even to mention the Jews. But the party of Schutz and Trutzbund opened the question again in 1918-1919 when a kind of anti-Semitism slowly began to take root." (p. 375) Like myself, Adolf seems to have no specific statistical data to substantiate his definite impression as to the link between Jewish persons and Communistic influences in these matters. Says Adolf, "In my eyes the charge against Judaism became a grave one the moment I discovered the scope of Jewish activities in the press, in art, in art, in literature, and in the theatre" (p. 50) though they "formed scarcely one percent of the population." (p. 51)

> [In matters of high-finance, day-to-day business transactions, and union organization, who has the temerity specifically to inquire as to one's past or present religious affiliations. When I (for example) am in need of a loan from a bank, I am in no position to diminish my prospects for that needed loan by impolite allusions as to the loan officer's particular race or religion - an impropriety which is apt to suggest my own narrow-mindedness.]

- - - - - - - -

The peace-treaty terms imposed upon the German Nation to end WW-I were harsh, and the subsequent political turmoil was hotly contested in the German states. Adolf's military loyalty, political insights, and his gift for public speaking did not go unrecognized, and he was soon assigned as an instructor in his military unit at war's end. He might have joined any of several old or new political parties contesting for votes to parliament, but now - as his political insights were nearing maturity - none seemed compatible to his views in regards to their notions as to what problems were most in need of being addressed; and none seemed willing to advocate bold solutions such as might actually be effective. Adolf was invited to join one particular small group of discussants recently organized - six members. Six members? Ha! His ideas and plans would require a much more substantial backing than that. But then . . . as he thought about it; at least their basic few tenants seemed reasonable. And . . . their congenial plasticity was such, that he might boldly guide and direct their growth into something more of his own making. He became the holder of the seventh card to what would eventually become the NAZI party. Their little groups were soon becoming large meetings. His oratorical gifts continued to improve, and the power of his rhetoric began to attract ever larger crowds. Having to speak ever more frequently, his preparations evolved into ever more well-considered and plausible plans, which slowly began to materialize with the ever larger basis of backing from his listeners. He inspired them with his hopes and plans for the common (German, or Aryan) man whom he was idealizing. "Never forget that the most sacred of all rights in this world is man's right to the soil which he wishes to cultivate for himself and that the holiest of all sacrifices is that of the bloodshed for it", he told them.(p. 440) The crowd could begin ever more to think of themselves as a noble (Aryan) race; with a destiny and a mission. Almost a sort of religious fervor.

The new Nazi group had to take special care that their new militant group not degenerate into a society for the promotion of parliamentarian interests. The first preventive measure was to lay down a program which of itself would tend towards developing a certain moral greatness that would scare away all the petty and weakling spirits who made up the bulk of their then present day politicians. It was realized that a new conception of the State had to be established, which in itself became a part of the new conception of life.

The Nazi rhetoric then deals with the term "volkish", around which a closely consolidated militant community could be formed. It was a vague term, such as "religious", for instance. And it was difficult to attach any precise meaning to the word, either as a theoretical concept or as a guiding principle in practical life. A word which acquires a precise meaning only when it is associated with a distinct and definite form through which the concept is put into practice. "The bulk of the people is not composed of philosophers or saints. Such a vague religious-philosophical idea will mean to the individual merely that he is justified by thinking and acting according to his own bent." (p.260)

"By helping to lift the human being above the level of their mere animal existence, faith really contributes to consolidate and safeguard his very existence. Take from humanity as it exists today the religious beliefs which are generally held, and which have been consolidated to education, so that they serve as moral standards in practical life, and abolish religious teaching without replacing it by anything of equal value, and the foundations of human existence would be seriously shaken. We may safely say that man does not live merely to serve high ideals; but that these ideals, in their turn, furnish the necessary conditions for his existence as a human being. Thus the circle is completed." (p.260)

"Just as the word 'religious' implies certain ideals and beliefs that are fundamental" (p. 260) to theological philosophy, the word "volkish" implies certain other fundamental ideas. The word can become a constituent element in the structure of a political party. A word that incorporates a certain worldview, "and demands arising from them cannot be realized by mere sentiment and inner longings any more than freedom can be won by universal yearning for it. Only when the idealistic longings for independence is organized in such a way that it can fight for its ideal with military force - only then can the urgent wish of the people become a vital reality." (p. 260)

"Any worldview, though a thousand-fold right will be of no practical assistance in molding the life of a people as long as its principles have not yet become the rallying-point of a militant movement." (p. 261)

As Adolf puts it "All great movements are popular movements. They are the volcanic eruptions of human passions and emotions, stirred into activity by the ruthless goddess of adversity; or by the torch of the spoken word cast into the midst of the people. The doom of a nation can be averted only by a storm of glowing passion; but only those who are themselves passionate can arouse passion in others."(p.82) And it was obvious to him, that "The largest forum of immediate listeners in not the parliamentary auditorium, but the public meeting." (p.80)

"The man who expounds the new truth must here go hand-in-hand with him who has a practical knowledge of the mind of the people, so that from the realm of eternal truth and ideals, what is suited to human nature may be selected and given practical form. A form which is derived from a specific worldview which is based on a solid foundation of skills and from them, to mold a militant community whose members have the same political faith. A community which is precisely defined, rigidly organized, and of one mind. Out of the army of millions who feel, more or less clearly the truth of these ideas, and may even understand them to some extent, one man must arise. (Guess who?) This man must have the gift of being able to formulate from the vague ideas held by the masses, principles that will be as clear-cut and firm as granite and he must be able to fight for these principles as the only true ones, until a solid rock of common faith and, will emerges about the troubled waters of vagrant ideas."

Hitler was by no means irreligious, but he steered clear of religious entanglement, realizing that Germany's long history of divisiveness between Catholicism and Protestantism would be counterproductive to his more all-inclusive theme of a folk-based nationalism, along with his notion of the importance of 'racial purity' and an ego inflating dogma of 'The German master-race'.

As Adolf explains it, "The function which dogma fulfills in religious beliefs is comparable to the function which party principles fulfill in a political party which is in the process of being built up. It is therefore essential to forge an instrument which, (like the Marxist party organization which clears the way for internationalism), can be used in fighting for this idea that is proposed by the National Socialist German Labor Party aim."

"The international ideology achieved success because it was championed by a militantly organized party. The reason for the failure hitherto sustained by our opposing Aryan ideology is that it lacked a United front to fight for its cause."

> [Thus arose the NAZI party with Adolph Hitler at its helm. But concerning the rise and success of Hitler, let us not overlook the essential importance of the book he wrote while in confinement after the failed 'putch' in Munich. That book sold millions of copies in Germany, and made Hitler a wealthy man. And "money speaks". One might well suppose that many of those copies were actually read; and were perhaps as influential to his rise in status as were his many orations at mass political rallies.]

Though it behooves us well to remember the evils of NAZIsm that came to fruition in the form of WW-II, we ought not neglect the valid insights on which Hitler's "*Mein Kampf*" expounds - concerning the equally great threat and dangers of Marxist Communism. More lives were sacrificed to Russian Communism - and again to Chinese Communism - than to Nazism. Nor ought we so soon forget what havoc arose from Communism in Korea, Vietnam, Cambodia etc.

Do I believe that the current president (Obama) is anything more than a specifically groomed tool for the moneyed interests of The Fed and CFR? Much the same forces which seem to have enlivened president Coolidge in the early 1900's. Assuredly, Obama is allied with the 'progressive liberal' branch of the Democratic Party, though how closely he is progressed towards actual Communism one might well yet wonder. I recall that some thirty years ago, my brother was used to rave and have fits about the CFR (council of foreign relations). I supposed that he might at sometime get around to saying something more specific and detailed (for my enlightenment) about his dispassion for the CFR, but we were both preoccupied with our work and efforts to become professionally established there in southeastern Washington State, and we had not all that much of leisure time together. I am left to suppose that he knew something of what he was talking about, for he was a very well-read person. And now (30 years later) that I have more time and specific cause for concern about the threat that has long been accumulating against our nation and its founding principles - to the detriment of the best interests of our American citizens - it seems to me a matter of urgency to become aware of what is befalling us. That is to say, time to acknowledge the threat at our door from the UN, CFR, Big Banking Interests (in cahoots with Big Government), IMF, Creeping Socialism, and One World Government advocates. Time to recognize; and begin to push back against these insidious and nefarious forces that wish completely to subjugate "we the people" to their supposedly 'good intentions' of 'social justice' across the face of the world. An intention of redistribution of the wealth of America's middle class, and 'the rich' (who have only barely and recently struggled out of the desperations of the poor and middle classes). Meanwhile, the 'super-rich', and the ruling elite of government officials and ivy-league professors, intend to persist as the ruling oligarchy. As in the Soviet Communist Party arrangement - the one percent who retain wealth, status, and privileges; and who maintain their sinecured situation by force of arms against an unarmed multitude.

- - - - - - - -

Adolf continues: There occurred an "action of France in occupying the Ruhr (in 1923) which really estranged Britain for the first time. From the political point of view it is not in the interests of Great Britain that Germany should be ruined still more, but such a development would be very much in the interests of the Jews who manipulate the international money-markets." (p. 41)

"Not only had France now assumed from the military standpoint alone, a position in Europe such as Germany herself had not held previously, but she thus obtained control of economic resources which, from a practical point of view, combined her ability to compete in the political world with economic advantage almost amounting to a monopoly." (p. 446)

"A considerable section of our (German) people who, thanks to a

(Jewish controlled) mendacious press, had looked upon France as the champion of progress and liberty, were suddenly cured of its illusion. As in 1914 the dream of international solidarity (a common religious-philosophical theme among the Germanic people) was suddenly banished from the minds of our German working class and they were brought back to the world of everlasting struggle, where one creature feeds on the other and where the death of the weaker implies the life of the stronger, so again in the spring of 1923." (p. 447)

"When the French penetrated into the coalfield of the Ruhr the hour of destiny had struck for the German people. If, at that moment, our people had changed not only their frame of mind, but also their conduct, the German Ruhr could have been for France, what Moscow was for Napoleon." (p. 447)

"If, at the beginning of WW-I, or even during the war, twelve or fifteen thousand of these Jewish corruptors of the people had been forced to submit to poison gas, just as hundreds of thousands of our best German workers from every social class and from every trade and calling had to face it in the field, then the millions of sacrifices made at the front would not have been made in vain." (p. 449) Think of it, "To hand over without batting an eyelid, millions of human beings to be slaughtered on the battlefield, and to look upon ten or twelve thousand public traitors, profiteers, usurers, and swindlers as the nation's most precious and most sacred asset and to publicly proclaim their persons inviolable." (p. 449)

"The situation in 1923 was similar to that of 1918. No matter what form of resistance was decided upon, the prerequisite for taking action was the elimination of the Marxist poison from the body of the nation, and in my opinion it was the first task of a really National government to seek and to find those forces that were determined to wage a war of annihilation against Marxism and to give those forces a free hand. It was their duty not to bow down before the fetish of 'law and order' at a moment when the enemy from without was dealing the fatherland a death-blow and when high treason was lurking at every street-corner at home. A really National government ought then to have welcomed disorder and unrest, if this turmoil afforded an opportunity of finally settling with the Marxists, who are the mortal enemies of our people." (p. 449) "Christianity was not content with erecting an altar of its own. It had first to destroy the pagan altars. It was only by virtue of this passionate intolerance that apodictic faith could grow up, and intolerance is an indispensable condition for the growth of such a faith." (p. 308)

Adolf continues: "I frequently implored them to let fate have a free hand and to make it possible for our movement (The NAZI party) to settle with the Marxists, but I preached to deaf ears. All of them, including the Chief of the Defense Forces, thought they knew better, until finally they found themselves forced to subscribe to the vilest capitulation in the records of history." (p. 450) "What places Mussolini in the ranks of the world's great men was his decision not to share Italy with the Marxists, but to redeem his country from Marxism by destroying internationalism in Italy." (p. 450)

I here make no apology for the existence of prejudice in the minds of men. It has always existed and I expect it shall, until the final demise of the last of our species from the face of this world. A whole race of men is perfectly capable of maintaining a prejudice against another race, or even against all others. One must suppose that there are historical reasons behind each and every prejudice, even though the specifics may have long past gone unremembered. We do well to remember the ubiquitous nature of prejudice - a part of 'the condition of mortality', one might say. But when that natural sentiment carries over into motive for action against one's neighbor, it then becomes reprehensible; and worthy of censure. It does not go too far to state that genocide is an evil that ought to be recognized as such by all peoples - and punished, when that is possible.

I have not yet become quite clear as to the intricate causes of WW-I, but one must suppose that the assassination of Archduke Ferdinand of Austria was nothing more than the precipitating event. Neither am I yet clear as to why - even for decades before WW-I - was there so much animosity in the German states against Russia. I recall that there was revolution in Russia against the royal family's oppressive grip on Russia. And that as that revolution was gaining momentum, this man Lenin was 'permitted' to transit through Germany - but on a 'sealed train'. Was that to protect Lenin(?); or was it to assure that he would not get free to cause havoc in Germany? As Lenin was quickly involved in the Russian politics and revolution, we must suppose that he had been invited by revolutionary forces as a sort of professional fomenter of chaos. As far as I know, Lenin was a Russian national by birth, and I am supposing that he had been exiled for political reasons. And I am further supposing that in his exile, he was probably in cahoots with Marxists in jolly old England and France. And I seem vaguely to recall that Lenin himself was of Jewish extraction. I know that Trotsky was. And I have heard it said that there were a great many persons of Jewish extraction that were involved in the Russian revolution - but that tentative assertion is very vague in my mind. In fact, it is my impression that that information is vague also in minds of those sources from whom and from which I have learned it.

> [I must apologize for all of the above vagaries. Through the past many years I have heard and read information concerning these things, but one becomes forgetful of details unless the memory is refreshed from time to time.]

We are all well aware that there has been more than just a little tension between Jews and Christians since they had a parting of their ways from a common source a couple thousand years ago. Early Catholicism was wont to inflame hard feelings against the Jews, claiming that the Jews were responsible for the killing of Christ Jesus. Since the Diaspora, the Jews have lived scattered as minorities, and attempted to live peacefully among the many peoples of the Middle East, Europe, and even beyond the Ural Mountains. The primitive imaginations of Middle-Ages-Man (and in some, even into our own times) has attributed all manner of sorcery, evil, and witchcraft as having its source among the Jews. In times of natural and man-made calamity, the Jews have usually been named as being somehow responsible. Scapegoats. 'Pogroms' of destruction and retribution by mobs of commoners have often flared up, here and there to vent wrath upon the astonished Jewish communities and their families. Jews have been expelled from Spain and from France, and where they existed (in towns and cities) they were belittled and confined; and locked away at night into 'ghettos'. Forced to settle anew, often into unsettled territories such as existed in central Europe, or into whatever realms might accept them. The Mohammedans have treated the Jews even more harshly than have the Christians.

David Duke ("*My Enlightenment*") elucidated some of the probable explanations as to why the Jewish people seem so continuously to have been reviled:

- Their cultural tradition of business acumen has enabled many of them to have acquired vast wealth.
- As creditors and money lenders, they have an ancient reputation as 'sharp dealers'. The poor and destitute, with little other option in times of travail, have regularly landed

themselves into debtor's prison and slavery in consequence of those dealings.

- With wealth, has come power - specifically, economic power. They certainly also aspire to temporal power. As do all peoples.
- They have not proven themselves to be benevolent or forgiving when in power, as one might notice even only in their rendition of Old Testament History. The Talmud is said to reflect even more onerously against them.
- Besides the control the Jews have wielded over legitimate politics and economics, they have also wielded their influence over its alternative world - that of <u>the underground and the Mafia</u>. How else would they historically have enforced the necessity of repayment from private debtors?
- As to the implications of what is written in "*The Protocols of the Elders of Zion*", it certainly is damaging to the character of the Jewish people. Even though it may never have been proven to have actually been written by Jewish authors.
- And the Jews have from ancient times been heavily involved in the slave trade. Auschwitz, by strange twist of fate, turns out to have been the center of the Jewish slave trade in Eastern Europe. As a part of their current underworld dealings, they are still heavily involved in 'white slavery', there being a large appetite for strange women in even modern Israel.
- Having had money and power among the races with whom they have mingled, lived, and had their dealings, they have also long known and practiced the art of <u>propaganda to their advantage</u> - beginning with the Old Testament and continuing into modern day media. There are those who suggest that they overly dramatize their own sufferings in this world, as though to suggest that other peoples have not also suffered life's agonies. Did they not come out with Egypt's spoil? Enough with which to have built golden idols? It seems to have been wealth that they acquired in their ordinary lives under Pharaoh, since nothing suggests that they sacked the kingdom.

And so, there does seem to be (at least some plausible) reason as to why peoples of a Christian nation might have cause to harbor animosities against (that small portion of) Jewish people who have come into wealth and positions of political power. Just also as they rise in anger from time to time against their secular wielders of economic and political power. But, insofar as I am aware, the larger proportion of Jewish people are neither economically, nor politically advantaged, nor influential. I could be wrong in that point, for my personal acquaintance with Jewish people is rather meager. Those few with whom I have been acquainted have seemed decent, affable, and honest. I can well suppose that I encounter quite a number of Jews who have no cause to make me aware of their Jewishness, for they seem not generally evangelistic. I have heard it said that well-to-do circles of Jews are 'cliquish', 'pretensive' and predisposed to nepotism. But those tendencies are by no means unique to Jews. My impression of the Jewish people is that they tend generally to be given more to intellectualism than other Caucasian groups.

It is my understanding that in the past couple thousand years the Jewish people have been more involved in trade, commerce and professional occupations than other European peoples. Forbidden, in fact, to own land or engage in farming in some countries. In fact, early Catholicism seems to have discouraged their own parishioners from occupationally dealing with 'filthy lucre', especially from involvement with 'usury' - the earning of interest from the lending of money. A very profitable occupation that would seem to have given Jewish money lenders and bankers a distinct economic advantage in accumulating personal wealth: and an advantage that one might suppose would have carried over into all branches of commerce. We are well informed of the enormous fortune accumulated by the Jewish Rothschild family that had its beginnings with Mayer Rothschild in 1764 in Frankfurt, Germany. A beginning that would eventually progress the Rothschilds into one of the greatest accumulations of family wealth in Europe. A fortune which would inevitably also make of that family a political-economic force to be reckoned with all across Europe and reaching even across the Atlantic into America.

Mayer Rothschild acquired his banking experience as an apprentice in the Jewish Banking House of Oppenheimer in Hannover where he advanced to chief clerk, before he declined a partnership offer, to return to Frankfurt to establish his own banking firm. I have never yet come across a source to inform me as to how many centuries the Jewish banking firms had been operational in Europe - perhaps eight or ten centuries? Mayer Rothschild had 5 sons, all attentive to enlarging the family's fortune and influence. They were eventually ennobled by the Hapsburgs to the status of Baron; and each of the 5 sons flourished, one each in England, France, Vienna, and Italy. There were ongoing generations of the family, and each of the ever increasing financial firm branches was kept in the hands of family. And by means of an efficient courier system of informers, they were enabled to act uniformly with always the benefit of advance and specific information.

The Rothschilds married within the family, to keep their economic assets concentrated and effective. Nobles, kings, and business magnates came to be financially attached to and intricately involved with the Rothschilds. Big finance transactions inevitably involved the family with politics. Their influence continues into our present era, though not necessarily recognized as such, since they operate behind closed doors, and are not infrequently represented by the names of sons-in-law - such for example as Warburg, whose voice was the dominant influence in the founding and evolution of 'The Federal Reserve System', in this country.

[I didn't wish in this essay to get into any of these rather covert connections of the Jewish influence into the politics and economic intrigue that transpires in the politics of this world, because the conspiratorial implications are slippery and cumbersome to have to elucidate. So, let the one above reference suffice. And without any much effort, any one who reads this essay can easily enough confirm this information on the Rothschild political-economic influence in this world.]

In the United States, 'The Federal Reserve System' itself, is an outgrowth of, and connected to an equivalent central financial cabal-cartel (implying, of course, secrecy and self-serving machinations) in England and other European nations. As to what is meant by economic power, back in in 1913 when 'the fed' was established in America, ¾ of the world's wealth was said to be held by the Rothschilds, Rockefellers, Warburg, and J.P. Morgan. The Rockefellers, of course, are not Jewish, but having acquired great wealth and large business interests, they have come to mutually beneficial understandings with the Jewish financiers. Economic muscle power is obviously intimately connected to political power. These holders of massive wealth have so much political influence that they are able to remain almost totally opaque in their high finance and personal lives from any scrutiny even by the governments to which they are connected. For it is their secretive money arrangements that have for centuries financed the debt of nations; as well as the massive financial arrangements of large corporations. All political and economic enterprise functions on the basis of debt and would be entirely at a loss as to how to manage their old and ongoing debt other than by way of the unseen manipulations which - as in "*The Wizard of Oz*" - goes on from behind the curtains. It seems doubtful that government scrutiny of their accounting system could comprehend the essence of what transpires in the high finance cabal-cartels even were they to consent to open their books: so intertwined are their doings across international borders. Doubtful even, that the political elite of nations would want to try to force an accounting, such as would expose their own treasonous and disgraceful past, and ongoing collusion with the rascals behind the curtain. Supposing that the whole business was even then discovered to be a scam or a Ponzi scheme. What then? The whole world must suddenly revert to a primitive barter system?

In particular, we must be aware of such of the above-said information, as we read what Hitler writes of, in "*Mein Kampf*". For he, himself continuously uses only vague reference to the Jewish influence in Europe - and indeed, in the world - which he saw as a definite menace to the best interests of his beloved German states. Let us not be immediately 'put-off' with his blasé usage of such phrases as "Jew-Russian", "Jewish Internationalism", "Jew-union", etc. Jewish influence which to his long considered understanding seems so real and obvious as to be in no need of anything more that mere mention.

Does any student of history doubt but that Jewish persons have for many centuries made themselves economic and political advisors and confidantes to even all the rulers of Christian Nations? Have made themselves useful and even indispensable. This, even while the Jews as a people have been scorned and suffered persecution in those same nations.

To personalize from the general situation of Jewish people, we can well suppose that one who has been abused and scorned throughout his whole experience of life could hardly be blamed - were he to fantasize and look forward to a time when the tables might be turned to his own advantage.

What Hitler saw in the Jewish-Marxist-Communist movement was that Communism was on the march towards a subtle world domination through occult political-economic manipulation from behind the scenes. It appears to me that he was <u>not mistaken</u> in his understanding that powerful economic resources are quite capable of swaying and dominating the politics of a nation - even against the will and contrary to the best interests of the people of the nation (such as is cause for concern right here in America, in current times). There certainly seems something akin to wisdom in Adolf's comment, that: "If a government uses the instruments of power in its hands for the purpose of leading a people to ruin, then rebellion is not only the right, but also the duty of every individual citizen." (p. 75)

In the intervening years since the end of WW-II, we have come to see clearly that Communism - contrary to its rhetoric - ends up with the enslavement, servitude, and abuse of 'its huddled masses, yearning to be free'. And with the outright murder of that ten or twenty percent of its population who dare oppose it. We are given to understand that the Bill Ayers/ Bernadine Dorn crowd of subversive 'Weathermen' matter-of-factly discussed the reality of that little detail when they were actively involved in robbery, sabotage, and mayhem in this county in the 1960's. Though they have taken a now different tack from direct violence, to behind-the-scenes manipulations, they remain subversive. One might well suppose that those very behind-the-scenes connections are the likes of International Communism with enough influence to have been made possible their serving as Chicago area college professors, rather than serving terms as prison inmates.

Adolf struggled intellectually and politically finally to have achieved enough political and military power to oppose the looming threat of Russian-Jewish-Red-Communism in Germany. Achieved that with a small group beginning with but seven members. Public meetings in beer-halls, and later, in stadiums - constituted the public forums of politics, and his public oratory might go on for 1 to 3 hours. Once his new-formed party had grown enough to seem a threat to what he calls Jewish Unionisms, the unions began to give orders to their members to break-up the NAZI party meetings. By hooting and heckling, originally. When that proved ineffective, then by inciting small riots and eventually armed conflicts within the crowd. Police protection was of no avail, for they only arrived after the fact, and themselves would absolve the meetings to dispel the ruckus. Adolf was innovative. Began to bring his own newly organizing force to patrol the audience and toss out the trouble-makers at the first sign of disorder. Eventually he organized them into a military force specifically trained in techniques for handling even the larger and militant disruptions. Thus, the origin of his 'storm troopers'. In 1923 his NAZI party was 'outlawed', and Adolf was tossed into the pokey for an eight month stint. It is not all that infrequently that important political leaders seem to have spent some time in prison. Not one to merely pace and fritter away his time, Adolf spent his prison time organizing his thoughts into his book, "*Mein Kampf*". I am given to understand that millions of copies were purchased in the German states. One might suppose that his book had something to do with his release from prison, the restoration of his political party, and his eventual rise to dictatorship in NAZI Germany.

- - - - - - - - - - - - - - -

Says Adolf, "The Jew reasoned that, 'The Bolshevism of Germany', that is to say, the extermination of the volkish and national German intellectuals, and the resultant exploitation of German labor under the yoke of Jewish international finance is only the overture to the movement for expanding Jewish power on a wider scale and finally subjugating the world to its rule. As has so often happened in the course of history, Germany is the chief pivot of this formidable struggle." (p. 414)

From the beginning of his speculations, it was Adolf's thought that the problems of the German states was primarily that the Germans did not have enough territory to meet the requirements of its large population which was, consequently, an impoverished and downtrodden people. Not enough land even to be self-sufficient to their own food supply. In addition to that, the states were only loosely federated, each state pursuing their own interests, and a drone-like class of political elite and ineffective parliamentarians primarily concerned with maintaining their own sinecures. Those things in addition to the fact that the Jews and their labor unions were ever grasping for administrative control, and inciting the chaos of discontent and contest among the masses to achieve their goals. The dominant grip on the news media by the Jews enabled them to use propaganda effectively - a very substantial advantage, in Adolf's view. A force which he was later enabled to turn effectively to his own advantage.

It was Adolf's hope and intent to inspire and infuse the masses with a sense of national unity and will to achieve the greatness for which this Aryan population was destined. He was a moralist of great persuasive power, preaching a message intended to inspire the proletariat with individual personal pride and a vision of better times just beyond the near horizon. He emphasized the virtue of family and of cultural values. And he wanted to make very clear, the threat of Red-Jewish-Communism within their very midst.

- - - - - - - - - - - - - - -

As to the German trade unions, says Adolf, "Only the uneducated classes joined the Marxists. The Marxist leaders have formed out of much less intelligent human material an army of party combatants who obey their Jewish master just as blindly as they formerly obeyed their German officer."

"Actually, the Jew is using the trade-union, as a weapon with which to destroy the foundations of the (German) national economic structure.(p.224) "The Jew turns the trade union movement into an organization for the exercise of physical violence. The resistance and antipathy of those whose insight has hitherto saved them from swallowing the Jewish bait, have been broken down by terrorism. The success of that kind of activity is enormous."

Adolf reminds his listeners that there is not within Russia a single factory capable of turning out one motor-car in good running order.(p.237) While his German people were certainly better educated and technologically advanced above the enslaved peasantry of Russia, it was Adolf's intention to replace the parliamentary (but ineffective and lethargic) upper class German intelligentsia with his own NAZI party intelligentsia. But, he surmised that "The strength of a political party never consists in the intelligence and independent spirit of the rank and file of its member, but rather in the spirit of willing obedience with which they follow their intellectual leaders." (p. 310)

He continues to iterate, "The aspiration of the Jewish people is to become the despots of the world. That aspiration is quite as natural as the impulse of the Anglo-Saxon to rule the world." [Each chooses his own way of attaining those ends and fight for them with characteristic weapons, so does the Jew] (p.438) "As soon as the Jew is in possession of political power he drops all pretence. The democratic Jew of the people, becomes the Jew lusting for blood, the tyrant of the peoples. In the course of a few years the Jew endeavors to exterminate all those who represent the (German) national intelligentsia, and thus depriving the people of their natural intellectual leaders he prepares them for their fate as slaves under a lasting despotism." (p.226) "The Jew follows his own methods, he insinuates himself into the very heart of the nations and then proceeds to undermine the national structure from within. The weapons with which he works are lies and calumny, poisonous infection and disintegration, intensifying the struggle until he has succeeded in exterminating his hated adversary to the accompaniment of much bloodshed. In Russian Bolshevism we must recognize the kind of attempt which is being made by the Jew in the twentieth century to secure domination over the world." (p. 438)

- - - - - - - - - - - - - - -

We here in America might do well to pay more heed to some of what Adolf had to say about the threat (today, in this country from what is clearly a resurgence) of Communism and the threat of one-world-government which has become embodied in the United Nations. Beware also the intent to entangle our nation even deeper into the prospect of economic suicide that lurks in the likes of 'cap-and-trade', an ever advancing 'nanny-state', the harboring and subsidizing of aliens within our borders, and the

IMF which continuously puts the American taxpayer on the hook for the repayment of multimillion dollar loans to third-world nations who have no hope nor intention of ever repaying those loans themselves. "Poor people of rich nations, gifting money to rich people of poor nations."

And lest we forget, our ineffectual congress is indecently coupled to The Federal Reserve System, which in turn is allied into a cabal of foreign and financial organizations which continues to drain the wealth of this nation and its peoples to the benefit of their separate private benefit. Though the capitalistic system is flawed, it has been far more beneficial to political systems than has communism. Once we get free of the current 'red menace' to the politics of this nation, we would do well next to begin the task of exposing and rooting out the canker of 'the fed' from our political-economic system.

\- - - - - - - - - - - - - - -

However much the reader of this little essay is repelled by Adolf Hitler; and the evil and havoc he precipitated upon most of the world in the form of WW-II, I am suggesting that his book, "*Mein Kampf*", is usefully instructive, and well worth the reading. Communism never had a more determined and analytic adversary. If the life, energies, and purposes of Adolf Hitler was about anything, it seems primarily to have been dedicated to discovering and combating the ever elusive but all-consuming threat of Marxist Communism. Though Hitler was primarily concerned about the threat of Communism to his own German nation, he certainly recognized Marxist Communism as having international goals and objectives. He recognized 'the contagion' of Communism as being slow and insidious - the more difficult to discern and diagnose. We, too, in America at one time recognized that and acted to outlaw Communism. But we seem to have a short national memory. And the patient protean nature of that social contagion - Marxist Communism - has permitted the ongoing danger to mount its invasive tactic in new guises; Ultra-liberalism, progressive socialism, Hope-and-change, Chicago Mafia Politics . . . .

R. Garner Brasseur
4 September 2011

Reference: "*Mein Kampf*", by Adolf Hitler (official Nazi English Translation; Copywrite 2009 Elite Minds Inc.)

\- - - - - - - - - - - - - - -

First Addendum:

I subsequently discover more details about the expeditionary military forces sent into Russia immediately after WW-I. Sent and remained there about two years. Little is said about these forces. But they were sent by Pres. Wilson because the Bolshevik Red Army was considered to be a dangerous threat with ambitions for world conquest or domination. Two detachments of about 10,000 men were landed, one at Valadstock on the Pacific coast, and the other into northwest Siberia upon the Northern Sea Coast. These forces were in support of the 'White Russian Army', representative of the monarchy.

And so we note that the threat of the Marxist Communist movement in Russia was seen also in our own nation as a world class threat. Not just a delusion that was seen and acted upon by Adolf Hitler alone.

RGB
10-19-2011

- - - - - - - - - - - - - - -

Second Addendum, from:
National Review Online
The Hundred Years' German War
By Victor Davis Hanson
12/15/2011

The rise of a German Europe began in 1914, failed twice, and has now ended in the victory of German power almost a century later. The Europe that Kaiser Wilhelm lost in 1918, and that Adolf Hitler destroyed in 1945, has at last been won by German Chancellor Angela Merkel without firing a shot. Or so it seems from European newspapers, which now refer bitterly to a "Fourth Reich" and arrogant new Nazi "Gauleiters" who dictate terms to their European subordinates. Popular cartoons depict Germans with stiff-arm salutes and swastikas, establishing new rules of behavior for supposedly inferior peoples.

Millions of terrified Italians, Spaniards, Greeks, Portuguese and other Europeans are pouring their savings into German banks at the rate of $15 billion a month. A thumbs-up or thumbs-down from the euro-rich Merkel now determines whether European countries will limp ahead with new German-backed loans or default and see their standard of living regress to that of a half-century ago.

A worried neighbor, France, in schizophrenic fashion, as so often in the past, alternately lashes out at Britain for abandoning it and fawns on Germany to appease it. The worries in 1989 of British Prime Minister Margaret Thatcher and French President François Mitterrand over German unification - that neither a new European Union nor an old NATO could quite rein in German power - proved true.

How did the grand dream of a "new Europe" end just 20 years later in a German protectorate - especially given the not-so-subtle aim of the European Union to diffuse German ambitions through a continent-wide super-state? Not by arms. Britain fights in wars all over the globe, from Libya to Iraq. France has the bomb. But Germany mostly stays within its borders - without a nuke, a single aircraft carrier or a military base abroad.

Not by handouts. Germany poured almost $2 trillion of its own money into rebuilding an East Germany ruined by communism - without help from others. To drive through southern Europe is to see new freeways, bridges, rail lines, stadiums and airports financed by German banks or subsidized by the German government.

Not by population size. Somehow, 120 million Greeks, Italians, Spaniards, and Portuguese are begging some 80 million Germans to bail them out.

And not because of good fortune. Just 65 years ago, Berlin was flattened, Hamburg incinerated and Munich a shell - in ways even Athens, Madrid, Lisbon, and Rome were not.

In truth, German character - so admired and feared in some 500 years of European literature and history - led to the present Germanization of Europe. These days we recoil at terms like 'national character' that seem tainted by the nightmares of the past. But no other politically correct exegesis offers better reasons why a booming Detroit of 1945 today looks like it was bombed, and a bombed-out Berlin of 1945 now is booming.

Germans on average worked harder and smarter than their European neighbors - investing rather than consuming, saving rather than spending, and going to bed when others to the south were going to dinner. Recipients of their largesse bitterly complain that German banks lent them money to buy German products in a sort of 21st-century commercial serfdom.

True enough, but that still begs the question why Berlin, and not Rome or Madrid, was able to pull off such lucrative mercantilism.

Where does all this lead? Right now to some great unknowns that terrify most of Europe. Will German industriousness and talent eventually translate into military dominance and cultural chauvinism - as it has in the past? How, exactly, can an unraveling EU, or NATO, now "led from behind" by a disengaged United States, persuade Germany not to translate its overwhelming economic clout into political and military advantage? Can poor European adolescents really obey their rich German parents? Berlin in essence has now scolded southern Europeans that if they still expect sophisticated medical care, high-tech appurtenances and plentiful consumer goods - the adornments of a rich American and northern Europe lifestyle - then they have to start behaving in the manner of Germans, who produce such things and subsidize them for others. In other words, an Athenian may still have his ultra-modern airport and subway, a Spaniard may still get a hip replacement, or a Roman may still enjoy his new Mercedes. But not if they still insist on daily siestas, dinner at 9 p.m., retirement in their early 50s, cheating on taxes, and a de facto 10 a.m. to 4 p.m. workday.

Behind all the EU's 11th-hour gobbledygook, Germany's new European order is clear: If you wish to live like a German, then you must work and save like a German. Take it or leave it.

By Victor Davis Hanson
(a classicist and historian at the Hoover Institution, Stanford University, and a recipient of the 2007 National Humanities Medal.)

THE CHESAPEAKE AND OHIO CANAL

by R. Garner Brasseur

Having read about the Chesapeake and Ohio Canal, and reminded repeatedly of its existence, from seeing it upon the map as I plan my occasional weekend excursions, I decided to spend a weekend hiking along its towpath. Its construction was begun about 1828, a few years after the opening of the Erie Canal in New York State. It was never heavily used, or a commercial success, because of competition from the Baltimore and Ohio Railroad, which was a privately funded project, started at the same time as the digging of the C & O Canal. The railroad followed the same course as the canal, through the Potomac River Valley to Cumberland; and its construction proceeded much more rapidly into Cumberland, Maryland and into the Ohio Valley. By the time the canal reached Cumberland and was opened to through traffic in 1850, it was outmoded and the railroad had already acquired the bulk of the commercial traffic. Nevertheless, the canal was used until the 1920's - for hauling coal and grain into the Washington D.C. area. The intermittent floods each damaged the canal and made its maintenance expensive, so that when it was severely damaged by an especially destructive flood in 1924, it was more or less abandoned. It fell into ruin progressively. A number of years ago - 1956 - there was a plan to construct a highway along the canal right-of-way. There arose a controversy over that plan, as there were those who wanted to set the canal aside as a historical national park and recreation preserve for the use and interest of the public at large. The weight of the voice of Chief Justice Douglas was a contributing factor to the final decision to place the canal into the hands of the National Park Service for development and usage as a recreational preserve of historical interest by the citizens of the land. And, thus, it came about, that almost the entire length of that canal - with the exception of its terminal facilities - is now available to you and I as a national resource for our edification and recreation, along its almost entire 160 mile route.

I determined this past weekend, to get down to the canal, in its more remote area, over by Hagerstown. I knew though, the recent flood would make that possibility difficult. Friday evening I prepared my gear for that outing; and then sat down to scan the Friday Washington Post, the only issue of any newspaper that I regularly peruse. It contains information specifically concerning weekend and subsequent week long events and happenings for the area. There was an article indicating that the canal was currently closed along most of its course, due to recent flood damage. This did not deter my intent, for I had planned to visit its course at a higher elevation in the mountains, where - to my mind - it seemed less likely to have suffered from the heaviest of the floodwaters. What concerned me were the weather prospects for the weekend - probable rain. Since my call schedule and other arrangements were already final, I would take the chance; and change my course as necessary.

I arose at 7:40 AM Saturday morning. There was heavy overcast and threatening rain. I loaded my gear into the pickup and departed. It rained most of the day with but a few intermissions. I occupied myself by stopping at a couple auctions and garage sales. I stopped at Antietam Battleground National Monument near Sharpsburg. There, in 1862, General Lee's Confederate Army was defeated in his first (of two) efforts to carry the Civil War into the territory held by the Union Forces. Twenty-three thousand men were killed or injured in a single day - one of the bloodiest battles of the Civil War. From there, I crossed the Potomac River into West Virginia; and crossed the C&O Canal, which was closed to usage at that point, account of the flood damage. No matter though, for it was raining and cold; and I would not have been able to tour it under that circumstance alone.

West Virginia is fast becoming one of my favorite state; account of its rugged and only semi-developed terrain; and the rural atmosphere and natural beauty. I drove northwards and west, arriving at 4:30 PM (in the rain) at Berkeley Springs, West Virginia. A lovely little spot - easily nicer than Ashland, OR. The earliest colonials seized upon it, account of natural warm springs that produce 2,000 gallons per minute at a temperature of 75 degrees F. It has always been used as a recreational area and facility. It is alleged to have healing virtues account of the minerals and gasses within the water. The area was originally owned by Lord Fairfax; and donated by him, to the public as a state park facility. Of course, the Indians who habituated the area for centuries prior to the coming of 'the white man', did not own property, so it is natural that Lord Fairfax's ownership was uncontested by them. They had no such concept as ownership of land. Said one Indian chief in amazement, "Can a man own the land?". Since 1774 the area has been progressively developed into a spa. One can still go there and take 'the cure', but needn't resort to that dubious excuse, to enjoy oneself there. Colonial people of sufficient means would come by carriage or by horseback; and stay a week or two at a time. They had four or five big hotels, which in recent decades have - one by one - been lost in fires. Gambling was a big thing, in conjunction with the bathing, to occupy their leisure; but gambling here has since become illegal.

On the side of the mountain, above the town, I noticed an old English style castle. How strange that seemed to me. And so I drove up to the castle to attempt to ascertain its cause and purpose. It seems that toward the last part of the 19th century, a wealthy 48 year old business man was resorting here, when he fell in love with a 17 year old girl, here with her family from far to the south - perhaps Alabama. She refused his offer of marriage. Five years later however, they ran into one another - here - again. The girl, in talking with the gentleman, dreamily suggested how fine a thing it might be to have a castle upon the side of the mountain, overlooking this lovely valley in its domestic tranquility. And so they bribed one another into a domestic arrangement contingent upon the construction of that castle. It was built upon a half-scale model to the size of its prototype in England. In addition to the castle, there came two sons and a daughter to that marriage. After five years of marriage, the gentleman died, leaving the fortune he had acquired to Rosa (the young widow). She regularly threw weekend and week-long bashes at the castle for years; and eventually came to the end of that fortune. Perhaps the 'protectors and conservators' of the estate got more of it than did Rosa. But, in any case, that wealth was irretrievably departed from her. Meanwhile, her daughter had died; and her sons had settled in the west. Rosa came down in her status of life, and left the castle to support herself by raising chickens in that community. Her son, finding her in her depressed economic circumstances, took her out west with him, to Coeur d'Alene, Idaho, where she lived to beyond ninety years of age.

I stayed there in the motel at Berkeley Hot Springs. I had planned to read, but instead was enticed into watching an interesting and informative documentary film on television - dealing with the recent history and course of events in Cambodia, which was currently occupied by the North Vietnamese Army. The conditions imposed by that Communist Vietnam Army are as a benison and great freedom compared to what the peoples of that land have had to suffer and endure in the hands of their previous despotic and dictatorial oppressors. And yet, the Vietnam Government is under severe censorship for invading and occupying that country. A fact that casts its own judgment into the face of the United Nations - whose censorship it represents. And thus, we are reminded - again - that all forms of government must eventually be opposed on various issues; sometime repudiated altogether and absolutely.

I arose at 8:00 AM on Sunday. There was only a partial cloud cover, which seemed to be dissipating. I had renewed hopes then of being enabled to find and explore the C&O Canal. And so I headed westward, up over what they call Cacapon Mtn. - its flat upper surface being the capon. This geologic feature forms there an elongated mountain ridge oriented SSW by NNE, perhaps fifteen miles long and three or four miles wide. In its southern extension, it gradually tapers down and buries itself beneath the other mountainous formations, but continues there to extend, embedded in those formations, to at least as far as southern Virginia. That particular formation is one of sandstone and is known as the Tuskarora Sandstone

Formation. I myself have observed it in the road cuts, on each of the three weekend trips that took me into West Virginia this fall. Most of the mineral springs areas, and the hot springs that abound in this mountainous area of Virginia and West Virginia, seem to be associated with, or located near this particular sandstone formation. That sandstone seems to be to be particularly unusual in its hardness and its light coloration. One has some difficulty in finally concluding that it is, in fact, sandstone. In places, it is manifest as great sheets and slabs of rock - appearing more like granite or andesite. Upon inspection of its small detail, it appears to have its sand granules cemented together and nearly marbleized by the limestone saturated water which has percolated through it over eons of time. In these areas then, it is truly in a hybrid state between say, dolomite and sandstone. Those well acquainted in the area, say there are areas where this sandstone formation is soft and granular - like sugar. I remember seeing that formation in one road cut, where its cross-sectional appearance was like a high round log some 200 or 300 feet in diameter. Whereas the well-water of the surrounding areas is often unpleasantly tasty, because of the high iron content; that which is associated with the spring waters of this sandstone formation are mostly pure and excellent to drink. Presumably, those waters of high mineral content are filtered and purified by their passage through the sandstone formation. And the hardness of the marbleized sandstone perhaps allows the water within to seep out only here and there, locally - where there are faults in its continuity. Weighing then upon the waters that have seeped beneath the formation; those waters are forced to rise and seep out as artesian wells from the base of the formation - just as the placing of one's water-impervious body into a tub filled with water, would cause the level of that water to rise and spill over the edge.

Wherever I travel through these mountains and valleys, I repeatedly see the name of George Washington. Said to have built a fort here; constructed a road there; led an army that way; encamped somewhere else etc. Obviously, he was personally acquainted with the territory and familiar to its people. What an amazing health, energy, and stamina he must have possessed. I should like to get my hands on a copy of his journal and observations. I was not surprised then, to find that he had been at Berkeley Springs, too. In fact, he owned some land there and a house or two for his recreation later in life, when he could get to it.

But I left Berkeley Springs and drove to Paw Paw. The name itself, is enticing - like a well thought out title for a book. But the bridge at Paw Paw had been washed away by the flood of the previous week. Trailer houses and truck-trailers lay scattered about, askew and in bent and sagging condition. Roads - as well as the bridge - had been washed away.

Mattresses and bedding were hanging from the topmost branches of trees along the river. Without seeing what had happened, one could see what had happened. Paw Paw was an important site for the amassing of federal troops during the Civil War.

I had to detour southward and then further west, to find a place to cross the river. I finally managed it at Greenspring - about 20 miles east of Cumberland. There had been extensive flooding there too; and the folks were occupied in trying to clean up their houses and land; and in trying to dry out their dirty and wet belongings. The bridge there was a one-lane toll-bridge with a flat bed; and without side-rails. Apparently it had withstood the flood because of that peculiar construction. The water was still high - up to within a couple inches of the road-bed of the bridge. And I was a little afraid to cross it. But I saw some heavier traffic cross it without incident and finally chanced it myself, since the toll shed was on the other side. I figured that if I washed away, at least I wouldn't then have to pay the fifty cents toll charge.

Immediately beyond the toll-bridge, I encountered the C&O Canal at Old Town. And what a lovely stretch of towpath and canal it was. Indeed, how lovely it all must be. I walked along it for a distance of a half mile - to where it was closed off account of flood damage. I inspected a couple of the old concrete locks, with their wooden lock water-gates; long since in a broken and sagging condition. I believe that we could do worse, than to take off a week in some September or early October of the near future, in order to hike and camp and chat along this canal right-of-way and towpath.

As it was already near mid-afternoon when I arrived at the canal, the (only short) excursion that I was allowed account of flood damage, enabled me to head back to Chevy Chase - arriving back at the house at 5:15 PM.

Ten days earlier, on the night of Wednesday, 11/6/85 I had a call from home inquiring about my circumstance in the midst of the hurricane and the flood. As I don't watch TV or listen to the radio, and since I don't read the newspaper except on Fridays; therefore I didn't really know much about it. I had looked out the window and noted some light rainfall and an occasional zephyr-like gust that moved the tree branches. Not a very serious storm, from my point of view. It did have serious consequences for this whole middle-state seaboard area though. Here is the way it came about. A hurricane had formed off the coast and was headed directly at Washington D.C. But the eye of the storm suddenly veered northward and crossed into the mainland, passing over Long Island at New York - about

250 miles north of here. That 250 mile diameter cyclone had absorbed a high content of moisture in its formative stages upon the ocean. Though the eye of the storm missed Washington D.C., the huge southwest wing of moisture-laden air brushed into the Appalachian Mountains of Virginia, West Virginia and Maryland. In doing so, it was forced to rise against that mountainous incline. In doing so, it cooled; and its then supersaturated clouds of moisture condensed, dropping torrents of water across the entire breadth of those mountains in a very short space of time. That torrent of water upon the mountain steeps, quickly found its way to the creeks and rivers of the valleys below. Those channels, fettered by steep embankments and narrow channels, rapidly rose to levels far above flood stage, backing up those waters almost to the topmost headwaters near the mountain crests. Those encumbered river waters traveling their long and devious north-south courses before finding their few and narrow eastward passages to the sea, did not arrive into their more spacious lowland outlet riverbeds until 18 or 20 hours later. The flood damage was extensive along the whole course of those rivers and streams, but more especially upland, before the waters find easier passage in the coastal lowlands. Such disasters are not uncommon; and their pattern is one of irregular irregularity.

R. Garner Brasseur
11/19/85

CRICKET SONG

(Written to help Miette on an idea for a story. She rejected it though, on the grounds that it was not a story. She was correct of course, for it is more like an essay than a story.)

R. Garner Brasseur

The song of the cricket, in early Rome, would perhaps be indistinguishable from that of his remote descendant, emigrated to the new world; and whose song you and I have heard. Is there any man who has not strained and listened patiently for an encore? No amount of applause will persuade the cricket to sing it once again; though a respectful silence may. Neither is the melody nor voice of the cricket lovely; though my several recollections of the total experience, never-the-less stands out sharply in my memory.

I expect that most people have heard the cricket under much the same circumstances which I recall. Late, upon a quiet summer evening, one suddenly becomes aware of a remarkably loud, even and high pitched buzzing sound. So familiar are we with the sound, that we instantly know from which creature it derives. Not, that we have ever actually seen the cricket in the act of 'singing' his song; rather, it is a phenomenon that actually perhaps has been witnessed by only a small number of patient observers. Though you nor I have ever visually witnessed the performance, yet we have each, perhaps, at some time taken the trouble to obtain indirect evidence of the fact.

The loud cricket song, against a background of lower pitched crickets in chorus, implies that the soloist is near at hand. Staining our ears and moving our head, we attempt to localize the directions of the source of that song. Approaching - no matter how quietly - the singer is startled into an abrupt silence. Now, closer to that source, we wait, motionless and quietly. Cricket breaks into song once more! This time, or perhaps the next, we can discover the cricket beneath some rock or growth. Exposing the singer, again stops the song, and the cricket scrambles for cover elsewhere. We virtually never find any suspect, other than the cricket. And removing the cricket puts an end to the nearby solo, though the distant chorus persists. These things, I think, are sufficient indirect evidence to enable us, tentatively, to agree with those few naturalists who have directly observed that cricket does the singing.

The picture on the urn is that of a boy dozing in the field beside his work tools; while the fox is feasting upon the boy's lunch. And cricket, nearby, has ceased his singing. Nature speaks through the sudden silence of the cricket. "There is no grape so bitter, that Wiley fox cannot enjoy. There is no bread so mean, as cannot fill a hungry boy".

RGB
11/1/84

Death Of The Dance

by R. Garner Brasseur

My spouse and I were sponsors last night for the sub-Debs's dance, held at the Junior College. The customs seem to have changed in the past thirty year, more or less.

There was a large crowd of high school folks, mostly. There were some up to perhaps age 22 or 24. No Junior High School students were included. The evening went smoothly - probably not as rowdy as they were in my generation. The customs of our times and the paces of the rituals perhaps, do not seem strange to us, as they are the only such, of which we are generally aware. By comparison however, the current happenings definitely seem remarkable.

The music to my ear was more or less pure junk, its volume, outrageous. It intermittently caused my ears slight pain. I went out to the pickup to get some cotton, which I wadded into pledgets, tucking one tightly into each ear canal. The music was then no longer painful to my eardrums. Live music? Oh no! Disc-jockeys, playing recorded music . . . if you please. And they flashed psychedelic beams of light about the dance hall! They paid these two show-men $170.00 for staging the program. They furnished their own equipment - speakers, flashing lights, smoke producers, etc.

Most of the 'music' was what is called 'rock'. They made some concession, however, to the 'cowboys' in the crowd (apparently considered to be of perhaps second class social status) by playing an occasional western cowboy ballad. It sounded to me like angel's voices, compared to most of what they played. The whole program was apparently pre-arranged (taped) and structured in that sense. First the rock-hard for twenty minutes, then five minutes of country western, followed by five minutes of slow and formless notes, during which time the lights were all but turned off and the dance step simplified to a slow walk so that the young romantics could explore the gross anatomy of one another, and count each others' teeth with their tongues. All of this without having to overburden their attention spans upon the details of footwork.

I would hardly have believed that their dance to the rock music sounds could be so formal, stale, and unimaginative. They formed up two long lines, the girls in one, the boys in the other. The parallel lines faced each other, separated by perhaps five or six feet of space. There, separately, each of the couples (with the person opposite, in the opposing line) swaggers about and rotates their various joints, without ever making contact with one another or seemingly even noticing the presence of one another. The lack of contact and all might lead one to conclude that it were a highly moralistic dance, but then, we don't really know the content of their thoughts.

Now and then, a cloud of smoke appeared, and slowly dissipated. I thought, at first, someone had started a fire. Actually, though, there was a smoke generator especially designed to produce those clouds, giving the ballroom the smoke laden, bluish appearance with which we were so familiar in years past. In our time however, the smoke was actually produce by the smoking of cigarettes by the youngsters. I presume from this curious situation, that smoking in the dance hall is strictly forbidden. I know that many of the youngsters still smoke - though no longer in the dance hall. Impinged upon by all of these moralities, the 'clouded room' mystique prevails yet and lingers in the mental imagery of man. Something akin to music abides yet too; though distant and strained.

Alcohol was not permitted at the dance. Those that attended the dance could not re-enter, having once departed. Nor was there an intermission of the dance, such as to leave a natural moment that might lead to a casual stroll out of doors for a breath of fresh air.

All in all, I thought the controls were frightfully rigorous. Perhaps a crowded urban population of irresponsible youngsters requires that, as their needlessly extended school careers engender permissiveness and anonymity.

RGB
11/18/84

Two Lads From Denmark

In the Autumn of 1984 two young men from Denmark arrived at my door one evening in Hobbs, New Mexico about 5:30 P.M. on Saturday November 24th. I was alone at home for several days just then, so I invited them to stay a couple days. They did so, and departed about 7:30 A.M. on Monday the 26th of November. They had arrived into the United States through the Port of New York in August. From there, they went first to Maryland, to the home where Hans had stayed a couple of years previously as an exchange student. There they borrowed a 1971 V.W. Bus with which to tour the United States. They made a bed in the back of the vehicle, on which they usually slept. They manage to get by on about $8.00 per day apiece.

They traveled up to Niagara Falls, westward through Cleveland, Ohio, and then to Chicago. Then up through North Dakota, The Badlands, and down through the Black Hills. From there, to the Grand Tietons and up through Yellowstone National Park, en route to Libby Montana. Then north into Glacier National Park and up into Jasper Park in Canada, where they stopped at Atomic Hot Springs. Then onward to Banff and once more westward to Vancouver, British Columbia before dropping down into Seattle along Hwy 5 into Portland. From there they headed south, staying on Hwy 101. In San Jose, they had an acquaintance through whom they met Real Brasseur, who at age 22 or 23 is about their same age. Real gave them our address in Hobbs and invited them to stay here on their way eastward. They visited the Grand Canyon, came through Las Vegas (but missed Death Valley) and down through Flagstaff, Phoenix, Las Crusas, El Paso and stopped at Carlsbad Caverns the day they arrived here.

I treated them to a pizza that evening and had them stay in Real's room. On Sunday they did their laundry in our machines. That evening my wife made for us a big meal and had over a current Danish high school exchange student, Lars, and his host family, the Simpsons. Paul and Hans stayed over with us also Sunday night and departed Monday evening after another big meal.

On Saturday night Paul, Hans, and I stayed up and talked until 4:15 A.M. and on Sunday night, until 3:00 A.M.

We talked of hospitals and socialized medicine. I discouraged the significance of hospitals and emphasized the only truly necessary parts of medicine and those most economical as being Public Health Programs, immunizations, and selecting good breeding stock. Apparently the Europeans are crazy too (like are Americans) with notions of romantic love. I pointed out that most other cultures do as well or better with other systems. I pressed heavily the need to select a healthy mate to produce healthy children. I told them of the 'country western' ballad theme of unrequited love and went into an explanation of the phenomenon,

We talked briefly of flying saucers and I gave them my opinion and limited experience and knowledge from having been once deeply involved with reading and believing it. That led on into a discussion concerning the discrimination between first and second-hand experience, and between knowledge and 'hearsay'.

As to superiority, the Russian MIG airplanes have a great engine with superior power, but the American F-15 and F-16 have much better maneuverability. We talked of the space race. I feel that we are fortunate to have Russia competing, else we would not be far along on the project—for want of any competitive stimulation. I told them of my respect for Russian Culture prior to Lenin, and of the great contributions to literature and music that come from these oppressed peoples. But that the Communists as a political entity are not to be trusted.

We talked of the problems of individual morality that must find remedy before war and hatred might ever be suppressed. Individuals must each finally refuse to pull triggers upon the authority of the officer - for we are each personally responsible beings. I suggested that moral individuals ought not also become tax collector agents for morbid government. I told them of my experience of tax collectors and the IRS; and of the circumstances of my arriving here in Hobbs, subsequent to the machinations of tax collectors within the federal agency.

We talked of Bishop Weakforce of the Catholic Church, who harangues the U.S. government to do something for the poor, while the church does nothing with all of their millions of dollars and world power status.

We talked of religion. I told them of its manufacture in Rome. Told them of Livy's History of Rome, to support my view. That there is even a question as to the validity of the person of Jesus Christ. The problem of Apollonius and of the supposed divinity of even Romulus.

I gave them a book, "*The Uses of the Past*", by Herbert Mueller - the only general history book of which I know, that is without the Christian bias.

We talked of: 1.) the importance of family and power in big and extensive families. 2.) The use of the family (not men) to power. 3.) Kings in Europe. 4.) The Cortez conquest of Mexico and Pizzaro conquistadors in Peru. 5.) We speak of the power of the Christian Church and how little it has accomplished throughout its long history. 6.) Talk of all the rhetoric about missionaries and the limited accomplishment of even the most energetic among them, as suggested by the lives of David Livingston and Albert Schweitzer.

We speak of the economic problems of the world and their relatedness finally to money problems of U.S.A. We discuss the actual usefulness of the Marshall Plan after WW II; and of the inevitable huge waste caused by throwing large sums of taxpayer money at third-world Africa, with similar hopes and intentions which were destined to end in failure account of the non-technological nature and history of the myriad of only primitive states which use those funds almost exclusively for war. We discuss the notion of stealing the value out of money, as is practiced by all governments now and past. The clipping of coins of valuable metals, mining the copper out of our pennies, the ever progression of inflation etc.

And we speak of education - for my children and for these two young men specifically. Possibilities in medical school or in the field of biology. My choice would be Biology—Genetics or Fisheries. Problems of cloning . . . .

Discuss: Democracy. The American Tradition. Possible fall to a dictator (as is common in Latin America). Why Reagan was elected, and how much political value can be present in a big smile and an optimistic outlook. Will there be new taxes this year? No. Other options such as "adjustments" etc.

On Geology, Giant Volcanic Calderas, and The Badlands. Unbelief versus disbelief. Man's relatedness to the chimps. The "Spaceships of Ezekiel"

But as I was pressed for time, I did not get around to making these sketchy notes until two or three days after the visit. The notes are therefore incomplete, as well as sketchy. But I expect that you can get the gist of the spirit of our conversation. It was sort of an exchange of ideas between us. They were curious. I did most of the talking, trying to cover a variety of subjects; and trying to elicit their comments and questions.

R. Garner Brasseur, M.D.
11/28/84

Re: Paul Sorenson
Ronshovedvej 4
Vejle, Denmark 7100
ph 05824771

Hans Ole Frokier
Nielsskovej 237100
Vejle, Denmark
ph 05826513

Echoes
by R, Garner Brasseur

I recently saw a play, "Echoes" by Richard Nash and produced locally at the Playhouse Theater here in Hobbs. Pepper Murray and Edd Wells had the lead roles. In fact, they were essentially the only roles. They were two psychotics, institutionalized together in a room. They occupied themselves in 'lets pretend' activities and games which they pretended at, very realistically and which they pretended to enjoy. But they were not of one mind in this, and so each game only barely started before its moves and activities crossed a sore point in the thought processes of one or the other of the two. Then the game came to a crashing end as one or the other displayed a psychotic sudden reluctance and rigidness to go any further. There, at some point, their commerce halted, as though the flow were crashed upon some painful fixed idea within the psyche of one or the other of them. Their pretend roles were vivid and believable but maintained only by dent of great energy and could not long be supported before they reverted to their blasé selves, depressed from the fatigue of their effort and further depressed by their current limped nothingness and feelings of guilt and worthlessness. They searched and switched then immediately to another game and new roles, hoping undoubtedly to be able to maintain those roles. But the result was always the same. They were stuck each with the core of themselves within a real world that they did not wish to acknowledge or accept. They plotted together to avoid communication with one other and the real world. They encouraged one another to not get hooked by, or even to listen to the real world, for fear that one or the other might be seduced back into reality; leaving the other bitter and saddened; and now also alone in the fragile and isolated world of make believe.

The whole play was one string after another of bright little fantastic plays, abruptly ended and punctuated, with spells of depressing reality. At the end, one did escape and return to accept family and the reality of the world as it is.

It was a story that was relevant to all large and small psychosis and to the various neurosis which we all tend to harbor in one form or another. It was also a interesting picture of a problem that is very real and rampant in our society. For it is precisely the thing that happens to many of our children as they advance in school to the seventh or eighth grade, but more commonly in high school. The pressures of peer-groups beckon and call our children; and have a tendency to infuse them and confuse them with ideas and information that challenges their views of things. Not that peer-groups alone are afar from reality, but that the real world, too, is somewhat schizophrenic and particularly frustrating to youngsters in that stage of life when they are beginning to exit the naiveté of childhood, and are casting about for the beginnings of a stable adulthood. Our schools have come to foster a climate in which peer pressure has become an overly dominant influence among the students who, of course have generated the peer system as a by product, which becomes so counter-productive to education in secondary schools, that it ought to make us reconsider what real value these schools serves. Perhaps they might be much more productive and useful, as well as less expensive, by disbanding them as requirements; thereby disorganizing the tendency they have to become social societies for runaway youth.

R. G. Brasseur. M.D.
9/4/83

H.L. MENCKEN

Through my middle years I had occasion to read both from Mark Twain and Mencken, and something about their wit, flamboyant style, and mild iconoclasms gave me to suppose that there was somewhat of a connecting link between the two of them. I recently read another anthology of H.L. Mencken writings. On a couple of occasions, he does mention Mark Twain. I get the distinct impression that he was very strongly influenced and inspired by Mark Twain. They were both free-lance newspaper men by dent of experience, and each broke into that trade at an early age; and on his own. Both were shrewd observers of men and both and processed good psychological insights. The style of each is bombastic, critical, and analytical. Each is good with the clever phrase and expression. Both sparkle continuously with a friendly thread of gentle humor that makes their brand of criticism less harsh to the reader and lends it a philosophical air.

Surely, thinks I, no one having read the two men can doubt the strong influence of the one upon the other. Both are prolix. They commonly use words that are usually used uncommonly. Many of the words they use appear to be colloquial, perhaps more commonly used in the times they lived, than now. They seem both to be in the habit of the coinage of words.

With both, the writings are diverse. They seem well informed, knowledgeable, and give evidence of having researched their topics well. Additionally, they seem each to have uncommon grasp of insight or valid intuitions which go behind the external appearances of the matters they discuss.

Mencken has some valid and unique points to make about persons such as Washington, Lincoln, H.C.Lodge, W.C.Bryan, Holmes, FDR, G.Cleveland, Hardy, Coolidge, Wallace . . . .

RGB
11/13//80

- - - - - - - - - - - - -

[Then, on 3/24/88, I came across an essay by Mencken, "I Discover '*Huckleberry Finn*'", which affirms the influence of Twain upon Mencken. Influence both direct and indirect upon Mencken, through the influence also of Twain even upon Mencken's own father.]

RGB

HAY FEVER

R. Garner Brasseur, M.D.

Saturday, March 31st, 1983, Miette and her friend went with her mother and I to see "Hay Fever" by Coward - a three act play. I believe I saw it once fifteen years ago, in Skowhegan, Maine. I enjoyed the play, and was able to comprehend the subtleties of the plot; and the complexity of humor. Yet, my grasp of the situation was intuitive, and based upon myself having been caught up in similar situations in real life.

Miette says she enjoyed the play, but she gave us to know that she was rather perplexed and felt she had missed a good part of what was being portrayed. During the play, I tried to explain it to her briefly. Yet, my explanation was too brief and too hushed as the play proceeded.

As to Miette's questions during the performance. Though I perceived the interactive situations of the play intuitively. Still, how, can I give an analytic and verbal explanation to someone whose life experience does not put them into a sympathetic intuitive perception with the flow of the play's content?

The Bliss family of four is an unusual family and without their being aware of that fact, that are a cohesive unit, tied together by unique familial cultural perspective. Father is a writer, and accustomed to psychological analysis of character. He is in fact a creator of characters of various psychological depth for use within his novels. He is the more aware of this variability of depth and levels of perception within people, by virtue of the fact that his wife is a professional actress, who by experience and by intent, can with 'perfect pitch' play any number of roles quiet correctly, just as some musicians can (without a fixed instrumental frequency) give us a vocal middle C with precisely 512 vibrations per second.

Every role that mother plays - on stage, in society, at home, or tending the flowers; is played with an intensity appropriate to one of her calling. Every joy, every pain, and every sorrow, is appropriately conveyed (even if only to her private internal audience) by body carriage, by facial expression, by phrasing of words, and inner stream of consciousness.

The children, exposed to all of this in their upbringing, are indeed psychologically attuned to all these subtleties of deportment, demeanor, and expression. This occurs for them at the intuitive subconscious level - later in life (as occurs in this play) they may then consciously increase by intent, their fluidity in these matters when they as adults become personally involved adult participants in their own family interactions. For they have come to perceive that there are many roles that we are all called upon to play. They can play their roles the more convincingly, because of their familial pattern of practice in daily life. And are attuned to nuances of meaning within the familial situational dynamic.

So it is too, with music. Perhaps originally came drumming, then drum rhythms, then flute and woodwinds, then strings, then more complicated systems such as piano, and finally the organ. As each instrument is added, the product can become more complex with multiple shades of musical expression and variation. Other factors can be added and altered. Major and minor keys, counterpoint, tempo, melody, higher and lower octaves. A versatile musician may play one of several instruments. If familiar with a wide repertoire of music he can enter in at any point in the composition and play well his lines. He may even improvise if he has the wit and the ear to do so, and play in the manner of a virtuoso, enhancing the overall outcome, making it more agreeable to all.

Again we may liken what goes on in this Bliss home, to views of the world geographically. From the moon, earth's physical features are readily recognizable. At ten miles above the earth we still see the earth but recognize different appearances and previously unperceived overarching features. Flying low, one sees earth's features of ever smaller scale. Walking over hill, plains, and mountains, one knows earth yet more intimately. Inspecting rocks with field lens magnification shows ever more subtitle aspects of our universal reality. And from thin slices of rock viewed with powerful microscopes, one's mind begins to conceive the miniscule realities of quantum theory.

In my mind, having recognized earth's features from all these views, we are called upon to combine them into a synoptic conceptually, knowing that they are all true views. Despite the apparent vastness of incompatible differences between the stepped gradation of views, these appearances are, in fact, perfectly reconciled. Our simultaneous awareness of the views, conjoined with whichever view we now behold, increases our perception of this current view and enhances our sense of relatedness to the unity of existence.

Each of the four guests in the Bliss household, is there for reasons of his own, exploiting the situation to his own advantage and enlightenment. Each of them too, is there playing his or her own little game at this or that psychological level. Yet, in that encounter within the Bliss family, each comes up against his own confusion and frustration and need to escape. The Bliss family is highly versatile at transiting up and down between octaves of interaction; and at recognizing the subtle clues of these transitions. The outsiders are dazed and lost; then challenged and frustrated in their attempt to stay in the game. Their bewilderment and frustration brings to us (the audience) the amusement. In the same way, there is humor in a situation where a versatile speaker gets others to repeat "If Peter Piper picked a peck of pretty pickled peppers, where is the peck of pickled peppers Peter picked". The humor arrives when the speed of repetition causes the least adept to garble, stumble, and then feel lightly foolish. So also do we become amused in watching clumsy little children (whom we love) try to imitate us, and stumble cutely - and then, good naturedly try again.

The Bliss family has won - in more than one way. 1) They have each achieved a new awareness of a comfortable sense of family unity. 2) They have learned to appreciate and understand each other a little better. 3) They have perhaps each transcended another rung in their perceptions of social interactions. The guests have each been somewhat frustrated, yet neither have they been losers. They were interested to know something further about the strange Bliss family - and they have achieved that. Also, they now better comprehend game playing, as a result of their new experience.

How often have I experienced this same sort of unity in my own family. When I get together especially with father or brothers, there is a sort of unique outlook on life, and manners of expression among ourselves that acknowledges that while we tend to see things differently than the world at large, yet our view is more real and worthy of being maintained in some degree. Perhaps because it contains a large element of resigned skepticism. Little things, such as inside jokes, and vague references to idiosyncracities of persons bring things immediately to focus in our minds, without having to go into lengthy explanations. The sense of communication with the familiar is exhilarating, as the mind moves rapidly from idea to idea, each in turn already heavily invested in rich emotional content. It is like the difference between slowly hiking from the national park (scenic wonder) to the mundane city grass patch; versus being able to fly and encompass each more rapidly, with less footage (and the more energy for capacity to notice, compare, and contrast.)

Yet, in all, while it is occasionally enjoyable and exhilarating to return to the homestead, the space there is limited and the outlook confining. Its element of skepticism is worthy, but the conversation tends to be too generalized and vague; and its participants too remote from an analytic rigor of specific details. It is as though those perched there (temporarily) regard themselves as arrived, their only aim being, a rigorous abandonment of any willingness to change any opinion - account of the ever present certainty of just cause for skepticism. For skepticism is but the first courageous step toward transcendence.

RGB
4/2/1984
Hobbs, NM

Hospital Politics
by R.G. Brasseur

Since I arrived in Lea County in January 1981, an additional thirty plus doctors have arrived, pushing the number of physicians of the county up to an unprecedented sixty-two in number. We then had four delegates to the state convention of the New Mexico Medical Association.

Starting at about the time that I arrived, the hospital (Lea Regional - owned and managed by Hospital Corporation of America) initiated a recruitment plan or bringing in more physicians to the area. They let it be known that it was their idea that bringing in more physicians would increase and maintain the hospital census. They further alleged that more physicians were definitely needed in the area. They ran some surveys (so they said) and correlated it with some nationwide data to back up their dubious claims of need for additional physicians. A large hospital chain such as this undoubtedly has a large propaganda staff of professional visionaries and self-serving strategies that can instantly supply the bogus concept with dubious data to support whatever plan and direction they wish to explore economically in the health field.

The Hospital corporation of America is a big business corporation funded by the invested dollar from the profits and savings of individual citizens and of retirement funds. Additionally, they have funds for investment from the yearly profits of the corporation. The more dollars that they control for investment in their field of expertise, the greater their political and economic power. They have no intention of limiting their growth (or influential political power). They plan to grow by a certain incremental percentage yearly. Thus, the men of business and administration within their organization enlarge the pyramidal base of their organization and their own individual power and income progressively each year when things go well. Besides the income, they enjoy the game - now that they have power, equipment, and leverage. Like football, it is a rough sport for the small boys without experience or equipment. Yet those grown large and strong and well equipped with pads, helmet, and protective gear can have a capital and enjoyable experience of euphoria, calling upon their unity and experience in defeating the poor and disorganized fellows who happen naively upon the field as random late-comers. They have no compunction about crippling or destroying the young and innocent. For that, after all, is the way the game is played.

On the other hand, the hospital does have a local board of directors to whom the hospital administration must justify its plans for growth in order to keep those plans in tune with the best interests of the community. And to continue to have the cooperation of the community. The local directors, of course, are impressed by the administrator's array of favorable statistics and correlations, believing vaguely that such diverse and esoteric facts are proof; and that the correlations are inevitably valid. The board members are local egotists, flattered by the professional hospital administrator into believing that their own local financial success is something other than mere chance and inherited wealth. Some are not even well off, but as minority people, imagine themselves to be enlightened and progressive minority leaders. They all nod knowingly and agreeably to the 'progressive' agenda and flattery. One might almost imagine they could see truth in those carefully crafted statistical 'facts and correlations'.

They are further mislead on other matters and implications of the HCA wizard. Hinting that the local doctors are greedy and perhaps overly ambitious. That they charge too much too; and that the competition will perhaps bring down medical expenses for employees and families. The local vested interests have an eye for business too, and they are easily convinced of what they want to believe. For they know that the younger doctors are notoriously bad business men and that they will be big spenders on homes, autos, and furniture; on country clubs, and racquet-ball clubs; on flying machines and commercial tips. That the spending of the overly many young doctors may have to be on a credit basis, doesn't much bother the local business men; for the doctors learn fast and though they leave here disillusioned within a year or two like dogs with their tails between their legs; yet, they will eventually make an economic recovery and be able to pay off their local indebtedness along with the big carrying charges thereof. They will sell off their big houses at a loss. Each may perhaps be expected to leave here, having spent and lost an average of perhaps $100,000.00 dollars. All and all, a nice little piece of business for the community.

Mr. McDonnell says that HCA has cleverly sold off the doctor's complex of offices that surround the hospital so that they are no longer interested especially in keeping the offices filled with doctors. By this time, the HCA has undoubtedly lost a little chunk of investor's money in income guarantees and have therefore abruptly turned off their recruitment policy, just as initially they switched them on abruptly. Dr Hood says they now want him to sign a permanent lease, rather than the original month by month agreement. He says he won't do so, especially now that they have pulled out the lab and X-ray facility. For he can as easily (and perhaps more practically) move his practice down close to town.

The first physician to come out here under the auspices of the hospital was Barney Bloor; then Dr. Laws. Then, a whole wave of physicians broke upon the new beachhead. Now that tide is ebbing away. I count 17 physicians that have left the area since I arrived. I know for certain of another 6 that will be gone within 3 months. By the first of the year, perhaps, another three or four. I am sure a couple more will leave next summer.

Recall now, that there is and has been a glut of physicians upon the market, and that that distortion will continue to enlarge. Perhaps the credibility of the HCA (in assuring physicians that they can do well, here) has become tarnished. Still, a little time for lapse of memory; and a renewed policy of enlistment and salary guarantee would certainly again bring a new flood tide of physicians to the shores of Lea County.

Opportunities come and persist for only a limited duration. They then pass, and perhaps recur quietly at a later time. Our economic well being as individuals nor as a group of physicians is in any way assured. The uninterruptedness of ever new rules continues to shift and change, requiring of one a constant will to perceive without which the unaided will to live is a null entity. Before the recent (now receding) flood tide of physicians inundated the area, NVMC (clinic with which I was associated) might, in retrospect, have been well advised to staff their clinic with units of earning power (physicians). The hospital policy has suddenly switched off their recruitment along with the amenities that nourished those recruits under artificial circumstance. The door of opportunity again is open to NVMC to replenish their loss of physicians. We might do well to enlarge our physician staff beyond what might have been considered prudent in past time. Thus we can take up some of the slack from physicians leaving the area and protect our group against attrition in the next drought brought about by a new reversal of policy.

RGB
7/22/84

VISIT TO ABO - 1983

By R. Garner Brasseur
7/12/83

We visited the old mission of Abo near Mountainair, New Mexico. Abo was established in early 1600's by the Spanish Conquistadores who came in the area already heavily populated with Native American Indians. They brought with them the Franciscan Priests. The soldiers conquered and subjected the Indians. The priests followed with peaceful apology and offered their condolences benevolently. In many cases, the novelty of the foreigners, with a show of arms and interesting goods of trade was enough to induce the natives to accept the entourage as guests and offer them hospitality and information.

The soldiers were commissioned to defend the priests, and support the establishment of mission colonies. Ultimately, the mission had the responsibility to support the soldiers. Common cause between the priest and the soldiers.

The priests paraded their devotion and peaceful demeanor. They were compassionate in forgiveness, and ever ready in dispensing absolution and the sign of the cross to soldier and native alike. The soldiers made great show in subjugating themselves reverently to the invisible authority of the priest. No doubt the native noticed this and in some instances found even that the priest intervened on behalf of the native in this or that just cause; and chastised the soldier with reprimand and harshly pious looks. The priests treated native and soldier alike with prayer and primitive medicinals in time of illness. They were gentle with women and children. That the priests did not openly solicit sexual favors from native women, while the soldiers to the mission contract were violent and demanding undoubtedly also predisposed the priest to position of both esteem and authority in the eyes of the native.

No doubt there was war within the individual native family units, even though that was not easily or soon recognized by those involved. The women enjoyed the novelty and chivalry of the civilized priests who took the time to give them attention and who appeared so concerned for their physical and spiritual welfare.

Reasonably intelligent beings easily perceive exploitation. The native peoples were intelligent and in many respects had a civilization of a higher quality than that of the Spaniards. Technologically and in armaments, the Indians were greatly disadvantage. The priests of the mission acknowledged that the native Indians within a tribal setting had lived together in peace and equality, though intermittently in contest with surrounding tribes. None within a tribe exercised authority over another in everyday matters, and no one seemed subject to the will of another. There was some small amount to slavery, however. And disharmony between tribes seems to have been a part of the Indian way of life in general; and we might presume that the pressure for tribal territory containing the food and wild game might require such a thing. And in time of drought, they were undoubtedly reduced to desperation in attempts to survive. Raiding parties may have been the last desperate measure in such times, though it had a tendency to gradually become a way of life. Remembrance of those desperate struggles undoubtedly left them with long enduring animosities between the tribes. These abide, at least vaguely, even in good times when tensions were greatly eased. Nor must we believe that all those within a tribe loved one another. Whatever government the natives had, it seems to have been effective in minimalizing any outward display of personal animosities and jealousies between tribal members. Those who disliked one another presumably merely avoided or ignored each other, or failed to display otherwise common mannerisms of respect for one another.

The men of the tribe, experienced in warfare and other realities of life, soon undoubtedly (if not immediately) recognized that the Spaniards meant them no good. The complicating factor of the priests confused the natives and made it difficult to recognize the obscure nature and form of the threat that they posed.

The progressive demands of the soldiers upon the natives for hospitality and the unrelenting pressure of the priests for the conversion to 'the true religion' to replace their natural religion soon caused the enforced and prolonged hospitality to wear thin. Rules and the enforcement thereof became progressively more necessary for protecting against the natives. The soldier must display ever more force and the priest, more covert coercion.

The war within the family grew, for the Indian men could sense the subtle assault against their religion, against their way of life, against their land, against their hospitality, and against their stature as men in the eyes of the women and children. Between the Spaniard (both priest and soldier) and the Indian braves, the tension mounted. Yet, the Indian women and children were swept up into this new thing represented by the Spanish.

The women and children of the tribe, first a few, then ever more were aiding and abetting the influence of apparently perplexing traits of the priest and the unexpected or unbelievable power he wielded against the technology of Spanish warrior. The priest had giant visions of an enormous structure of worship. The women and children helped him to realize that dream, with their hours of labor and supply of materials. As the enormous structures slowly materialized, so did their enthusiasm for they hardly themselves believed that they could accomplish such a task. Perhaps it was a miracle as the priest insisted repeatedly. If it were a miracle (of their own hands) perhaps the god of the priest was a more powerful deity than their own.

With but few exceptions, the men of the tribe cherished no such delusions. They could see what was happening to their authority and prerogatives. They saw the tensions mounting in their homes. They saw delusions growing in the minds of their own people. They became progressively disenchanted with the newcomers; and later, hostile. These hostilities began to show and brought them into open individual conflict with the Spanish. They did not fare well in these. Small guerilla tactics brought them ugly and massive reprisal.

The men had no hand in the building of the church for they could see the trouble it was to bring within their territory. They saw their power and prestige being expropriated. Eventually, years later, their loss and recognition of the slowly encroaching outside force was sufficient, that the Indian tribes eventually overcame their intertribal disunity to throw off the Spanish yoke. But that unity between tribes was insufficient to be maintained and the Spanish eventually re-conquered the tribes and the land, accepting those Indians who submitted voluntarily(?) to the priest and defeating those who would not. The Indian religion has not though, been purged from the Indian; and the church has been obliged to tolerate some Indian practices and customs. The church has found it useful - to accept some Indian saints and holidays. The great mission period wherein the church ruled the people as vassals; and owned the land; and demanded labor, love, and money eventually declined. The new system was a Spanish Colonial System administered by regents and governors through the military. The church however, remained; and Catholicism remained the official Spanish religion.

Why, in the mission of Abo was there found along side the mission church, a large kiva? Quien sabe? Why do many Indians still worship their ancient gods? Do they more seriously honor the new imported deity? Quien sabe?

RGB

DEATH OF A MIMOSA

by R. Garner Brasseur

The circadians are gregarious insects, occupying together a single tree, where they can vocalize in a deafening unison. What they lack in quality of music, they redeem in sheer volume. And the quality is amiss by a great deal.

In our front yard stood a large mimosa tree - related to the Mesquite Bush, so common in these parts. That tree was heavily populated by the cicadas in the summers of 1982-1983. A low rose bush with a heavy trunk stood beneath the rain-drip shadow of the mimosa. That rose bush partly died - the part nearest the mimosa - in 1982; then died completely in 1983.

That rose bush did not die a natural death, as I can now perceive in retrospect. It was murdered - and pointlessly - as that death in no way benefited its killers. Here, I gather, is how it came about. The offspring of the cicadas hatch upon the branches of the large tree and burrow down into it, in order to reach the tender roots, where they attach themselves to feed on the tender sap rising from the roots. I wondered as I began to puzzle this out, how it was that these plant nymph parasites were clever enough to attach themselves at the roots of the rose bush, causing its corresponding near branches to die without yet harming the tree of the home of their ancestors. Clever creatures! The following summer of 1984, the nymphs had to dig a bit further to find living succulent rose bush roots - and the remainder of the rose bush thereafter died. Still, there stood the tree, seemingly unharmed. Clever creatures, those nymphs.

I was surprised in the spring of 1985 to notice that the mimosa was showing no evidence of life. And yet, I never can adjust my thinking to the time scale of plants, so that it took me a few weeks to consciously perceive that the tree had actually died, and that it wasn't about to be resurrected. The cicada nymphs were not as circumspect as I had imagined. Those that reach adulthood in 1985, had to find some other homestead to repair to, than that of their immediate ancestors.

As the interrelatedness of all of these strange things was slow in dawning upon my full awareness - the noisy choruses; the hemiplegia of the rose bush; and its complete death a year later; followed by the death of my beloved shade tree. Jauhn stopped by for a visit in his battered old Luv pickup truck. And during his stay, he removed the corpse of the mimosa. He planted in its place, an oak leafed volunteer which had poorly situated itself in the back yard the season past. I see that now, after three weeks, it is starting to put forth a few sprigs of green new leaf. But it will be years before it gives me the shade provided by the mimosa - it's predecessor. And henceforth, I shan't put up with any rowdy choruses from any residents of its branches.

RGB
7/29/85

Preying Mantis

Only since having lived in the southern USA (in the past 3½ years) have I chanced to become aware of the preying mantis. I am sure it lives in the northern climates too, though probably they become larger in the south. Consulting now my small pocket guide on insects, I see that the insect is supposed to have been imported to this country from Europe and from China, and that its range is indeed in the south - and spreading - in this country.

I took particular notice of one last year, late at night. I was at the kitchen sink and looked out the window. A mantis was perched on the edge of the screen window, with his head twisted towards me, so as to observe better (perhaps) what sort of thing goes on in one of the dwellings of Homo sapiens.

And I have been vaguely aware previously, that the mantis doesn't flinch easily. He has an unshakeable courage or philosophic disinterestedness concerning threats of danger to himself. Two of them were perched upon the front door the other evening as Miette, coming home about 9:00 PM, shrieked and declined to pass the threshold into the house, because of their refusal to give her passage.

The little creatures are harmless, but since that fact had no effect on Miette's fears, I undertook to dislodge and remove them aside for her. Using a stiff magazine, I tried to shovel them aside. My efforts did not excite them or cause them so much as to move a limb. Once by force dislodged from their grip on the carpeted door stoop, and alighted nearby, they simply dug in their heals once more and remained calm observant and immobile.

The rotatable head, the sticklike form, and the upheld arms make it easily recognizable as a unique species. Yet its studiousness and observing ways; and its quiet resolve even in the face of danger and death, are what makes it truly what it is - the mysterious preying mantis.

RGB
9/13/84

To Tina
(in 2010)

Through the years, I have written a lot of essays, letters, and (in more recent years) quite a few of the more brief e-mails. Written also, a couple of books and a couple of what have become voluminous genealogy manuscripts. And in return I have received a modest amount of correspondence. As I have been unemployed and in desperate economic straits from time to time in the course of this life, I have had a lot of time to reflect and agonize over all sorts of real and imaginary problems. There seems a natural tendency for the themes of one's thought to sort of 'short-circuit' and become sort of endless loops (like Mobius strips) leading to nowhere; and destitute of any useful or interesting conclusions or ideas - just the sort of thing that is wont to progress to sleepless nights, for example. To avoid the futility and needless dissipation of my time and energy, I make an effort to stay in touch with my many relatives and a few friends. A large part of that effort keeps me preoccupied with various form of writing. It is hard work, and I always find myself reticent to make each new beginning - account of my natural laziness. But it feels so good thus to have thoughtfully dealt with and put behind me each burning deed and thought, that it seems well worth the time and effort it costs me. Wrapped in pleasing delusions, I then can sink deeply into the arms of morpheus - and cease to be. And having slept well, arise rested and renewed. Free of yesterday's worrisome theme, and ready to face the inevitable dilemmas of the every new day.

MEN ARE JUST HAPPIER PEOPLE

from Tina

Men Are Just Happier People - what do you expect from such simple creatures? Your last name stays put. The garage is all yours. Wedding plans take care of themselves. Chocolate is just another snack. You can be President. You can never be pregnant. You can wear a white T-shirt to a water park. You can wear NO shirt to a water park. Car mechanics tell you the truth. The world is your urinal. You never have to drive to another gas station restroom because this one is just too icky. You don't have to stop and think of which way to turn a nut on a bolt. Same work, more pay. Wrinkles add character. Wedding dress - $5000. Tux rental - $100. People never stare at your chest when you're talking to them. The occasional well-rendered belch is practically expected. New shoes don't cut, blister, or mangle your feet. One mood all the time.

Phone conversations are over in 30 seconds flat. You know stuff about tanks. A five-day vacation requires only one suitcase. You can open all your own jars. You get extra credit for the slightest act of thoughtfulness. If someone forgets to invite you, he or she can still be your friend.

Your underwear is $8.95 for a three-pack. Three pairs of shoes are more than enough. You almost never have strap problems in public. You are unable to see wrinkles in your clothes. Everything on your face stays its original color. The same hairstyle lasts for years, maybe decades. You only have to shave your face and neck.

You can play with toys all your life. Your belly usually hides your big hips. One wallet and one pair of shoes - one color for all seasons. You can wear shorts no matter how your legs look. You can "do" your nails with a pocket knife. You have freedom of choice concerning growing a mustache. You can do Christmas shopping for 25 relatives on December 24 in 25 minutes.

No wonder men are happier.

From Tina
About 2005?
RGB

A SUMMARY CONCERNING: "A STUDIED IMPRESSION" of That Which Is"

The writer has come to view the overt life as a struggle and a journey - not unlike that of Odysseys - while his personal covert avocation has come to be a quest for the answers to the riddles of being and reality even while struggling with the necessity of full time employment to support the biological imperatives of one's mere mortal nature. That quest is a race against time; and a goal towards which civilization as a whole seems also unconsciously destined. In the slow halting advance of civilization, some few great men have paved the way for his own hope - of some measure of success in that personal quest by the force of their ideas and the shaping influence of the energy of their lives. For civilization - having no mind nor perception of its own - is dependent upon the minds and perceptions that we mere mortals possess; and which we edge to ever greater incisiveness.

While the lives of the millions are consumed in life's fundamental imperatives and in the sharing of the plentitude of common agony that is the universal lot of mankind, yet through some strange twist, fate has decreed for (some fortunate few) some little excess of free time and good health to dabble now and then into metaphysics and to reflect upon the causes of the residual superstition and ignorance in which we are all yet immersed. The major negative and counterproductive aspects of man's being first exposed; one might next take note of man's positive potential for individual personal enlightenment - and a limited potential for the comprehension of the nature of reality. By dint of persistent effort and hard work, each and any mortal can acquire language, personal skills, and the tools necessary to moderate some of the harsher aspects of his life, advance his own civilization and well being, and begin to divine and advance his own purpose and objectives of life.

The book is an accounting of the many questions and notions with which the author has wrestled in trying to comprehend the reality in which mere mortal man is embedded on this journey of life into which each is thrust. What are the causes for the clogging of man's channels of thought and for the obstruction to open, informed, and honest conversation that only slowly abates, down through the ages? It becomes obvious that superstitions are deeply imbedded indeed; and encouraged to remain so by the private agendas of organizations and individuals to their own benefit. Valid information widely available and unopposed by superstition ought have some power to expedite the understanding and to uplift the condition of mortality. But our species is only just beginning to acquire some valid information, even while private agendas have cause to oppose it by the encouragement of misinformation.

One may elucidate some of the great ideas that have facilitated evolution towards a more just society of individual freedom and personal rights, and towards an economy that provides some reasonable standard of living to all who are willing to behave with civil decency towards one another. Ideas such as humanistic concern and understanding, and reciprocity of civil decency. Men and societies of men can be beneficially uplifted by acquaintance with such notions as: The Golden Rule, the Silver Rule, the Iron Rule, and a dedication to an ideal of truth that is compatible with man's obligation to be intelligent, and made to realize the moral value of reality. One might advocate that men are well served to be schooled in the scientific method, instructed in natural history and evolution, and made fully aware of the obvious inevitability of human sexuality and genetic imperatives. And well informed that there is cause aplenty for skepticism concerning historical texts, and human testimony.

With hope and a hearty skepticism concerning man's superstitions; the limits to the cryptic information of myths (and in lieu of the contradictions of our chaotic world, schizophrenic society, and contradictory information) one might put forth his honest effort to reason and to reflect upon the reality of this world and of his being; and to give honest purpose to his own life by way of gratitude for the great thoughts, ideas, and actions of noble men who have paved the way for that possibility to each person. And in the end, an author might hope that this book be his testimony concerning the nature of reality - a testimony that must reflect his honest views, arrived upon by dint of honest and wide study of many resources, and tempered by a practiced and informed power of reason, based on valid sources and information . . . all of which is in conformity with a first-hand broad personal experience of a long life well supplied with many personal interests. And often humbled by personal tragedy, failure, grief, and disappointment.

R. Garner Brasseur, MD
14 December 2005

WILEY SPRINGS REST AREA

R. Garner Brasseur
January 1986

Broke again, and unemployed. The days are mine to spend as I will. But they are troubled days, for I am aware that I must be up and doing. Would that I had a calmer disposition - one that might bid me take my ease by the quiet waters of Babylon, without the requirement of expended effort and subsequent fatigue; and without the anguish of a burdened psyche. But I have not yet found a lead to that pathway of wisdom. And so, my wandering continues as I pile mistake upon error each day, always in a hurry to make up time that I have lost. To work each day with fixed mundane routine is far easier, for such a day's production in dollars accounts to one the work and effort that assure me I have earned my night of quiet rest. My justified soul then may rest upon those laurels. The task of seeking the productive employment, however, does not in itself produce the where-with-all upon which to sustain the physical reality of one's being. Each failed day so spent increases incrementally the weight of tomorrow's failure.

The job search began in earnest on 6 January, 1986, as I took my leave from the unearned and unwanted repose of home, gathering my clothes and a few boxes of such useful gear as I might need as I head to California in search of a job. I loaded my gear into my Toyota Pickup camper shell of 1979 vintage. The pickup is an unwashed red of somewhat faded color, with scattered dents and chipped glass light-fixtures and cracked windshield. It looked as rough in its unadorned features, as I felt in my condition of jobless disrepair. I headed westward along the southern desert of New Mexico, into the even more forbidding desert of southwestern Texas, towards El Paso - a place new to my experience. The Toyota Pickup is a thing of inspiration in its obedient and responsive deportment - a tribute to the engineering genius of mankind. Besides its dependability, it is enduring and economical. And the system of well-maintained roadways in this land of subtle hostility suggests again the genius of that same creator. The marvels of the desert and its expansive naked beauty, bespeak another system, of which man himself is but a fragment of the organizing laws of nature.

On the outskirts of El Paso, one can see the Rio Grande riverbed. On the other side of the stream is the relative squalor of lean-to shanties and cardboard huts upon an unimproved landscape, bespeaking the relative economic disparity between the effectiveness of the governments of Mexico and the United States. Driving westward into the wind, across New Mexico between Los Cruses and Lordsburg, I could see - as though upon a cross-sectional view - the heavy moisture-laden clouds to the north, piling up against the western slopes of several mountain cordilleras a hundred miles distant. There they were generating the first snowstorm of the new year. A couple of hours before sunset I passed into southern Arizona. There was no rain nor snow there, but a huge dust-cloud filled the air with haze, and made the westerly sun invisible, as the winds whipped the dusts from the dry desert floor. The Southern Pacific Railroad runs alongside Highway 10, and scattered here and there are the remains of the old railroad locomotive watering towers, as well as the intermittent small and medium sized towns that were spawned into existence by the coming of the railroad, in the days of its original construction. The bright steel rails are alive with the traffic of the numerous trains making this desert passage. A couple of the trains are in sidings, awaiting the arrival and passage of some oncoming train whooping along on the main line. They must all take to the sidings at the approach of Amtrack's passenger train, which sweeps along at its steady unobstructed westward pace. As it passes, the multi-unit freight locomotives begin to promptly snake their strings of cars back out onto the main-line.

I stopped south of Tucson for gas in the early evening, and thought I might have a bite to eat at the same time; but the adjoining café seemed nearly full; implying the probability of a long wait - so I continued on westward. The Tucson suburb was all strung out for miles in this wide flat geographical corridor through the otherwise barren landscape. Tucson seems on the verge of becoming continuous with Phoenix, to the north and west, but I turned westward on Highway 8, near Casa Grande, before I got as far as Phoenix. There I was almost immediately back into the desert darkness, and surrounded by the multitude of armed saguaro cacti that dominate these wastelands. Late in the night I saw a large green fireball meteor flash low through the darkness, and burn out far to my left, about ten miles distant. I had seen one just like it a week or two earlier, as I was driving westward on a dark night in western Arkansas. And my mind was brought to a recollection of a similar but much more spectacular fireball that blazed silently a thousand feet over my head in the wee hours of the morning some ten years earlier as I drove alone through the Willamette Valley. How curious I am to know more about the specifics of these phenomena, but they were mere passing ephemera. Who besides myself - if any - were apt even to have caught sight of them. They were too remote, too high, too large, and traveled too fast and far to have any such explanation as mere fireworks display.

I made my first passage through Yuma, Arizona later that evening. There I crossed the Colorado River onto the mountainous side of the river and began my ascent from the flat lowland, into the high desert. Within a few miles I was stopped at the agricultural inspection station. I feared they might confiscate my several delicious grapefruit. They did harbor the unwanted "scale fungus", but as they had been produced in California, I was allowed to keep them. Within about ten miles I was past the Algodones Sand Dunes area and flat out onto the floor of the heavily cultivated Imperial Valley, the great produce-gardening area of year around importance since the early part of this twentieth century. In a couple of places, they were working in these fields by night. The area is supplied with irrigation waters from the Colorado River, for it is otherwise far too arid to be fertile. In 1905, one of the irrigation canals disintegrated under the pressure of floods on the Colorado River. In consequence, a huge inland body of water was formed - The Salton Sea - before the flooding was finally checked, two years later. That whole valley, east of the San Jacinto Mountains, is somewhat below sea-level. I stopped for the night at El Centro to stay at an older motel that cost me $17.00. The town itself is situated on dead-level flat ground. There is a tendency for dust and silt to blow about the streets as it is blown in from the deserts, and fallen to the streets from the muddy wheels of farming vehicles, fresh from the irrigated mud of the fields - as they carry produce to the local depots; and out of the area.

I arose in the morning to the enchanting spectacle of naked and towering mountains that encircle the area. It was a mild and clear day. As

I drove westward to ascend into the San Jacinto Mountains, gusts of wind began to arise. Dropping down on the western side, toward San Diego, across the deep and spectacular canyons, the gusting winds grew into a rage. Now and then a mighty blast would sway the pickup, or momentarily retard its progress. A bit of litter and a few tumbleweed were moving about in response to those blasts of wind. A tumbleweed rolled part way up the road-cut, at a steep incline; then, when suddenly released from the waning blast, it rolled down into the bar-pit and settled there, as the veering flaw vented its rage in another direction. Before mid-day, I escaped the wrath of these mounting Santa Ana Winds, as I winded my way down into the lower body of a more tranquil air mass that encased the verdant Spanish architectural flavors which grace the San Diego area.

Later that day, those gusts of Santa Ana Wind reportedly tipped over a truck in one of the passes - a truck that was standing still at the roadside. Another truck, an eighteen-wheeler, was bodily lifted over the rail of a concrete bridge, and dumped casually into the ravine below. The Santa Ann Winds are said to be caused by a high pressure area over Colorado, causing the clockwise flow of air outwards, from its center. Those masses of air are compressed and increased in velocity as they come through the mountain passes of the rugged San Jacinto Mountains. I was fortunate that day, to have gotten an early start.

I drove onwards to Long Beach, and felt immediately more or less lost, once away from the one-dimensional entity of a numbered freeway. Here, in a strange city, there are hundreds of ways to get oneself lost. But I found the address I was seeking, after stopping to inquire brief directions from a man who spoke but very little English. Departing later that day from a meeting with Dr. H__, I got lost several times before finding the work address of a former grade-school and high-school classmate of mine, Lynn Fitz. But, he no longer worked there, and I could not find his name in the telephone directory. I had not seen him since graduation from high school, thirty-three years previously. I took a motel room on the Long Beach Boulevard, and had supper at a cafeteria. Returning to the motel, I felt constrained to empty out all the contents of the pickup, as I began to sense the circumstance of this slightly sleazy area. I remained in Long Beach the following two days, to use the public library facilities, and from there to search out employment leads by telephone. The library was large and beautiful, but did not have a section devoted to aiding the search of the unemployed to locate job opportunities. On my second night there, I found a motel room near the beach, in which I felt more at ease.

For a long while, the idea of attending Starr-King Seminary in Berkeley, California had been at the back of my mind, and slowly maturing into a plan. The medical climate of Ophthalmology in this country has so much changed in recent years that I am well advised to consider a change of occupation. I thought I might yet work a few years in some well-paying medical job to stabilize my economic situation, while preparing for a new profession. But the possibility of obtaining that income, seemed now to be fading faster than I would have supposed. Nevertheless, on the second day of my library stay in Long Beach, I searched out the Starr-King Seminary Catalogue of microfilm. Then I called the office of the president of Starr-King to speak with his secretary, Mrs. Bishop. She arranged for me an interview with the president himself, for 11:00 AM, the following morning. I was elated at the possibilities that seemed to lie in this new prospect.

I departed the Long Beach Library about 4:00 PM, en route to Berkeley, via Highway 5 North. I was disgusted with myself, not to have departed an hour earlier; for the Los Angeles traffic soon began to thicken, and I had never experienced traffic as unpromisingly slow as what I was now beginning to encounter. Besides being slow, it was difficult, and I lost thirty minutes when I had to stop for gasoline in passing along 'the grapevine'.

As I scooted past Ft. Tejon and into the San Joachin Valley, I found myself submersed into a heavy fog. And I realized, too, that I was short of time, since I now discovered the distance to be about three-hundred-fifty miles - some seventy-five or a hundred miles further than my original vague supposition. I sped along, despite the fog, knowing that it was hazardous, and that I was in the hands of blind fate. I tried for the most part, to follow the red tail-lights of speedsters or truckers that passed me by. But I would generally lose them suddenly, as when the fog might thicken suddenly. Then, I sometimes increased my speed to bring me back into visual contact with those lost tail-lights. That failing, I would sometime speed on alone, in blind and senseless faith. I judged that it seemed best to use the faster left-hand lane. Other drivers seemed to have the same idea, but by no means all of them. That fog did not lift until I reached the mountain summit near Livermore, in the bay area. Meanwhile, my plan to stop off at some small town to the east and south of the bay area fell into ruins in the heavy fog. None of the three towns I tried had any motel, and thus I wasted another forty-five minutes.

I took a motel room in Livermore, hungry from having had no meal in the past twenty-four hours. No café was nearby, so I settled merely for a candy-bar, before I showered and lately turned to bed. I arose at nine in the morning, and hurriedly departed, not knowing the actual remaining distance to Berkeley, the traffic conditions, nor the probability of becoming lost upon some devious pathway - in a territory new to me. The roads proved to be well marked, however, and I arrived easily in Berkeley within the hour. I stopped there for gas, and a helpful young service station attendant directed me to the area I was seeking. From the microfilmed catalog in Long Beach, I had copied out a more detailed map of this particular small area of my interest, and I easily found the Starr-King School, and parked nearby. Having not had a meal for over thirty-six hours, and with now an hour to spare before my interview, I elected to have a breakfast of eggs and toast. I was fearful though, that the meal might excite a speedy gastro-colic reflex at the very hour of my scheduled interview. I chanced it, never-the-less. Awaiting the preparation of my food, I noticed the clock on the wall, which registered a full thirty minutes ahead of my own watch. The attendant assured me that it was indeed the correct time. I had but thirty minutes to eat and make that appointment time.

Bolting down my meal, I departed in a hurry. My little hand-copied map guided me directly to the administration building of Starr-King Seminary - I was ten minutes early. Mrs. Bishop pointed out to me the office of Dr. Gordon McKeeman, and bid me knock to gain admission. The president was quite cordial as we began our acquaintance. We sat within five feet of each other in a matching pair of chairs, as though co-equals - like knights at the round-table of King Arthur's Court. The night before, I had taken thirty minutes briefly to outline the history of my life, the circumstances that now brought me here, and the purpose for which I now hoped to gain his approval. I had planned to refer to that outline, to keep my train of thought intact, but suddenly, eyeball to eyeball, as we were, that seemed inappropriate. I left the outline untouched, in my coat-pocket. My memory of the act of composition of those notes was itself sufficient. In the space of about forty-five minutes, I had said what I intended. Dr. McKeeman watched me and listened. Upon completing my harangue, I put to him the specific questions, regarding which, I wished his opinion and advice. And he obliged me. Might I be a candidate for admission to Star-King? Might I take the preparatory courses such as language requirements, as home-study extension courses? Might I extend the course-work to an extra year, so as to enable me to work part-time while attending seminary?

To my surprise, the average age of the students in seminary is somewhat above the age of forty, the oldest being a little above sixty years of age. They prefer the somewhat older candidates, such as might have a varied and fuller experience of the world. Some of the candidates do stretch out the coursework over a period of four years, rather than the customary three years. The training leads one into further options, in addition to that of the ministry; and those options are determined by the student himself, during the course of his training. Those other options are things such as group therapy sessions, writing, teaching, etc. At just about noon he led me back to the reception office to speak with Mrs. Bishop, in order to obtain appropriate information and directions concerning admission application procedure and forms. And I then departed the campus.

I walked about in that area - a small business district - to get the feel of its charm, there upon a hillside adjacent to the north edge of the Berkeley Campus. I then drove across the Oakland Bay Bridge, into San Francisco, to seek out the office of the American Academy of Ophthalmology. Here I hoped to obtain a listing of available job openings. Map in hand, I did locate the correct address with only moderate difficulty. It was a handsome building, both inside and out, but it was empty - and there was no forwarding address to be found upon the premises. The Academy meets in San Francisco only every second or third year. It would appear that they only furnish up handsomely for those specific occasions; and that they must then promptly remove to some hole-in-the-wall location to save expenses, immediately after each intermittent event. I called their phone number, and they suggested I complete the transaction by mail, as they didn't usually handle such matters directly in the office. It seemed a stupid thing to me, but I didn't trouble myself to either say nor imply that.

It was after 3:00 PM., and I was anxious to get out of San Francisco ahead of the traffic rush. I departed on Highway 101 south to Santa Clara. There I got lost trying to locate Main Street in what I knew would be the old section of town. But the old town is small, and is enveloped to near obscurity by the surrounding giant structures of the Silicone Valley production plants. Nor was the sun visible through the clouds to aid my sense of direction. And my prejudice - that South 101 actually ran south - added to my confusion once I was off of the one-dimensional freeway, and once more involved with the multiplicity of ways of being lost in an unfamiliar city. I was soon reduced to the necessity of asking directions.

There seemed to me to be reason for doubt, concerning these directions, but I stayed with them despite my doubt, and did thereby finally locate El Camino Real, which appears to transect the very heart of all of these west bay cities at the core of their older central sections of town. But Main Street of Santa Clara quite surprised me, for there were not but few business offices or establishments upon it. El Camino Real has always been a more attractive location for business - I supposed - due to its long history and always constant flow of traffic along its long established thoroughfare. It was originally developed to connect the twenty-three mission sites that extend from Baja California, up to the San Francisco Bay area.

I followed the house numbers as I drove along Main Street, looking for Pierre's address. Just as I approached his number, the street appeared as though it were apt to end, and I dreaded the possibility of having to relocate the street's extension beyond the upcoming railroad tracks and industrial complex. Mercifully, however, Main Street took a ninety degree left turn, and continued, in disregard for what seems logical. In this extension area, each large housing complex - each with perhaps forty to fifty families - had a separate and conjoint street number shared between its apartments. And so, I drove a very long way to cover the span of those few numbers that finally took me to Pierre's address (the final number on that street), where it abutted upon a ramp embankment that led to an overpass of the tracks. Pierre, Rochelle, with baby Jessica - now six months of age - lived in a second-story one-bedroom apartment flat whose patio porch appeared to be almost level with the traffic of the ramp at that locus. Still, one hears there, but little of the traffic noise. I talked a while with Rochelle and cooed a bit at the baby before Pierre arrived - within a few minutes of my arrival there at about 5:00 PM.

Pierre and Rochelle are on a fast of a week or ten days, subsequent to what they supposed was a fete of overeating, during the Christmas and New year Holiday, when they were at our home in Hobbs, New Mexico. Pierre was tired from the combined effect of the hunger fast, and that day's twelve hour work-shift. Later, about 8:00 PM, I drove out alone on el Camino Real to enjoy a taco ensalada for my evening meal. It filled me with its potent flavors - and shortly thereafter, it also purged me. Thus did I receive a double value for my money. When I returned to their apartment, we talked a while. They were discomforted about the sleeping arrangements. I assured them I would be most content to sleep upon cushions, upon the floor, and in my sleeping bag. And so it was - and I rested peacefully through the night.

The following morning I called to Rancho Mirage and arranged to meet with Dr. M__ on the following Thursday, thus leaving me free to spend the coming weekend with Pierre and family. They had planned to go to Berkeley, to shop the bookstores and it pleased me to join such an outing as that. They had never been in Berkeley previously, so my recent acquaintance with the area served us well. I found a few books that I couldn't resist among those amazing collections on Telegraph Street. I bought some bagels and cream-cheese, and we got back to the apartment at 8:00 PM.

The following day - Sunday - I arose about 9:30 AM. We drove out to a local flea-market of grand proportions, and spent the day there. There, they purchased some chairs, and we hauled them back to their apartment in the pickup. Monday morning we arose at 8:30 AM. Pierre biked off to work, and I drove again to Berkeley, to spend some time at the public library and to scout about the area for possible living quarters and work. I composed the required two-page letter of introduction of myself, to Starr-King Seminary, and had it typed - at three dollars per page - and then mailed it in. I stayed two nights at the same motel, on University Avenue, where it was clean and I felt secure in parking the pickup in its inner court. Contrary to my general custom, I watched a television show one of those nights. For they were playing "Apocalypse Now", a much talked about film; and I felt constrained to have seen and thought about the film. Its message concerned the American involvement in the Vietnam War. Its details, I am sure, were essentially true; as were the ironies and absurdities it offered one to ponder. The specific plot, I expect, was fiction.

Berkeley is continuous with Oakland to the south. Berkeley is pretty and quaint, but there are many old houses in various states of disrepair. Large remodeled houses and new apartment dormitories seem favorable to the needs of college students, and cater to their limited budgets. Though some of the facilities appear slightly seedy, they are also advantageous in that they are proximal to the campus. A good many young adults - presumably, students - hang about the streets. Not uncommonly, one of these can be seen at some busy street corner, to beg a dollar from some prospective passer-by. Contiguous with Berkeley to the north is Albany, which is neat and clean, and seems to me as though more hospitable for living, due to its lesser commotion and clutter from transients. As a place to live and work near to Berkeley, it more appeals to my taste.

In the afternoon of my third day in the Berkeley area, I drove on down to Santa Clara again, this time via Highway 17, on the east side of the bay. It seems to me to be about ten or fifteen miles shorter than the route through San Francisco. I had supper with Pierre and Rochelle that evening. The baby had learned to roll over by herself, and she cooed and smiled for me a long while. Pierre gave a long and eloquent speech on the subject of dealing with the government as a freeman, by breaking one's contractual arrangements with the various agencies of the government. A theme he seems to have acquired a few years ago, while residing and working for his uncle in Washington state. In our nation which is intended to be governed from the bottom up, his argument seems perhaps technically correct, but as a practical matter, that uncommon approach has been difficult to sustain and has largely been lost from the grip of the common man. The bureaucratic government truly is becoming ever more and autocratic, and legalistically troublesome. Perhaps such information as Pierre expounds, ought to be fed into the public school system, and taught. The latent power of those ideas might then be more effectively and efficiently released into action.

On Thursday morning I departed from Pierre's home in Santa Clara, for I had an evening appointment with Dr. M__ that day in Rancho Mirage - just west of Palm Springs - for shortly after 5:00 PM. But, unbeknown to me, I was destined to be troubled again, and precipitated into difficulties by a want of specific relevant detail of fact; and by circumstances of chance and fate. I thought I had allowed myself sufficient margin of time for error, such that I ought easily be able to meet with Dr. M__ at the appointed hour.

Leaving Pierre's home, I made the wrong turn at Santa Thomas and got lost briefly before retracing my steps, and heading south on Highway 101. From there, I took Route 52 over the San Luis Mountains, toward Highway 5. Then, my headlight switch began to chatter, and it became my suspicion that the headlights might no longer be functional. So I stopped at the visitor center at the top of the pass and confirmed that suspicion. Being unable to make this amateur repair, I quickly abandoned the attempt, in hope of reaching my destination before I were to require the use of the headlights this day. The visitor's center was situated above a huge man-made reservoir of water, whose now completed construction was only begun in 1962. It is part of a system that conveys water from the north end of California, all the way to the southern part of the state. Seventy-five percent of California's usable fresh water comes from the northern part of the state; whereas seventy-five percent of the state's requirement for that water, is in the southern part of the state. A curiously suspicious incongruity, suggesting that the laws of nature care not a whit for man's wishes as to supply and demand. The waters of this San Luis Reservoir are pumped up into it from the American River and the Shasta River systems of the north, whose natural outflow is into the San Francisco Bay, somewhat to the north of this location. As I approached the visitor's center and speculating as to the type of rock I was seeing in these mountain formations, I noticed some huge boulders that reminded me or those one sees along the ocean beaches of Oregon and Northern California. Inspecting them more closely, one can see that they indeed are of the same gender, and that they are also even barnacle encrusted - though perched here high atop the mountain range, and quite inland from the ocean. One begins to see how Darwin gradually acquired his speculative audacity. This uplifted formation too, at some time not geologically long past, seems likely to have been situated at the ocean shore-line.

I turned south onto Highway 5, toward Los Angles, and it began to dawn on me that in addition to the distance from here to L.A., I must also drive a long congested stretch of highway 10, eastward across Los Angles itself, and out onto the desert east of L.A. to reach Rancho Mirage - between Palm Springs and Indio. How far was that, after all? My estimate began to grow, the more I considered it. It turns out to be a very long way - an additional one hundred forty miles! I drove fast and steady, so that I was past the Grapevine, and westward onto Highway 210 by 3:30 PM. Then the traffic began to thicken and even clot occasionally. But it never quite halted or even steadily remained slow. I hurried onward at mostly sixty-five miles per hour. It was becoming obvious that not only would I <u>not</u> reach even Palm Springs by 5:00 PM, but that now I was in danger of the possibility of having to drive in the early darkness without the benefit of headlights. Fortunately, at least my parking-lights and tail-lights were functional. My wristwatch, though not of vital necessity, had stopped at 5:00 PM - as though, perhaps, an omen - to inform me of my utter rejection by the fates.

I stopped at a convenience store to phone Dr. M__, and inquire for specific local directions to his office. He was still seeing patients, and his nurse gave me the directions. In my urgency, I went off into the wrong directions and into the gathering darkness. After driving about three miles, I became certain of that, and headed back to where the lights of the city were concentrated in the darkening sky. I could hardly see the road now. The headlights of the oncoming traffic aggravated my visual handicap.

Arriving back at the convenience store, I took the only other alternative direction, and soon began to mingle with the flow of traffic, following the tail-lights of the cars ahead. In the darkness, I missed the street name of my turn-off point, and found no further tail-lights to lead me forth. And I now knew that my driving for this day was ended.

Right there, I found a post-office substation and a service-station. It was now 6:00 PM, and I parked the pickup there. I again called Dr. M__, who had just finished with his last patient. I told him my location at Veldt and Highway 111, and he came down to pick me up in his plush new van at 6:30 PM. He seemed to be about my age, and I had the impression that he was perched upon the verge of expressing his sympathy concerning my being broken down and transient upon the roadway of life in my weather-beaten old vehicle. He had lived and worked in this area for about sixteen years, and had only a month earlier moved into his new office facility, which included a new outpatient surgical facility. The place was so plush, and he seemed so modest a person, that I had the impression that he was out of place. He had taken his Ophthalmology training at Johns Hopkins, and had been in training with Dr. Gil, who was currently at Newport Beach, Florida, where he was said to then be doing a full one percent of all of the cataract surgery in the country! Like myself, Dr. M__ had three sons, even the youngest of which was now in college. I had called his office several times in the past few weeks, but he had been always running late, and had been too busy to talk with me. His nurse had been always cordial to me, as though she was personally aware that he was in need of some physician assistance in the running of his overly busy practice. Now, at 7:00 PM, he was casually showing me through his ultra-modern clinic and surgical facility. He introduced me to two attractive women that assist him. They too were genial, polite, and modest - and they were on their way out from this day's work.

We talked about the oversupply of Ophthalmologists in this country, and he too seems fully aware of that situation. He seemed reluctant to pry into my personal situation, and so I took it upon myself to roughly apprise him of my situation and current status. He gives me to believe that I might be the right sort of person to assist him with only the clinical end of his practice, if only I have grasped that - here, at least - that is the way it must be. His office and facility; his rules. He tells me that he shall speak with his accountant, concerning the financial aspect of that possibility; and then he will be in touch with me. So, to ease his mind, I say what he seems to be thinking: that we could try it for a few months, and discontinue if it seems not to be working out well.

Dr. M__ drove me back to my pickup and left me there with slight hesitance, as though he didn't feel quite right about leaving me alone in my broken down condition. I assured him that it would be a simple matter to get the headlight switch replaced in the morning. I then walked a couple of miles about the area in several different directions to see if there were not a nearby inexpensive motel to which I might readily repair for the night. There wasn't. I spoke to both of the two young service station attendants, who assured me it would be fine to park the pickup there at the service station until morning. Shortly thereafter, a young deputy sheriff came by and I told him of my problem, requesting him to pass the information on to the night shift, so that they wouldn't have to trouble themselves to investigate my transient status there in the night. And so I parked the pickup there at the service station, in a spot more remote from the traffic. I ate a bagel at 9:00 PM and then settled myself for the night on the cot and in my sleeping bag, in the camper shell of the pickup. I spent there a comfortable night.

I arose the next morning at 7:00 AM, filled up with gasoline, asked directions, and promptly found the Toyota dealership nearby, about four miles down Highway 111. The service foreman couldn't take on my problem this day. He asked one of his service men about a possible diagnosis for the pickup's problems, but came to no definite conclusions. I went to the parts-man to ask if he had a light switch in stock, for the pickup. He queried me about the model and the part I needed. And then, as though by inspiration, he took it upon himself to check out an idea that occurred to him. He asked me to release the hood latch, and he looked within. Fiddling with, and poking upon the positive battery terminal fitting, he seemed to conclude that his hunch was correct. On that terminal are two fusible links, one of which is for the headlights; it seemed to be malfunctioning because of corrosion deposits. With difficulty, he disconnected that link and replaced it with a new part, which cost me but $3.50. Behold, the headlights then worked. I was pleased, relieved, and chagrin. Chagrin not so much because my own diagnosis was in error, but rather because of the obvious untidiness about the unattended battery terminal. The battery stay bar had become unbolted, and the battery terminals were both badly corroded. One of the two sets of three battery cell-caps had been lost in Arkansas three weeks earlier, and I had merely plugged those holes with a paper towel, and covered that with tape. The tape was loose, the paper was wet and torn, and the whole thing was an unsightly mess. He calmly then removed the tape and debris; and then found me an old set of cell caps to use on the cell openings on the battery. And I went on my way rejoicing; and in my mind, commending this parts-man to the spirit of goodness in the universe.

Next, I lost myself a couple of times in trying to get to Palm Springs. There I stopped to see the desert museum, in order to apprise myself of some desert facts before heading out onto the solitudes for the next couple of days. Parking here at the museum was difficult because of the many vehicles that were present - account of the Bob Hope Dessert Classic Golf Tournament. A young girl attending a parking lot entrance, called to me as I slowed to read her "lot filled" sign. "Circle around and come back - then I'll have a spot for you", says she. It was an impersonal business offer with no covert implications, but the thought conveyed a certain uplifting charm to a gray-beard outcast such as I. The other circling traffic was plentiful, and I was certain that what she suggested could not happen. Never-the-less, I did circle back, remembering that a great much of one's life experience is founded upon improbabilities. But upon this occasion, my first guess had been correct. I finally located a parking spot some three blocks distant, and hiked back to see the museum. Completing that tour, I stopped to get some soda-pop, bagels, and cream cheese, by way of preparation for taking myself up unto a high mountain wastelands for the weekend.

I drove up toward a mountain peak, heading north on Indian Road out of Palm springs, then up highway 62, to Yucca Valley at mid-afternoon. There I stopped for enchiladas and beans, before driving up to the altiplano and rock mountains to a spot which they call Joshua Tree National Monument. Its distinctive feature is that the Joshua Tree abounds here. Someone once defined history as being "just one damned thing after another". In that same sense, one might define a Joshua-tree as "an unlikely thing, among the plant species". I guess it belongs to the genus of Yucca. I don't know why the Mormons named it a Joshua-tree. It was my intent to stay out there a couple of nights, sleeping in my pickup camper shell, and spending the days in writing, and in clearing my thoughts. I even had some distant hope that there I might find the loose ends of some thought processes that might empower me to write some few lines of poetry - a difficult thing indeed. The campsites however, were all filled with folks on their weekend excursions. I am sure that this time of the year is, in general, the very best for visiting the area, as the temperatures are comfortably cool in these winter months. In the summer, the daytime temperatures can rise to 160 degrees F. upon the desert floor (150 degrees at one foot above the earth, and 125 Degrees at four feet above the earth). A camel is designed to tolerate such conditions as that, but not mere mortal man. As I entered the area, the sun was setting and I hurried up to the panoramic view obtainable at Little San Bernadino Mountain, which overlooks Cochran Valley below. From there, the view is exquisite and far. One can see a sentinel peak far to the south of The Great Salton Sea. That peak is in Mexico. From this view point, one can see San Gorgino Pass to the west, set between Mt. Jacinto of the Jacinto Mountains, and San Gorgino of the San Bernadino Mountains. At this place the winds can be a mighty force. Highway 10, and a constant stream of traffic pass below - to and from the Los Angeles area. The atmosphere off in the direction of Los Angeles is always murky, giving the sunset colors a deep red hue. There in Gorgino Pass, man has raised already, perhaps a thousand wind powered generators, and it seems likely that many more shall follow. From this view point, one can see the famous San Andreous Fault Line, which has the appearance of a long low ridge of hills set upon the valley floor between these two mighty ranges of mountains, and running parallel to the San Jacinto Mountains.

But here at sunset, I was hoping especially to see Halley's Comet with the naked eye. As the light of the sun diminished, the half-moon directly above became brighter. Then Jupiter, far to the west and upon the ecliptic became visible. And the constellation, Orion, above, showed its features. A flashing red/white/blue star in the east catches one's attention. This is Sirius (The Dog Star), of the constellation Canis Major. But Halley's Comet was not visible to the naked eye on either of these two nights when I was searching for it. Mark Twain was born in the presence of this comet a hundred fifty two years previously, and died seventy-six years ago at its last previous appearance in our heavens. Perhaps something or someone else of human significance had now had its beginnings on this new occasion, for co-incidence in time is inescapably common - however un-common among those instances be cause and effect.

I stayed at a motel in Yucca Valley, and returned the next morning to the land of the Joshua-trees. Seeing them once more, I was less doubtful that they existed. And I viewed again the sunset and nightfall from the Keys View Area. Then I headed south, hoping to camp at the Cottonwood Spring Camp Site, but they too were full - even early on a Saturday. I expect that the camps may largely empty out on Sunday afternoons, but I didn't wait to find out. I headed east on Highway 10, toward Blythe, planning to stay at a rest area that night. Rest areas are sparse on that great desert, and I drove about eighty miles before I finally came upon Wiley Well Springs Rest Area, still twenty-five miles to the west of Blythe. I arrived about 9:00 PM. Mobile-home campers and trucks had stationed themselves in the parking spaces, and there were some even upon the adjacent dusty soil beyond the black-top pavement. I too parked upon the dirt area. I owned a vague sense of assurance of there being safety in our numbers for the night's encampment, even though we campers and truckers were unacquainted with one another. I located a picnic table near a light-post, and sat me down in sweater and jacket, to complete my log book entry for the day, and to write a few pages of this script. About 1:30 AM, I climbed into the camper-shell, and into the sleeping bag, to spend a restful night.

Arising about 9:00 AM, I pondered what my course should be that day. It was again clear, calm, and mild, and there were no insects about at this time of year - neither by day, nor by night. None of those eternal mini-distractions to torment one. I began to write, and it flowed easily - not a common thing. I knew then, that was my proper task for this day, and I applied myself to it contentedly. Freshening up in the toilet facility, I saw a note taped there to the mirror. "Three women with three kids need help. We have spent all of our money on gas and car repairs, and are trying to get back home. We would appreciate whatever help you could give us - either food or money. God bless you. We are in the yellowish car with a Jartan trailer, and parked out front." One of those women - a comely wench with pleasant demeanor - had stationed herself at one of the tables out front. Mildly, but with determination, she approached each automobile as it drove in from the freeway, briefly telling them each of her plight; and offering to wash their car windows in exchange for a contribution. Most, I think, consented to give her a dollar. Only myself, and a Native Indian man - whose pickup had broken down - did she exclude from her solicitations. Only we, perhaps, seemed to her more destitute than herself. Actually, there appeared also to be two or three men in company with these stranded women, but making themselves inconspicuous in the background. But what could they do, anyhow, out here on the desert where they could find no employment . . . . What were they likely to accomplish, as compared with the efforts of this fine woman who seemed to have just 'the right stuff' for this particular difficulty. Her charm and grace reminded me of my own dear daughter. And so I later bought from some Indian vendors who had stationed themselves there, a native crafted necklace with correspondingly appropriate design for Miette.

Even in this nice weather, a fair number of vehicles came limping in with various mechanical problems. Four people pushed in a heavily laden small red vehicle of about ten years vintage, and left it there. Another, finally started after stubbornly resisting that effort for about thirty minutes - probably a vapor-locked gas line. Three young men a VW Rabbit, had a broken fan belt. Another young man's auto coasted in with a nearly empty gas tank. He was now concerned as to how far it was to the nearest gas station.

I should like to have remained here another couple of days, but I was nearly out of bagels, and I had about caught up with my self-required writing project. And "I had promises to keep; and miles to go before I sleep . . . ."

I stopped to spend the night at the home of my brother, Gene, in Mesa Arizona before then returning home to Hobbs.

RGB
Jan 1986

A White-Collar Street Person
By R. Garner Brasseur, M.D.

On 9 February I again headed west into California, where I explored the possibilities for employment in the areas of Tracy, and Vallejo.

My note of 2/25/86 describes the situation:

I believe that I have been out here in The Bay Area of California about three weeks again, now. But it requires of me a distinct effort to recall that with any degree of certainty; for I see no evidence of any accomplishment from my time and effort to acquire a job. No 'Eureka' days of victory therefore, such as to make them distinctly memorable to me. Rather, each is tainted with the same pallor and distaste of failure; and with it, discouragement and a little anxiety. For the reality of one's physical being and necessities, needs must eventually be solvent, within one's capacity to earn what those things cost. Nor are my personal expenses all; for I still have a wife, a daughter, and a son to help along. And I needs must bear the expenses of the costs of a little more personal education, including tuition, books, and big city living expenses.

I am attempting to set in motion, the wheels of events that will ultimately bring me that employment which I seek and need; for there can be no realistic expectation that that can happen, except through contact with individuals and organizations that have medical facilities, and access to patients who might require my services. To set in process - through chain of events - shall inevitably require some certain minimum of time before that effect of finding a suitable opening for my employment, can come into being. It may be the case - and it is a comforting thought - that the wheels are now turning, that will soon produce to me that opportunity for an income producing occupation. Equally probable however, is that no such process has been grinding that will, in fact, secure me employment. I must in fact, presume that my efforts, to date, have not been effective. And I must press continuously in my efforts and vary my tack, in my quest for employment here, in the face of an overly abundant supply of Ophthalmologists. The health plan groups of physicians, such as Permanente and ITM, by their nature, are incapable of making any quick decision concerning the expensive hiring of any such employee as a physician. And when the applicants are many, their decision processes become more complicated to them; and lengthen. The private physicians who are contemplating the hiring of physician, become great procrastinators, knowing that they are personally doing well economically, and that an added physician may often initially cost more than he produces in income. Only those with fairly substantial surgical volume are likely to be seeking physician assistants - and their egos tend often to be so large as to make them difficult employers. In their presence, one often has difficulty breathing; for their tumorous egos often consume almost all of the oxygen in the air.

Realistically, it may well be the case that the only way I shall find employment is to start or buy my own practice. Both are difficult to accomplish, account of the expense. And me with no assets. Such expense is no special problem to a 'going concern' with the heavily surgically oriented practice; for surgery a-plenty will bear that cost. A medically oriented non-surgical practice however, will barely - or perhaps not quite - pay that expense in the field of Ophthalmology, where costs of equipment are exorbitant. Yet, I must consider that possibility; and soon get started in that direction unless something else turns up or my employment. Before doing so however, I think it best to consider going into some other medical field such as ER coverage, or urgent care centers. Perhaps I might even find employment as a general physician or a staff physician in one of the state hospitals. Henceforth, I shall include those possibilities among my investigations.

On this Wednesday I spent the entire day in the Vallejo Public Library. To do such a thing; rather than spend the day in beating the bushes, troubles me psychologically; for I always wonder if this might not have been that very day when I might have flushed out that ideal lead and connection to a employment opportunity. And yet, I needed time to read and rethinking my premises - and to search about the library for other leads that I might have overlooked. In actuality, I didn't find those new leads in that library; yet, at least, I know now that they are not to be found there. And that too, is useful and comforting in its own way.

I left the library at 5:30 PM, and stopped at a fruit stand on Alameda Street to buy four pounds of oranges for a dollar. Then I headed up the hill, east of Vallejo, to spend another night there, at the rest area that overlooks the whole north bay area. A fine sight - either by night or day. The orange-red sun was setting into some cloud banks overlying the ocean just as my pickup began to ascent the hill. I was tired; so I lay down on the cot in the camper shell for a couple of hours, after changing into my sweater. There to listen to my soul music while dozing and half asleep. Two tapes of Neil Diamond, three of Roger Whittiger and among my favorite. "Song Sung Blues", "Brother Love's Show", "the Unicorn", "Dream America", "Peace Train", "Imagine", "Calypso", "Kentucky Moonshine", "Gitshe Goomy", "Walk on Water", "Canta Libra", "Captain Sunshine" . . . . Reading, writing, and listening to music - such pass-times are essential to divert the mind from futile ruminations over one's ongoing troubles in this world.

After my rest period, I take some bagels, crème cheese, salami, and root-beer, along with my note book and reading material down to a picnic table just below the parking area. There, I eat a little, then sit me down upon a pillow, to write and read for a few hours. About 11;00 PM it becomes cool enough to make my jacket a comfort. The moisture in the air dampens my writing pages ever so slightly, though the skies above are clear. Orion is a little west of the vertical meridian at 9:00 PM. The moon is gibbous, and far to the east - it was full two nights ago, arising in the east just as the sun set in the west, while I was south of Hayward driving to Pierre's place in San Jose.

Many cars and campers are parked here at the rest stop a few miles east of Vallejo. Perhaps three fourths of the parking spaces are occupied; about half of them will spent the entire night here. The rest area, utility building, and picnic facilities are pretty, clean, and well maintained. There is no other such rest area so close to the urban bay cities area as is this one. With the rainy weathers now resolved, I have not had to take a motel room for the past seven nights. Again, at least at this time of the year, there are no insects of any kind to disturb one's thoughts or comfort while spending the evening at the picnic tables. No one - other than myself - is eating or sitting at these picnic tables. I expect that will change when the summer weather returns. But I find it pleasant just as it is; all the more so, because I have it mostly to myself. A few people walk about and stretch for a few minutes, but most that are staying here in their campers, seem to turn in early - by 10:00 PM. I usually stay up until 1:30 or 2:00 AM.

Despite the evil times and my condition of unemployment, my aloneness here, and my external freedom are things that I enjoy. Throughout each day a thousand observations and thoughts impress themselves upon my mind. Yet, I have not nearly the time nor opportunity that I would like, to record these things, by way of working them out, to derive from them, their lessons and benisons. I actually have more time for such things as writing and reading, when I am regularly employed. For then, my free time is unburdened from having to dredge up ideas and schemes for the search for employment.

The traffic roars by here continuously. It seems quieter in the evening, when most of the truck traffic is homing on down the hill. In the early morning, it begins to get more noisy as the traffic increases and the truck engines are noisily straining to ascend the hill.

3/1/86

For three successive nights I returned to the Hunter Hill Rest Area - my low budget retreat - to spend the evening and the night. At least two or three other vehicles, like myself, had returned on each of these occasions, too. Perhaps there were others less conspicuous to me because they were not vans, pickup campers, or motor homes. The restrooms were cleaned and grounds picked up each day - by what are apparently private contractors. Sometimes two or three young men, or a man and woman together; another time by three women. There were two each of women's and of men's toilet areas in the same building. The servicing squad would close off one for servicing; then open it as they closed and cleaned the other. Each day new graffiti was written upon the walls. The cleaners removed what would easily come off. Despite the heavy duty stool and stall facilities, they are relatively rapidly degraded by the brutal element in mankind. The picnic tables and benches are fixed to the concrete slabs. Most, are poured concrete. Those of heavy plank are soon defaced with initials and carvings. The concrete garbage receptacles are lined with plastic sacs, that are daily toted away and replaced. I never saw any person in the act of doing any damage or mischief to any of those facilities, which indicates that in general, the public persons do appreciate, respect, and conserve these public facilities. Many individuals, at some phase of their life, do however manifest some destructive behavior - from perhaps a sense of bravado, or at a time of anger and frustration in their lives; the accumulated such instances may easily account for the continuing evidence of destruction which we regularly witness. Presumably, the facilities are intermittently overhauled and fitted up with new fixtures. Rarely do I see a highway patrol car drive through one of these roadside rest parking areas. I have never seen an officer stop to use these facilities but once - on this very day.

For the most part, folks at these rest areas remain anonymous from one another. Rarely does one greet another; and there is very little talk - no conversation. Someone might ask - and receive - information and directions, but always the tone is impersonal. The middle classes and the upper lower classes of people seem most to use these facilities. Always, there are a great many truckers that stop for short and medium length rest and break periods. It is my impression that the measure of security of person and property engendered in these spots is that which can be attributed to the ever present truck drivers. For in their occupational roles, they are courteous, sober, and well behaved. These rest areas are as oases to them and partly designed and intended for their use. One senses that they possess a certain pride and respect for these areas. Their omnipresence at these spots make of them a potential but unspoken force that helps to ensure the security of individuals and of property here. The ubiquitous public telephone, further assures the roadside guest and the facilities against wanton abuse.

Between Livermore and Tracy - at the edge of the delta area - I encountered heavy fog at 7:30 PM last evening when I was driving eastward, toward this rest area south of Tracy. The fog was so thick that I had difficulty locating the turnoff, though I knew approximately where it was. The outbound traffic - a Friday night - was heavy. But there was only a moderate usage of these rest area facilities, since most were probably headed to rural areas and other cities for the weekend. I sat at one of the picnic tables in the fog, and read. I finished the second volume of "*The Admiral of the Ocean Seas*".

The fog was exceedingly wet. Though I could feel no wind or breeze, the foggy air was drifting past me toward the SSE, as I discerned from the condensing vapors of my breath. Soon, I began to feel cool and damp from the penetration of the fog through my two sweaters; and I put my jacket on. The pages of the book dampened as I read. I did not wish to bring out my writing materials, as I feared those pages might get wet even as I was writing. At midnight I retired to the pickup camper and read until 1:45 AM in my sleeping bag. I had to replace two of the six 'D' type batteries to obtain sufficient light from my fluorescent bulb. Perhaps a dozen cars spent the night here. After I retired, a young couple in a small car pulled in next to my pickup, to spend the night in the back of that car, its carrier compartment laying flat to accommodate them more easily. Even I enjoyed more comfort than that.

I arose at 7:45 AM and had an orange, some chocolate and a coke for breakfast. The couple in the car slept until 10:30 AM. The morning was cool and foggy. By noon the fog had lifted somewhat and twenty minutes later, I began to see some faint shadows cast by a bright sun sitting above the haze. There was a film of fine water droplets on the picnic tables and benches which I wiped off; and covered these wet areas with newspapers. At noon the surface began to dry, rather than to accumulate additional moisture. By 1:00 PM the sunlight was fairly bright, with still some diffuse haze. I set up my work space and materials upon one of the picnic tables and began to read and to update my journal. Sort of what you might call a day off to the unemployed such as I. No need to endlessly plow through with the motions of groveling about for employment on the weekends, which was beginning to seem as somewhat of a forlorn hope. Not a weekend of what one might call 'easy leisure', for the retired and the unemployed are never entitled to the peace of mind that accompanies that.

It seems intended that folks should toilet their dogs towards the back of the lot. Several signs there say, "pet area". Others say, "pets must be on leash". Neither rule seems well observed. One man brought forth a horse - which he did keep on a leash, while he, a woman, and a child had lunch at one of the near picnic tables. The grass at the back of the rest-area lot was long and green. You would have thought he might have staked out the horse to graze back there rather than confining it to the scrub growth up here near the front of the lot.

As the flies took possession of the now shaded area about the tables, I removed to a spot in the sun at 2:00 PM. The angle of the sun was perpendicular to the right side of my face. I squinted my right eye shut for an hour while I wrote. Then I turned my back to the sun, and opened both eyes to read. The bright colors seen with my left eye, were then all faded and pale as seen with my right eye. I removed my sweat shirts and t-shirt to get a 15 to 20 minute exposure to the sun on my back, to allow the skin to manufacture a free dose of Vitamin D-3. I then lay down on my back on the picnic table bench, to harvest the suns rays onto the front of my chest and the arm-pits.

Looking to the east, south, and north, one sees a vast expanse of low flat delta landscape of the conjoined influence of the meeting of the northbound San Joaquin River, with the southbound Sacramento and American Rivers. Today, at least, I could not yet see the Sierra Nevada mountains a hundred miles to the east. This whole vast inland valley represents the silt depositions of the weathering and water run-off, from the mountains of California's coastal and central ranges. The valley is flat and low, so that the rivers flowing along the north-south axis of the central valley move along at a sedate pace. The waters from the mountains that feed the San Joaquin from the east are, of course, sprite and energetic as they originate high in the Sierra Nevada's. When those rivers gather momentum from rain or from the snow melt, they bring down large amounts of weathered gravels and silt. The run-off from the snows is a slower process which extends far into the summer months; and these waters come down cold and clear over the rocky stream beds, depositing only relatively small amounts silt. The young Sierra Nevada's set back to the east from the much older range that now constitutes the foothills of the range. That previous and older range is transected by the many high mountain streams that egress westward into the central valley river system. That older range - the foothills of the Sierra Nevada's, is very weathered and worn. The rock formations that form the backbone of the range are of a greenish coloration in their freshly exposed fracture surfaces. They seem to weather very rapidly to a rusty reddish color, implying a relatively large iron content. And the weathered surfaces are very irregular, forming a fibrous crystalline texture of the rock itself, a great deal of which appears to be of a rock type called, serpentine. Other local areas appear to be of the nature of cert - also of greenish coloration, but of a hard and sedimentary origin which does not readily decompose into silts, clays, or micas. Its texture is grainy and hard like flint or sugar agate. But again, the spinal core of this range seems more fibrous; and as it weathers irregularly, large fingers and stumps project vertically through the overlying weathered rocks and silts to stand naked in the rolling meadows of those foothills. This visible - and presumably subterranean fingerlike physical character - tends to hold and retain that soil, which sifts and compacts itself downward into the crevices. Thus, it resists somewhat, the effect of water, to carry away the top-soils in heavy run-offs. The eastern slope of the costal range, by contrast, being of heavy mudstone and silt formations uplifted from the valley floor, runs off easily and weathers rapidly in response to the force of moving water. And the muddy slope when heavily saturated becomes a gel-like mass that creeps and slides in response to that weight of lubricating water and the force of gravity. Here, there are no underlying upward projections to restrain the creeping hillsides.

The foothills of the Sierra Nevada's are volcanic in their origins, with cherts and silts being somewhat retained upon their slopes by the fingerlike projecting which resist weathering somewhat. Scattered about, at various localities are the evidence of volcanic flows of lava, forming flat-topped buttes with columnated faces and cliffs, much the character of those seen in central and eastern Oregon and Washington - though nowhere nearly as extensive. One might suppose that this ancient well-weathered foothill range with its highly colored minerals and serpentine, is the source of the gold that has been taken from nature's bosom in this state. The heavy weathering from rains and snow melt and the elements has freed the nuggets and flakes and slivers of gold, while yet retaining those heavy riches, which work their way downward into the superficial ledges and cracks and spaces between those finger projections. Thus they tend to be conveniently concentrated by the combination of natural weathering and natural sluicing. The location of the gold-rush towns along these foothills, tends to confirm such a theory. Or shall we rather say, that it suggests that theory.

RGB

From Beaver Campground at Table Rock Lake - in the Ozark Mountains of NW Arkansas

Written March 30 of 1986

I had arrived home again on 7 March 1986, and next called Dr. L___ in response to an ad in the AAO Placement Bureau publication. What I read ("immediate opening, a going concern, 2nd office, availability of equipment", etc.) led me to hope that here - in southeast Maryland - was a potentially ideal opening, well suited to my requirements. Speaking with him by phone - twice - before making the journey out there, seemed to affirm that opening as a viable opportunity. As Mick Rosskoff was hoping to do an internship there, he accompanied me. We took turns - one resting in the camper, and one driving - and drove that 1800 miles in about 32 hours.

Just prior to making that journey, I had obtained an additional lead in response to an ad I had answered a week earlier. Therefore, en route to Maryland, we stopped a couple of hours in Webb City, Missouri to look at that possibility. It seemed also a reasonably good prospect provided only that they might actually furnish all the necessary tools, equipment, office, and a salary guarantee: as implied in the phone discussions with this rural hospital administrator. That, always a dubious possibility because they are simply naïve about the cost of those requirements. Such an ad is likely to be merely a sort of 'fishing-trip' for a pushy hospital administrator casting about for an additional device by which to increase the stream of income to a struggling rural hospital.

We found our way into and about Baltimore, but Mick's job prospects there did not seem to have materialized, despite what he had been promised. That same day, I dropped him by to the N.I.H. at Bethesda, to look into possible job openings there. Not good, says he. From there we traveled to Leonardtown and there I took a motel room ($35.00). I called Dr. L__, and he picked me up at 7:00 PM to go with him to a Hospital Staff Meeting. The doctors were a mixture of East Indians and Gringos. A nice hospital; and a good meal. A boisterous fifty plus year old Mohammedan surgeon interjected himself repeatedly into all of the social and business aspects of the proceedings. Following the meeting, Dr. L__ and I talked. Dr. L__ took me to his Leonardtown office. It is new and attractive, but outfitted as a one-man operation, with no office assistants other than the secretary - the same one for each of his two widely separated offices. He went on at length about the various options to which we might agree. One, being that of purchasing his second office (some twenty five miles distant). The more we talked of business and of potential, and possibilities; the more uncertain I became as to what exactly he had in mind. He prided himself on being open, face-to-face, and 'up front' in all his dealings, but he was an expert at keeping things vague. The only way to define how such an operation might actually work out, would be to work with him for several months, to observe and discover from the course of events. But his guarantee of a yearly $40,000.00 was so minimal as to suggest that the circumstances and conditions that he expected, would provide me with very little opportunity to put charges on the books; and that my hours indeed would be filled with non-profitable exertions such as chasing from city to city, seeing patients without any screening or technical assistance whatsoever. I had vivid recollections of that from my experience with Dr. C., in Oregon. As to the highly touted laser equipment, it was located in yet a third office; and so remote as to make it almost useless on a time-cost-effort basis. He, himself, had been laid up for two or three years in consequence of a severe auto-accident in 1981 - probably not unrelated to long miles of driving between the various components of his one-man three-base operation.

Dr L____ dropped me off at the motel about 11:00 PM. I thought I might look at his other office the following day, but within an hour, I formulated and reviewed my impressions; and concluded not to waste further any of his time - nor of my own. Mick and I returned the 1800 miles to Hobbs, in again about 32 hours.

I then again toyed with the possibility of working out some arrangement with the people of Jane Chinn Hospital in Webb City, MO. They are a private enterprise corporation out of Los Angeles, about four years old, and with the concept of buying or managing small hospitals in rural areas; and to retain these patents and this business into their rural setting. They update and re-equip their rural hospitals after acquiring them. They then encourage physicians to associate with an Independent Practitioner Association (I.P.A.) to settle about their facilities by giving them a contract of guaranteed income and benefits. They also manage the physicians' office practice expenses and office-help by supplying these along with the office, at a cost of 50% of the physician's net income. If they would actually do this for the Ophthalmologist, including the obtainment for his use of all the surgical and office equipment, that would indeed make it an attractive possibility. But would they? It is doubtful that they know what they are getting into on that score. For the cost of that office and surgical equipment would be in the range of, perhaps, nearly $300,000.00. To remain competitive, the Ophthalmologist must have access to all of that equipment. Only by having the equipment, could one hope to attract a large enough patient base to build a practice from scratch. Not to have it, would seem to assure him that he could not build a practice income equal to his one year guarantee; and that he would assuredly then be seeking a relocation site one year hence, in - an environment of hard feelings between himself and this recent hospital management group. Nor are mere promises of equipment - deferred to be purchased later - adequate nor realistic considerations to the ophthalmologist; for that is mere theoretical equipment, and can produce no income . . . except theoretical income. To be established on such a basis, is like unto giving-it-a-try, without a sincere effort; and to guarantee of economic failure. To be sure, one could also similarly fail even with that equipment; but the possibility of success (from the inception of the opening of one's practice) needs must be the minimum requirement for a year's effort and hope.

Returning home on March 14, I was awaiting the arrival of papers for application to the State of Missouri for medical licensure. A week elapsed, and it becomes obvious that they have forgotten to mail out the forms. A phone call ($5.00) is sufficient to cause them to be mailed the same day; and they arrive after the weekend. But the Missouri Licensure Application for is impossibly cumbersome. As to the exact dates and preceptors of individual medical school clerkships taken some twenty-five years ago; well, that seems to me an impossible feat of memory. Thus, though Webb

City, Missouri did look to be a reasonable possibility; yet this large inertia of unaccomplished necessities - not even yet set into motion - relegated the concept to that of mere remote speculative status.

Previously, at about Christmas time, I had received a letter from Dr. H___ of Winfield, Kansas, about 175 miles west of Webb City. Running down that reference in my correspondence, I called them. Several things about Winfield conspire to suggest it may be a viable possibility as a practice situation. First and foremost, they already have nearly all of the ophthalmology equipment that is required - except the YAG-laser. And that equipment sets there unused and costing them money for the past year and a half. Furthermore, it occupies office space which thus returns to them no rental fee. And they have had an ophthalmologist there for many years, with the exception of this recent interval. It is a nice little town of about 10,000 people. It draws patients from surrounding towns; the clinic even has satellite clinics in some of these outlying towns. I was greatly surprised by the clinic building itself. For it is spacious. A two story building, and well appointed with marble floors, marble stairs, and marble and tile inlays. It sets on two acres of ground and its total floor space must be twice that of Hobbs clinic. There appear to be about nine or ten doctors there; and they have each a large personal office. A flyer from the chamber of commerce says they have sixty plus employees - a large ratio, to physicians. I wonder that they are able to support it all. The building itself was originally built by Snyder Foundation - a privately endowed entity founded by the Dr. S___ family (of whom a third generation S___ physician remains with the clinic). A couple years ago, the clinic doctor's corporation purchased and is making payments upon the clinic building. The S___ lab is attached but remains a separate entity for medical research. Large portions of the building are not productively occupied. Two dental office are no longer in use. The ophthalmology offices and equipment are idle. The Octopus field test device costs them dearly in its quarterly maintenance charge service contract. They are undoubtedly also paying installments for all of the equipment they bought 2½ years ago for the eye clinic. The optical shop is well-appointed and spacious. It is leased to an optician, who is, of course, anxious to get an ophthalmologist on board. An ENT physician comes out once weekly from Wichita (about 35 miles distant).

The clinic may have gotten a hellish bargain in the purchase of the clinic building - I don't know or have any clue to guide me on that matter. Still though, it appears to be quite too large for their group size

- by perhaps 30 or 40 percent. They are thinking of taking in two other physicians in addition to the ophthalmologist. So far as I know, they have not any other ophthalmologist now looking at them. They had an older ophthalmologist for many years. He died or retired. Then they got their most recent ophthalmologist - a Dr. W___ - a few years ago. He was with them just over a year; and departed 15 months ago. He was said to be talented and skilled. But there was some domestic difficulty. His wife was a resident physician in L.A. and the young Dr. W___ got involved with one of the clinic staff girls, causing the breakup of her marriage etc. Also, he was said to be not facile in dealing with patients. In short, despite his technical strength, he seems to have caused some embarrassments to the clinic.

In all, considering their investment in ophthalmology equipment and space - as well as their potential for losing the leasehold income from the optician; it seems probable that the S___ Clinic may be anxious indeed to obtain ophthalmologist in the near future. And the potential seems good, for supporting one. The State of Kansas is congenial; and easily grants temporary licensure to physicians entering the state to practice. There is an ophthalmologist 15 miles to the south (Arkansas City), but he is busy. From what I have learned thus far, I think that Winfield is my most likely and earliest available option. I need yet to get them a C.V. and three reference names that they can call. And I think that I got along congenially with the physicians of the clinic with whom, I met.

Departing Winfield, I drove eastward 100 miles to Independence, Kansas. A Dr. B___ had placed an ad with AAO, saying that their community needed an ophthalmologist; and that an office previously used by an optometrist was available. That office - not surprisingly - turns out to have been owned by this same Dr. B___, who himself has been retired for the past year. I spoke with the hospital administrator - a young man with a badly pox-marked face - who occupied a sumptuous office elegantly appointed and isolate from intruders by a set of corridors and two tiers of secretaries at stations remote from one another. I got there about 2:30 PM. I easily got past the secretarial guard and found the administrator not apparently unhappy at my un-appointed arrival. I knew therefore, that he too must needs want to obtain the services of an ophthalmologist in the community. The town has never had one; and I am given to understand that the hospital is prepared to spend some big money on equipment to attract one. But do they have any realistic idea of what that might cost them?

The town round about where the hospital sets, is of older houses - not particularly well kept. One, here and there has been gutted out by fire. The hospital, by stark contrast, was new, and of ultramodern design, with a far older hospital building appended at the rear. Driving in towards the center of town, I realized that the town was far greater in its extensions than I had originally surmised. The older section of town - in which the hospital is located - is surrounded by a horse-shoe shape suburb, so that the size of the community seems some five times larger in area than I had thought. And many of the homes and estates located here are very nice - some, even elegant. A fairly nice community, all in all. But, so far as I know, the ophthalmologist would have to supply his own office space at $880.00 per month and supply all of his own office equipment - a not inconsiderable expense. And the hospital backed guarantee seems rather unpromising. And there are ophthalmologists but 15 or 20 miles distant; to the north, and to the northeast.

And so, I drove to Webb City, Missouri again that evening. I took a motel room in Joplin and refreshed myself with a long hot shower, hair wash and a good nap - preceding a long night of restful sleep. I called home and learned that Jane Chinn Hospital had been trying to get in contact with me. The next morning I drove over to that hospital and talked with Ms. R___, before departing to the Ozark Mountains of Northwest Arkansas for the weekend - there to collect my thoughts and impressions on March 30 of 1986.

3/31/86
From Beaver Campground
In The Ozarks

About Beaver Campground

About 2:30 PM on Saturday, I arrived at Beaver Campground - a lovely place. There, the river has carved a circular oxbow channel (more like a half-circle, perhaps) deeply into the limestone bed, so that the opposite (outside) wall of the channel is a sheer cliff ranging in height from 35 to 55 feet. On the backside of this wall runs a creek, that has carved out an opposing oxbow quarter-circle. A mere 30 foot thickness of vertical stone wall separates the two partial circles. Here, man has cut through the wall, to make a gap. An old railroad line was built across this gap - with a span of bridge immediately adjacent, on both sides. Picturesque indeed. The railroad line is no longer in use.

I walked upon the ties to cross the railroad bridge. Then spent an hour or two checking out the rock and stone accumulation in the stream bed. It is not all clay and limestone/shale shard. The whole formation seems to have been permeated to some degree with silica, which seems to have infiltrated the porosities and hollows of the limestone - which seem especially to occur at the interfaces between layers, and along the vertical fracture lines that interrupt these horizontal layer. As these cavitations develop, incrementally, the silica accumulates in what appear to be layer upon layer, to occupy the space left vacant. Actually, these layers are not discontinuous, but represent only 'fortification lines' - color changes, due to chemical fluctuations in the proportions of those chemical through time.

In addition to the calcite - composed of the compacted soft shells of prehistoric creatures - which is the base of the huge volume of geological formations around the world, a large portion of that calcite is compounded homogenously with a granular silicatious material. That silica is present in some layers; absent in others. When present, it greatly hardens and strengthens the rock, so that it may exist in large blocks - and sometimes in large sheets. That granular silica is known a "cert", and it has been shown to represent the accumulated skeletal remains of zillions of tiny prehistoric one-celled creatures called radiolarians and conodonts. There are morphological differences in these evolved skeletal, from age to age. Differences which enable one to date the deposition periods of the various strata.

The stream beds of the Ozarks are interesting, in that they contain the hard and insoluble remnants of what were once, predominantly calcite base geological formations. There are shards of cert, and many nodules of fortification agates of variable sizes and interesting shapes.

RGB
3/31/86

ROUND-ABOUT WICHITA

March 3rd of 1986

Wichita lies 30-35 miles to the north of Winfield. To the west and south lies some gently rolling farm land. The Arkansas River has been dammed-up, and creates a large body of multi-fingered lake that makes the area to the south and southeast a sort of recreational area. To the east of Winfield, the hills become more formidable; and there are road cuts and engineered highway inclines to facilitate motor vehicle traffic. The geological formations are layer upon layer of limestone with gray to yellowish hue, and alternating with layers of brittle clay and shales. The gray to yellowish overlying soil is often two to four feet thick at the top of rocky road cut. The rocky strata tend to ungulate in their horizontal alignment; and at some places, the formations sag and tilt, threatening to continue to melt or slide or topple from the face of the road cut. The road cuts themselves, having been freshly exposed, weather rapidly into a gravel of clay and small slate-like shards to collect as talus at the base. Here and there are layers of thick blocks of limestone that appear to have been metamorphosed into a variety of shale which has been permeated (and cemented together) by silica; and then re-crystallized into the limestone. The combinations of cert and limestone seem to be somewhat resistant to weathering; yet seems soft enough to easily quarry - making it good material for buildings. Each of the rolling ridges or mounds has an underlying limestone base formation at its core - supporting it, as a skeleton supports an animal. The gullies between the mounds and the fingers of the ridges seem to cut unnaturally deep. Perhaps because the water that occasionally carries the surface particles physically down stream, is supplemented in its effect by the subterranean flow of waters which carry off the calcium carbonates in their dissolved and ionized components; this leaving the overburdens above to collapse in those subterranean chambers and passages which it creates. Here and there, I find an occasional flagstone-shaped block of limestone, or calcified shale/limestone complex, whose flat surface is etched by a network or rivulets coursing between the horizontal layers of limestone-laden formations. Now, a million years later, we see the block and channels, after they have been weathered free of their original parent formations. In the road-cuts through similar formations (through which I traveled at the end of December 1985) in Tennessee, some 20 or 30 individual streamlet channels were seen, frozen in position, in randomly scattered sites, at various levels and locations, in the face of that road-cut; lending support to such a theory. Additionally, glaciers tend to produce similar rivulet channels to be found once the glacier has melted away. Except that, it is the undersurface of the overlying ice that becomes eroded into the rivulets. These channels then tend to silt and clot, thus leaving casts of the rivulet channels - the reverse of what we see concerning the limestone rivulet channels.

South of Joplin, Missouri - and somewhat east of it - the ridges and valleys of this large limestone/shale formation increase in depth to become known as the Ozark Mountains. From what I have heard, this is supposed to be an area rich in minerals and many unusual kinds of semiprecious rocks and stones. That puzzled me, for the entire formation had the appearance of mere limestone and shale - the two elements combined - to make it mostly an easily weathered rock that fragmented into clay and large and small shards. Only an occasional outcropping was of durable building quality. Yet, that must be at least reasonably plentiful, as the towns in this area have many very handsome old buildings that are built of this local rock.

- - - - - - - - - - - - - - - - - -

Driving westward out of Wichita, Kansas, on Highway for about sixty or seventy miles, the earth was level and under cultivation. The soil was black and thick, with a slightly reddish tint. Thereafter, the land surface again developed into a gradual and gentle undulation, and soon again I was into the ancient weathered red-butte formations, presumably continuous with those seen at the corresponding longitude in Oklahoma ten days earlier. And very little of this area was seen to be under cultivation. The rainfall progressively diminishes westwardly across the state; forty inches in the extreme east, to fourteen inches in the far west. Never-the-less, in the far west of Kansas

- south of Garden City and round about Liberal - the earth again is more level upon this high plateau, and a considerable proportion of the land is under cultivation and irrigation. The water source is, presumably, the ground waters of the Ogallala aquifer formation, which extends far southward from the Black Hills area of South Dakota.

For the first time in my life, I actually saw the cyclonic high cloud formations, consisting of concentric large spiral rings of cloud extending a hundred miles to both the north and the south. I passed beneath one such ring after another as I continued to drive westward. It was the leading edge of a cold front, and the temperature dropped some fifteen degrees in the space of about an hour. The radius of the huge storm cloud seemed to be between a hundred fifty and two hundred miles; as I encountered the eye of the storm center just west of Dodge City. The low cloud pattern was one of multiple small white cumulus clouds, which displayed some tendency to fuse and enlarge, the whole formation moving to the east and north. In the process of coalescence, the rearmost cloud would slowly overtake the one in front, or one cloud might slowly drift at right angles to another as they both continued to move in concert with the entire formation. It was late in the day, and it was becoming cool, so that there was not much further tendency for the large accumulation of thunderhead cloud masses. Yet, fifty miles to the southwest, I did note one large thunderhead cloud. Within two hours, at 7:00 P.M., it was just to the northeast of me, and was dropping its load of billowy formations to the earth. I presume I would have encountered an intense squall in that area.

- - - - - - - - - - - -

4 March 1986—from Taos, NM

It may be the case that I will get an offering of a job site from either Winfield or Webb City. Both sounded quite positive when I communicated with them last week; but there is no way for me to guess as to what other options either of them is considering besides my own candidacy. Of the two, I am more interested in Winfield, for there, things are ready to begin immediately - should they once agree among themselves to proceed with the project. There too, licensure problems will be much less an obstacle. One might suppose that they might be anxious to move with the project, for it is costing them money every day the office and the equipment sits idle.

But I dare not optimistically neglect my continuing effort to locate other options. For those who must ultimately decide the course for their respective group, have but little experience of what might be happening in the field of Ophthalmology at this time, and thus, plenty of motivation for procrastination. My own needs require that my efforts be ongoing, for the psychological trauma of lost hopes and having to initiate a whole new search efforts are just too painful and burdensome. Too, a better possibility may yet arise from my current search effort, such that neither of the above two options will appear to serve me well, by comparison. Therefore, the search and effort needs must continue.

As to the Webb City possibility, it is a far more remote possibility than Winfield, both in terms of a starting date, and in terms of it ever becoming a viable and real option. Without their allocation and release of funds, the necessary equipment will not materialize - leaving that merely a vague option. Until then, it remains a non-entity, rather than an option. The starting time, in any case, could not be earlier than July, with October being more probable. That is a long while from now, nor could I possibly wait that long, if other options arise.

In-so-far as the possibility of my returning now to school, that now seems a dead issue, since I have not received an acceptance from application. But, apart from that, my efforts to date have turned up no part-time work in the bay area of San Francisco. A moderate employment of twenty-five to forty percent of my time would be pre-requisite - to enable me to support my family, and to finance my continuing education. Having now spoken or communicated with a dozen more-or-less of these eye-doctors that are each toying with the idea of using a part-time Ophthalmologist, it is obvious that they remain undecided and fickle about what they want. Certainly they would not be dependable as employers. From my experience, to date, I couldn't feel comfortable in working for any of them.

The next tack, then, is to consider the possibility of setting up my own Ophthalmology Practice. The big difficulty in that, is in getting the use of the expensive equipment. And the only hope for that, is to find a hospital that would be willing to acquire it, in exchange for the possibility of deriving some regular income from it. That possibility could exist only if no other Ophthalmologist in their community already has his own such equipment, for then there is some chance the hospital may get usage fees enough to pay for that equipment. But the possibility is remote indeed that they would purchase any such expensive gadgetry with the mere hope of cutting into the volume of an already established Ophthalmologist outpatient facility.

The final possibility is then to merely open up an office of general medicine, and take care of whatever problems come through the door. The advantage of that, is that it is a real and reasonable possibility, however archaic it would appear. And what could be more practical than that which is both reasonable and possible?

RGB

THE SAN BERNADINO MOUNTAINS AND EASTERN CALIFORNIA

written 10 April 1986

DAYLIGHT HOURS IN ARIZONA: 9 April 1986—This is My first trip through southern Arizona during daylight hours, using Highway routes 10 and 8. Rest area facilities in the south part of the state are poor. The route is all set in double-lane highways. The land is desert, with mesquite shrubs - many Segura Cacti beginning 75 miles south of Tucson. There are many interrupted ranges of intrusive and uplifted sharp and high peaks - their deep substance often of large blocks of igneous - many areas of multiple intrusive. There are uplifted table lands of desert floor which has a thick accumulation of conglomerate rock, mud, clay, and gravel. That floor has been deeply scoured, to form prominent gullies from the occasional flash floods. In various places there is also a dense population of volcanic basaltic rock upon the desert floor. Basalt does not readily break up, decompose, nor readily become scattered, but the forces of the desert are relentless and their operations are continuous through eons of time. From Casa Grande, highway 8 heads directly westward, with a nearly flat desert floor and a gentile upward incline toward the west. One large wave of mountain ridge then to cross, before dropping down into Yuma, some eight mile further. Here, there are heavy accumulations of clay and gravel in large hills and banks. Likewise, just before climbing over that last ridge - as though the river once flowed on that side of the ridge.

Once in California, there is again a high ridge of intrusive rock to climb before dropping down into the Imperial Valley, which is heavily irrigated and lies far ahead in stark green contrast to the desert we are about to escape. But the eastern most edge of the valley has accumulated an eight mile wide strip of large sand dunes which we must first traverse. The dunes diminish and disappear as one approaches and then enters the lush green fields of crops. By no means is all of the Imperial Valley under cultivation - only a thirty mile wide strip of the central valley - south of the Great Salton Sea - is under cultivation, as is a similar expanse north of the Salton Sea, as one approaches Indio. Driving this last leg just after sunset behind the San Jacinto Mts., shows gorgeous many-colored hues of several mountain ranges, one behind another. The hue of shadows and color is magnificent.

Now in California, I spend the night in the pickup at a rest stop off of Highway 10, north of Palm Springs - Whitewater Rest Area. This morning I came north on Highway 215, just west of Gorgina Pass. Thus delivered to Highway 15, I followed it up into the San Bernardino Mountains. Here I find large intrusive igneous blocks and sheets of stone, with areas of accumulated and uplifted conglomerate gravel and rock waste. My travels this day and the next would keep me upon that high plateau. Between the scattered communities, the landscape is barren high desert with greasewood and a few shrubs. Too dry for any dry-land farming, and no reasonable way to get irrigation waters up this high. One sees only some occasional cattle, by way of agriculture.

Victorville (10,000 population) and Apple Valley (30,000) are both beautiful desert areas - apparently they are primarily retirement communities. The Victorville hospital has an Argon and Krypton Laser, but no Yag-laser. Here, there are three resident ophthalmologists, with Dr. Reed having his own laser equipment, including a Yag-laser. There are a couple of additional eye-docs who commute into the area from Las Angeles to work these trap-lines here in the high country.

Barstow (24,000 population) has one resident Ophthalmologist, as well as one that comes in part time. The hospital there however, has no ophthalmology equipment. The hospital is negotiating for sale to private enterprise, and one might then suppose they would be willing to purchase at least some instruments and an operating microscope - perhaps more. It remains a possible practice site for perhaps a year hence.

Ridgecrest has a least two resident ophthalmologists, and two that fortify one of the two by working here on a part time basis, with outpatient facility emphasis and heavy advertisements. The other ophthalmologist is associated with a general medical clinic, it in turn being closely associated with the local hospital. On would have to say the town is already fully saturated with ophthalmologists.

Bishop, in the central portion of far western California is located in Owen Valley, a remote, isolated, and scenic area. The city of L.A. takes some of its water from even so a remote an area as this. I spoke with the hospital administrator, Herm Spenser, who was very accommodating to my inquiry for a place to set up a practice. He had on his agenda for the following week, the consideration of encouraging an ophthalmologist to come into the area to practice. Dr. H___ was here until a year and a half ago. The hospital has a Wilde Operating Microscope and surgical instruments, but no laser equipment. And the town itself has only a population of 7,000, with another 3,000 in the adjoining area. They will not extend surgical privileges, except to a resident of their community - that would indeed increase the possibility of a ophthalmologist surviving here ... if it were to prove an enduring truth. Still, the population is just a wee bit too small - unless they would offer one a guarantee of $65,000.00 to $70,000.00 of annual cash income. For the eye doctor would have to supply his own office and office equipment. Still, there remains the problem of no laser equipment. I mentioned these things to the hospital administrator, only to learn that he had already been independently apprised of these things by a search agency. Apparently though, the hospital board did not grasp the economic implications of risk to the poorly financed young eye surgeon, and refused to agree to any additional financial amenities. Thus was I rather disappointed, though not surprised, since I fancy I might have been quite content in Bishop.

R. Garner Brasseur. MD
written 10 March 1986

MEXICO ODYSSEY - 1995

by R. Garner Brasseur

Friday, 10 March of 1995, I completed my forty hour work week at Las Vegas Medical Center and departed the hospital at 4;33 PM. And I need not return to my medical duties until the first Monday of April. Some two or three months ago I conceived the vague notion that I might make a tour of Mexico during this time-off period. I located a book ("*The People's Guide to Mexico*" - by Carl Franz) that deals with the subject. It was chock-full of the author's tips, ideas, and suggestions; matters and details born unto him through his apparent wealth of personal experience on the subject.

I had toyed with the idea of going into Mexico with one of my brothers, or perhaps with Bob Brown, an old friend of mine. But they were unable or unexcited about the idea. And I myself was in a state of vacillation as to whether I would prefer to make the trip in solitude, or with a companion. In the end, I was quite content to have it come down to this . . . traveling alone. For the trip is destined to be little more than a mere blundering along on a whim from day to day; into areas and circumstances of which I have no previous personal experience. It is only my own personal interests and curiosity that urge me foreword. I shall be an alien in a foreign country, where I have no personal acquaintances nor relationships. Their religious and customs are all rather different than my own. My ability to read, speak, or understand their language is merely rudimentary;, and among them I expect to encounter only rarely, the occasional person who might speak some small amount of English. I'll be making decisions and choices based upon mere whim, vague preferences, and a small store of only general sorts of ideas concerning these peoples and their various societies. A society of factions and subcultures. No . . . it isn't likely that any of these whom I have considered as possible traveling companions would make the trip in any way easier for me. Most folks have enough regularity and order in their lives, that they would most likely feel rather uncomfortable to travel on the loose and informal schedule that I propose for my own choice. And though it is my trip I would feel obligated to grant them some minimal guarantees as to physical comfort, mental tranquility (that the leader knows with some assurance, what he is doing), and some definite notion of what I expect to see and do. But I can promise none of these things.

Mexico, in fact, is always a little dangerous in its potential for Americans. Potential danger from disease, bandidos, and civil unrest. Civil unrest to the point of revolution is a special possibility because of a severe economic crisis in the past six months. The value of the peso had fallen from 2.3 to 1, now to 7.5 to 1. The president of Mexico has recently announced new stringent economic policies, including a 5% use tax on sales. Already the Mexican People are poor, and the amenities of their lives are few. They certainly see the wealthy of their own nation as an adversary to their own ongoing destitution - an elite that fortifies themselves in walled and guarded villas. And they also have a vague nationalistic sense that the wealth of the United States is also in some manner partly responsible for that poverty that so meagerly sustains them. Concomitantly, they tend to perceive all Americans as being rich, and thus harbor a vague and thinly veiled hostility toward us "Gringos". In the underworld of Mexico, the easily identifiable Gringo tourist is certainly a target to robbery and extortion; and in the event of outbreak of civil unrest, that same target would surely be much more at risk.

I might have departed for Mexico on Saturday, the 11th of March, but the logistics of getting oneself organized and the settling of personal affairs is not an easy matter. Laundry to be done. Bills to pay. Letters to write. People to call . . . . I know that I want to travel light, so as not to get separated from those vital necessities, nor be caught in the frustration of chasing lost baggage. My baggage needs to be enough limited that I can handle it alone at all times - and personally carry it for miles if necessary. For I cannot let the weight of the baggage dictate the limits of where I might choose to stay in each city upon my itinerary. If I don't like the price or quality of where I have stopped to inquire, I wish to easily re-shoulder my load, and move on.

I left my pickup at home and departed Las Vegas on the bus at 6:15 AM on March 13th. I was surprised to discover that the bus stopped in

Albuquerque at the airport, before stopping at the bus terminal. It seemed entirely too practical to be a likely thing. There was a thirty-five minute stopover at the bus terminal, to change buses for the southward journey. I quickly hiked the six or seven blocks over to where I knew a cluster of banks to be located, in downtown Albuquerque. It was only 9:00 AM, and I worried that the banks might not yet be open - I was relieved to be wrong on this matter. I stopped first at The New Mexico Bank only to learn that they did not handle any foreign currencies. I tried The Norwest Bank across the street, where I was told that I might there buy Mexican currency, but that they would have to have been notified a day in advance, in order to arrange to have some on hand. "But life is short, and time is fleeting . . . ." I jogged another five or six blocks up 3rd, to Loma Blvd., in order to find Sun West Bank. There I stood briefly in the customer service line for access to a teller, only to be told that I must speak with a teller at a special foreign exchange desk. She did have $560.00 of Mexican pesos on hand, which she sold me for $98.00 American. I then headed back towards the bus terminal, stopping en route at a branch of the 1st Interstate Bank, near the city convention center. A sub-executive officer directed me to a teller's booth with a long line of depositors. The bus was soon to be departing. My anxiety mounted as I watched the minutes pass upon the face of my wristwatch. When I finally reached the head of the line, the teller directed me "over there to the other teller, Joyce". There, I stood another several minutes in line, before she informed me that she was not Joyce and that I should stand in that other line which she points out to me. After another wait in line, I was at last speaking with Joyce. Yes, she would sell me some Mexican currency. Opening a drawer, she took out a 5 x 11 x 4 inch cardboard box filled with Mexican currency. I asked her the rate of exchange. Not knowing, she lifted the phone to speak with an executive; then informed me that the rate was 1.6 pesos to the dollar. "Really??" says I, "I just got some at Sun West Bank at a rate of 5.5 to the dollar". "Well", says she, "we have had this currency around for some time, and we got it at a 1.6 to one ratio; so we need to sell it for that rate." Even to a country bumpkin like me, that seems peculiar - and I declined her offer. I jogged back over to the bus terminal, and arrived there just as my bus to El Paso was loading. Soon after departure, I became a little concerned as we appeared to be approaching access to the north-bound Hwy 25; and knowing that I needed to be headed south. Did I get on the wrong bus? And how would I get off this bus and redirected onto the south bound bus towards my destination. I dread to have to approach the driver to inquire about this (to thus expose my naivety). Thus do these little fears and insecurities take hold of one who ventures alone into places or by routes foreign to one's personal experience. But long experience with such cruel uncertainties, and embarrassing premature conclusions makes me cautious about the taking of any rash and unconsidered action - lest I expose my provincial naivety. Quickly, I must rationalize some theory to explain to myself why my first fears are unfounded. After all, there is sufficient reason for me to believe that the bus driver is not apt to have allowed me on his bus after having examined my ticket which clearly states my destination. For me to be on the wrong bus is apt to cause the bus driver as much inconvenience as myself. I thereby concluded that this bus would probably be going south via some other southbound highway than Hwy 25 - perhaps to the east of the Manzano Mountains. Such a route would enable the bus to serve many smaller communities in those rural areas - certainly plausible and logical. I reached for my printed bus schedule to affirm that which I have now already concluded. And I am quite then at ease, even before the bus exists Hwy 25 North, to head eastward on Hwy 40. We journey to Moriarity, and then southward through Willard, Corona, Carrizzozo, Tularosa, Alamagordo, and Las Cruses; arriving in El Paso, Texas about 4:30 PM. I was anxious to get to the banks in El Paso, in order to pick up some more Mexican currency. Here again, the new and unfamiliar is ever manifest as a source of frustrations; to place on trial and exercise the fiber of my physical and moral being. Because I am at least slightly familiar with El Paso from one single previous trip through the city, and because I had been observant for the locations of the city's banks as the bus was arriving at the terminal; therefore I was aware that at least several banks were close at hand to the bus terminal.

It was now my urgent objective to get into one of those banks yet this very day, if that be possible at this late hour. But I had some grave reservations on that score, for I own an ancient and deep prejudice which informs me that banks tend to open late in the mornings - and close in the early afternoons. And yet, the above experience of the banks in Albuquerque reminded me that I had already been at least partly wrong in this matter. So I was ready to believe that I could yet be wrong a second time in a single day.

I shouldered my two bags and promptly entered the bus terminal lobby in search of a locker in which to deposit my baggage, so as to expedite my search for a bank. But now, I was thwarted by an obstacle new to my experience. Rather than operating by a key, these lockers operated by an electronic code. Frustrated, I strained to becalm myself in order to concentrate my attentions to the printed operational instructions. Next, one must fathom the further mystery of commuting paper into coin. The coins of course are worthless, since the silver was mined from them thirty years ago, but the undiscerning machines swallowed them without demur - just as though the coins had some actual value. My learning seemed to run in slow motion and I was greatly relieved to finally be free of the baggage and into the street, upon my search for a bank. My scouting eye had provided me clues enough to set out on some probable course without further delay, toward the taller buildings several blocks distance. Ten minutes later I walked through the front door of the large Texas Commercial Bank, some five or six blocks from the bus terminal. An 'information desk' was in the center of the spacious lobby. There I asked the young woman attendant as to how I might obtain some Mexican currency. "Right there", she said, pointing to a cage twenty feet across the lobby, "but I think they might now be closed for the day." I was a bit confused and perturbed that she wouldn't give me some definite answer. "I am sorry, I don't quite understand", said I, "will I be able to get a currency exchange here today?" She too seemed genuinely uncertain about it. As I turned to look to where she had pointed, I saw the "CLOSED" sign in the teller's window. I continued my about-face, feeling disappointed and dejected, but before I had time to march away, I heard a sort of whispered, "Psst". Looking past the "CLOSED" sign in the teller's window, I saw the Hispanic teller beckoning me. He pushed aside the "CLOSED" sign as I approached his window. I told him I needed to exchange $300.00 for some Mexican currency, and asked him the rate of exchange. He pointed to a sign indicating the non-negotiable 5.8 peso to 1 dollar rate of exchange. Then he counted out the 1740 pesos to me. Later, as I reflected on this strange sequence of events in that large bank foyer, a couple of interesting points began to dawn on me. I must presume that the Mexican Currency Exchange Desk in that large Texas Commercial Bank must be of the nature of a special concession to some private and separate business interest, or to some separate Mexican National bank . . . for it would appear to be autonomous. That would explain why the "INFORMATION DESK" clerk seemed so uncertain as to what to tell me. Explain too why a teller - operating by any regular house rules - would suddenly re-open his post to me in the late afternoon. Secondly - as I would learn on the following day - while the rate of exchange was 5.8 to 1 on this day, the clerk already knew that the peso was slipping . . . and that the exchange rate would be 6.0 to 1 upon the following morning. Ah, what a curious and complex place this world seems to us pilgrims. And wonderful are the realities that force themselves upon us, one and all.

I immediately crossed the street to another bank, but it was closed. I walked then to yet a third bank a couple blocks distant. There I exchanged three, hundred-dollar bills for twenty-eight American ten-dollar bills and twenty, one-dollar bills. Knowing nothing of the practical realities of what consequences might result from a sudden dramatic devaluation of the Mexican Peso, I thought it might well be wise to have bills of usable size in the relatively far more stable American currency - to facilitate my passage and deliverance from the midst of troubles, should such need arise as I journey through Mexico.

And now, at 5:00 PM, the banks were all closing. And I was content to have accomplished as much as I had - under such marginal circumstances of timing. The tall and substantial International Hotel was only three of four blocks away; and only four or five blocks from the bus depot. I walked to the hotel to take a room for the night. The clerk seemed a bit surprised that I would arrive without baggage, and it placed the bell-hop into an unusual situation wherein he had no baggage to seize for profit. Taking my room key, I next walked back to the bus terminal and returned with hands free and baggage slung across my shoulders. A uniformed security guard stood beside the hotel entrance. Though I was clean and in clean clothing, I was not overly well-dressed; and there are, perhaps, some faintly rough edges to my appearance. Except when I am on duty, I nearly always wear a head-band. And I was sporting a full beard, held together with a couple of rubber bands. And I was also wearing an old quilted vest. At about twenty yards, as I approached the hotel entrance, the guard suddenly spotted me and instantly made a move to intercept me. Perhaps his first impression of me was that of a rag-man type of street person . . . just the sort of ruffian he doesn't wish to have in too close a proximity to his entrance; there to offend tastes of the more well-to-do patrons of that establishment. But his instinctual movement was based upon his early impressionistic judgment. My carriage, strength, and rapid un-intimidated advance seemed to cause him to quickly re-evaluate his primary doubts as to my legitimacy, and he circled back to his post by the entrance. For, at closer range, it perhaps now seemed to him more likely that I was merely somewhat eccentric in my attire, rather than a homeless vagabond. He and I nod at one another as I enter the lobby. I approached the elevators and retired to my room on the ninth floor. It had already been a long day for me, and I was weary from the hours and silent planning of my vague and uncharted voyage. A journey whose ends will continue to be loose and which will necessitate changes and adjustments over the course of the next three weeks. I have now a nice quarters in which to lodge for the night. I now took the time to rearrange my caches of the Mexican pesos and American dollars, in order to fit myself for travel into Mexico. In my wallet I carry the equivalent of about three thousand dollars in Mexican, and not overly large American bills. In my right front pocket I carry my smallest bills and coins of Mexican money. The three hundred dollars worth of American small bills, I divide into two equal parts for positioning into the self-made pair of elastic garters, and fit each thus concealed pile snugly just below the popliteal fossa at the top edge of my below-knee length stockings. The remainder of the Mexican and American moneys, I then place into my cloth elastic money belt, which I wear about my waist at the top outer edge of my shorts, pulling my t-shirt lower edge over the top of it. I wear the money into bed as I sleep; and also bring my wallet to bed with me. It sounds eccentric, I know, but it sleeps comfortably and enables me to rest in security of mind. The thought of being suddenly broke and destitute as an alien in some foreign land is unsettling to my mind. Cash on hand . . . and paid out only slowly and in relatively small quantities is the precise lubricant that enables one to move fluently and at will, in an alien society. Not that the people are greedy, nor that their society is unyielding. It is only just that eliciting their sympathies is inadequate to the purpose of lubrication. And in Mexico, there are already far too many things that draw upon their limited stores of sympathy.

About 7;00 PM I lay me down to nap and restore myself from the cares of the day, thinking then to attend to an evening meal in an hour or two. But I didn't awaken until 1:00 AM. No near cafes were yet open at this hour, so I walked down to the bus terminal cafeteria for eggs and bacon, and then back to the hotel to finish my night's rest.

The next morning I returned to the Texas Commercial Bank to pick up another hundred dollars worth of Mexican currency. It was this same teller, now looking down at the mouth and grumbling because the peso continues to fall. He gave me now the six to one exchange ratio on this day.

I then walked the few blocks to the post office and mailed the text of my recent divorce proceedings deposition - along with corrections which I had been asked to make; and on which I had spent an hour or two last night, and again this morning. From there I walked to a tourist information booth. I was told that the easiest and least expensive way to get to the main bus terminal in Ciudad de Juarez, is to return to the El Paso Chihauharese Shuttle Bus. It runs hourly and only costs five dollars. I returned to the hotel for my baggage and then took that shuttle bus. On the Mexican side of the border all of the passengers and all of the baggage was unloaded for inspection. While that was in process, I was instructed to walk the fifty yards to Mexican immigration. Showing them my passport, they willingly issued me a three-week tourist pass; and I returned to my bus, whose passengers and baggage were now being reloaded. There, an advance sales ticket-agent sold me a bus-ticket to Chihuahua for sixty-five pesos (about eleven dollars). I continued on the shuttle-bus and arrived at the Juarez Bus Terminal twenty minutes later. Juarez is among the largest cities of Mexico.

At the bus terminal I was then faced with the problem of discovering which bus I was to board, at which dock it was loading, and when. I found no one there to speak English and I was not surprised that my small acquaintance with Spanish seemed inadequate for this problem. I ran across the driver of the shuttle bus I had ridden; and he pointed out the information on the ticket from which I could determine that.

Traveling towards Chihuahua I have chosen a seat on the left side of the bus, to stay out of the afternoon sunlight. The countryside was desert ruble rock with scattered clusters of low mountainous background. The asphalt roadway stays to the east of the western Sierra Madras Mountains. There is little evidence even of ranching in this forbidding terrain - that, sustained by irrigation wells and watering circles. The dingy communities are few and far between. The winter temperatures here are quite suitable for travel and I am comfortable with shirt and quilted vest. Halfway to Chihuahua is a restaurant stop that seems to be regularly used as a lunch and pit break for most of the many busses that transit the area. Here, one can purchase tortillas, sandwiches, and soda pop during the twenty minute stop. Six or eight other busses were parked about the parking lot. Some arrived and others departed during our brief stay. Trucks too, but rather few automobiles seem to travel the roadway. Twenty yards to the north of the establishment is an open-faced concrete blockhouse about the size of a small one-car garage, with a cross atop of it. Obviously a religious shrine; a very common feature along the roadways of Mexico. For that matter, not uncommonly seen even in southern new Mexico, Arizona, and southern Texas . . . though far less commonly. To my surprise, a fair number of the travelers who are stopped to use the restaurant facilities, will also make a brief homage at the shrine - perhaps about 5% seem to do so. I would see it as a deeply ingrained superstition perpetrated by their strongly Catholic religious tradition; and only slowly waning, in a world which is increasingly technological and ever so slightly more affluent. It has been said that a superstition is a premature explanation that has overstayed its time.

As we approach Torreon, the desert began to green account of the increased availability of irrigation waters of the Naca River which flows nearby. There are extensive systems of watering canals to be seen. Arrival in Torreon is at the Central Comionera, a couple of hours before sunset. From there I take a taxi up to "circa de la Centro" . . . (near the center of town) - generally considered to be the old plaza de arms area. Cost . . . About twelve pesos. There I get out and shoulder my two bags, to wander the streets in search of a clean but older hotel. I first explored one that was far too mean and shabby even for my rustic tastes.

Along the route to Chihuahau, we picked up a passenger who sat in the seat next to me. He appeared to be thirty-five or forty years of age, and carried a large artist's sketch pad. He told me that he lives in El Paso and was coming down to Chihuahua for a week of vacation time, to visit friends and relatives. He was born and raised in Chihuahua; and says he owns a small piece of land down here. He is employed doing sculpting work in the jewelry trade; and studied at an art school in Chihuahua. We approached Chihuahua about 8:30 PM, in the darkness of a mountainous desert terrain. The bus stopped at the edge of town, at the large bus terminal, designated as "La Centro Comionera", which I presume means something like "the central common carrier depot". My fellow traveler tells me it used to be located in the central part of the city, but has now been relocated to the periphery of town. This change of location of bus terminals to the outskirts of the cities appears to be a prevalent trend throughout Mexico. I am told that there are two hundred thirty different bus carrier lines in Mexico, for the busses are far the most common public transportation system here; and they carry that burden of humanity efficiently and economically. Their large numbers of vehicles require a large area of loading and parking space. The lobbies tend to be quite large in the bigger cities, and - as with our U.S. Airlines - each carrier company maintains a booth where the tickets are sold; and where one can scan the posted departure time, destination, cost, and hours of travel time to any destination. There are usually a number of options from which one can choose his destination - with variations in time of departure, but with less variation as to prices. Some of the busses are slower because of their making local stops along the route, while others are express. As a "Gringo", being unable to speak the language, I am wary of getting into the wrong line and missing my scheduled bus, or getting onto the wrong vehicle. So, when I purchase my "bolito", I generally ask them to give me the individual number of the bus - "a que estationemiento?" (at which number of loading platform?). Gradually one acquires enough of these little Spanish phrases and experience of the routine, that one's level of anxiety begins to wane. Curiously, I don't know whether these little phrases I construct from my limited vocabulary are anywhere near to being grammatically correct or not, for I have never heard anyone ask such questions in Spanish. It would appear that the majority of these Mexican people travel thus so regularly, that they have a firm confidence about these elementary matters that seem to me more complex. I must presume that my Spanish phrased questions are somewhere near correct, because I have depended upon their feedback to keep me upon my intended destinations. But, I needs must be careful with my phrasing - so as to try to get the simple "Si" or "no"; or "Aqui" or "Adelante" answer; for if they should retort in regular Spanish sentence (or even phrases), I can't easily follow their meaning.

Well, it's a humbling experience to be aphasic and in need of so much information because of one's vast inexperience at what he is trying to do! The learning process always seems so painfully slow. Sometime it is discouraging, yet the pace of it is so steady that there isn't much time to dwell on that. Always busy trying to construct some new phrase because of some recent misunderstanding; or to figure out where one is going tomorrow, and why, and how . . . For no one has furnished me an itinerary, either specific nor general.

There are other benefits to the peripheral relocations of each city's Central Camionera. The mass of Mexico's peoples are poor, with not a high standard of living. Tourism is the country's number one industry. And unemployment is high. The relocation of the bus terminals seems to create a lot of extra jobs for taxi drivers. The streets within the cities are horribly narrow and tortuous; and heavy with unpredictable vehicle and foot traffic. Meanwhile, neither are they being upgraded, and the size, weight, and maneuverability of the busses is individually increasing; as are their numbers. It seems as though the entire population of Mexico spends part of each day on some bus or another. The central part of most Mexican cities would simply not have the space to contain the number of busses that use the Central Camionera.

In Chihuahua I paid the taxi driver twelve pesos (two dollars) to drop me off near the central plaza area. He stopped at a hotel and took me in, expecting me to sign in. I presume that some sort of commission then falls his way. I inquired the price and was quoted seventy-five peso (twelve dollars). But I didn't like the part about being manipulated this way, so I told him I might scout about elsewhere first, or said something in Spanish that I thought might imply that. In retrospect I came to see that as a mistake. I hoisted my gear upon my shoulders and began to check out the area on foot. After thirty-five or forty-five minutes of that, I finally checked in at a place where I was charged a hundred twenty-seven pesos (twenty-two dollars). And as I was a bit tired of hauling that gear about, I wasn't about to argue. Nor was the room a whit above marginal. I note that the sliding window of the room didn't have any lock or stay of any kind, so I fashioned a barricade post from a closet hanger bar before I went out for a walk about 8:00 PM. I promptly managed to get myself lost, while now the dingy streets and alleys were becoming deserted before I finally found my way back to the hotel two hours later. Actually I had passed right by my hotel a couple of times before I recognized it - which at least says something for my native sense of directions. During those two hours of wandering, I was quite alone and vulnerable, with plenty of cash. I would have been easy picking's. My rough and shabby appearance undoubtedly offered me some disguise protection. And I can run pretty good when sufficiently motivated. In truth, I was rather relieved when I found my way back at 10:00 PM. And I was also hungry; so I went into the hotel café and ordered up a fine and tasty meal for about twenty pesos (three and a half dollars). Having had no nap, and being physically and mentally fatigued, I retired into bed about midnight.

I was up about 9:00 AM to a calm and sunny day. I stopped to have breakfast of eggs and bacon with a glass of orange juice (huevos con tostados, y jugo de narajan): and then hiked out to explore the many streets and by-ways of stores and shops. Of course I didn't purchase anything, because it would increase the burden of that which I needs must then carry about with me for the remainder of this trip . . . and for life. Actually there were three things which I sort of planned to acquire somewhere upon the three-week course of this trip: a fine guayabera (perhaps even two of them), a good leather belt, and some nice bandannas of unique pattern or theme. And there is always a sort of vague and exciting hope that I might suddenly come upon some small and easily portable article so unique and affordable as to bring me some definite satisfaction in return for a relatively small amount of trouble. Perhaps an unusual sample of mineral or stone will meet that standard, for example. Or, to find something uniquely appropriate to be used as a gift. Everywhere one turns, there are stalls and shops of trinkets and jewelry articles; and people hawking such from the steps and pavements of the streets. They are called "joyeria". About the only stalls and shops more common than the joyerias" are those of the vendors of the host of temptingly delicious things one might buy to eat - and they are well patronized by the native throngs. Appear even to find their native customers even when those strands and mobile contraptions are situated afar from the milling crowds. One might get the impression that the only thing more perpetually hungry than a Mexican, are their Mexican dogs. I don't recall actually seeing anyone crowding up to the "joyeria" stall: I wonder how they make their living? Perhaps it is the case that most of those same folks of the hungry masses have also some dark and hidden passion for some one or another of these trinkets of jewelry. A passion perhaps that is too expensive, or too obviously evil, as to permit the common exposure of that passion . . . a thing such as one might generally prefer to be unnoticed. And then, when the closely nurtured cache of funds has been hoarded away, the gleeful miscreant portion of his being surges forth with cash in hand to sate his or her lust for the hitherto forbidden and long coveted trinket. The lust thus sated, he may then revert to the open decency that occupies the major portion of his customary work-a-day existence and life.

I did stop to get a small Espanol-Engles Diccionario; and then had to hunt about for a place to get a magnification loop, finding it difficult to read from any amount of unsteadiness of a moving vehicle, or when the light is slightly dim. I am rather careful about what, where, and when I eat - because of my vivid memory of an episode of bacillary dysentery that laid me low in Mexico City back in about 1968. And, because I generally eat but one meal daily, I often manifest a strong gastro-colic reflex, especially if it is anything more that modest in quantity. So I generally like to get a room either before or immediately after I finish that (usually) evening meal. I certainly try to avoid eating anything in the hours just before I am to travel. For when the intestinal reflexes begin to pressure one, the struggle for control of the sphincter can be long and grueling, leaving one with little potential attentiveness for the passing scenic countryside; or any reading one might have intended.

I returned to the hotel about 1:00 PM with intent to rent the room another night. Checkout time is 4:00 PM. It was the same clerk who registered me last evening. Her response now was a sort of smug NIGYYSOB, "oh no o o o . . . ." At least that was my interpretation of her response. It surprised me - in a poor county: and in a not very classy sort of a hotel. Surely they can't be booked with swarms of reservations. Then it dawned upon me, that last night after I had paid cash for my room, I stopped at the desk on my way out for a hike, to get a receipt to protect me against charges of non-payment here in some foreign country where I can't even speak well enough to protest on my own behalf. I recall that at the time, she was sort of flustered and difficult about the receipt business. And the one hundred twenty seven peso charge did seem a bit steep in proportion to the low quality. Perhaps she had already pocketed part of the money; for the receipt she gave certainly has something of the quality of make-shift about it.

Actually, I was entirely pleased now, at this necessity which required me to relocate to another hotel. It would give me some actual basis for comparison of value. So I set my mind upon the San Francisco Hotel, which I had seen while walking about. Quite a nice looking place. And I was curious to find out just how nice - and how expensive - this quite first-class place might be. It came to only two hundred forty pesos . . . actually only forty dollars. Though more expensive, it was surely much more of a bargain on a dollar for dollar basis. And I enjoyed my stay there. It was clean, plush, quiet, and secure. That evening I sat in the lounge to have a Margarita before taking supper. With the drink they brought me a large serving of peanuts. When I had finished all of that, I was a little too full to consider taking a full meal - also a little too woozy. So I returned to my room, contemplated tomorrow's plans and then went to bed a little early, because I was developing a head-cold.

Earlier that day I had taken a taxi out to the depot of the ferrocarril (railway), with rather a firm intent to having some experience of this mode of travel. The cost of the taxi was twelve pesos each way. The structure of the depot was old, but of firm and handsome construction. The lobby was the size of a basketball court. But to my amazement, there wasn't a bench, a chair, or a stick of furniture anywhere within! The ceiling was enormously high. There was a set of small ticket windows at one end of the building. One was open, with a clerk in attendance. Several sets of tracks ran in front of a wide concrete platform out front - the whole thing, covered by a high roof. A string of four or five passenger cars had been let standing, while a single-unit diesel-electric locomotive was lazily shifting a couple cars to nearby locations. The passenger-cars of the train were perhaps of early 1950's vintage, but unwashed and unmatched. A few of the natives in simple clothing were about the premises. They and some vendors were in and out and round about the idle passenger-cars. Everyone waiting the lapse of perhaps an hour, until the train might finally depart.

There were twenty or thirty people inside the vast and nearly empty depot. Most were grungy in their appearance. Most were propped-up sitting against the walls, with their boxes and baggage beside them. Some, lying on the floor with baggage as a pillow. I knew that I wanted to travel at the first-class status, if that were an option.

I approached the ticket window to get some information as to destinations and schedules, and to acquire a ticket. But the ticket agent knew less English that what I knew of Espanol. No schedule was posted anywhere on those expansive bare walls, nor was there any printed handout of schedules. No shred of any information whatsoever. Nor could I find anyone round about, or of the idle work-crews, who could give me any information.

3/23/95

Yesterday, in Guatalajara, I took a taxi down to the central area of this second largest city of Mexico, with a population of three million. There I exchanged some American currency, at a 6.8 to 1 rate of exchange - the best rate I have yet obtained. A morning newspaper in Guatalajara, this morning listed the exchange rate at 7.23 to 1. But I notice this evening in Puerto Vallarto that they are giving an exchange rate of 6.2 to 1. It would appear that the American tourist trade here is so heavy that they can get away with paying out the substandard rate. And along the streets of Puerto Vallarto and the contiguous communities, one can see the American pressure physically upon this bustling spot. American couples walking and gawking upon the streets which are crowded with American being.

I was up at 9:00 AM this morning to shave and comb before wandering across the street to get my bus ticket (eighty pesos) to Puerto Vallarto. I then walked about the general area of the Central Camionera for 1½ hours and was again amazed at the number of shops in this (and all) areas that sell only, just shoes. Shoes(?) . . . Yes, and some boots, too. But I have never seen any customers in these shoe store. I wonder if they actually ever sell any shoes. Or, perhaps, these shoe stores are just some form of bogus investment 'opportunity' that someone is selling 'en-mass' to some gullible investors. Actually, there are more of these shoe shops than there are "joyerias"; and they don't seem to be making any more sales. Obviously, something here that I am not grasping.

Well, I circled about a one-half mile area, and as I came up to the last half of the circle, I discovered that I was in front of a long building that housed the ticket booths of a half dozen different bus lines; along with the usual central cafeteria of the building. It was just the same arrangement at the terminal which I have been using, but it houses different ticket vendors. I stopped to examine the prices and destinations being offered. Now, how could I - as a tourist - guess that there was this other bus terminal near at hand; and one that offered destinations not offered at the other. In fact, when I first arrived in Guadalajara - and ever since - I have been puzzled as to how it happens that only six or eight bus lines (of Mexico's 230) are represented here in this second largest city in all of Mexico. And now as I continue my encircling walk, the pieces of the riddle become apparent, and I begin to get a completed answer to my earlier questions. To my surprise, there are six or eight of these other identical buildings, each about a hundred yards wide, that are set side-by-side upon this half mile long and slightly curving concrete driveway; and a huge auto parking lot is set at the center. Between each building, is an empty hundred yard space - where additional similar buildings can be set, when need arises. It only happens that just by chance, I arrived at the endmost building of this string of buildings; and thus failed to notice that the rest of this string of buildings were also sub-units of the same giant Central Comionera.

I turned in my key, and left my motel room about 12:40 PM; and packed my gear across the street to prepare my departure on a bus of the Primero Plus Line at 1:30 PM. I passed through the departure turnstile and stood before the bus designated for Puerto Vallarto. The driver nor attendants were at hand, so I stood awaiting. A handsome thirty year old Mexican woman was already standing there, also awaiting to board. Three large cardboard boxes stood beside her. I presumed they were hers, and that she was awaiting the arrival of personnel of the bus. She was a bit extroverted; attempted to make some casual conversation with me. But she couldn't speak English; and I could comprehend only a few words and phrases of the Spanish. We stood there some three or four minutes before the bus personnel arrived to board us. She continued to attempt to get some words of conversation through to me . . . a forewardness rather uncommon for a Mexican woman. Their customs generally mandate that they be unto themselves and withdrawn in the presence of men - especially with men with whom they are unacquainted. Yet, she was becoming ever more friendly. She introduced herself as "Candy", and we shook hands. She indicated that she was going to Puerto Vallarto, and wondered where I was going. It crossed my mind that she might have had a shot of hooch or some psychotropic just before arriving here, and that she might just now be beginning to get a little high from it, as the substance was now beginning to make its way into her central nervous system.

I was assigned to seat #16, and stored my one bag in the overhead compartment upon entering the coach. There were only three or four of us passengers upon the bus at this time. She was approaching the outrageous in her familiarity. She suggested that I sit further back in the bus - with her, but I declined, indicating that this was my assigned seat. Well, at this point, I wasn't just sure what to think, as she proceeded to seat herself beside me here about six rows from the front of the bus. Soon she had her hands upon me; and then became openly suggestive in her squirming motions. I would not say that she was not a little tempting, even in her outrageousness; not that even an aging fellow such as myself was not a little flattered by such attentions. But I am still thinking about the intoxication theory to explain her progressive misbehavior. And I began checking the various places upon my being where I have tucked away some little bundles of cash. The money-vest beneath my T-shirt at the waist; under the elastic bands at the tops of my B-K socks, below each popliteal fossa; my wallet in my hip-pocket; and in the zipped inner pockets of my reversible vest. One of those pockets contained a roll of twenty one-dollar bills. I also had smaller Mexican bills and coins in my pants pockets. Patting myself down, I note that all areas are secure. As I am pushing her hands away and attempting to calm her down for a long four or five minutes, a handsome young American man of fair complexion and perhaps twenty-two years of age entered the bus and sat across the aisle from me. This Mexican gold digger then abandoned me and sat herself next to him, giving him now the same sort of routine. It was a relief to be free of her, and I rechecked my caches of cash once again. About five or ten minutes of this, and the young man suddenly abandoned his assigned seat in this un-crowded bus to move into the front-most row of the bus, adjacent to the bus driver. Several minutes later, she again sat herself next to me, again to probe me with her delicate fingers, and I was once more on the defensive. Another ten minutes of this, and seeming to grow discouraged at the effort, she moved further back into the bus. I checked my caches of cash once more, and was a bit astonished to discover that her efforts had met with some success. She had managed to make off with my roll of twenty, one-dollar bills from the zipped inside pocket of my vest, as well as the few loose paper pesos from my front pants pocket. Fortunately however, what she got was only relatively slim pickings from me. I wondered how much she might have taken from the young fellow that had been sitting across the aisle from me. I considered lodging a complaint with the bus conductor or the driver, but why would they want to believe me without any evidence - even if our language barriers did permit an exchange of ideas and details between us? Or, what if the Mexican police were to get involved into the handling of such unprovable accusations: she and I might both end up in a Tiajuana-jail - for God knows how long. No! As it was, under these circumstances, perhaps I got off real easy. About forty-five minutes later we reached the first bus stop several miles down the road. There the bus driver got off to get a coke, and the little rip-off artist stepped off the bus right behind him. But, or course, she did not resurface, and the driver promptly departed with no apparent thought of her absence. I had adequate time to ponder the matter before she made her get-away, but as I reconsidered the intensity of the this girl's actions, it seemed to me improbable that neither the driver nor the conductor could have failed to notice her impropriety. Surely they ought to have intervened. So there seemed reason enough to suspect that the bus driver, the conductor, and the girl were all part to this little swindle. I am pleased at least to suspect that her heart sank some, too; when she later privately opened my roll of bills to discover that each of the twenty was merely a one-dollar bill, and that the paper pesos were only small pocket-change bills.

It might be best if no one ever heard of this little incident, because it sure does make me look foolish.

We arrived in Puerto Vallarto about 7:30 PM - a total of about six hours driving time. The main town is quaintly handsome, but obviously very Americanized, with many American tourists milling about. At the south edge of town, the big mountains came right down to the Pacific Ocean shore, so that the bus must pass through two or three tunnels beneath these mountain buttresses in order to get to this outlying suburban sector where the busses make their regular boarding and discharging of travelers. There certainly are an uncomfortable over-abundance of Americans in this sector of town, too. Here, the shops and streets are fairly bustling with people. Now as I reflect upon the matter, I can see that this area is - in fact - the original and current Puerto Vallarto. The streets are cobbled, the buildings are crowded. Most of the streets tend to be narrow. The buildings rise at most, to five or six stories . . . most are one and two stories; and their architecture is decidedly Spanish in the exterior, with many of the business section of town being of whitewash large grained course stucco. But a look inside the buildings tell one that this rustic Spanish interior is decidedly more real and true than a mere mock-up appearance.

From the bus-depot, I shouldered my two bags and hiked back along that street of main traffic the bus had just traversed. I hiked six or eight blocks, passing a couple hotels before seeing one that caught my fancy, about a half block off of this main street of traffic. There I take a room for a 126 pesos. The building is about six stories high and appears to have been built in, perhaps, the 1930's, in a handsome Spanish design. There was no television in the room, nor an air conditioner. A little information card on the dresser advised the hotel guest that one need not be disturbed by the small lizards one may see about the room - as they are quite harmless. And besides that, they help to keep the mosquito and insect population at a minimum. I walked out from the hotel after depositing there my bags; to find a place to eat. There appear to be a lot of these, including plenty that are quietly Spanish in flavor, inviting in appearance, and not overly expensive. The one I selected served a very tasty meal and cost me only thirty-five pesos (less than seven dollars), including the Margarita. I stopped to get a couple cokes to take back to the room. This, my regular custom, in order to assure myself an adequate daily fluid intake - to minimize the chance of any recurrent episode of renal stone, such as I once experienced several years earlier . . . an experience inevitably long remembered. In my room, I spend a few hours writing before getting to bed about 2:00 AM.

The moist tropical climate of the Pacific coast of Mexico, along with the lack of air-conditioning in the hotel both contribute to the rather musty odor of the bed clothing. A factor that perhaps weighed overly large in my initial overall impression of moderate disdain for the area of Puerto Vallarto. Mid-morning of the next day (March 24th) I arose, packed my gear, hiked back to the bus terminal, and paid my eighty peso bus fare to return to Guadalajara. Once more I was greatly impressed by the long climb up to the altiplano; and by the more pleasant climate of the huge plateau areas of these fertile agricultural lands; and by the more distant towering volcanic formations whose eons of intermittent activity have given rise to this expansive highlands area.

But, in fairness to Puerto Vallarto, I must say that there are many things about it which might seem to make it an interesting and pleasant place in which to retire. In the first place, its low elevation would make it ideal for persons with cardiac and lung conditions. Additionally, there is good access to easy transportation by sea, land, and air routes. Though there is the disadvantage of a fairly heavy American tourist population, they seem generally to spend the most of their time in those separately developed tourist spas to the north of Puerto Vallarto. I have the impression that one could perhaps, take an apartment in the more compact area of old Puerto Vallarto, and then live relatively inexpensively and not even have to own a vehicle, as one would be in easy walking distance to mercados for one's groceries. And, though perhaps the area is a little more expensive than the interior, still rather inexpensive compared to costs in the U.S.A. Should I retire, I think I might well consider coming to Puerto Vallato to take up a three to six month trial of living.

From Guadalajara I continued eastward across central Mexico by bus, enjoying the rugged landscapes and scenic fertile agricultural valleys. I was interested now in attending a bullfight to satisfy my curiosity and enlarge my Mexican cultural experience. It being Saturday when I arrive in Queretaro, and this being the bullfighting season, I thought my chances of seeing one in this large city might be excellent. Queretaro is some 220 kilometers north of Mexico City, and I specifically wished to avoid Mexico City entirely. For in the past few months the Mexican economy had declined considerably; and in the past few weeks the rate of exchange of the neuvo peso to the American dollar had fallen to about 7 to 1. And in consequence, I feared an undercurrent of seething animosity to Americans, along with the anger and hostility which the Mexican populace is more openly apt to direct toward their own form of government corruption. For months there had been intermittent armed insurrection in Chiapus Provence, south of Mexico City; and there is always the possibility that it could spread even into the capital city. I had a great reluctance to expose myself to that possibility except by some necessity, as I had already once visited Mexico City on a previous occasion some twenty years ago. Well remembered, because Montezuma reeked his full revenge upon me on that occasion.

I soon learned that there was no bullfight stadium in Queretaro. I would have to go to Mexico City if I wished to see a bullfight. I thought that I might just accept the fact that I was now destined to miss seeing the spectacle, at least on this trip. But as I contemplated that during the evening, I became progressively dissatisfied with that conclusion; and it disturbed my sleep intermittently through the night. From what I had been seeing of Mexico on this trip, the possibility of open riot and insurrections seemed to be remote. These people impress me as being family oriented and peaceful. Everyone, everywhere seemed quite preoccupied upon the streets, trying to make a few pesos by selling tacos, helados, etc.

In the morning I awoke late, but resolutely determined to see the bullfight in Mexico City, on this very day. It was already 10:00 AM. I quickly packed my two bags and took a taxi to the Central Camionera. By 11:15 AM, I had boarded a first class bus, bound for Mexico City. I had grave reservations about my chances of actually arriving there early enough to get to the stadium in time. Yet, it now seemed to me the central and single most important element of this entire trip; and I could not permit myself to pass it by without at least having made a mighty effort.

The bus arrived at the terminal in Mexico City by 3:00 PM; it was a large, clean, handsome, and busy place. But I was unable to find anyone that spoke enough English to facilitate my need for directions and information concerning this afternoon's bullfight. And time was working against my hope of getting to the stadium in time to gain admission. Finally I did encounter a cab driver who knew at least as much of English, as I, of Spanish. It was communication adequate to get him to understand my two objectives. First, to attend the bullfight this day; but before that, to get situated into a hotel where I first might drop off my luggage.

Off we went at a rapid pace, jumping lanes and skirting the slower traffic. I fumbled about for a seat belt and finally had to ask him where it was. His indication was that there were none, and no apparent need of one. Meaning, I guess, that he always drives like that; and that it is in no way dangerous - not at least in his view. There appeared to be some truth in what he said, for traffic conditions were wild. It was a 15 or 20 minute drive before he dropped me off at The Hotel Plaza Madrid on Calle Madrid, just off of Paseo de La Reforma. And he waited for me in the lobby while I rented my room (200 pesos). I dropped my bags into the room and returned to the cab, to continue the trip south to the bullfight stadium, near the Plaza de Torres - arriving just after 4:00 PM. Traffic was snarled and jammed for a radius of several blocks about the stadium. Foot traffic was moving faster than the taxies, so I paid the driver his 60 pesos, thanked him and went afoot the remaining several city blocks. Cars were double and triple parked; and upon the sidewalks and curbs, so that even the foot traffic was greatly slowed as people wound their various paths between the erratically parked vehicles. I ended up amid the milling throng, crowding their way toward the ticket booths and entrances. Fortunately, the lines at the ticket window were not very long. People with scalpers ticket were standing near the ticket line, negotiating prices with those yet seeking admission. I didn't attempt any such dealings on the side, for my Spanish is not adequate to the task, and I was greatly suspicious that it might lead me into some unheard-of complication. By dumb luck, I arrive at a ticket window labeled, "Sombra" (shade). Just what I wanted . . . not having to face into the afternoon sun. I was about to pay 91 pesos for a ticket, when someone returned one to the agent in the booth . . . which he let me have for 51 pesos (about 8 dollars). The throng was crowding towards the entrances; and the musical fanfare of bands could still be heard from inside the arena; and I was in fine spirits, knowing that I was going to be able to see the bullfight after all. Amid the noise and the shuffling crowd I move, straining to decipher the markings upon my ticket. Here was tunnel 4 - just where I needed to be. Through the tunnel and into the stadium I quickly found my seat assignment and sat me down. I had paused to rent a cushion, to set upon the concrete stadium bench seat. People were still milling about in search of their asientos (assigned seats) when the preliminary fanfare ended about five minutes after I had found my seat. The spectacle was about to begin. There were some announcements and some introductions of various worthy citizens over the P.A. system. And the matador and his retinue, readied and stationed themselves for the entrance of the first bull. At the center of the stadium was a large round ring of about 75 feet in diameter, enclosed by a 6½ foot high solid hardwood wall that is painted red. The floor of the arena is covered with fresh sand. The enclosure is interrupted by four gaps of 20 inches width space, 90 degrees apart from one another. A gated segment of the ring enclosure is opened as fifty thousand awed spectators watch a mighty, muscular, horned bull come charging and snorting into the arena. There is a solid baffle wall - of about 7 foot width, centered before each of the four gaps in the wall enclosing the arena. There, behind that baffle, one or another of the cape men frequently escapes from the charge of the bull, as they take turns in taunting and "running" the bull about the ring. Thus do they advance the bulls animosity and rage - at the same time, sapping away his limited reserve of energy. Spotting one or another of the taunting capes, the bull increases his pace toward the insult, lowers his head, and charges; as the cape man ducks behind a baffle wall. At the next baffle area, another cape appears, and without having lost his full momentum, the bull again picks up his pace, and charges once again - and misses -this second retreating cape man just as he inevitably missed the first one. Thus do the cape men endeavor to work the bull about the ring, six or a dozen times. Now the bull may come to a halt standing, frustrated, and breathing heavily;

perhaps aware the he is a little tired. And then appears the matador, his straight and masculine form wonderfully arrayed and light of foot, advancing slowly, surely, and cautiously, in face-to-face encounter, step-by-step towards the bull. The instinct of the bull at this point is to hold his ground for a moment; and to catch his breath . . . while dimly pondering this new tactic he now faces. The matador's close-fitting short trousers end snugly just below the knee, to override the top of his tight stockings that rise from his trimly slippered feet. The jacket is also close-fitting and brief in front. Jacket and trousers glint and sparkle in the afternoon sun. He wears a white shirt. Matador approaches the bull, having removed and displayed his loosely fitting cape to its full width before the bull. Holding the cape open with both hands, he shakes it gently towards the bull and drapes it off to the right beneath that outstretched arm . . . may even stamp a foot to further tantalize the momentarily stymied creature. In a moment or two, the bull lowers his head and makes a halting charge at the flaming red display of the cape as the matador pivots the cape aside. Having not made contact in the charge, the bull stops and pauses once again. The process is repeated, again and again; progressively draining the energies of the bull, rather than permitting its replenishment by any prolonged rest. The rage and determination of the animal seem to increase, even as its energy surely diminishes. The bull unwittingly preparing himself for his own final mortifications.

As to why the bull is so dim-witted as to repeatedly charge the red cape . . . that to me remains a mystery. For the frame of his adversary, the matador, is fully exposed beside the flashing red color of the cape and its relatively large surface area. That might also explain the next mystery; as to why the bull should suddenly go to the attack of the horse being ridden by the picador, who has suddenly entered the arena while the bull was preoccupied with the futility of charging an empty cape. The matador, or one of his cape men, leads the bull into the proximity of the heavily padded and blindfolded horse - the one truly innocent by-stander in this ritualized drama. A fate peculiar to that role. Well trained - and against all his instincts - restlessly to await that fate, stands the horse, however unhappily. Surely as the sun doth rise, the bull lowers his head and charges the horse broadside. On one of those several contests of that day, a particularly husky bull lifted the horse with its rider several feet off the ground, nearly hoisting them over the very top of the 6½ foot enclosure wall, before setting them back to earth as the rider forces the point of a spear deeply between the bull's shoulder blades. In fact, that seems to be the basic function of the mounted picador - to inflict perhaps a half dozen such deep wounds there just below the base of the neck of the bull, using this lance which is tipped with a broad based steel point about 3 ½ inches in length. Having accomplished that, the bull is much less inspired to continue that confrontation; and either backs and drifts away, or is easily distracted to another direction by the work of the cape men while the picador and his mount then exit the arena. Then the matador and his cape men taunt the bull into making several more passes at the cape. Now the picador holds in each hand a 2 1/2 foot long barbed dart. He attracts the bulls attention and then takes cautious steps towards the bull to close the thirty foot gap that separates them. Having approached to within fifteen feet of the bull, and from an attack angle of about forty degrees, the picador suddenly dashes across in front of the bull with the darts held high in each hand. While yet on the run, the picador reaches above the outstretched horns to jam the darts between the shoulder blades and then dances away to safety before the bull can make the quarter-turn and chase him down. Then a brief respite of a minute while the bull comes to an angry pause in a state of confusion. A second . . . and then a third picador successively repeat the planting of additional darts. Six of these embedded banderillas now dangle and bob about from his upper back with each step the animal now takes . . . festering and irritating along with the injury to his pride. Now again the matador strides magnificently into the arena to confront the bull. From this moment he now is allotted not more than sixteen minutes to bring the bull to its knees and demise. Again he removes his cape to challenge the bull by flourishing the red lining a few feet before its eyes. It is his intent to keep the angry beast piqued and on the move so as to weaken and fatigue - in preparation for the risk he must face in his final and most dangerous task in this grand ceremony; that of thrusting the long sword deeply into the bull's chest. The reluctant bull seems to summon forth some new source of strength to resume a new series of futile charges into the empty cape, as the matador demonstrates the deftness of his form and slippered feet to whirl and pivot, inducing the crashing creature to follow and circle with the movements of the cape. Sometimes charging straight through the suddenly withdrawn cape to stop short, turn about, and charge again towards the lure of the repositioned matador who faces him. There is the roar of the crowd of fifty thousand spectators, with each new charge of the bull and each unscathed escape of the master of ceremonies; his flourishes becoming ever more elaborate and risky as the bull weakens from fatigue and his bleeding injuries. From the bull's mouth a string of saliva trails out along his flank; and breathing heavily, he stumbles to his knees, re-groups, and slowly rises to charge again. Finally then, the bull is enough slowed and weakened that he stands motionless; can no longer be enticed into yet another charge. The matador is ready then to try for the kill. An assistant hands the matador a long, straight, narrow sword. Taking the sword in hand, he holds it at arm's length and thus poses a few seconds while facing the attentive bull. Then, aiming for a spot between the ribs and the shoulder blades on the left side of the creature's back, the matador lunges to close the gap of ten feet that separate him from the sacrifice. The bull lowers its head and begins its countercharge just as the matador reaches over the horns to thrust the sword up to the hilt, and into the creature's chest . . . hopefully piercing the aorta or the heart. A minute or so of staggering about, and the bull totters down upon its front knees, and then the hind quarters settle down to the earth. The head droops, but the body is still tense. If the creature then makes no further attempt to rise, one of the matador's assistants cautiously uses a six inch blade to reach over the horns and quickly transect the spinal chord just below the base of the skull. The extremities jerk but once, and instantly the creature becomes unstrung, and topples helplessly onto its side, having taken its last breath.

It is finished.

A team of horses pulls a small two-wheeled platform into the arena. The bull's head is lifted by the attendants onto the platform, where it is secured in place by a chain; and the limp monster carcass is then dragged from the arena. The matador and retinue then stroll in manly leisure triumph about the perimeter of the arena; receiving the applause and affection of the encircling sixty rows of aficionados in the stands. The rows rise steeply, the topmost, perhaps one hundred twenty feet above the floor of the arena. The seasoned spectators have judged the matador's performance upon his restraint, posture, command, style, timing, and finesse; and their response to the matador's triumphal promenade (paseo) is roughly proportional to the excellence of that performance. But the darlings of the slate of matadors own a certain grip of command which they exercise also over the crowd - in addition to the command which they have learned to exercise over the bull in that encounter in the arena; and the command of self-discipline which they must exercise upon their own fears and inhibitions so as to enable themselves to gracefully perform this show of bravado.

The encircling paseo of triumph may continue on to a second, third or forth lap . . . . Perhaps more. From the front-most rows of spectators .

. . hats, jackets, leathered flasks, and even an occasional boot is thrown into the arena towards the feet of the matador as he passes. The matador, smiling and waving to the crowd, maintains his leisurely stroll and now and then deigns to stoop to retrieve one or another of the articles which have landed at his feet in the arena; and with a good-natured ease, tosses it back into the crowd, to the approximate locations from whence it has arrived. His trailing retinue of attendants participate, in similar manner, returning the majority of the articles. Where the rain of enthusiastic outpouring is large, the triumphal paseo moves more slowly . . . requiring more time to restore the generous display of the outpouring of goods and affection. Now and then, a past hero of the arena, or an official or local magnate makes his way into the ring, to shake his hand and embrace the matador; and arm-in-arm attend the paseo for several steps. All very grand and spontaneous, on the one hand. On the other hand, all of this has become routine and customary onto the point of ritual . . . by dint of customary repetition, through some hundreds of years of established pattern.

So soon as the triumphal paseo has ended, a large part of the crowd is headed for the urinals, in preparation for the next round of the bullfight; and for the next wave of cold beer that is first being conveyed and peddled into the tiers of spectator. Meanwhile, a work crew of eight or ten men has entered the empty arena to shovel out the clots of blood and sand, sprinkle in some fresh sand, and then to smooth the sandy surface anew, in preparation for the next round of contest between man and bull.

I am told that the fighting of the bulls generally goes on for about two hours; and that usually four are thus sacrificed on any given Sunday of the bullfight season. On this particular Sunday however, the event continued on for four hours; and eight bulls breathed their last. I gather that - as on this day - an unusually enthusiastic crowd may demand and appeal for an additional round; and sometimes get their way.

During one of the rounds of this day, the pace of actions had slowed and the crowd was protesting its displeasure at the famed matador, whose every tactic failed to keep the bull upon its futile attack. Instead, the bull had taken up a defensive stance upon some favored spot. While the crowd was booing, the matador was waving his upraised hand in questioning appeal, toward the official behind the wall of the closure and towards the owners at the topmost booths of the stadium. As if to say, that the fault was in this bull which was docile, and that he demanded another bull such as might allow him to prove his virtuosity and high reputation - a bull with some fire in its belly. The ranch that supplies a bull that proves thusly docile, is disgraced thereby. But, as it happened, this same docile bull then suddenly came to life! And provided one of the grandest contests of the day. At one point early in this revived contest, the bull tripped the matador into the sand as the tip of a horn caught his ankle in a charge at the cape. I was surprised at my own spontaneous gasp of horror as the bull then again quickly turned, lowered its head, and butted the downed man . . . yet, somehow, failed to injure him with either the flashing horns nor weighty hoofs, and in its rush the bull passed over the man and rolled him into the dust. A murmur of dissatisfaction went up from the crowd . . . as if to say, "Can we call so dishonored a man by the name of matador?" It all happened so very quickly that I can't easily piece together just how it all occurred. Ending up in a cloud of dust behind the bull, the matador sprang immediately to his feet and regained his manly composure in a state of righteous indignation. Dusting off his bangled attire, he snatched his cape from the floor of the arena, shook the dust from it, and promptly returned as the matador indeed, to face the now inspired bull. Two lost souls, restored to honor. The crowd too, was restored to a rousing enthusiasm by this unusual heroic change of circumstances in the contest, as the matador began his task of working the bull into fatigue with a series of spectacular cape passes. That accomplished, he then flawlessly buried the sword to the hilt within the bull's deep chest. And the bull dropped immediately toward its final demise. No victory so sweet as that snatched from the jaws of defeat! The crowd was on its feet in ecstasy. It seemed as though the triumphal paseo might never end.

Throughout this afternoon of splendor and spectacle, the air was of a perfect balmy temperature of comfort; and there was the very gentlest of a breeze - just enough to make one aware of the very perfection of this waning afternoon in Mexico City. And I was enthrall to the magnificence of this grand event and all of its ancient evolving pageantry. All about the stadium, and woven into the fabric of these customs and proceedings are the many levels of creature and creative psychodynamics. And too, by chance, yet another magnificent element contributes itself to all that I experienced at that grand stadium on this enchanted day. Directly above, the great birds of modern aviation were roaring toward their landings some ten miles to the east. Thunderbirds . . . mystic harbingers of things to come. Modern parade and spectacle, perfectly combined with the ancient. What a tribute to the ever evolving imagination and mind of man.

The End

R. Garner Brasseur

Addendum:

Mexico is going down in flames over the control of drugs by rival cartels and gangs, and the problem is spilling over into the USA. At the heart of the problem is what has become an enormous appetite by gringos. I had no idea how big a problem that might be until we catch news of the tons of illegal substances coming across the borders. And hundreds of murders and of those killed in the cross-fires by and between the rival gangs.

Even when I lived in Southern Oregon in the late 1960's there was already a drug problem there, which seemed to be centered around the Cave Junction area and radiated to all the surrounding areas. As I have never had any personal experience with either alcohol, MJ, or other illegal substances, I was only remotely aware of it all. That whole area between Hwy 5 and Hwy 101, from Roseburg down to Redding is rather of the nature of a wilderness which seems to have been used increasingly for the illegal growing of MJ. As the lumber industry was going out, people from all over the country were moving in to grow MJ along with those now unemployed lumber industry people. MJ began to sell at a thousand dollars a pound. Mendacino County became then the heart of the problem. There was a helicopter crackdown on this illegal substance farming in the 1980's, and the price rose to $5,000 per pound. It became a good living if one didn't get caught. Many of these 'farmers' became wealthy - strong income on which no taxes were being paid. Some enterprising high school students were raking in fifty thousand or a hundred thousand dollars in their summer vacations. People began to be able to live in comfort with this new income source. The illegal growing persists. In some towns MJ is the only major business, and what other businesses there are, can offer no comparable wage. One Humbolt County resident is quoted as saying that of 300 families in her community, only five were not growing MJ. (These figures and details gathered from THE WEEK, December 3, 2010)

Alcohol had caused a great deal of social difficulties throughout the ages, but when it became illegal, the associated problems became a great deal more troublesome. MJ and possibly other substances may end up in needing to be legalized similarly. Along with alcohol, it may continue to ruin health and lives, but the government will never be big enough to protect people from the detrimental results of their own indiscretions and folly.

> "Everyone wants to save the world; no one wants to help mom do the dishes."

AUTUMN TRAVEL AND VISITATIONS - 2001

by R.Garner Brasseur, M.D.

INSTALLMENT ONE:

I returned home 24 October from six weeks of travel having visited the Northeast, the Northwest, and territories in between. And have now spent the past couple weeks in an intense effort to produce new and updated Brasseur Genealogy family group sheets - necessitated in order to debrief myself of the details while the information was still fresh in mind; and to file away the clutter of accumulate notes, data sheets, and scraps of paper from my pockets. That project now about 90-95 percent completed. Will get copy out to you when completed in the near future. Not that you or anyone would have cause to more than merely peruse the data, but mostly just 'for the record', as they say. And of course to bolster my own delusion that I have actually accomplished something of possible value or interest as I loaf about the country making a general nuisance of myself. Like Socrates' horsefly, buzzing about among the population of horses to keep them enervated with twitching skin and swishing tails - lest they otherwise slumber away their transient mortality in an excess of lethargic contentment.

On the morning of the 11th of September (earthquake day\ there are traces of age in my one-horse shay\ a general flavor or mild decay\ but nothing local, as one might say\ there couldn't be, for the deacon's art\ had made it so like in every part\ that there wasn't a chance for one to start) I stopped in Springfield, MO to get an oil change for $15.00 at Wal-Mart.

There, I learned that New York City had just been attacked! The first tower was in the process of collapse as I watched the television monitor. Now here was something to ponder! It was truly news to me as it had been my good fortune to have had the radio of my one-horse-shay cease its function several months earlier. I stopped that night at a nice roadside rest stop in Indiana to sleep and ponder the news. And to puzzle out a possible solution as to what action I might have taken were I to have been aboard one of those fated flights. In the morning when I awoke and yawned to yet another fine day, I continued eastward (part of the autumn migration of odd birds). (And then of a sudden . . . \Ah, but stay. I'll tell you what happened without delay\scarring a person into fits\and frightening a fellow out of his wits.) Immediately I was aware of a noise from the odometer cable (traces of age in the one-horse-shay). The noise suddenly ceased. But so did the function of the odometer and speedometer. (And yet as a whole, it is past a doubt) that I am free to continue upon my route. Frozen in time was the odometer reading - at 324,500 miles. Henceforth I must gauge my speed by that of the trucks which cluster and hover all about me. The log of my mileage no longer continues. A certain moral there - not all of history is or has been recorded. We can merely suppose and speculate at much of what might have been. That, of course, true also concerning history that has been recorded - since most or many are written from some particular individual and political-religious point of view. We are ever free to temper our own view of matters upon the basis of what seems likely in lieu of other information, probability, and our own experience of the nature of reality.

On the night of the 12th, I stopped over with cousins Earl and Barbara Youmell in Cleveland where we spent the evening in interesting speculations about this day's events which have transfixed the attention of the nation. They seem to be contentedly retired and plan now to spend a part of their time in Florida.

END OF INSTALLMENT ONE.

INSTALLMENT TWO:

This nation was stunned and became suddenly introspective at the enigmas facing it in consequence of New York's 'earthquake day'. Individual citizens escaping to fortress of solitude to puzzle out the meanings of this as it pertains to their own immediate and national concerns. My Cleveland

Youmell cousins abandoned their prearranged plans for visiting with cousins, Frank and Glenna Youmell, with whom they had intended a get-together in the Finger Lakes Area of New York for this very weekend. Contrails in the skies were not to be seen for several days henceforth. Was this an internal conspiracy or the work of an alien nation? Was the nation at war? Were further assaults to be expected? Who was the enemy and where was he hidden? How and when would we acquire enough additional information to decide such questions? I too pondered these questions as I departed eastward from Cleveland, skirting the northern edges of the Finger Lakes en route to Massachusetts. Answers to these questions would require time and the evolution of further developments. Meanwhile, the national security was in the hands of the legitimate government and its military establishment.

The advancing years find me increasingly confined to my own fortress of solitude, and seeking my own answers concerning the nature of reality and a valid view of the historical past. No reason that I can discern for these new concerns to deter me from my current investigations and travels. And the official pronouncements specifically affirm that point of view. Each citizen must now (and always) come to his own conclusions as to the probability of personal and national risk; and be regulated thereby, as we live our lives through the individual gestalt-like (vague and shadowy) perceptions of our day-to-day reality. We are officially advised to be cautious, however, and the experience of my entire life seems to affirm the wisdom of such caution. Thus did I arrive in Massachusetts to continue my investigations into genealogy. Within the past eight or ten generations, some of the Brasseur descendants have taken to using the name of Duhamel, rather than Brasseur. Specifically how that came about remains to me a matter of conjecture. I have engaged in this particular improbable search because I have lost the trail of the descendants of many of the Duhamels of some three to four generations past, and have wondered if many of them might not have emigrated into manufacturing towns of Massachusetts a century or so past.. Armed with information from the social security death lists as to what Massachusetts communities might have Duhamel residents, I began to check out town hall death records - community by community. The employees of the town clerk office of Southbridge were helpful to me but none of my investigations into Duhamels there showed any connection to the families I was seeking. There appear to be many Duhamels who are not derived from Brasseur families - most of them, in point of fact. Among the many other communities I checked into, the town clerk employees who are charged with collection of this information (supposedly information of public record) are in no way cooperative to making that information available. The citizens of Sweden seem more aware than most - of the reality that governmental agencies tend to be more than useless in their function. That they are often, actually obstructing their actual intended purpose - unless and until an informed citizenry can find a will and a way to make them behave themselves. And thus I found no evidence of there being any Brasseur-Duhamel people in my limited search in Massachusetts and Rhode Island. I did find death records of a Brasseur death in each of two communities there, but there was not enough information on the death certificates to take me back far enough to make a definite connection to either of the two Brasseur families I know to have emigrated there (and from which they most probably derived). I do have limited records of those Brasseur families being in New Bedford, Massachusettes and in Woonsocket, Rhode Island. There is a fairly good French-American Genealogy society and library located in the basement of the Unitarian Church in Woonsocket. I spent most of one Saturday there, but came up far short of what the reality of their numbers and existence must have been.

Before departing Massachusetts, I stopped in one afternoon to re-visit Donald and Elaine Brasseur in North Andover (from whom I obtained excellent information on a previous sojourn) to collect a little more information of their family and have supper with them and two of their granddaughters. Their Brasseur ancestor is the only one of our French-Canadian Brasseur family to have served in the Civil War. And I also stopped at the Haverhill city library and city hall, as well as at the Groveland city hall to collect just a few other scraps of information as are to be reflected on the "A-1" family group sheets. In all, I spent four or five days in Massachusetts, enjoying the finest of weather conditions and sleeping in one or another of their few rest areas. I spent one of those nights at a private campground so that I never went overly long without a chance for a good shower. I keep root-beer in the ice chest I had borrowed from son Real; and often have some bread or crackers to eat with cheese, bologna, and sardines before I turn in at night. Massachusetts is very woodsy, quite covered with rocky hills and mountains, and laced with widening streams and valleys through which are scattered large and small communities. There are old factory buildings in many of these communities - buildings that appear to be a hundred years old or more. Many of them are still being used. I happened to be coming out of the library at Athol - toward the northwest of the state - right at noon and was surprised to see a couple hundred people pouring out upon the street from one of those very old factory buildings. It reminded me of how we used to pour out of school at noon and head home for lunch before returning to the afternoon session.

I spent a night in southern New Hampshire before driving up highway 89 into Vermont. There at Newport, I had a great deal of difficulty before finally locating cousin Yves and Yolanda Brasseur who I first encountered back in 1989 when they were living on a big dairy farm about 5 miles north of town. Pious, generous and pleasant people. That was the year I talked him into going with me into the interior of Quebec Province where his ability to speak the French and his remote connection with the Brasseur families in the Granby area helped me acquire some of that genealogy information. He was pleased to see me again. Says he had been trying to get in touch with me but couldn't find out where I had moved to, and his cousin - the Laliberty woman (with Brasseur ancestors) from Granby area had a stroke and couldn't come up with the information for him. Yves and Yolanda are now retired and living in town and sharing the occupancy of a house with one of their daughters and her family. They had their 50th wedding anniversary just a couple months ago, and had wanted to have me to come up for the celebration. Yves had severe Rheumatic Fever when he was a young man and secondary valvular heart disease which precipitated upon him a cerebral embolus which severely disturbed his ability to read some five years ago. But he has now gradually recovered some of his reading ability once more. I stayed over for supper with them. Their English is only very slightly limited, but they appear to generally speak French in their home. He told me the story of all of the farm-loan and legal conniving that robbed him and his family (13 children) of the farm and dairy herd upon which he had spent his life in acquiring, working, and developing.

The good weather stayed right with me, and that night I drove on west across northern Vermont and into New York state where I slept out in the Plattsburgh Wal-Mart parking lot. (Wal-Mart specifically makes their lots across the country available for the shoe-string traveler.) Part of the next day I spent at the Messena library, checking my E-mail and catching up on some journal reading. I had some old travelers checks of a couple years vintage that were getting pretty ragged, and I thought to cash them in before they become finally illegible. Then, later in the day I stopped by Brasher Falls (perhaps fifteen miles distant) to look up Frank and Glenda Youmell. I had become acquainted with all of these Youmell cousins some eight or ten years previously, when they had invited me to the first international Brasseur-Youmell Family reunion at the Andre and Yolande Aubiscon cabin on the Regis River, just north of Brasher Falls (she being born a Youmell).

Frank Youmell had just gotten retired a month or two ago and was involved with a bit of a water-system and small carpentry job on his home. Glenda will continue to drive the school bus during the current school year. She is involved with the union functions and appears to me to be in danger of having the telephone grow upon her listening ear. Their three daughters are grown and gone, one married and living at nearby Potsdam - the mother of their only grandchild, Jacob. I stayed overnight and had a nice visit with them. She and I are a little skeptical and questioning of one another on philosophical issues. They have been motorcycle enthusiasts through the years and I suspect they may have some intentions of another motorcycle odyssey in to coming summer. Meanwhile Frank will get a chance to do more hunting than he has in previous years. He showed me his little collection of rifles and told me some of the history of his older prizes.

END OF SECOND
INSTALLMENT.

INSTALLMENT THREE:

Shortly after I had lunch with cousins Frank and Glenda Youmell at Brasher Falls, NY, I headed northward, to cross the bridge near Messina into Canada. The traffic from Canada was backed up for a mile or more account of large scale searching of vehicles at the American immigration port, where the national guard appeared to be assisting the immigration officers with the searches. More trouble from terrorist plots seems to be anticipated. I was still considering events of the recent twin towers bombing and my views have been congealing only gradually as the limited and sometimes vague information is gradually accumulating and being made available. A sophisticated and obviously well planned and well coordinated attack. It is astonishing to conceive that there could be some 15 or 20 foreign young men to volunteer to the assignment of hijacking 4 large airliners upon a mission that promised certain death to themselves. Were they volunteers(?), or perhaps just misinformed as to their ultimate destination. Or perhaps they were enlisted soldiers to a non-uniformed terrorist army. Possibly ordered to those assignments, with a sentence of death to themselves and their families should they decline or fail in their assignment? Where do they come from? Do they just walk in off the farm plot or away from the herd of livestock to sign up at a recruitment center? The name, Osama Ben Ladin has been bantered about upon occasion concerning other previous terrorist activities aimed against this nation, including a previous bombing attack upon one of the twin towers several years earlier. A Saudi and an inheritor of a vast family fortune, who does not reside in his native land. A jet-set terrorist who is able to purchase his admission to whatever nation of the world he finds to be useful to his heinous personal agenda. An assassin who maintains and operates training facilities in remote hidden camps and caves in run-down, third-world nations of the middle east; and whose personal wealth, energy, determination, and program of propaganda against the U.S. has been known to U.S. intelligence operations for many years. Said to have been involved in the bombing of American Embassy buildings in Africa, the bombing of U.S. military barracks in Africa and the Middle East, involved in the defeat of U.S. military forces in Somalia, and more recently, the bombing of a U.S. Navy vessel in the Middle East. So there is a long history of this campaign of terrorism against the U.S., in which he has long been the prime suspect as the moving force. Are there other similarly funded and trained operational terrorist organizations whose prime target is the U.S.? None other has been mentioned, and we must conclude that there are not hundreds, or even tens of such organizations. Such terrorist forces were apparently operational out of Libya in the mid-1980's, though we hear nothing more about them subsequent to their being the object of a U.S. counterattack in 1986 when Reagan was president. And now, subsequent to the twin towers bombing, anthrax contaminated letters are being sent anonymously to various government officials, and a few people have died of that contamination. Not likely to be coincidental and independent from the twin towers assault. A scare has begun to oppress the folks in government and in the post offices. A fear spreads across the nation, for who knows when contaminated mail may begin to arrive at the homes of private citizens. Who knows what form of terror may threaten the nation next, and where it may suddenly appear? There seems the possibility that major targets of the nation's infrastructure could be at risk. Major bridges, dams, tall buildings, and nuclear power plants. Steps must be taken to defend ourselves and the nation. One can see that we must immediately be involved in defensive actions upon our native soil. It soon seems that we are forced to the conclusion that we are, in fact, at war. Our nation with vast assets in people, real property, and technological capacity can hardly expect to be able to fight merely a defensive action. There must be an aggressive action against the 'fifth column', the training bases and the supply lines that permit determined enemy actions against this nation. But are we sure who is the enemy? Where are the soldiers of the enemy located; and where are its leaders seated?

It begins then to appear that our nation has not been attacked by a foreign nation, but rather, by a guerrilla force which is derived from the Muslim religion and nations of the middle east. Individuals who are steeped in what is being called "Muslim Fundamentalism". One might suppose that Ben Laden himself is a fundamentalist religious fanatic. Why else would he not avail himself of the opportunity to live a life of comfort and ease, and to get a kidney transplant to prolong and ease his limited life span with his kidneys in failure. As to those he recruits to his agenda, however, we might well suspect that many of them are drawn by a whiff of money and relative economic security. Some of them appear to have been recruited while in the U.S. on student visas or work visas. We do not know that those who come from his terrorist camps are numerous: just that they are well trained and firmly bound to the risk of their lives (perhaps economically?) by participation in his projects. And it appears that at least those who are on assignment to their missions are well supplied with outside funds for their travel and living arrangements. A large part of their anti-American ideology appears to be founded upon the Muslim religion and the antipathy of this terrorist group towards Christian America - or, at least, that is the pretext. But why against "Christian America", and not also against the Christian nations of Europe, and the other nations of the American continents? Is there any nation of the world that admits more Muslim middle-eastern peoples to their country (on student visas, green cards, and even into U.S. citizenship) than does the U.S.? Is there any nation of the world to which more peoples of the world would rather immigrate? Do the Muslim middle-eastern people believe that their economic prosperity would magically bloom if the U.S. were suddenly to withdraw into 'fortress America', or that the wealth of our nation would simply revert into their hands if the U.S were to cease to exist? Is their irritation with the U.S. based upon our cooperation with the Israelis (whom they hate so passionately)? Or is their antipathy based merely on a lust for power? It is true that no nation of the world has recently had its fingers into more of the business and affairs of the foreign nations of the world than has the U.S. - with the possible exception of Russia. But the Russian involvement has been declining since its economic collapse.

Are the masses of people of the middle east consumed and preoccupied with antipathy towards the U.S.? In the living of their busy daily lives do they give any thought whatsoever to the U.S.? Are they unavoidably subjected to a constant bombardment of propaganda, or to any news whatsoever? How many sources of news do they have? and how much diversity of opinion? We have reports that Ben Laden maintains a powerful radio station in the Persian Gulf from which flows his steady stream of invective and one-sided rhetoric that reaches far across the middle eastern world in his effort to cultivate a favorable image of his person and his cause against the evils perpetrated by the U.S. One might readily conceive that the people of Iraq might harbor strong feeling against the U.S. subsequent to the Gulf War, and we are led to believe that the masses of Iran harbored such animosity subsequent to their revolution which ousted their monarchy a couple decades ago. But is that necessarily even so? Undoubtedly the body of the religious establishment and the 'student' minorities in Iran's centers of population seem to have been charged with invective - a large enough segment of the vocal minority to seize and hold the reins of power and project an 'official' viewpoint. But at the present moment, there is evidence that the Iranian grass roots masses have had nearly their fill of fundamentalist theocracy. And it is obvious that Saddam's military hold upon Iraq was not disrupted by the Gulf War, though it seems not improbable that his oppressed masses would welcome his removal. We have reports that the Palestinian masses are divided from the regime of power that controls and speaks for that movement in their struggle against the Israelis. Obviously, the ruling juntas of various political states do not necessarily represent the preferences of the people they control. Even in our democratic countries the will of the masses is often thwarted, though our peoples tend to be far better off economically.

The Russian Army seems to have withdrawn from Afghanistan in defeat after trying to defeat them in a ground action a decade ago. Ben Laden is said to have had a hand in that outcome. The ruling coalition that has ended up in political control of the country since then is another junta that goes by the name of "The Taliban", whose major strength is in the northern part of that remote country, though the country is politically divided into contesting segments. It appears that the Taliban has been maintaining an ongoing alliance with the bases and forces of Ben Laden: willing to continue to harbor and shelter Ben Laden's presence and bases in exchange for the political, economic, and military support of the Ben Ladens rebel terrorists. The Taliban and its forces have not been at war with the U.S. and they had supposed our nation had no cause to malign or attack their regime or their forces. Our nation has had to recognize that any regime which shelters our enemy, and from which even non-nationalist forces are arising to promote and perform terrorist acts of aggression against the US is an enemy to the US and a fair target for retaliation from US military strikes. The logical conclusion to which our nation has arrived is that <u>we are at war</u> and must attack Afghanistan to: 1) destroy the Taliban, the force it commands, and the territory it holds, 2) Bring about a legitimate ruling coalition in Afghanistan that is more fully representative of the peoples of that nation, and which will distance itself from any continuing ties with the Ben Laden group, and which will maintain non-hostile relations with U.S., and 3) and to capture and destroy the forces of Ben Laden, Ben Laden himself, and disrupt the political and financial backing that permits such groups to operate.

<u>Smallpox</u> is one of the most highly contagious and deadliest of diseases known to mankind. It has been proclaimed by the World Health Organization to have been eliminated since the 1970's, and there was the proclamation that vaccination against that disease was no longer necessary. I have protested that notion since first I heard its announcement. What better way to kill off large populations than to discontinue their immunizations against the deadliest of diseases. But what voice do I have? And immunizations against smallpox did go on to become discontinued. Word now comes forth to the effect that the smallpox virus may indeed be upon the agenda of terrorists for germ warfare attacks. I note that immunization materials for smallpox are again being produced and will be made available once again. But the current supplies are inadequate. Be sure to move heaven and hell to get immunizations for your children as soon as possible; and for yourselves as well, if you have not yourself been vaccinated.

Note this copy of smallpox information. (THE DEMON IN THE FREEZER: How smallpox, a disease officially eradicated twenty years became the biggest bioterrorist threat we now face. The New Yorker, July 12, 1999, pp. 44-61) I wish you be aware that there seems to be downplaying the actual danger from smallpox. I have been telling people of this eventuality (that we are now facing) for 25 years:

1. The mortality rate (death rate) may be considerably greater than the stated 30%. In the historical past it may have been

in the range of 80-90%. Recall for example that it wiped out the entire tribe of the Mandan Indians in the 1890's.

2. There seems to have been recent official government orders to step up the production of the vaccine. Will it then be widely available? Is it available to any doctors and clinics at this moment??
3. The disease has an explosive contageousness!!!!!
4. Some benefit from vaccination may last as long as 10 or 20 years. Since no such materials for vaccination have been available since the mid-1970's, that means that every person in the country ought to be immunized.
5. What is actually being done about this?? and by whom??
6. And how are we situated concerning the possible threat of Diphtheria?? A pharmacist friend tells me that immunization material for both Diphtheria and Tetanus have been very difficult to obtain in the past several months.

A man such as bin Laden with his vast financial resources, powerful political allies, effective organs of mass propaganda, a sizable body of religiously indoctrinated agents to suicidal missions, and well supplied with heinous effective weapons of political mass destruction is a threat not only to the U.S., but to any possibility of peace within the entire world. He undoubtedly has covert allies, such as Saddam's Iraq from which there is the possibility of his obtaining germ warfare materials; and even material for nuclear warfare. There can be little doubt that something must be done about him. If the enemy confronting us has access to biological warfare tactics, it is my suspicion that he may well have access to nuclear material. I am tempted to suspect that we might soon see some nuclear attacks on a small scale. Such for example, as the destruction of some of our nation's aircraft carriers in the Persian Gulf and the Indian Ocean. Thus far only, have my personal musings brought me concerning this new crisis being faced by our country.

The line of traffic entering Canada on this day was not long, and I came quickly to the inspections station. I appear to be one of the very few whose vehicle they elect for a thorough inspection. Nasty people, these agents, but they manage to cloak their hostility beneath a mantle of indifferent formality. And I cloak my irritation with them beneath an air of patient tranquility. Their search is superficial and not prolonged. I inquire of these customs officials as to what sort of paper-work and documentation would be required were I bringing my miner grandchildren with me across the border. Required would be certified copies of birth certificate and certified letter of permission from the legal guardian of each child - about what I had expected, but had not yet been able to confirm from any authoritative source. The border authorities would also separate me from each of the grandchildren and ask them if they were accompanying me on a voluntary basis.

Having gotten through emigration, I drove on in to Cornwall, Ontario where I stopped off at a bank to make exchange into Canadian money. Long lines of people there making deposits and exchanges and a great many teller windows, only half of which were open. A good many bank personnel wandering about behind the teller cages as though they might open more teller booths to service those of us waiting in these long lines. And yet, that wasn't happening, and it seemed not to be a concern to the dozens of bank officers hanging uselessly about. One gets the impression of a certain contempt they manifest against the ordinary man of the street who is condemned to an unnecessary wait in silence.

I had previously contacted cousin Yolande Youmell-Aubischon of my impending visit and my hope that she might accompany me into the interior of Quebec Province where I hoped to locate and drop in on a particular Brasseur family from whom I some hope of obtaining some additional genealogy information. I knew that Yolande had some reservations about our dropping into the home of private relatives unexpectedly, and I had no idea as to whether or not she would actually consent to assist me with the project. The rural folks of Quebec Province mostly speak French in their homes, and many of them seem to be able to speak no English whatsoever, and so I was destined to have great difficulty with this genealogical project if I were to be without the assistance of Yolanda. I arrived at the home of Andre and Yolanda Aubischon about 5:00 P.M., just as she had gotten home from work. She and I went out for supper, and returned an hour and a half latter to eat some of the dessert treats she had prepared. We talked an hour or more before she turned in for the night. I stayed up a couple hours to catch up on my notes and then read a while. When I awoke the next morning she made us breakfast of bacon and eggs. She and I then departed in her new Hauyandi station wagon. I gather that her vision is not quite perfect even subsequent to her cataract surgery and implant, as she preferred to have me drive her new car. Though I have driven through Montreal several times before in the past several years, I do occasionally miss my intended turnoff; as I did on this day also. We found our way back to the route we had intended without too much delay and continued on Highway 10 to Granby where we stopped at a rest area for directions to our intended destination. We found the village of Bethane and stopped there to inquire of the village folk for directions to the farmstead of Rita Brasseur Demers, and proceed there without further confusion. As we drove into the yard, the woman of the house and her two teen age children came out to inquire of we strangers. And the husband came up from his work in the farm yard. She is the daughter of Rita Brassuer-Demers, and is married to Pierre Bonin. Yolanda conversed with them in French while I looked on in ignorance. After suggesting that we might do better to look up her mother in the nearby village of Valcourt, she began to give us a few scraps of information herself. The interest of her curious children and spouse then became aroused by the genealogy subject and they soon invited us into the house. It seems they had originally thought we might be Seventh Day Adventists out upon a campaign of weekly annoyance to the local residents. Yolanda having gotten us past all of that, we were now seated at the kitchen table in their simple but clean rustic dwelling. The woman grew positively enthusiastic and prolix with information. She drew down a couple of blank pages and proceeded to sketch out the names and diagram the relationship of the members of her immediate and extended family from memory - calling her mother now and then to get clarification. She handed a couple blank pages of paper to her nineteen year old daughter and soon had her working to produce information of another part of the family. The husband stood near the table hungrily awaiting his overdue noon lunch as the very interested wife and children eyed us with interest and Yolanda gave them further information about ourselves and the nature of the project upon which we were working. The 11 year old boy wondered if his name was in my thick Brasseur Genealogy Work Book. No, but it would be, soon. Yolanda relayed to them the information that when I got my materials all organized, I would send them copy for perusal and request from them whatever corrections and addition that were relevant. We finally completed our information collection about 3:00 p.m. and made our departure. What nice folks we had encountered here! They had made our genealogy outing a remarkable success. The boy goes to grade school in Granby, as the census in this area of Bethane is too low to permit the local school to stay open. The girl attends college level career training classes at Sherbrooke. I gather that the mother works as a nurse at the hospital in Granby, while Pierre Bonin works for the county, and in his spare time cuts and sells wood from this farmstead.

Yolanda and I drive over to Magog to visit her friends Joan and Gerald for an hour or more before making the return drive to Ile Bizzard. We stop at a restaurant for supper and then return to their apartment about 9:00 p.m. Yolanda and I talk for a while before I take my leave and head over toward Vaudreuil and Ontario to the west. We have had a good outing and a successful mission.

END OF INSTALLMENT
THREE
13 November 2001

INSTALLMENT FOUR:

A few miles to the SW of Vaudreuil (where my Brasseur ancestors settled in the 1760's) is Rigaud (onto whose grant lands settled 4 of the 7 sons of our original ancestor from France). Just a couple miles to the SW of Rigaud one crosses over into Ontario Province. Having failed as yet in my attempts to learn something of that branch of the family which goes by the name of Duhamel, I had it in mind to contact a Duhamel in the village of Alfred, Ontario, where I had an address for one that was just a few years younger than myself. And so on this bright calm and warn autumn Sunday I drove about in that small community looking for the address, but was unable to discover the street I was looking for. The streets were deserted and no shops were open in this generally French speaking community. I stopped at the police station to inquire directions. The bilingual police officer was acquainted with Raymond Duhamel and told me exactly how to arrive at where he had lived. But Raymond had moved recently and he did not know exactly to where - somewhere into far beyond this same general area. I drove over to the old address I had, and inquired of a neighbor (who spoke so little English that I could not communicate with him) as to where Raymond had moved. They knew exactly where he was now living, and gave me directions. And so I drove a few miles to the west of town to find the trailer park and inquired of the camp owner for the exact address. It is a pleasant well kept area that also takes in overnight campers at $22.00 per night.

My knock on the front door was answered by a handsome woman of about my own age who comprehended English only moderately. I explained my request for genealogy information concerning the Brasseur-Duhamel connection. A part of her reticence was probably due to the fact of my inability to comprehend French, and her only modest comprehension of

English. She called out her husband (Raymond), who seems to have been working at a computer in the next room. I briefly explained myself again to him. They exchanged a few words in French and he, seeming to have no special enthusiasm for the subject, dismissed her to answer some question for me as he returned to his preoccupation in the next room. She hesitantly looked at my Duhamel Family sheet and seemed to approve of some the entries, but indicated some perplexity concerning some of the others on my list. I gather that she was previously married and had children from that marriage before she married Raymond. But she was hesitant or hard put to explain the details of these relationship and she referred me to Juliette Duhamel Lacombe, who was living in a nursing home in Alfred. I had hopes that here I might be finding a warm trail. I located the facility and wandered about its dilapidated hallways until I found the room of her residence. She was perhaps eighty and rather somber with modest residuals of an old stroke hemiparesis. She did seem to understand what I was seeking by way of information, but indicated that she did not want to remember. "They are all dead. It is so sad." And so I took my leave. Stymied again on the Duhamel trail. I drove back to the rest area near Rigaud where I was able to take my customary two and half mile walk, have a modest picnic snack, and then read before turning into the sleeping bag for the night about midnight - feeling a little discouraged as it had begun to seem that I was doomed to defeat concerning my quest for the Duhamel connection.

I arose the next morning to the customary question of "where to this day, and what I intend to accomplish?", for it isn't as though I have any firm schedule or agenda. It was somewhat overcast and I had thoughts of scavenging the Archives in Montreal at 1945 Rue Mullin to see if they might have acquired any new information since my last visit there a year ago. But on that last pass through these territories I had picked up one piece of information that did actually confirm a relationship of the Duhamels (of Alfred, Ont.) to the Brasseur family. That, in Hawksbury, a mere 15 or 20 miles to the west. And I recalled that they had been gradually acquiring a store of French Canadian Genealogical information in their public library over the past several years. There, my long search for additional information of the Duhamel family and their connection to the Brasseur family came finally to fruition. Among their collection of genealogy reference books was the list of parish information from the community of St. Victor Parish of Alfred, Ontario. It had been published in 1999, and probably had not been available upon the shelf for longer than the past few months. I spent the day making copy of the relevant information for my own records. I then drove to Plantagenet to take a room at one of my favorite motel spots, but discover no room at the inn on this rainy night. I drive back to Rigaud in a downpour and take a room. I stretch out my damp sleeping bag and other gear for drying, have some crackers with sardines, followed by donuts and some chocolate milk and then submersed myself into the organizing of my new found Duhamel information. When I next looked up to the clock, it was 5:00 AM. I slept in until 10:00 AM, then shave, shower, and reloaded my gear into the pickup and head west just before noon.

I was still a bit tired and resolved to have a day of relative ease. I drove to Plantagenet and took a room in the early afternoon. I called Pauline Brasseur Groulx with whom Vic and I had visited a couple years ago. Several months ago I had gotten communication from her sister in Ottawa, suggesting that we three might get together to go over their genealogical line a little more closely to try to iron out some few uncertainties there. She was to call me the following day for confirmation and a time. I had a fine nap, worked upon my new material, had a regular full meal, and read before turning in about 1:00 AM.

I was expecting a return call the next day and expected that I would probably get together with these two distant cousins. No call came, so I made a return call just before check-out time. It was my impression that they must have cooled luke-warm about the trouble of it. I was told that the sister could not come because her car wasn't working, and that she had not yet gotten around to doing the research she had intended to do concerning her own branch of the family. As though I were owed some sort of explanation. And her own husband wasn't home at the present time. I notice that these French Canadian women seem to maintain a rather strong sense of personal subservience to their spouses. Much more at least than what I am impressed with in my own ordinary experience of daily life. The failure of this meeting was of little concern to my interests, since I had already figured my way through the confusions of the limited details to its most likely resolution, and had only intended to show them my corrections and possibly get some little affirmation of the accuracy of the parish lists from which I had come to my conclusions.

New information about the background of all this terrorist activity comes now to my attention even as I am composing this section of my notes. It turns out that in addition to the Sunnis and the Shiites of the Muslim faith, a new and very radically fundamentalist sub-sect (Jihad organization) has been developing from sources in Saudi Arabia and spreading into Chaostan (Pakistan and the other four adjoining -stan countries to its north) in the past couple of decades. At the time when the Gulf War was developing, the tensions of internal strife within the Saudi nation were escalating over the issue of Saudi alliance with the west against the aggression of Iraq - the fundamentalists disinclined to be at war with fellow Muslims and in alliance with the 'infidel'. The Saudi royal family and the governing classes had been holding the radical militant impulse of the evolving sect in check, but the Gulf War heightened that internal conflict, and the radical sect was given more freedom and internal control by way of appeasement, so that the royal family and government could devote greater attention to the Gulf War conflict and global politics. Saudi Arabian oil has made them a fabulously wealthy nation and their religion requires them to give 10% of their income to charity. The country being split between governing and religious sectors, the radical new sect has stepped up its repressive policing and is diverting the 10% obligatory religious charity funding into the various nations of Chaostan. There they are building and funding new mosques, and schools, and drawing in the young masses of itinerant and unemployed peoples. Proselytilizng them into the beliefs and agenda of the newly evolving fundamentalist terrorist sect. Taliban is a word that means seminary school. The young children and youth with little by way of alternative opportunities in their lives were being drawn into the schools where their learning consists of memorizing the Koran scripture and its prejudiced particular fundamentalist interpretation as the sole curriculum in their schooling. The essence of the radical teaching being emphasized, is that Islam must be carried foreword - even by the sword, were people otherwise to refuse to accept it. That even traditional Sunni and Shiite sects are eventually to be coerced into this new version of Islam, if necessary and when the time is ripe. That (this version of) Islam is to be eventually the solitary enforced religion of the world.

After a couple of years of 'schooling', the boys in their early teens were then initiated into the organized terrorist military camps (al-Qaida) and tactics for the training in the use of various weapons and explosives, before being sent out onto missions of local and international warfare. I presume that the immense personal wealth of Bin Laden, in addition to his personal fundamentalist beliefs and education, and his personal connections to the powers that be in the Islamic nations of the Persian Gulf area, all combined to catapult him into the position of leadership of this gradually evolving fundamentalist organization and grand dragon of al-Qaida over the past couple of decades. The influence of their wealth, schooling, and force of arms in an otherwise impoverished and backward nation, enabled them to subvert the whole established government of Afghanistan to their will and agenda. In effect, the fundamentalist terrorist sect has clandestinely become the government of that nation. Our nation in recognizing that reality has finally come to call that regime by the name of Taliban (the seminary school). Pakistan and the other Chaostan nations have been reluctant to distance themselves from their co-religionist Moslems (especially in alliance with the infidels), but have finally (reluctantly) been forced to stand against the Taliban in order to maintain the sovereignty and control of their own separate governments. This, again, is as far as I have come in my recent and ongoing attempt to gain some little understanding of what has recently been happening in this "war against terrorism", and how is has come about.

END OF INSTALLMENT
FOUR.
18 Nov. 2001
RGB

INSTALLMENT FIVE:

I drove down highways 9 and 20 to reach Queen's Highway 401 at Cornwall and continued westward towards Toronto, stopping at a service area for an hour's nap before arriving in Toronto about 5:00 PM. I had hopes of being able to locate cousin Namoi Spreitzer - to meet her, take her out for a hamburger and chat a while. She is descended form my father's oldest sister, Annie Grimes. In the past 8 or 10 months I had become acquainted with her through E-mail via connections with cousin Yolande. I was particularly interested in conversing with her, as she had informed me that she was a college graduate with a major in Philosophy, and I was quite interested to discover the particular flavor of her philosophical views of life and reality. I stopped for gas and to get my bearings. And I picked up a good map of the city, to facilitate what promised to be otherwise a long and complex search to locate her place of residence. And of course there were the usual obstacles of torn up streets and nebulous detours to negotiate in the darkness and the rain where the street signs are always placed in print that is overly small and elevated on top of poles that are high above the reach of one's headlights. But the well seasoned philosopher generally maintains a temperament and a powerful flashlight such as to obviate such inconveniences as populate this world and impede him from his objective.

With no great loss of time, I located the address only to learn that she was out of town to visit her mother's home in the north country. Not a great surprise, as she had previously sent me word that she too had some travel plans which might interfere with our chances of getting together.

Then it was that I got lost for an hour before finding my way to Hwy 400 north. Just north of Vaugh, I stopped at a service area to get some wonderful fresh crisp sour-cream donuts at a Tim Horton's outlet. Tim Horton's seems to be the predominant coffee and snack shop in Quebec and Ontario Provinces, scattered everywhere at the service areas, at the edges of the towns and scattered along main routes of traffic that penetrate the cities, towns and villages. At this particular place, they actually have two outlets that stay busy. A main shop in the service area mall, and a second outlet 60 yards away, at the edge of the parking lot, which services only drive up traffic. I even came across some or them in Massachusetts and in Michigan. Would that I could so consistently find a supply of tasty donuts as I travel elsewhere about in the U.S. After refreshing my supply of donuts, and after reading an hour in the cab beneath the lights of the parking area, I retreat to my sleeping bag in the camper shell about 11:00 PM.

I awoke about 5:00 AM to head up into mists and northward towards Pentanguishene. Even at this early hour I am confronted with a continuous stream and triple line of headlights from traffic that is headed towards Toronto. North of Barrie, the traffic slackens remarkably even as the road narrows down to two and then to one lane of traffic each way. About 6:30 AM I reach the Midland and Pentanguishene area and park at a shopping mall situated halfway between them. I stretch out in the cab to get another two hours of sleep before awakening at 9:00 to a bright sunshine which is dissipating the mists. I stop at the home of cousin Art David Brasseur, in Penetanguishene, but he is not home. I drive out to make some genealogy copy to leave with him, and to get a few groceries. Since he is still not home, I leave the genealogy copy hanging on his doorknob. I'm sure he will find it interesting. I drive down to the waterfront and look back at Penetanguishene which is perched on an incline and rolling plain above. The handsome stone Catholic Church and its taller towers impose on ones imagination, looming like a judgment from above the very tree tops. How many man hours of labor did its construction require of this not large community, and over how many years? And not more than 8 or 10 miles to the south is an equally impressive Shrine of the Martyrs Church.

I continue north to Sudbury where I take Hwy 17 westward. The route bypasses the city to the south and west, and I have to detour 6 or 8 miles into the town, past large piles of mine tailings serviced by industrial plants and railroad spurs to get some gas in this otherwise sparsely settled north country that is situated in the heart of this great mining area of rolling stone outcropping interspersed with a sort of small structured tree and brush. It is the site of an ancient giant meteorological impact. After a couple days of intermittent light rain, my bedroll and canvas baggage is wet, so I stop at Espanol a little after seven in the evening to take a motel room. It is a pretty little lumbering area with a nearby hydroelectric plant situated above a handsome cataract of river which I cross by a bridge span to enter the community. I spread out my dampened bedroll and clothing upon the furniture to dry and then drive out to have a Chinese meal. there are little oriental restaurants in even all these little towns of the north, and more than one even in this small community.

Heading west next morning I stop at Webbwood, having heard there were several Brasseur families in this general area years ago. I stopped a middle aged woman to inquire about the location of the local cemetery. "I don't know", says she. Says I, "I am told that some of my relatives are buried here." She inquires, "Catholic or Protestant?" "Catholic", says I. Pointing to the west end of town, she says, "the Catholics are buried that way, the Protestants, on the other end of town." Folks often know more than they readily admit. I drove to the Catholic Cemetery and read a hundred fifty tombstones - no Brasseurs. So I drove on through Massey (whose cemeteries I had searched a few years ago) and on into Sault Ste. Marie, from whence I crossed over into the U.S. Traffic was backed up a mile coming into Canada, but I drove directly up to the U.S. customs booth with no wait whatsoever and casually chatted a minute with the agent there before passing on with no inspection whatsoever. After crossing the colossal two mile long suspension bridge across the Mackinac Straits into the Michigan lower peninsula, I stopped an hour at the Cheboygan City Library to pick up a couple pieces of Brasseur information just before their closing time. I stopped for my light supper at Burger King and then parked at Wal-Mart while I walked about 3 miles for exercise. Then I napped and hour and read a couple hours before proceeding down highways 27 and 75, where I stop for the night at a rest area just south of Vanderbilt, The next morning I proceeded down to Lansing, where I spent the day at the Michigan State Library and Archives. An impressively large and well appointed building. I didn't come up with very much additional information there. There must be some explanation for why it is that there is almost no information publicly available in the US concerning Catholic Church records of births, marriages, and deaths; while such information of Canadian Parishes is readily available in many libraries within Canada. After library closing at 5:00, I stopped for gas and a snack before driving up to Saginaw to look up cousin Dr. Jim Brasseur, with whom I had first visited about ten years ago. There are areas of the city that appear to be in a kind of dilapidated condition, and I am told that the population is down to perhaps 75,000 from its high of maybe 100,000 a few decades ago. I finally had to get myself a good city map before I was able to locate cousin Jim's home.

It must have been about 8:30 when I finally located His home. He invited me in and proceed to cook up a batch of ribs which he shared with me from a rotisserie. They were as good as any I have ever tasted. It recalled to mind that when I was last here, his wife Jean served me an equally excellent lasagna. But Jean was out of town this particular night, Jim and I talked a little about genealogy and an about current war and politics. He put me up in his basement apartment, as he turned in about 11:30. There I found an excellent book on the history of Medicine by Garrison of about 1929 vintage which I had read perhaps thirty years ago. I spent a few hours refreshing my memory with its contents before drifting off to sleep. The next morning I had a shower before cousin Jim made up a mess of eggs and toast for my breakfast before I departed and he was making preparations to get together with one of his sons for an outing. I promised to send him copy of my recent genealogical findings after I had gotten a chance later to get it organized. I then headed up across the Mackinac Bridge again to follow the upper peninsula westward along highways 2, 117, and 28 on this fine colorful autumn day, stopping ten minutes in the Indian gaming casino at Christmas, MI this Sunday afternoon to watch a small crowd of senior citizens pretending to enjoy themselves at the slot machines. It does at least seem to ease their passage through time. I stop in Marquette to get a few groceries and use the opportunity to exercise the cantakerousness which society not uncommonly overlooks in the senior citizen. I had waited some five or ten minutes in the checkout line while the middle aged woman ahead of me used food stamps, coupons, and a store discount card to pay for her few articles of grocery. I was beginning to wonder if they might not yet also give her cash before she eventually walked out with her groceries. I had picked up some chocolate milk and some donuts that were marked with a sale price, but was then told that I must pay the full and usual price for these items. I quoted the sale prices that were on display, but was told that I would need a special store sponsored discount card in order to get them at the discount price. I thought to bargain with her by offering to pay the sale price in actual cash, rather than with coupons. She was new on the job and seemed to see my point, but had not the authority to barter, so called her manager over to settle the issue. They did finally offer to let me fill out an application form and issue me one of those discount cards to go into effect right now. But the application form was so discouragingly long and involved, and I was so unlikely to pass this way ever again, that I finally offered to pay the full price, rather than to hold up the line of purchasers behind me. When I asked about the possibility of installment payments, her smile did not seem genuine and so I tried yet the old gag about would they accept cash, for which she willingly held out her hand. I tendered her a few old one dollar bills, wondering if she thought they might still be spendable in their wrinkled condition. She seemed at that moment a bit less out of patience with me, but then on the other hand, she now had good prospects for finally getting rid of me.

And I continued on into Wisconsin and the sunset. About dusk I thought to follow the signs to a state park campground to spend the night. Having had to drive ten miles to find it, I was out of patience when I arrived there. And there was a 3.50 fee to park in this dark forest with no showers and no lights to read by. And with no one else parked here, it seemed to me that I might be in potential danger from bears and moose, in addition to your ordinary highway men. So I drove back to the highway and continued west until I arrived at the Wisconsin-Minnesota border. There, was a very nice rest area. I had a little picnic snack, read the roadside information about the regional iron mines, and then walked about three miles under the lights, before reading a couple hours and then turning into my sleeping bag for a solid night of rest.

The next day I continued on through upper Minnesota and arrived at North Dakota about 4:00 PM. There I stopped at a combination rest area and information booth. A woman in attendance wanted me to sign the guest register before she would give me a North Dakota map. I signed my full name, which she thought an unusual one. I told her that I was born in North Dakota, and that I was the first boy in the US to be named after both the President Roosevelt, and the vice-president Garner; and about having gotten letters and gifts from each of them. I waxed into a sort of dramatic mood, saying that the portents for my life at that time had seemed auspicious, and that my family seemed since then to have certain lofty expectations of me. It isn't likely that she noticed the old pickup in which

I had arrived here, and my apparent freedom to travel may have further suggested that I might be a person of substance. In retrospect I can see that she seemed to be preparing herself for a Horatio Alger success story as I mentioned the years of determined energy to which I had dedicated myself "And after all these years, look what I have become" says I philosophically, opening my palms to the heavens. "Nothing!" She gasped in astonishment and stuttered, "Oh . . . there, there, there, there . . . ", as if to console me. And I was instantly a bit embarrassed to have misled her expectation, so I turned on my heal and made a quick exit, muttering something to the effect that the realities of life are often inexplicable.

Minot was only about 180 miles distant and I intended to get there early enough to spend an hour or two in the city library to do a little genealogy research. West of Devils Lake the traffic was stopped for 20 minutes as they were doing construction work on all four lanes upon a stretch three or four miles length. And still, I arrived at the library before 8:00 PM and managed to complete my project before the 9:00 closing hour.

END OF INSTALLMENT FIVE

INSTALLMENT SIX:

It was a pleasant autumn evening as I stopped for gas and considered my options for the passing of the night. I wanted to spend the following day doing some genealogy research in Bismarck, and to visit with Dick Morgan at Falkirk, just north of the rest area at Washburn. I made the call to "dad" Dick Morgan to ask him if he would mind my parking in the yard of his rural home to sleep in my pickup. He is an ex-professor of History and much visited by his former students of years past. I stop to visit him a couple times a year in recent years - we were buddies and neighbors in the 7th and 8th grade. He welcomed the idea and encouraged me to come right on down to watch with him the rest of the Monday Night Football Game. Another good idea. It is only about a fifty mile drive so I was wheeling into his driveway by near 10:00 PM. We watched the game to near its then obvious outcome and then discussed the philosophical intricacies of some such interesting subjects as History and Sex. About 2:00 AM we agreed to give it a rest for the night. I was about to climb into the sleeping bag in my pickup camper when I noticed some inexplicable lights that seemed to hover at an uncertain point beyond the house and somewhere far short of the horizon on this dark night. Puzzled, I grabbed my flashlight and set out to explore - only to discover that they were actually only a set of decorative lights strung out along the side of the house itself. Returning in the dark to my pickup, Dick and I startled one another when we suddenly met as I was circling his pickup, to which he was retiring to spend the night. I was previously aware that he not infrequently elects to sleep naked in an old buffalo robe, in his pickup camper shell. He tells me now of an apparition that he has sometimes seen in the grove of trees near which I am parked. But he is a teller of stories and one can never be sure but what he is pulling ones leg, and I am not a believer in the supernatural. Near dawn I awoke to a call of necessity and heard some stirring in the yard of this solitary rural home-site, but Dick had mentioned the night before that his wife gets up early on Tuesday to wheel the garbage out for collection. When she had withdrawn, I did my duty and returned to the comfort of my warm sleeping bag for yet a couple hours of sleep. A little breeze was stirring wonderfully through the grove. When wakefulness began again to stir within me, I heard more rustlings and random intermittent touchings of something against the camper shell. My thoughts turned briefly to Dick's last night tale of the apparition in the grove. But reason returned with full awakening as I sat up to reach for my glasses and stared about to re-apprise myself of current reality in time and space. The wind had increased in volume, and twigs, with a plethora of leaves were raining down to glorify and enchant the wonder of an Indian Summer midmorning. It was 9:30 AM. I went to the house and knocked to entrance and to continue my talk with Dick, while his wife prepared for us a bit of breakfast. He later told me what his wife had said. That she was probably the only woman in the township to have two loony old men sleeping in her driveway. And he reaffirms to me his vague belief in the 'apparition of the grove' without the citing of any supplementary body of fact or legend, except there seems also to be a second apparition of the house itself. We finished our conversation about noon and I continued south on Hwy 83 to Bismarck.

I stopped again into the same building on the state capitol grounds where I had spent a day doing genealogy research some 8 or 10 years ago. As I entered the lobby I noticed an information desk about forty feet away on the other side of the room. How difficult can it be to find ones own way around this building? I shunned the information desk and sauntered off to the left on my own, as did everyone else, leaving the two career receptionists with no apparent duties to perform. The sign above the door said "North Dakota Archives and Genealogy Library". But it was rather a limited and smallish collection, whereas my recollection was of a far more voluminous assortment of tomes. The room was very well appointed and staffed with several personnel who kept themselves all but faintly concealed behind an enclosure of heavily tinted glass. One came out to speak with me when I stopped at the main desk. What had happen to all the rest of the books through which I had previously browsed? The young man assured me that this collection had never been any larger than it is currently. Puzzled, I spent the afternoon going through the collection of individual history books of the various communities in the state which had each produced its anniversary collection of the names and families that settled and lived in each since its founding. About 4:30 PM I finished my survey and asked the man to make me copy of some the pages before I departed. I was still curious about the discrepancy between my memory of the place and the actual smallness as I had noted. While discussing it with him, it suddenly dawned upon him that I must be referring to the State Library - a separate entity. "And where would I find that?" I inquired. It was the next building here on the mall, about a hundred feet to the south of this building. I hiked over there. Sure enough. Here was a voluminous library! And of community history books, their collection was significantly larger than that of the other library. Both libraries are state owned, and managed with state employees, but there is no coordinating mechanism or even informal cooperation between them. Why they exist separate from one another is a mystery to me. Nor does either of them have any cooperative mechanism with the Germans From Russia Heritage Society Library a mile or two away.

In the large state government employee parking lot, I napped an hour before stopping to have a submarine sandwich and then heading west on Hwy 94. I had stopped at the home of cousin Gordon Neuberger, but nobody was at home. Of the 4 or 5 previous times I have stopped, I have only found him once to be at home. He seems to live a busy life in his retirement. I stopped at the newly constructed rest area near Glen Ulen to spend 35 minutes walking. I was astounded at the huge cathedral-like structure so well appointed to such a modest usage. I then continued west to the Roosevelt State Park and Rest Area, where I stopped for the night, getting to bed about 1:00 AM after catching up on my notes and reading a while.

I arrived in Terry Montana the following day about noon and had a caramel roll and a cup of coffee with sister Kate as we spoke of local and world events and looked at history philosophically. In the mid afternoon we drove over to visit sister Skippy for an hour. She had recently been so severely ill with a respiratory disorder that they had even called in her son, Billy, whom I have not seen in more than forty years. But Skippy seems alert and recovered. The perkiest I have seen her in a couple years, in fact. The long history of her bed-ridden status draws upon my sympathy to the point that makes me uncomfortable. I was looking at Kate's book collection and about to depart, when she insisted on making me a gift of the book of my choice. I took "*East of Eden*". Then drove on in to Miles City, hoping to get my oil change before closing time. There, I had a sandwich while waiting, and then drove over to see Malcomb and Beth Winters. They were just sitting down to supper and asked me to join them, but I had eaten. I talked with them while they ate. Mal has had some heart problems for a number of years - cardiac arrhythmias - and has had some endocardial surgery which seems to have benefited him. They are currently planning a trip to Australia, to visit a daughter. I was trying to gain some insight on the origin of the friendship between Malcolmb, Zeek Mosby, and Gene. Gene graduated from high school in 1946, and we arrived in Miles City in the autumn of 1942, which means they met in high school. We reminisced about the trip the four of us took to Yellowstone Park in 1950, and about a couple of Beth's classmates from Swedish Covenant Hospital Nursing Program, with whom I was also acquainted.

A bit later that evening I drove over to the home of nephew, Steve Kransky, to visit him and the 11 year twin daughters, Christina and Alexia, whom he is raising alone since his wife departed through cyberspace to more promising romantic arrangements for her life. Steve works at a minimum wage as a taxi driver while now completing by internet connections to Eastern Montana College, the final semester of college credits prior to his expected graduation in December of this year. Harold (Aloha's first husband) was there also. We talked about an hour before Harold and I headed over to his place, to leave Steve to continue with his studies. Harold is his usual thin self at now age 84, and is still alert, healthy, and talkative, but with just a little trouble in hearing. The divorced son Jeffrey is a trucker and maintains a sort of home base in one of Harold's bedroom. But he is only rarely around. Harold has been subsidizing Suzy's vagrant and expensive life style to help her raise her two sons, who are now of age and departed. Suzy has recently told him that she no longer needs financial aid from him, as she has now gone into a communal home living arrangement. Yvonne abruptly died at age 50 this past summer.

Harold entertained me with a few tunes on the piano, and we sang a couple of songs before he turned in early to bed. I read a while and then slept in Jeff's room. Harold fixed me some eggs, toast, and coffee in the morning before I departed westward about mid-morning. I stopped in Billings to get some information and proceeded west. I decided to drop in to see Janet Potter - my high school classmate who has organized our high school class reunions through years. So I turned south at Columbus to drive through Absorka, to Fishtail, Montana. It is an area of Montana I had never previously seen, and is quite worth seeing. Who knows? She might even invite me to stay for a home cooked meal. But alas, I missed her entirely, as she was visiting her daughter in Billings. I visited a bit with her spouse, Ray, and asked him to leave her a message to contact me by the E-mail address I left with him; as I had been unsuccessful in getting my message to transfer to her address. There was an intermittent misty rain that afternoon, and now is was beginning to be mixed with snow. I was in a hurry to get on over the pass into Bozeman before the snowfall should force me into the use of tire chains.

The threat of snow did not mature. From Hwy 94, I followed Hwy 287 and arrived in Townsend about 7:00. I stopped at a cafe and ended up with a meal that was only barely acceptable, and then I drove out to locate my nephew Gordon Huft and his wife Mitzi. I hadn't seen them for ten or twelve years and it was not an easy place to find, and harder in the dark. A big house for two people, and a nice place overlooking the headwaters of the Missouri River. They were very cordial and we had a nice visit, catching up on the family news and happenings, and getting into the discussion of world events and history, and touching on the inevitable points of philosophy and my own whimsical ideas that are sometimes wont to cause the rolling of eyes among such folks as have little sense of humor. Gordon manages some grain elevators in the area and I proposed to extract some information from him concerning yields and distribution of grain. I had become aware that early in the evolution of civilized urban centers it was the development of agricultural grains that made them possible. That early in their evolution, the agricultural yields had been small, and that there were times in the middle ages of history where the yield had been as low as a two fold increase. But man has gradually developed stronger and more productive strains of seed stock, and agricultural methods have greatly improved. What then is the current yield in the planting of wheat? Might it approach a one hundred fold increase, for example? Probably not that high even under the most favorable of conditions. I have subsequently checked the encyclopedia, where I discover that a mature head of grain may contain from 30 to 50 kernels of grain. If true, that means that yield could never be greater that a fifty fold increase, and possibly only a thirty fold increase under the very best of conditions. I learn from Gordon that there is at any one time only enough stored wheat in the bins of the world to feed the world for not more than 3 or 4 months. Thus, if there should suddenly be world wide crop failure - or even failure of only the crops of the northern hemisphere - there would quickly develop a famine of world wide proportions. The repetition of the explosion of Tambora - as in 1815 - might well bring that about. A massive collision with a mile wide meteor would most assuredly bring that about as the skies of the entire planet darkened. Few of our species would be apt to survive.

I took my shower then read and spent the night at Gordon's place. In the morning I bid them adieu as I headed west about 7:00 AM. It was a cool morning and I spotted a lightly clad young fellow walking out along the shoulder of the roadway. He was headed towards Seattle and was repentant of last nights drinking spree that had gotten him dumped to the necessity of walking through the night to keep himself warm. I took him as far as Missoula where I stopped for gas and to say hello to Annie, but she was not about, so I headed out west. I arrived in Spokane about 2:00 PM, and stopped to cash the last of my ragged travelers checks before arriving at Phil's. He and Dot temporarily have a EWU student staying at their place, but offered me the use of a couch for sleeping, if I were to be around for a couple days. There I spend a couple of days reading and do a load of my dirty laundry. From there I drove out to spend a couple days with Duane and Georgia on the farm where I was able to get my daily hike and read at leisure from books and other material Duane has at hand for my perusal and enlightenment. I only go half way through "*My Awakening*", by David Duke, but I will get a chance to finish it when I return to the Northwest in early December of my pre-Christmas journey. I then drove through Yakima to look up Vic and Marg, but just missed them by four hours as they had taken off to San Francisco to spend about a week of get together with Yvette, Jay, and Guy. Meanwhile, I drove on into Vancouver, Washington and stopped at the home of Jerry and Anita Fisher about 9:45 PM. She is on a Sabbatical leave and they will soon be upon a prolonged trip around the world. I talk with them about an hour before they go bed and assign me to Cindy's old bedroom. There I read an hour or two before having cookies and milk and then getting off to sleep.

The following morning I stop at Jauhn and Massy's place in west Portland. Massey serves me a breakfast of eggs and toast and fills me in on local domesticities. She tells me that Miette and her two children will shortly be down from upstairs. They and her mother are visiting in town a couple days while Bart is on brief trip into Mexico. And so I had a brief opportunity to visit with Miette though I had to leave by 12:30 PM to get to Pierre's place. There I got a little nap before Jackie stopped by with Chris and Sam. She spends an hour and a half filling me in on what is happening, before she heads out upon her errands. About 7:30 Pierre stumbles in, exhausted from work and the frustrations of the complications of life which move ever too slowly towards their uncertain resolutions. He goes early to bed after we talk a while and I get a relaxed evening for reading and contemplation. He and Jackie attended a homeowners conference the following day, while I catch up on my rest and reading. That evening I stayed with the kids while Pierre and Jackie had an evening out. The following day Beans and I went out upon a biking excursion through the neighborhood streets and parks. He is giving me the grand tour and explanations. As I follow him through the rough paths on the fringe of the park, he beams as he turns back to me saying, "I just love this place." He leads me around a back route to his mother's apartment, to elude a police car that is parked in the area. It dawns on me that we have neglected the necessity of wearing riding helmets. We talk a while with Rochelle before we head back home. Later that same afternoon, I went with Belle, Chris, and Sam to the nearby school grounds to spend an hour playing football Frisbee. Chris and I were really dragging by the time we arrived back at the house about 7:00 PM. I stretched out on the floor of the living room near the entry vestibule and dozed toward recovery of my strength. While lying there, Rochelle entered with an agenda through the open doorway through which the children had been entering and exiting without closure. She sat upon the step of the stairs and to speak with me what she had on her mind, and to interact emotionally with the children as they circulated in and out the door. After about 15 minutes of that, Pierre and Jackie returned from grocery shopping, and Pierre struggled to control his aggressive impulses as Rochelle tenaciously attempted to engage him in futile dialog. I was uncomfortably in the middle of this, and went outside to sit and await the outcome. Ten minutes later, Pierre came out looking for me, with Rochelle right behind him. At that moment, Jackie closed and locked the front door. The ruckus did not thereby end in a physical altercation. Having been evicted from territory where she was not to have been admitted, and having no way of getting back in, Rochelle got into her car to depart, with something cryptic and unpleasantly spoken to me: "You are all so passive." Ah, yes, domestic relations like all of life are a challenge and a contest.

Each of us having enough troubles our own, is well advised to avoid getting entangled into those of others. ("Laugh and the world laughs with you/ But cry and you weep alone./ For the world would share in your pleasures/ But has troubles enough of its own")

Pierre and I discussed the incident, the evidence of which to me suggested that she was certainly under the influence of alcohol. The following day I took my leave of Pierre's household and drove over to spend a day or two with Jauhn's family. In the evenings, Massey and I occasionally find time for a talk while out upon a 2 mile hike. When she expects I will be about - for a meal - she usually takes the trouble to prepare some food of which she knows I am especially fond. Jauhn is still working half time at Intel, and attends classes at Portland State University in pursuit of a degree in Geology or Archeology. And so he tends to keep preoccupied with these and other projects. The kids and I play some sort of board game at the table that centers around the subject of Geography. The various states of Chaostan are brought to our attention one by one, as are the ever evolving states of Africa. Who can keep track of all those strange names and capitols?

I next drive to Medford and spend a couple nights at Real and Catherine's place. They both teach in grade school. One morning I drove over to speak with Tina for a few hours. She knew that I was in town, for my pickup had been spotted by the 15 year Cowboy who was in hiding from his father at the time. It is difficult to keep secrets within a small community. Tina always takes the trouble to give me an interestingly earthy and informative interpretation of the domestic situation in her household. I left her in the mid-afternoon to pick up the kids from school. They are a cheering and dynamic bunch of rascals. Three of them I then drove out to their karate lesson and looked in while they went through their routine. And that evening the kids and I had supper at Real's place, where we all spent the night.

From Medford I headed south en-route home to Albuquerque. I stopped in Redding to visit Raymond Horton. It was my first meeting with his wife, and with his daughter and her family who are visiting. They were very cordial and seemed to expect that I might stay over to visit . . . which I did. The next day they all headed out to the daughter's home in the Bay Area, leaving Raymond and I to loaf and visit another day. From there it was eastward past Susanville and down to Carson City where I looked up my med-school classmate, Bob Brown. We visited a couple hours, and I then called Jean Brown to visit by phone with her for about ten minutes before continuing my journey eastward. I found a nice rest area at a state park were I spent the night. The following day I continued upon the seemingly endless roadways of geologically naked Nevada to finally enter a vast Pampas-like grassland in the southwest corner of Utah. That night I got as far as the Barringer Meteor Crater, where I spent the night in a rest area before finally arriving home in the mid-afternoon of the following day, having been gone a little over six weeks. Before I entered the apartment, I tossed my head-band in to assess the risk. Peace reigned. After Bayloo and I took a two and a half mile hike along the arroyos, I even got a restful nap and a full supper with puddin' and everything.

I was then faced with the challenge of organizing my newly acquired thoughts, experience, and genealogy research. The genealogy project came first. It took a little over a couple weeks to complete the revisions of the Brasseur Genealogy manuscript. And only now, four weeks later am I finally completing the travelogue.

Why does the bear go over the mountain? Why(?), one might ask, do I trouble myself with all of these time consuming projects? Because I have the health, the time, the curiosity and yet enough energy to do so. Because I have not yet learned how to sit quietly (in blissful peace with myself) in the sun. Because even an unwanted and essentially useless life might just as well be lived and endured with some little courage, energy, and hope; just as though it were of some significance. Because life challenges one to think. Because one must eventually charge oneself with the responsibility for discovering whatever he can of reality. Because a responsible adult being must ultimately define his own worthy agenda of life - even in the very act of living and enduring the agony of one's existence. And so I too must sit a spell to contemplate - beneath the Banyan tree.

END OF SIXTH
INSTALLMENT
AND END OF TRAVELOGUE
R.G.Brasseur
25 November 2001

The Passing Summer
(with grandsons, Beau and Ribs)
2 July to 24 July 2002

Having arrived in Medford 30 June I stayed over at Tina's place on Diamond Street for two nights. The house is being sold and she is in the process of casting about for new lodgings. Being thus preoccupied with seven children and other things, she was willing to have Beaux and Raubaex travel with me for 3 or four weeks as I return to my home in Santa Fe after now being absent for about six weeks.

Tina made us some waffles for breakfast before we departed south on highway 5 after stopping in Phoenix for gas, ice, and soda pop. As we started out, I explained to the fellows the concept of frugality. Its definition and its importance to folks of limited means. And that my travels were necessarily attended by the practice of frugality. I also mentioned something about the magical powers that a man with money commands, and how that power departs him when the money is no longer in his possession.

It was a clear but mercifully cool day over the Siskiyous and down to Redding, California - a mere 150 miles. About 2:30 PM we arrived at the home of Raymond Horton. His wife Betty is away and he plans to drive down to the Bay Area tomorrow to pick her up. Beau and Ribs were in and out of his backyard swimming pool a half dozen times throughout the day and evening, and spent the interval of their time ramming about on their scooters. I chat with Raymond and some with Jim. The usual subjects having to do with philosophical discussions of current events and the nature of reality of times past and present.

About 7:00 PM Raymond, the boys, and I drive to the In-And-Out to get hamburgers, fries, and milk shakes for our evening meal. Raymond and Jim then got out the trundle beds for the boys to sleep upon and they turned in about 10:00 PM. We watched the tail end of a movie on TV and I then turned in about 11:20 after reading a bit.

July third we were up about 7:00 AM. The boys had some cold cereal and I had a roll and a cup of coffee before we take our leave of Raymond and Jim to continue south on Hwy 5 on this progressively warm day. We stopped to gas up and bought a watermelon before we got as far as the turnoff to Bakersfield. We arrived at Tehachapi about 7:00 PM, and there we stopped for a few more groceries and then stopped at a shaded picnic table upon a strip of grass beside the railroad track on the front street of this growing community. We made sandwiches of bologna, cheese, and hard biscuit to wash down with cold soda pop. And then we opened the now cold watermelon from the cooler. The watermelon was wet but not otherwise satisfying to the taste and after eating about half of it, we threw the rest away. And I later found that Ribs had surreptitiously disposed of his sandwich in the grass beneath the table. Meanwhile they had gone across the street to the gas station/convenience store to spend some money and use the restroom. I put our gear away and then pulled over there to gas up. To my astonishment, they had each spent some ten or twelve dollars on some laser light gadgets. At a gas stop earlier that day they had each spent money on a plastic cap pistol with caps and little plastic bullets. I had had to instruct them that the caps were not to be shot off in or from the cab of the pickup, and they were not to be pointing the guns at the vehicles and pedestrians in our stream of traffic. They follow the instructions pretty well, the younger one requiring an occasional reminder.

They had each brought a certain amount of spending money with them from home, and I, unfortunately, had no exact idea of how much; nor of what instructions they might have had from their parents as to how the money was to be spent. Beau later indicated that they had each about twenty five dollars. Ribs later indicated to me that he had spent the last of his money before we reached Santa Fe.

Near Tehachapi we saw perhaps two or three hundred large jet liners in storage on the tarmac. A few miles beyond that, we stopped at the rest area near Boron on the Mojave Desert just before sundown. There I stretched out a bit upon a concrete table top while the boys raced about the sidewalks on their scooters and played with a dozen other kids that seem to have stopped over there for a bit with a few people who were stretched out upon blankets on the lawn. The restroom facilities appear to be taking quite a beating in at least this season of the year. Perhaps the state of disrepair is related to the current financial crises of California. I note the agricultural check station at the northern border of the state is closed at this time too. The evening cools down very nicely as I watch the bright evening stars beginning to appear.

In anticipation of a hot day on the morrow I had the notion that we should get started early while it was still cool. Shortly after 10:00 PM we turn in for the night, with ideal sleeping weather. The occupants of about a dozen or more other cars seem also to be settling in for a rest, in addition to the many trucks that one always finds in these rest areas at night. Beau sleeps in the front seat of the cab, while Ribs and I climb into the camper shell and sleep upon the cushions. We are troubled the whole evening and night long by not a single mosquito, for we are in a dry desert, with no standing puddles of water about.

Up about 8:30 as the retreating shadows of the trees exposes us to the baking warmth of the sun. We are headed down Hwy 395, 15 S, 10 E, and 86 to El Centro on the edge of the Sonora Desert. About 9:45 AM we stop at a MacDonald's for a little breakfast. The place was filled to capacity and we had to wait a bit to place our order. Meanwhile, the lines to the bathroom facilities require an extra 10 or 15 minutes of waiting. The Fourth of July and the temperature is rising, surely reaching at least 110 degrees as we travel along the western fringe of the Salton Sea, south of Indio. We consume liquids and sweat abundantly to keep cool. No air conditioning. About 2:30 PM we reach El Centro and stop by the apartment of Lynn Fitz, a high school classmate. He arranges for us a room at the Imperial Motel. The four of us then spend a couple hours in the comforting refreshment of the swimming pool. About 7:00 PM, we have supper at the Burger King, and then drive out to have a dish of ice cream. The boys decide on the "bubble gum" flavor - two scoops. The mass of bubble gum balls in their portions was more than they could get around. It was rather a mess. No more bubble gum ice cream for them under my auspices. I rather guess that they too were a little dissuaded from it. Back at the motel, they were again into the swimming pool a couple of times before they finally got to bed about 11:00 PM. We spend the following day also at the motel. After breakfast at Denny's, back to the swimming pool intermittently all day long. I put my foot into the hot-tub waters and they seemed to me uncomfortably warm, so I stayed out of it. The boys tried sliding down the aluminum banisters into the pool. Ribs then thought to try sliding into the hot pool in the same manner. He hit the water, touched bottom, yelped, and leaped out almost before he got wet. I checked the temperature again with my hand. Indeed it does seem to me perhaps even dangerously hot. We went out with Lynn and Laura for Chinese food that evening. Ribs being a fussy eater, grabbed the whole bowl of plain white rice (intended to be divided among us all) and dumped it on his plate, and then ordered yet another bowl of the same, eating nothing else.

The morning of the 6th we checked out of the motel and stopped to bid farewell to Lynn before heading east on Hwy 8. We stopped at MacDonald's in Yuma to get breakfast and then continued upon another hot day of travel. As we approached Tucson, we saw the smoke of a great forest fire to the east of Tucson. We stopped at the grocery in Tucson to get some eatables, then continued on to a very nice rest area about 30 or 40 miles east of Tucson. There we had some rolls and some watermelon; and spent about two hours there while the boys goofed off with their scooters. About sunset we continued up through Stafford and then headed up the steep Highway 78 into southwest New Mexico's Mogollon Mountains. There we saw another forest fire blazing through the night - perhaps five miles north of the highway. Near the summit, we came upon a public campsite about 10:00 PM. There we pitched our tent in the darkness and turned in for the night.

The following day I had intended to take them up through the catwalk park where I know they would have been thrilled at the interesting climb in the cool of the canyon on so warm a day. However, the catwalks were closed for repair, and so we moved along through this sparsely settled area to Reserve, where we stopped for gas, and for a milkshake. We arrived home in Santa Fe in time for supper that evening. They spent three or four days and nights with some folks of their acquaintance who have moved here from Medford. While around the house at our place they got along famously with our two foster daughters, Heather and Chelsea. Heather, a Navajo girl age 19, and Chelsea a Pueblo girl about 16. And they were as attracted to Heather's 4 month old baby as was I.

They had agreed to exchange letters with Heather and she was asking me for their new address.

On the 13th of July, Bayloo packed us a picnic lunch and the boys and I drove out past Los Alamos to Bandallier National Park, some 60 miles distant. There we visited the cave dwellings of an ancient people and then had our picnic lunch before returning home for supper. And the we watched a video movie, Moby Dick. On the 14th we drove north to Tesuque to walk about the grounds of a sculpture park. They were especially fascinated to watch a glass blower fashion a vase from molten glass.

On the 16th we visited a few goodwill and thrifty stores to look for books and whatnots. The fellows found a living room putting hole at our first stop And so we also picked up a couple of golfing irons so that they could practice with them. We have a log hallway down which they putted into the golf hole trap. Though they managed to burn out the rejection mechanism within a day or two, it is still usable. They took it with them when they went back home. I also had perhaps 400 golf balls on hand at the time we departed for Oregon, and I asked them to take along all they wanted. They each filled up a sack full.

On the 17th the three of us made an outing to the south of Albuquerque to visit the Salinas National Monument and the Valley of Fire. We stopped at Santo Domingo Pueblo to gas up and stopped at the Wal-Mart in Albuquerque to get an oil change. It was late in the afternoon before we had covered the 60 miles to the Abo Pueblo site. A deserted and ancient Pueblo site which has been uninhabited the past couple hundred years. Just as with the other two independent sites of this national monument, Abo is dominated by the ruins of a large mission church some 300 or 400 years old in the midst of the now partially excavated pueblo apartment dwellings. When we finished our tour there, we stopped in Mountainair to enjoy some rather tasty Mexican food before continuing southward to the San Isidro ruins, where we arrived about 7:00 PM. But it was past closing time, and finding no camping facilities there, we continued on south to Carrizozo, arriving there about dusk and having just enough daylight to set up our camp on a BLM or Forestry Service camp site which cost me 2.50. And then the fellows got out their scooters and roared about the camp site asphalt roads for an hour or more. When full darkness arrived, the starry skies were magnificent. I lay back on the hood of the pickup and the boys laid on the top of the camper shell as I pointed out some of the constellations and some of the brightest stars before we turned in for the night. We had cushions enough to facilitate a night of comfortable sleep.

We were up shortly after 8:00 AM the following morning as the rising sun began to focus its heat into the tent. For breakfast we had only muffins and root beer. In restoring order to the living space in the cab of the pickup, I discover that the fellows had inadvertently left a large mess on the drivers space of the course cloth seating bench. It was the same plastic silly-putty material that Poco Uno had rubbed into the scalp of Cui on our outing last year. There, in Dunseith, the women of Don Richard's family had to resort to a special shampoo to get the stuff out of Cui's hair. Tenacious stuff, once it penetrates and sets into strands and fibers of materials. It had returned now to plague me in now this new form.

The valley of fires is a relatively young flow of black lava that appears to have coursed like a river through a deep ravine some 1500 or 2000 years ago on a course of perhaps 40 or 50 miles and now lies in solidified fractured chunks some 20 or 30 feet below the embankment upon which we were encamped. The fellows had brought a golf club and some golf balls with them, and spent a half hour driving the balls as far as they could into the lava fields, and then scrambled down the embankment to search for the balls before repeating the exercise. We gathered the tent and other gear into the pickup and departed at midmorning, to return to the Grand Quivera ruins that we had missed seeing the night before. We explored those ruins about 45 minutes, though the fellows were naturally much more interested in chasing down the small lizards that skittered about the place. So quick, these lizards, that I was surprised that they were able to catch them. They seem to have figured out the method as they tell me that the lizards are fast but that they tire easily, so that one can wear them down and finally capture them.

It was lunch time when we again reached Mountainair. And we so much enjoyed the food we had there last night, that we went back to same rustic little hole in the wall where we had eaten last night. And then we drove on north to the third such site of similar ruins which constitute this national monument. They again caught a couple of lizards before we got out the watermelon to eat our fill on this rather warm day. And from there we again passed through Albuquerque and drove north to Cochiti Lake with the thought of camping out again this night. A good place for boating perhaps, but seemed to me entirely unsatisfactory as a camping or a swimming site. And so we drove back to Santa Fe to eat at home.

I had an appointment in Las Vegas the 21st and the boys rode along with me. I dropped them off at the city park 2 blocks from my appointment for an hour and then interrupted their fun to take them first to the goodwill store and then to MacDonald's for a bite to eat. Returning home, we stopped off at the Pecos National Monument and arrived there just as a thunder storm was sweeping over the area so that they closed the trails account of the lightening. This pueblo was a center for the selling off of stolen Spanish horseflesh to the Comanche and other natives all over the west, but it was vacated and fell into ruins a couple hundred years ago. In recent years the park system has built up what appears to be an unnecessarily expensive visitor's center and staffed the place with a lot of expensive personnel. At the time we were there, there were 4 uniformed career officers on duty bending backwards trying to be of service to us while yet forbidding us to explore the site. We watched the short documentary movie of the history of the area and then drove up to the picnic area which overlooked the ruins. The storm was more exciting to the fellows than the ruins were likely to have been. Ribs was inhaling large gulps of his beloved electrically charged fresh cool air while the rain pelted down atop of us all safely away from the electricity in the Faraday Cage that we call the pickup cab. One could appreciate the reason for the closing of the pathways as bright bolts of lightening crashed all about us. Soon then, the storm ended, as abruptly as it had started.

The boys and I have been taking our evening walks regularly but Ribs accedes to its inevitability only rather reluctantly. Always specifically indicating that he doesn't want to come along. But it is part of the program and he follows along without the necessity even of threats. He generally tries then at least to establish some condition - such as that we rent a movie to watch. But I brush those timid suggestions aside, as they already watch plenty of TV and an occasional library movie. He continuously straggles along behind sort of dreamily to display his want of enthusiasm. About three-fourths of the distance upon one leg of the walk is a bus stop bench, and he often just stops at that point to sit or goof around and awaits our return to join us again. About two blocks beyond where Beau and I usually turn about to return, is a golf driving range enclosed by a very high wire netting. The hard hit balls apparently sometimes burst right through the mesh, or over or under the mesh. If someone has not been there hunting balls ahead of one on a particular day, one is apt to find a dozen or more loose golf balls to pocket. I thought I might use the story of this possibility to prod the enthusiasm of the fellows for walking a longer route and doing it with some spontaneity. And so I put it to them that we might explore "the promised land". There was curiosity, and then enthusiasm for the idea. Not wanting them to reach through or under the fence for balls that were yet within the boundary of that private land, I told them that was not going to be permissible. And that a fellow called "Peter" was the guardian of the property of this promised land. It was his job to protect that property and to keep us out of the "promised land". That if they reached beyond the fence, they might end up in the "pokey" and needing me or their parents to bail them out. It was on that night of 14 July that we came home with a record 27 golf balls to add to our collection.

The other leg of the walk is in the dry cactus strewn tract of land behind the golf course. One can find an occasional golf ball almost anywhere there at some time or another. But perhaps nearly half of them I find are in a small dry steam bed where the 'sliced' ball can easily clear the fence and end up in the tall grass and weeds. Ribs is sluggish on that leg of our walk also, but seems quite less so since I pointed out that most of my finds were in that area which I have taken to calling by the name of "the happy hunting grounds". The mysticism of these names has a wonderful way of piquing their interest. Once, even on the high, dry, and barren "purgatory" march we found a half dozen balls, though that march is usually sterile except for cactus. "Heaven's Gate" is the shortcut to the housing tract of our home through a loosely toothed barricade of railroad ties planted like fence posts at the end of the pavement. Given a choice of how to reach home, Ribs is always quick to suggest that we go by way of heaven's gate.

Fortunately, the radio of the pickup ceased operating several years ago, and so my trips are now free of the proven futility of trying to find or follow any interesting radio programs in my travels. Beau and Ribs could scarce believe that it didn't work, I think they still believe that it does. In any case, they managed too, to find their own ways for filling in the hours of sit and travel. They scarce paid any attention to the wonderful evolving landscapes running continuously about us. They dozed and slept 30 to 60 minutes a couple times a day. Otherwise they occupied their time in playing with the several gadgets they purchased along the way, and there was a constant flow of chatter between them. Good-natured arguing and fighting about whose turn it was to sit by the window and over what was what. There was also considerable shoving, wrestling, and pounding upon one another in their various versions of "gotcha" games. They had some occasional questions for me as to which of them was right on this or that, and other questions about "how long till we get there". Other sorts of questions too which I had to make a stab at answering. Beau likes to tease and pick at Ribs a bit. Often followed by a flurry of fisticuffs. Ribs may pretend to be injured in order to bring the fight to an end. Or he withdraws to magnify and shelter his supposed injury and shouts "you idiot", as Beau laughs it off and nudges him a little further.

Even while we were traveling, it appeared to me that they were each upon the phone several times every day to be in contact both with Tina and Real. They seem to have their own calling card, and yet it seemed to me a bit like overkill, besides possibly being expensive. I inquired into this while speaking with Tina. She tells me it only costs 3 cents a minute and so she doesn't mind the excessive calls. And though Ribs is only 10 years old, I had not realized how closely attached he is to the comforts of home. Apparently, upon several occasions he has gone off to spend the night at the home of a friend, only then to call his mother in the wee hours to come and get him because he is "homesick". And I can see that he has a certain gift for manipulation and so it seems not unlikely that he has patterns of behavior that enable him towards the utmost of the comforts of home. And yet, during the three weeks he was with me, I saw no other indications of his being homesick apart from the frequent phone calls. He has rather a serious and romantic aspect to his outlook. I am given to understand that he likes to listen to mellow melodies and even to some classical music. Upon occasion, I sometimes sang in the car. Often at the beginning of the day, "Its up away at the break of day, at the peep of early morning. Staff in hand and eager band, our hearts as light as air. In a drum and fife there is joy and life as our feet the earth are scorning . . . etc". Or, "I'm going says I, to that land in the sky. Away upon the mountain". Followed by a yodel. They sometimes sang along with me. And then Ribs might sing one of his own favorites, such as "Yesterday". It seems odd for a 10 year old boy to sing so romantic a song so earnestly. "Yesterday. All my troubles seemed so far away . . . ." And, he knows all the words and the verses. A nice tune, and I could sing it along with him, since he has the words down pat.

On July 22nd we three headed back for Oregon. Before we left town Ribs managed to stub his big toe jumping off a swing barefooted. Pealed back a thick layer of skin from the front of the toe but no other damage. We soaked it and cleaned it up before then keeping it covered with tape. It didn't slow him down much. We drove north through Espanol where we stopped for some soda pop and ice before continuing up thru Taos and ran into a small rain shower that cooled us off for a bit. Headed then up through Tres Piedras but stopped 5 minutes at the high bridge of Grand Canyon of the Rio Grande to walk out to the middle and peer down into the river some several hundred feet below. Deep enough to make me a bit nervous. We drove on up hwy 64 through the Sangre de Christo uplands and finally into Chama. From there, on up into the territories of the southern Utes in Colorado, passing through Pagosa Springs en route to Durango and on to Dove Creek and Monticello where we turned north to pass through the canyon lands National Monument territory. We had stopped at Mesa Verdi National Park with the intent of camping out there, but the camp ground was occupied by a mob of fire fighting personnel, and so we had to find other arrangements for sleeping. About midnight we arrived at the hole in the wall rest area. A rest spot in the shadow of a huge monolithic red sandstone mountain some 500 feet high - about ten miles south of Moab. There along with a dozen other outfits we settled down to pass the night in the vehicle. Beau in front. Ribs and I in back. And it was just cool enough to make sleeping conditions good. Up the next morning at 8:00 in the shade of the red monolith mountain and had a muffin and a can of pop before heading up through the land of the Moabites to highway 80, up hwy 6 through Price, and over Soldier Pass. There we stopped at the beautiful Whitewater rest area to have some watermelon and give the boys a chance to work off some steam in the chasing about of a few chipmunks. Then, down to the Spanish Forks and up Hwy 15 towards Salt Lake City which we by-passed on Hwy 215 to reach Hwy 80 West. As we proceeded those 150 miles through the salt flats in the afternoon, it became excessively hot. The temperature must have approached 120 degrees. We stopped for gas just across Nevada border, into Wendover, and from there we started climbing into the mountains of Nevada as the temperatures cooled pleasantly. About 6:30 PM we reached Elko, where we stopped to get some information about possible camping areas in the state and to buy some groceries for an evening picnic. A very pleasant town of perhaps 15,000 population. What is so nice a town doing way out here in the middle of Nevada? I wouldn't mind living here my self. The University of Nevada was originally sited here before it was relocated into Reno. We stopped at a city park to consume our picnic supper, and after the fellows had worked off some steam on the swings and slides, we loaded up and continued west to arrive at Winnemucca.

In Winnemucca, we drove by a cemetery located right on Main Street, and turned the corner to drive past a second side of it. No protecting hedge or wall to hide it from the view of every passerby. Ribs says "gosh, I wouldn't want to be buried in that cemetery." "Why is that, what do you mean?" says I. "Gosh, anyone that might be there to cry upon the grave could be seen by everyone", in his opinion.

My map indicated that there was a public camping area just a mile or two out of town. But when we asked around about it, no one there seemed to know of it. We finally located it ourselves out in water canyon, but there were no other campers there in that isolated place, and it was overrun by Mormon crickets. And so we went back out past the cemetery to the Wal-Mart to spend the night there.

We were up the following morning by 7:30 to use the restroom facilities before heading up Hwys 95 and 140 into Oregon. This is one of the most solitary and most beautiful drives I know of. Barren desert country covered with desert greasewood, volcanic mountains and gigantic frozen rivers of lava plateaus. Mid morning we stopped at one of the few rest areas to have a sandwich and some watermelon. At the edge of the plot, an artesian well flowed continuously so that a small stream flowed off into the brush. A few wild burros are to be seen round about. Continuing once more westward, we crossed into Oregon's Stein Mountain country to be confronted first by the Albert rim upthrust fault and stopped at its lip to survey the view for a hundred miles to the north, south, and west. Then we eased our way at 25 miles per hour down the 5 miles of winding narrow roadway perched upon the face of the fault cliff and made our way the remaining hundred miles into Lakeview where we stopped for gas. From there, again along Hwy 140 through Klamath Falls, past Mt. McLaughlin and into Medford by about 3:00 PM

Beau was blowing a whistle in the cab as we drove along. It had a piercingly high and irritating sound. A couple minutes of this and Ribs says, "Grampy, make him stop". The thought had already crossed my mind. And so I suggested that might be good idea, since it seemed perhaps to be even harmful to one's hearing. Says Beau, "well it doesn't bother my hearing". I explained it more earnestly and he says, "what?". The wind was whistling in the open windows so I repeated myself a bit more loudly. He says, "what?". I started to repeat it once again before I finally caught the tenor of his humor. We all had a good laugh at his wit and then heard nothing more of the whistle. Beau is rather a "take charge" sort of fellow and, like Huckleberry Fin, he likes to have his fun. Just as it was with Poco and Cui on last years trip, so also this year; the older likes to tease and torment the younger in a companionly sort of way, with plenty of give and take in both directions. Each little round of conflict dies out like the brief summer rain squall. At the end of one such, Ribs was venting to Beau his complaints of how he was being unkindly treated by Beau. Telling Beau he didn't appreciate being made fun of. He was especially upset that Beau had said to someone that he (Ribs) sucks his thumb. "But, you do", says Beau. "Well, gosh, you don't have tell everyone", says Ribs. Minutes later, Beau was giving him syllable by syllable lessons on word pronunciation to help him overcome some of his slight speech impediment. One hot afternoon in Santa Fe it rained a bit, and Ribs immediately stepped out onto the porch to get a big whiff of one of his favorite smells - that of fresh rain upon the pavements. And it seemed to recall to his mind the stories that Poco and Cui told him of their having gotten to swim in the flooded streets of Bismarck at the German convention last year.

Ribs has a sort of passion for throwing quarters away into the arcade machines that one finds in nearly every gas mart, shopping mall, and department store as we travel. A sort of vice mixed in with all his little virtues. I noticed that some two or three years ago while we were out for pizzas one evening. And now, he had run out of money about the time we reached Santa Fe. One day as we were headed into the Wal-Mart store, he suddenly claimed that he had found a one dollar coin on the parking lot pavement. As I thought about it, that seemed rather unlikely, for those coins have been a failure, and there are very few of them in circulation though I keep two or three of them around. Of course the whole thing was spent before we left there to make a stop at the bank. I asked if they wanted to come into the bank and Ribs indicated that he would wait alone in the pickup, so I didn't lock up. And yet, before we got to the bank door, he had joined us, seeming to have gotten lonesome rather quickly. We then drove back to the Wal-Mart to pick up my prescriptions. And he now has two quarters which he says he found on the asphalt at the bank. Again, it seemed to me highly improbable that he would find two quarters on that short stretch, especially since as with the dollar coin, he was treading in my footsteps and I would certainly have been the finder. This second find recalled to my mind that I keep a large handful of loose coins upon the floor of the pickup cab next to the drivers seat. I had even drawn their attention to those coins when we had stopped to get an oil change in Albuquerque, explaining to them the necessity of removing the coins to my pocket before leaving the vehicle in their care for the oil change. Some two or three times previously in past years, my coins had thus been lost to me. In the store, after he had squandered the two quarters in the arcade, Ribs nonchalantly picked up a package of batteries as we strolled down an aisle. I asked him if he had enough money to pay for them. He didn't, and so I had him put the batteries back. I pondered these things a few minutes to organize my thoughts and then I gently related to him the above details and something about my doubts pertaining to his ability to find money. I then asked him directly if there might not be another version of his finding of the money that he might now wish to "fess up" to. OR, if he was going to stick to his story. With an earnest expression upon his face he looked me in the eye and said "I'm sticking to my story". I don't say that he convinced me, but it seemed enough that I had confronted him. And so, I let it pass. But I never had further cause for any subsequent suspicions with him concerning money. I do notice however that in their various interactions, his own brother has occasional cause to suspect him of lying. And that he (Ribs) one night lied to me by calling from the home of their friends to suggest that he had just talked with his mother, and that she had specifically told him he could spend the night there, AND that the mother of the friends had agreed to that. Both statements I investigated and found to be untrue.

(I had sent this very summary to Real and to Tina, thinking they might be well advised to deal with what seemed to be these little dishonesties in his character) I bring such matters to your attention suspecting that you yourselves have had similar experiences that have sometimes roused your suspicions, and knowing that you are continuously in the process of ironing out these little character flaws in your children. I might have let these observations pass unreiterated, but there seems to be something perhaps within my genes of the missionary predisposition concerning what I perceive to be valid moral principles. Especially concerning moral discipline of my own people. Thus it is that I am predisposed to nudging and intervening in order to encourage reform. I am particularly concerned about the passion to spend quarters in arcades, not only because it is frivolous and the habit of wasting of money is counterproductive to character development. Additionally, you are, no doubt, aware that homosexuals and other deviants are known to sometimes haunt arcades with the express intent of feeding quarters to youngsters with uncontrollable spending passions.

None of the above two paragraphs stood in the way of my enjoying the time and experience we shared in July of 2003. I was especially attracted to Ribs because he reminds me very much of my brother Vic, when he was a lad. Facial appearance very much like him with the same curly hair, and mannerisms and expressions that seem almost identical. Even a mole similarly located upon his face. The day I dropped them back home in Medford, I laid back on Cui's bed a few minutes and closed my eyes while Ribs put one of his discs on for me to listen to. One of the songs was that which he sang a few times in the pickup, "Yesterday". Suddenly he was standing next to me saying "Grampy, look". I opened my eyes as he was a foot or two from my face with a huge spider in his hand. I instinctively raised my arms in combat and jostled his arm to keep the spider at its distance. Says he, with a suddenly worried look upon his face, "Grampy, don't! . . . I'm afraid too", as he tried to retrieve the now excited spider that was climbing up his arm and onto his back, to put the pet back into it's aquarium of confinement.

Concerning Beau, I am struck with amaze. He seems as logical, pure, and upright as Huck Finn himself. And as full of innocent fun and pranks.

The boys liked to watch "King of the Hill" and "The Simpsons" on TV and Beau likes to imitate some of their voices and some of their pithy expressions. I checked him out to be sure that he could actually drive the pickup in the event that something happen to me on the trip. It seems to me that he can do it, except that he will have to sit upon the pillow to see over the steering wheel. As I worked the clutch the man in the middle got to shift back and forth through the gears as we traveled.

Cowboy offered me the use of his bed that night in Medford, and I headed back to New Mexico the following glorious day. I slept a few hours to the east of Winnemucca and then had to press on with steady determination in order to get through Salt Lake City by 8:00 AM and the traffic rush. Coming downhill into Price, Utah, the highway patrol stopped me for speeding in the ancient Pickup. Said I was doing 70 in a 60 mph area. I didn't argue with him, for I don't know - my speedometer doesn't work. He seemed to have a strange fear that I might harm him. He had me step outside the pick-up and step in front of the headlights to keep an eye on me as he looked into the cab of the pickup. There, he noticed, and was curious about my rock hammer. I told him that I collect rocks occasionally, and that I was just now returning home from having spent a couple of weeks with my young grandsons. He suddenly softened at the thought of these things. Apparently, a Mormon fellow, and now seeing me as a guy with 'family values'. And thus we parted, on good terms - no citation having been issued.

Heather and Chelsey ask about the boys. Want to know their new address and phone number so that they might get in touch with them. They asked me to say hello to the fellows.

I plan to attend the German convention in Rapid City South Dakota on Sept 4 through 7. I would be glad to drop by and pick up a couple of the grandsons to take along with me in this fine season of the year. But, I expect of course that it is improbable, as school may well have started by that time.

R. Garner Brasseur

Late Summer of 2002

(With Poco and Cui)

by R. Garner Brasseur

On 31 July 2002 I received an e-mail message from Tina to the effect that grandsons Poco Uno and Cui would be willing and able to make a trip with me to the German Convention in Bismarck. I began to organize and pack my gear in preparation for a trip of about five or six weeks, as I completed my current business affairs and projects. It was late into the evening of 1 August when I finally loaded the last of my gear into the pickup after a busy day of preparation. So late, and I was tired enough that there seemed every prospect for a natural and cozy nap of a few hours before departure. About two hours later I awoke refreshed at 1:10 AM and departed with an easterly gusting wind to speed me along Highway 40, and then Northward on Hwy 666 from Gallup. I stopped at Cortez just after dawn to gas up and get some donuts before continuing along through Dove Creek and Monticello to the beautiful rest area at the great red sandstone monolith which is situated on the north side of the same rock that houses the "Hole in the Wall" tourist trap. I arrived there at 8:00 AM, tired enough for a pleasant nap in the shade of that great dome. This old fellow swallowed his medications and followed them up with a boiled egg from the lunch basket before stretching out on the mattress in the pickup camper. There is something satisfying about bumbling about alone, like a desert tortoise, in a silent barren land without a pressing time schedule; and self-contained with the modest necessary accouterments for one's humble existence.

I awoke three hours later on this pleasantly overcast day and continued north to Highway 70 west and up Hwy 6 across Soldier Pass, then down and through Salt Lake City just before the evening traffic contest. I continued westward on Highway 80 to the rocking excitement of terrific blasts of gusting wind that jolted my awareness to the wisdom of reducing my speed. At 8:00 PM I stopped at a rest area in the wilderness of Northern Nevada to satisfy my hunger with sardines, crackers, cheese, and boiled eggs, and then lay down with a pillow on the pickup seat. There I fell into a blessedly tranquil state of semi-sleep and reminiscence for a couple hours before continuing westward. Just to the east of Winnemucca, I stop at another rest area and sleep in the pickup camper another four hours. A dozen other vehicles are similarly there encamped. Someone on motorcycles has even pitched a tent there.

At Winnemucca I gas up about 5:00 AM, and then head across Hwys 95 and 140 towards Lakeview, Oregon. I encounter about a half-dozen cars on this 200 mile stretch of road. There has been some rainfall in this vast stretch of the Great Basin Desert within the past 24 hours and it is gloriously cool and blooming. Blue sky and blue-green desert brush and sprigs of grass amid volcanic tablelands and valleys as I climb in third gear toward the ridge ahead. I stop at the springs of a rest area at 8:00 AM to take my meds and breakfast upon a couple more boiled eggs, before heading over the magnificent Albert Rim and winding my way far down its face along the precariously perched roadway to the valley below at a cautious speed.

Already in Lakeview there is smoke in the air on this otherwise clear day, and its density increases as I continue westward. Past Mt. McLaughlin and down into the valley of the Rogue the smoke causes a dimness akin to that of an eclipse of the sun, though the orange sun is full above at an hour past mid-day. I stop at Real's place and notice the car of his mother parked up front; her and Real in earnest conversation in the driveway. A conversation that seems to run-on inordinately long - and uninterrupted by me. An issue of some sort, I should guess. As I step out of my rig, I am pleasantly confronted with some of my grandchildren: Mijita, Nombres, Joss, Izzy, Beamer, Chad, and Rachel. We do our little three-step dances together and engage in our wee conversations, before they and I return to various little games and interactions on the front lawn. A half hour later, the grandmother departs with Joss and Izzy, and I talk a bit with Real. But something is weighing on his mind, for he is doing all of the talking and the subject seems to have something economic at its root.

Presently, Catharine stopped by to pick up some of the youngsters for swimming and my attention was captured by the absence of any of the customary feminine pleasantries. Soon after she departs I drive out to the library before returning about 6:00 PM. It seemed as though I might get a bit of a nap on the floor while Real was at the computer; and perhaps a free lunch later. But when Catharine and the children returned, there was again a coolness in the air that was beyond my zone of comfort and I drove out alone to have a hamburger.

I stopped by Tina's place about 8:00 having earlier had an invitation to spend the evening and the night there with the grandchildren. Guests were beginning to arrive for an evening of cards. Poco Uno and I drove out to pick up Cowboy (and Lindsey), whom I hadn't seen for over a year - he was out on parole for the weekend. At age 16 he is now taller than I and filling out into a trim masculine form. He says he has been working long hours on the farm the past 8 or 10 months and yet has found enough time to study and complete his GED requirements. We return to the house and spend the evening in the basement where the youngsters play a few games and the adult card games proceed upstairs. Tina presents us with the traditional root beer and ice cream treat about 10:00 PM. About midnight the card game guests depart and I have a chance to talk with Tina about 45 minutes before we all turn in for the night.

Arise about 10:00 AM. Tina, Perry, and Cowboy have gone to church. Poco, Cui, and I gather our gear into the pickup and head out about 10:30. We stop at Lakeview to get some groceries on this pleasantly cool and overcast day, and then head up Hwy 395 beneath the towering Albert Rim to Burns, then east along the Malheur River, and at days end cross over into Idaho at Nyssa. In another fifteen minutes we arrive at old Ft. Boise just before dusk. There we pitch our tent, build our sandwiches for supper and then turn in for the night about 10:00 PM. The following morning (5 August) we are up at 7:45, pull up steaks, load our gear, and drive on into Caldwell where we stop at a cafe to have large pancakes for breakfast. Cui can't even finish off one of them. Though he is about the same height as Poco, he is quite thin. We drive through Boise and on to Mountain Home where we turn off of Hwy 84 and onto Hwy 26 (Goodall's Cutoff) to get to Craters of the Moon National Monument. Presently we come to an area where there are some black pieces of material scattered upon the roadway. I supposed that some loose asphalt material had cascaded down from an overloaded Highway Maintenance truck. But the boys observed that the black things were moving, so we pulled off to the side of the road to investigate. These things were mature plump grasshoppers; the first black tribe that I had ever seen. Part of a swarm about a mile in width that were crossing the highway here. We stopped near the entrance of the national monument to lend some tools to a fellow who was trying to replace the solenoid from the starter of his car. We then look at the exhibits before taking the seven mile drive through the lava fields, taking time to climb a couple of the cinder-cones and spatter-cones on this mercifully cool day. Then, on through Idaho Falls towards the Grand Tietons as the day is waning. We stopped at the Burger King in Briggs for supper and then drove to Victor, where we take a camping site at dusk. There the boys use the swimming pool while I take an evening stroll before we turn in early for the night.

The following morning (the 6th of Aug.) we stop at McDonalds in Jackson Hole to have egg McMuffins for breakfast. Then through The Tietons, DuBois, and Riverton where we stop for groceries and to get myself a swimming suit. Then on through the spectacular Wind River Canyon and Thermopolis. Just to the east of Worland I noticed that the temperature gauge was rising so we stopped to discover that I had broken a fan belt. We limped back into Worland without delay by 4:00 PM and delayed about an hour while the mechanic replaced the fan belt. About 20 miles west of Buffalo we stopped at a forest service camp and pitched our tent at dusk.

I rouse the boys each morning with song. "Its up away at the break of day, at the peep of early morning/ Staff in hand and eager band, our hearts as light as air./ In a drum fife there is joy and life as our feet the earth are scorning/ Off we start, with boy and heart, with never a thought or care./ Up, up stepping along as we keep in step with the marching song/ Up, up marching along. And the scouts are up and away!" Never any applause, of course, but they arise without demur; and we work efficiently together, both to make and to break camp. On 7 August we drive through Buffalo and Gillette to arrive at Devils Tower National Monument. Within fifty miles of the place, the number of motorcycles we encounter begins to astonish us. We were in a very long line of cycles and were 30 or 45 minutes in line just getting past the gate. Parking was another problem. There were a couple of climbers trying to reach the top of the tower. We watched them for about 45 minutes as they struggled upwards. Not a sport that appeals to my instincts. As we head north, the motorcycle traffic becomes even heavier, and in one of those small communities it took us an hour of creep and stop before we finally got out of the mess. We learn that this is an annual rally of motorcycle enthusiasts that attracts cyclists from all over the nation. I later read in the paper that there were somewhere between 300,000 and 500,000 gathered in this area, this year. "Stugis Rally Days", they call it. It doesn't seem to me like a good situation in which to enjoy the riding of a motorcycle. Far too much traffic! There must be something else that attracts them into such an uncomfortably large crowd. Surprisingly, many if not most of them are older and middle age people.

We continue north on Hwy 85 and reach Belfield ND at the approach of days end. There we take a camp site, set up the tent, and make our sandwiches for supper, having to pace about the area while eating to keep off the Mosquitoes. And then we stopped at the pool to swim for an hour and a half before finishing off the last of the watermelon, showering up and turning in.

We awoke about 8:00 AM with tent wet from rain through the night, and even some patches of wetness upon our sleeping bags where they had come into contact with wet tent fabric. We pull up stakes and toss our gear and the wet tent into the pickup in the morning drizzle. Then east on Hwy 94 to New Salem where we stop in the late morning to have Pancakes and French toast for breakfast before continuing on into Bismarck. We arrived about 12:30 at the Raddison Hotel where our room was awaiting us. I registered us in to the Germans From Russia Heritage Society, and then the fellows were off to enjoy the use of the indoor swimming pool while I went to the GRHS resource room to plough about for new genealogical information. At 9:00 that evening I joined the boy in the use of the swimming facility and hot tub until 10:30 PM. For the next couple days the boys are on their own to swim, watch TV, and play games, while attend some genealogy lecture. We get together for noon and evening meals with the Germans, and the fellows show up mid-afternoons to get their fill of Kucken. And we swim together in the evenings. Friday night there was a heavy rainstorm and the fellows thought it great fun to wander through some of the nearby flooded streets in water up to their waists.

On Saturday morning the three of attended dance lesson to learn to Waltz, Two-step, Polka, and Shottish. It was a sunny day and we set up the tent upon the lawn for a couple of hours to dry out the fabric. That evening we attended the dance from 9:00 to midnight. I danced a couple waltzes and a polka. Poco danced a chicken dance and schottish.

We slept in until 10:00 Sunday morning and the quickly loaded our gear and departed the Hotel by 11:00 AM. The boys had breakfast a McDonalds but I stopped at The Doughnut Hole to have a caramel roll. We then looked up the address of my cousin Gordon Neuberger in Bismarck, but he was not about. I next located the residence of Ray Walton whom I had not seen since 1942. I talked with him only about ten or fifteen minutes at the entrance of his apartment. He is retired from his post of attourney general of ND and tells me that only Alice and Ruby among his siblings are still living. In the early 1940's he was a buddy of Duane and Gene. The three of them jumped into the Mouse River to save my sisters, Aloha and Skippy from drowning in the summer of 1942. We stopped in Bismarck on C Street to look at the old house were we lived in 1939. About 1:00 PM we stopped for gas and each had a root-beer float before we headed north. We stopped by the cemetery in Beulah to visit the graves of my Boepple grandparents, Uncle Victor, Aunt Bertha, Aunt Ann (and George Schnaidt), and Aunt Lydia (and August Neuberger). All of them buried in a cluster in lots that grandfather had purchased many years ago. We drove out to the farm but cousin Elmer was not at home. We drove 7 miles further to Hazen where both Gene and I were born, and then another 7 miles west on Hwy 200 to Stanton where my mother had attended and graduated from high school. There we looked up the old house where the Boepple family had lived from about 1917 to about 1941 - when grandmother had died.

We crossed the muddy Missouri River at Washburn near where our family often crossed on an old ferryboat in the 1930's. We stopped at Washburn (were sister Ookie was born in 1934) to have a pizza for supper, and then drove north another 7 miles to Falkirk where we dropped in to visit my old school chum, Dick Morgan. We set up our tent in his large rural yard, and then the fellows played croquette while Dick and I conversed several hours on old times and on various philosophic and historical topics. We turned in about 1:00 AM.

I was up at 8:30 the following morning to a brisk wind and awaked the grandsons a half hour later. The tent had just then collapsed upon them. We collected our gear into the pickup and then had some breakfast with Dick. His womenfolk all sort of ignored us and his wife, though smiling, made a rather snappy remark to him - all of which suggest some current tensions within that household. Perhaps our presence among them aggravated the situation. Thus it was that I was rather anxious to leave directly after breakfast, rather than to linger and reminisce.

We drove on north through Minot and Rugby to reach Dunseith about noon. Here in this small town our family lived two years beginning the autumn of 1946. Two of the most pleasant years of my youth and childhood. Here is where Dick and I were chums and classmates. We stopped into the visitor's center where I ran into Stella - the sister of another old friend, Don Richard. The family of one of her daughters was visiting, and she informed me that Don would be at her place this evening from Bottineau to visit. And suggested that I drop by to see him. Outside the visitors center is huge turtle about 40 foot long, composed of auto tire rims that are welded together. The fellows climbed on this a while before we then drove out to St. Louis (Catholic) cemetery to look up the graves of my Grandparents, Xavier Brasseur (died 1927) and Philomene (died 1910), and Uncle Pierre (died in France near the end of WWI.), and Aunt Leah (died about age 93), and the infant Aunt Lena who died in 1910, not long after her mother died of tuberculosis. Aunt Leah had imported a ten foot high replica of 'The Pieta' which stands near the top of the cemetery hill facing the visitor as he enters to gate. We then drove another six or seven miles to the old town-site of Tarsus and located there the cemetery were Aunt Aurora was buried in 1899, having died about age ten of pneumonia. We were unable to locate her unmarked grave site. Many of the headstones that are broken off and unreadable are stacked in a pile at the center of the grounds.

We whiled away part of the afternoon in driving to the international peace garden about ten miles north of town, and then returned to Dunseith to get some groceries and have a modest picnic in the small city park.

Throughout the trip the boys age 12 and 14 were commonly shoving, wrestling and pounding upon one another, as lads are wont to do. They are approximately the same height and both are very energetic, though Cui is more than commonly thin. I ignore their little spats, only seeing that they don't become to vigorous. In the glove box is a little Petri-dish that contains some silly putty. A rather pliable plastic material that I sometimes squish back and forth between my fingers to exercise my hands. Like water, it will flow, but only very slowly, taking about 30 minutes to settle level in the bottom of the dish. In the course of the many contests between the boys this day, Poco had taken a dab of this material and rubbed it firmly into hair and scalp of Cui. I thought that it might simply slowly run out of his hair like water, given time enough. But, not. Apparently some such force as capillary attraction prevents that from happening.

Stopped in that evening at the home of Stella in Dunseith to visit with Don Richards, one of my pals from the seventh and eighth grade. While there, the women folk became aware of the gooey green stuff in the hair of Cui. They undertook the job of shampooing that junk out from his head of hair - not an easy task.

RGB

Another Trek to the Northwest

Prior to my departure to the Northwest at the end of November 2002, I had noticed a thin caking of oil and dust accumulating on the left half of the rear end of the pickup on the lower part of the tailgate and especially below that. I generally carry a quart or a part of a quart of oil in the pickup and I presumed some of that might have leaked out onto the bed of pickup and seeped out below the tailgate. That quart was lying on its side within a foot of the rear end of the bed of the pickup and there was very little oil yet within the container. And there did appear to be an oily film in that area to confirm my guess. I thought nothing more about the matter until later in the trip.

I was also aware in the past several months that there seemed to be some slipping of the clutch. To hit the accelerator upon the roadway in second or third gear did not produce the customary instantaneous accelerating thrust, though the engine responded immediately. Inquiry at a local garage suggested that it might well cost me over six hundred dollars to repair the clutch mechanism. As the slippage was only minimal and I had already been aware of it for a few months, I had some hope that the clutch might yet survive one more trip to the Northwest. And I entertained some vague notion that I might thereafter replace the old vehicle which now had in excess of three hundred fifty thousand miles on it. A mere estimation, as the odometer had ceased to function just short of attaining its 325,000th mile.

Bayloo departed to spend a few weeks with her daughter in Arruba on 29 November. I had to organize my gear and finish up a couple other projects before I was finally ready for departure in the old 1989 Toyota pickup to the Northwest on 4 December. I departed westward from Albuquerque about 5:00 PM. Ten hours later, at 3:00 AM, I stopped at a rest area just to the east of Barstow, California, to stretch out and sleep on the bench seat of pickup cab. I slept well beneath my 'quilt of many colors' in those cramped quarters for just over four hours and then continued on through Barstow and Bakersfield to Hwy 5 North. Ten hours later I was passing through Sacramento at 5:00 PM. The oncoming traffic towards San Francisco was ferocious on the other side of the median strip, but heading northward, I was moving easily and without delay in only moderately intense traffic. I stopped at Williams an hour later to have a whopper at Burger King. I note again how nearly uniform is the fine quality of their burgers from one location to another across the western states.

About 8:00 PM I arrived at the home of Raymond Horton in Redding, California. I startled his wife, Betty, by tapping on the kitchen window where I saw her working at her kitchen sink just a few feet from the front door. I spent two days of leisure and three nights at their place, catching up on our dialogue and finding time to read one of their books on the history of the Klamath Indians, "*Ancient Tribes of the Klamath Country*", by Russell S. Bowen. Betty is a native of Chilloquin, Oregon. Raymond and she lived a few years in the Klamath Falls area in the early years of their marriage.

I left Redding the 8th of December and drove the 150 miles to Medford, Oregon, where I arrived about 4:30 PM and stopped into Tina's place on Driftwood Street. She and the children have just moved again to this location in consequence of some deep dispute between her and her second spouse, Perry Miller. Cui and I took one of his friends home to Central Point and then stopped in at a shopping center to pick up Poco Uno and David. Then, back at Tina's place, we shared a couple pizzas for supper, followed by a treat of Root Beer Floats. After supper I had a few hours to talk things over with Tina as the kids are getting off to bed. Talked a couple minutes with Cowboy on the phone. He is to finish his one year contract with the mission program in Sunny Valley, and then return to home and civilian life in about three weeks. While engaged in this program, he has completed his high school equivalency studies and received his GED certificate. He is about 16 1/2 years of age at this time and is faced with choosing the direction of his education and training in preparation for his life's work.

The following morning I am up about 8:00 AM as the grandchildren are getting off to school. I chat a bit with Tina and watch the antics of Nombres before leaving behind for her perusal, an older copy of my manuscript, as I head north after stopping to pick up a couple donuts. I stop to visit Larry and Nancy Otis in Grants Pass to discuss a little philosophy and learn something of their recent trip into the "Chaos-stan" counties. Nancy gave me a copy of a book she had recently read, "*Sophie's World*", by Jostein Gaarder. I then stopped at Sunshine Valley to look up Cowboy, but there was nobody about the place, so I continued north of Hwy 5. After stopping at a rest area to nap for an hour, I continued on to arrive at the Hillsboro Library about 7:00 PM to check my e-mail before stopping at Pierre's place about 8:00 PM. They were eating out and arrived home an hour later. All of them - including Pierre - were in bed by 9:30.

Pierre is now long into the process of trying to demonstrate (and document the fact) that he is capable of both earning a living and running a household. Especially difficult in the face of all the court inflicted interference with that process. A process which is being driven by the mother of the children. An ongoing process of harassment that has now been going on for the past two or three years. I am worried about his health under the burden of stress being inflicted on him. I have followed (and attended some of) the farcical court proceedings concerning the ongoing issues of the settlement of this divorce, the division of the estate, and the issue of custody of the children. It appears to me that the court process primarily involves the inflicting of an adequately punitive bleeding of the estate such as perhaps to encourage the contestants eventually to settle the issues themselves. The court sessions that I attended where each terminated abruptly under the pretext that the court did not have adequate time allotted for the proceedings and requiring that the process be continued at subsequent time in some remote future. The judge clearly demonstrated his own contempt (for court, and for intelligent citizens alike) by his obvious want of any preparation by way of familiarization with any of the earlier relevant court proceedings.

I stayed over a couple of days with Pierre to keep any eye on the grandchildren and run them about to thither and yon, thus permitting Pierre to work long and uninterrupted hours at his job for few days and enable him to get a good lick accomplished on a couple of his employment projects. Unfortunately though, both the youngsters and I were aware that I owned no actual authority to compel them to daily tasks. Thus I was more an observer of the function of their individual consciences than an enforcer to them of their responsibilities. As one might suppose, the younger one's were more oblivious to their responsibilities than the older.

While the kids were in school, I had time to spend at the library to review the latest journals. I hopped on a bicycle to ride over to the school about a half mile from the house, to arrive there at 2:00 PM, when Beans finished his classes. I would then stand and pace about another half hour waiting for Bam-Bam's release from school. And then the three of us would ride our bikes back to the house. It was yet another half hour before Belle finished her seventh grade classes, and she arrived home alone in the space of fifteen minutes. Finally, about 3:30 PM, Bah and Boo arrive home, having been bussed to within a couple of blocks of home. Both are in their Junior year of high School. Bah is a year older than Boo. She busies herself with school work, piano practice, laundry and personal care during now this brief thirty to forty five minutes before their mother comes by to claim them to her custody which ends at 6:00 PM. At which point, Pierre or I then pick them up at the home of Rochelle's 'friends' - with whom she has been living since Nora and her spouse, Daryl, took her in on 24 April 2002.

Three weeks earlier (in April 2002), Rochelle had appeared before the judge armed with a certain batch of deceit and lies under the inspiration of another of her church friends, Robyn. Unbelievable as it seems to me, the judge permitted an in-chambers quick hearing of those misrepresentations of reality. And on the basis of that one sided testimony, the judge authorized her to occupy Pierre's home and family without even requiring that Pierre's side of the story be heard. A rash and inexcusable decision. One that ought to have enraged any decent red-blooded American man. The so called "Due Process" for Pierre was to be in court some three weeks later. Meanwhile, Pierre was given two hours to vacate the premises. Rochelle and Robyn summarily moved into Pierre's quarters with the help of Nora and Spouse, in apparent full confidence that they were now entrenched forever into the new Nirvana. With a vengeful audacity they began to 'clean out' and rearrange the personal property of Pierre and peruse and lose his personal papers. $3,000.00 worth of his guns sort of just disappeared and was never heard of again. Subsequent court hearing failed to specify who had taken them, or where they went. ($3,000.00 = thirty pieces of silver, perhaps?). The obvious explanation is that Rochelle stole them (a felony), and that she handed them over to Daryl (also a felony for receiving stolen goods). Presumably he sold the guns and they split the money between them. To the best of my knowledge, the case was never investigated by police and no charges were leveled at the perpetrators.

When 'Due process' belatedly arrived April 19th, that judge immediately recognized the previous injustice that had placed Rochelle in charge of Pierre's life and home, and ordered Rochelle out. Apparently feeling compelled in law to do so, despite his obviously harsh dealings towards Pierre and without so much as a word of admonition to the scheming Rochelle and her churchly buddies. The perpetrators of this injustice (judicial crew) apparently unable to ever quite forgive their victim. On April 24th Pierre was finally able to get back into his own home and again get custody of the children. But, how it is that any supposedly rational system of justice would permit such gross temporary injustice and disruption of the life of the citizen without a full hearing from both sides, is quite beyond my poor powers of comprehension.

Yes, and even in all these past six months since Rochelle was forced to vacate Pierre's home, she continues to live in with her co-conspirators who have been party to this affront on Pierre's rights and tranquility. From what I can gather, she has not found work; is probably not seriously looking. In her ongoing legal contest with Pierre which is hoped will eventually come to finality, she appears to be getting legal assistance from public coffers. I am curious as to what is the nature of the hold she has upon the household she has "adopted". Surely they must weary of her burden upon their lives and the endless contest. One must presume that they are awaiting some final remunerative settlement, and that they are anticipating then some final fiscal payoff for the role they are playing in the evil and turmoil that she continues to perpetrate. Or, perhaps they are merely congratulating themselves upon some anticipated measures of fat that is accumulating to their accounts in the barns of eternity - as though their misbehavior were a virtue.

And among the other inanities of the justice system, the court mandates that in the interim until final settlement, the children are to be with their mother from 4:00 to 6:00 PM of each school day. She and Pierre apparently interpret this to mean that Pierre is responsible for them until they are all gathered in his home after school. No consideration whatever to the reality that this strange inconvenience must greatly intrude on Pierre's regular schedule of employment. And as though the older two, Bah and Boo (both over age 16) were not of sufficient age and judgment of discernment to baby-sit their own younger siblings.

Without authority to direct the children, there was some inevitable difficulty in my getting the younger children to do their school and home assignments, so that I was not enthusiastic about playing that role for more than just a few days, even if I might have had more days to devote to the task. And I was not therefore disappointed to learn that Pierre's mother was soon to be about to take over that role. Until then I had a little time to spend with the kids. The kids generally eat supper at home with their father. One evening, Belle whipped up a terrific batch of spaghetti for us. Apparently, she and Bah alternate in this responsibility. Pierre encourages the children to speak up and have their say around the supper table. They are not yet overly facile in expressing themselves, though each gets his turn and his say.

\- - - - - - - - - - - - - - - - - -

Upon this Thursday late afternoon between about 4:00 and 6:30 PM, Bah, Boo, Belle, Bam-Bam, and Beans were taking their turn at the piano instruction from the teacher who comes by every second week to oversee their progress. In fact Chris and Sam also come by a bit later for their instruction sessions too. Meanwhile, knowing that the kids were scheduled, after piano lessons, to be carted off to spend the weekend with their mother, and having no clue as to what eating arrangements were to be, I cooked myself a hamburger steak and sat down to eat. Whereupon, Bah having just finished her piano lesson set about to cooking up the rest of the hamburger package into a granular consistency for a meal of tacos to serve the family.

I had spoken with Massy, and she invited me to attend a high school production of "*A Christmas Carol*" with her and the children. I departed Pierre's home in the rain and darkness fifty minutes before opening curtain and headed towards Sunset High School. Portland is pretty much cut up with street running off a odd angle etc., and if one misses a single turn, he is apt to find himself soon into very unfamiliar territory, and without much clue as to how to get back toward the intended destination. In fact, that was my fate again this very night. I was reduced to the process of dead reckoning as the window of my time frame was closing down upon me. Fortunately, I have a long history of being frequently lost during the hundreds of thousands of miles that I have been driving about the North American Continent in the past twenty five years. All of that misadventure seems to have left me with a sort of instinct for bumbling back onto the correct course by a sort of process of dead reckoning. I have never found the process of local inquiry to be the least helpful, most particularly in areas of high population density. Folks are unfamiliar with the names of their own nearby streets, and in their lives they travel only a scant few major concourses to arrive to their few destinations - the shopping mall, the school, the church, the Pub, and to Aunt Tilly's place.

But being lost and nearly late for the opening curtain, I stopped in at a convenience store to try my luck again with finding directions from the locals. Naturally it ended up with my being lost into just another dead end street. Resorting once more to the necessity of vague dead reckoning, I sensed the window of my time frame closing upon my opportunity. I was about resigned to my defeat when, lo, I discovered myself to have arrived. I quickly located a parking spot on a remote street and hurried along to the large school facility where I followed a few stragglers into the hallway and off at the end, a small knot of people clustered about. Surely, this must be the right place. And half way down the concourse I encountered Massy, who seems to have been searching for me. We were seated in the auditorium not more than a few scant minutes when the lights began to dim even as I was greeting this group of grandchildren. (Always a nickel short, 5 min. late, or by the skin of my teeth). It was by no means the quality of a Broadway production, but we were adequately reminded of the plot of this story by Charles Dickens. I stopped by at their home for an hour or more after the performance to chat and help them consume some of their Christmas sugar cookies. And then returned to Pierre's place a bit tired by 11:00, and turned in shortly thereafter.

And on the next morning I got myself over to the grade school by 8:00 AM to attend the awards assembly. A few rows of chairs were being set up for the handful of adults that would attend as spectators. I took a seat and read for a half hour while all the various preparations were being made. Finally, not long after 8:30, the children were marched in, class by class with their teachers. The children all squatting upon the gym floor. Finally the few general announcements are made and then the various instructors call forth each student in turn to receive some sort of certificate attesting to his or her special virtue, talent, or skill. Recognition for such things even as having turned in all the assigned homework, and for being genial to fellow classmates. In all, I suppose about half of the pupils got at least one certificate of special recognition. I can believe that the pupils enjoyed a little bit of a buzz, each not knowing but what he too might receive some sort of certificate of honor. But for me and (as I suppose) those pupils who did not receive recognition that day, the whole process seemed a bit tedious. A part of the step by step training to endurance and practice in patience that go into the civilizing and education of our youth in preparation for their adult participation in our modern world.

While reading and awaiting the commencement of the awards program, I was surprised to suddenly be confronted by Bah and Boo, who are supposed to be off and into their high school classes by this time in the morning. Their mother has sent them in to give me the word that Beans has neglected to pack any of his clothing into his backpack for weekend stay with his mother. And could I take him home to accomplish that after the awards assembly? They had no sooner departed than Pierre showed up. He told me that my name was on the list of those who were authorized to pick up the children from school. When I later appeared at the administrative office to run that errand, I was told that my name was not upon the list. By then, Pierre had departed and they had to reach him by cell phone for authorization.

And thus it happened that just past mid morning I picked up Beans and we drove back to the house to get his clothing. While waiting for him to pack, I noticed still a little ice cream and some root beer in the refrigerator. Apparently, it was something of which Beans was already aware; and to which he had already given some thought. For as soon as his packing was finished, he went immediately to the refrigerator to check the supply of good things there. And quickly proposed that he and I finish off what little ice cream and root beer remained. I allowed as how it seemed like a good idea to me, and in a spirit of good fellowship we finished it off together before I returned him to his school.

And then at about 11:00 AM I headed through Portland, across the high bridge, and northward on highway 5. I managed to whiz through the usually congested area of Renton to arrive at the home of an old high school classmate, Jean Buchanan, in Bellevue about 2:15 PM. She told me the story of how her sister and mine (Skippy) had once hopped a train on the Milwaukee out of Miles City to run away together - they took them off the train at Melstone, Montana and sent them back home. Jean has read my autobiography and most of my most recent manuscript; and we seem to be reasonably close together in our philosophical outlook on reality. She fixed me a bit of a lunch as our conversation proceeded to various historical and philosophical subjects. About 5:30 PM I took my leave and she was determined to send with me a few things to eat. Northward on Hwy 5, the traffic was now beginning to thicken and slow.

I arrived at sister Ookie's place in Marysville (just north of Everett) at 7:00 PM. She was slow in responding to my knocking - had already gone to bed. Not unusual for her to retire quite early, as she suffers from chronic fatigue. "Oh, it's you again", says she. I do sometimes stop by to visit her two or three times a year. We talk about an hour, and then make her couch out into a bed where I may sleep before she heads out to her bedroom for her own night of rest.

The next morning Ookie made some French toast for breakfast. I had been traveling with homemade banana bread and my supply was depleted. And so I thought to ask her if by chance she might have a recipe for mother's Christmas date bread which I hadn't tasted for forty or fifty years. By chance and to my surprise she did have it - along with many of her other recipes on 3" x 5" cards. She said I was welcome to have it, along with whatever other of those old recipe cards I might wish to take. And so I sorted through and found a half dozen recipes that I would take along with me. She and I chatted for a couple hours and then each took a morning nap, before we went out upon a leisurely walk of about a mile and stopped at a goodwill store to go through their stock of used books. Returned to her apartment, we talk a while and have a sandwich before getting down to the business of now also an afternoon nap.

For supper we had a nice roast stew, followed by some pie; then again discuss what is and was, but avoiding any discussion of what shall be. It was about nine o'clock before she went to bed. I got a shower and then read a few hours before getting to bed about midnight.

I had planned to leave the following morning, but on our walk we discover that my pickup is missing. Presumably towed away. Checking with the manager of the apartment complex on this Saturday morning, we learn that it was she who has perpetrated this evil yesterday afternoon - after I had been parked there less than 24 hours. She says that she didn't know who it belonged to, and besides, people are supposed to check in with the managers when they park in even those spaces which are not specifically assigned to a particular resident. And that she was concerned that it might have been a stolen vehicle (so what if it were? how does that make her mischief a matter or urgency?). In reality, none of Ookie's visitors have ever gone through this process in the 10 or 12 years that Ookie has lived there. This manager says she called around to find out who owned the pickup, but that no one answered the phone when she called Ookie's place. If that phone call actually happened, it must have been while we were out on our walk. As to what was the urgency in getting the pickup towed away, there was only the pretext that a car parked next to mine needed a jump start. The more likely explanation is that seeing my New Mexico license plate and the reality of the aging of the vehicle, she thought it probably belonged to a Mexican, or some other person of no account. And that she was thus apt to be able to get away with abusing her authority as an agent of a governmentally sponsored housing project.

As it was now Sunday, the towing company would not even come out to release my pickup to me - except that a special holiday penalty also be applied to the tow-away and storage' charges. As this manager would not act to straighten out this problem, I called and spoke with her supervisor in Tacoma on Monday. She put me off with the explanation that she would review the incident with the manager; and that if she had erred in her judgment, the managing company would refund the expenses I would now encounter in getting my vehicle restored to me. Naturally, this "investigation" could not be done immediately; and the probability of small claims case be pursued by a non-local resident from far away New Mexico would be small.

Having raised as much ruckus over this as I could, I was finally constrained by time and circumstance to the necessity of putting out $329.00 to get the vehicle out of hock. Poor old Ookie was rather agitated at being in the middle of more trouble than she has seen perhaps in many years. Her own economic and medical problems are alone more than she can comfortable cope with.

RGB

Juarez Trek

And so in Feb of 2003 I found myself wandering about Juarez, Mexico in search of a Guayabera shirt. It was crowded with people, both the locals and Americanos. Even this main Avenido Juarez is dingy, battered, and the sidewalks cracked and irregular. Every store front seems to have poured its own sidewalk of concrete or set its tile many long years ago with no attempt since then to maintain its physical condition. They are fractured, and uneven from section to section, and many have potholes. One must watch his step lest he stumble into one of its irregularities or even an occasional mud hole. Difficult to watch one's every step as there is so much shabbiness of the buildings, store fronts, and street venders to distract one into the status of gawking tourist. Women, men and even little children are everywhere about, trying to attract one's attention - and a plea for a donation to relieve their economic destitution. Even with a whole pocket full of money one could not possibly hope to meet all their requests for coin and paper. Older boys and younger men stand as hawkers in front of many of the store fronts and the mercado entrances with an outward cheerful aggressiveness requesting one to step inside to look about, and asking if there is anything in particular they can help you find. They will even follow one a few paces down the street as one trys to avoid getting engaged with them into any patter. They all but grab you by the arm or shoulders - as though they were all aware of the potential of that for igniting an altercation. Many of the side streets have been closed to traffic and are occupied by double rows of merchandise stalls under canvas or wood. Some limit their enterprise to the sale of jewelry, or shoes, or toys, or women's shirts and blouses; others have a conglomerate of colorful clothes and hats, and leatherworks. About one in twenty five or thirty are limiting themselves to the cooking and selling of various Mexican fast foods and soft drinks. The locals partake with relish, but I notice none of the tourists partaking. I would be reluctant to do so. Considering the crush of shops, stalls, and people, they keep the streets and sidewalks fairly free of debris. The walkways are narrow so that one must often dip the leading shoulder to narrow the profile in the face of the oncoming foot traffic. The people appear docile and unthreatening, though certainly always potentially volatile. They only wish to do their business and sell you something. The pigeons hover about any open areas and make their rush to forage crumbs in spots where and whenever there is a lull in the traffic.

Of the local young women, there a only a few that work as clerks in the shops; more work in the few scattered larger stores. There are not a great number of schoolgirls and younger women walking about the streets - at least not in these mid-day hours. Of those that do, most seem to parade about in pairs, exposing their midriffs. Short tight blouses and tight fitting jeans with body sufficiently high to cover only to above the hairline of the pubic triangle - and so closely fitting as to expose the contours of their private parts and buttocks. One could count the outline of the coins if they were to carry some in the pockets or these jeans. I am aware that they tend to marry young, while in the bloom of their rapidly declining youth and beauty. Those yet in school are wearing short-skirted uniforms with white socks up to the knees.

There are many taxi cabs painted all much the same, parked about the main avenues: their overly eager drivers so anxious for a fare that one is certain to be plagued by their zealous solicitations at every street corner. Eager and anxious to serve one. There seem to be very few takers. One wonders how they manage to sustain their seemingly optimistic enthusiasm. Most appear to be in their late twenties and up to the age of about forty.

A few blocks deeper into the teaming city, the tourist density diffuses away to nothingness and the locals are interacting mainly among themselves. I presume that they must catch just enough of tourist traffic to make an occasional sale. Barely enough to sustain their livelihood. The early hope and enthusiasm of the young men aspiring to make their fortune upon the streets is apparently squeezed from them in some few short years beyond their early years of wedlock and the gathering of a few children. There is a deficiency of numbers of those beyond the early twenties of age. Have they all fled to brighter hopes north of the border?

I was soon lost in the narrowing side-streets that branch out at various odd angles so that I was soon in doubt about directions. No tourists at all here. Except for the youth, there appears very little spontaneity among them. Many middle aged people sitting upon the sidewalks, leaning against the walls. Most are plainly dressed; many in shabby clothing. Some holding out the hand for alms; more perhaps just waiting for time to pass. Occasionally a small knot of colorfully dressed native Indians sitting upon the inner part of the walkway near the building. One among them has some jewelry or trinkets spread out before them on a cloth for display and the hope of sale.

The larger of the streets are busy with automotive traffic. Half of those vehicles are busses carrying the local traffic. They roar and screech as they duck and weave their way through the congestion of two or three lines of traffic. One must watch for the opportunity to cross the street in safety. One wonders at the instincts that guide the drivers. For, like a flock of birds in flight, they seem never to collide. Apparently always some minimum civility and silent understanding among them despite their continuous headlong rush into traffic.

Many of middle age and beyond, ambling as though aimlessly upon the street; some lame and prematurely stooped. If they are upon personal or family errands, they would appear to have plenty of time for the task. More time than they know what to do with. People involuntarily unemployed who have long past relinquished all hope of bettering their lives, and now reduced to the bare subsistence of livelihood. I suspect that some not insubstantial proportion of them spend their nights upon the streets or in hovels not far removed from that. For, indeed, just these dozen or more blocks from the main avenues, the one story buildings are rapidly diminishing in quality even further, to give the vast majority of this neighborhood the appearance of a shanty town. The gentle slope in the wide valley enables me to see over their diminutive shanties that extend on for miles to at least the next low ridge. And yet, I am not at all sure that any majority of them notice their own despair with the quality of their own lives. Many, I should guess, have never entertained hopes of a better quality of life and livings circumstances. Many have entertained such dreams only for their offspring and see themselves as fortunate to have raised at least a couple of children of their own.

The situation of the huddled masses in China is apparently about the same. Millions of hopeful younger people jammed together in crowded narrow quarters with only the dimmest of prospects of ever finding a way to better their lives, while those in middle age and beyond shrivel away to early deaths on meager fare. A hundred years ago, the situation in the larger cities of this nation was much the same. In China, tall strong buildings are arising in the cities and the skylines are dotted with the booms of balanced structural cranes. Will prosperity ever arise to the vast majority there? Vast sums of money are flowing into "third-world' countries from the World Banking Association, but we hear no word that these "loans" are being repaid - or that there is any prospect of that ever happening. Nor is it anticipated that the millions that they loan to Latin America and third world countries shall ever be returned. Where does all of this free money come from?

I am reminded of Buddha, who wandered out from the enclave of his luxuriant palace and sumptuous existence to be startled and astonished at the world of destitution that surrounded him. A world of human agony and hopeless millions.

Some eight or nine years ago Zaszco gave me a quart of whiskey for X-mas, and it has been sitting about and unopened. As we are planning soon to move to Santa Fe, things here are getting sorted and some things being tossed away. We won't be able to have any alcoholic beverages about the house, and so I decided to get rid of the whiskey by drinking a shot of it every night before I go to bed. I had never partaken of any whiskey previously. It is really terrible tasting stuff - quite unpalatable, as it seemed to me as I sipped it away. So unpalatable that I had to mix honey into to it to tone it down.

And then the other evening I noticed that my hard palate and the back of my tongue seemed to be irritated. What was going on? I thought about that a couple of days and then finally came to the conclusion the whiskey was actually chemically burning my mouth. I then recalled that in the movies, the cowboys order up their whiskey in a little shot glass, and then "toss it down". I had never given any thought to that ritual previously. And I have now come to the conclusion that it is more than just a ritual. The truth must be that whiskey is so mean tasting and irritating that nobody can stand the taste of it. That in fact, they don't actually drink the stuff because they like it. No! They drink it because of the systemic effect that it has on their being. As it is absorbed rapidly from the stomach into their circulation it quickly gives one 'a bit of a lift', as the expression goes. Instead of sipping and savoring it on the palate as I do with a liqueur, or a wine, it is meant to be literally tossed to the back of the throat and swallowed down quickly before it chemically irritates the mucus membranes. And now that I think about it, I recall having seen quite a few angry looking palates over the years, for which the alcohol must certainly have been the explanation - though I am only now realizing it.

And so the education of this country bumpkin needs must continue on from day to day even as I am approaching my seventieth year. And I sure do hope that nobody ever again decides to give me a gift quart of whiskey.

R. Garner Brasseur
Early March 2003

Some Final Thoughts - Poetic

True Confession

by R. Garner Brasseur

In this world of feigned belief,
do I stand alone in awe?
Dumbstruck as the innocent
in docked dismay before the law.

Where 'certitudes' all uttered forth
in contradicting oath,
Still beckon me to ponder deep
Yearning yet for valid truth.

While pipers sanctimonious
Misguide with siren song.
Maligned is noble science
By ever glib impatient throng.

As I lay dying some years past,
Unsettled yet in my affairs,
My end of time had come at last,
And so far gone I little cared.

Sons and brothers sallied forth,
accounts to reckon and resolve,
This evil spell that held me fast,
Might they assault and yet devolve?

Having owned a life of thought,
Now by my troth must I confess,
Ere misfortune end this trial,
Sacred truth to swear at last.

And summarize this little light,
'Twas gleaned by one mere mortal.
That unto me was not revealed
In mystic insight heaven's portal.

But, when magi bare illusion's lies
and disenchant the fable,
Benign and free stands Natural Law
whose profits bring the bread to table.

RGB
30 Dec. 1999

- - - - - - - - - - - - - - - - - - -

Western Spartans

by R. Garner Brasseur

Through the years when we were young,
We climbed our ladders rung by rung.
While near at hand or at the door,
The wolf was present evermore.

Before the winds from home to home,
We little band of pilgrims roamed.
Drawn by fate and circumstance,
Required to grasp at every chance.

To cuddle down in want each night,
Arise resolved to each day's fight.
Every hand aboard required
To face his destiny inspired.

R.G.B.
30 March 1999

ATLAS SHRUGGED

by R. Garner Brasseur

As Atlas then to shrug the world
When once I had my fill.
Satiate of duty's guilt,
Widely wandered vale and hill.

This weighty sphere had vexed me well,
And tried me to the core.
By vague and futile hope and dream,
From un-kept promises of yore.

Did I request this mortal frame?
Upon this ageless rock I pout.
Enslaved within this land of shame,
Beset by certitudes I doubt.

Why do we tread this beaten path?
Why yet to sing and dance and spin?
Why do we brave this threat of death,
Why yet pursue in love to win?

With patience yet to stay the course,
Not full contentedly be sure.
Though filled with outrage and remorse,
Resigned a while yet to endure.

R.G.B.
21 Oct. 1998